Restoring Responsibility
Ethics in Government, Business, and Healthcare

In this important collection of essays Dennis Thompson argues
for a more robust conception of responsibility in public life than
prevails in contemporary democracies. He suggests that we should
stop thinking about public ethics so much in terms of individual
vices (such as selfishness or sexual misconduct) and start thinking
about it more in terms of institutional vices (such as abuse of power
and lack of accountability).

Among the questions Thompson addresses are: How can we
hold officials in large organizations accountable for policies
shaped by many different people? Are advisers responsible for
the consequences of the advice they give? How can the conflict
between secrecy and accountability be resolved? Why do political
campaigns corrupt even honest legislators? Why do elections fail
to make representatives accountable? His institutional approach
also shows why the ethical principles needed in hospital decision
making differ from those needed in doctor-patient relations; why
good character is neither necessary nor sufficient for the ethical
management of corporations; and how democratic responsibility
should be promoted in a global society.

Combining theory and practice with many concrete examples
and proposals for reform, these essays could be used in courses in
applied ethics, legal process, political science, and political theory.
They can be read with profit by professionals and by students in
graduate schools of public policy, law, public health, medicine,
journalism, management, and business.

Dennis F. Thompson is Alfred North Whitehead Professor of
Political Philosophy and Director of the Center for Ethics and
the Professions at Harvard University.

For Dan
Best regards
Dennis

Restoring Responsibility

Ethics in Government, Business, and Healthcare

DENNIS F. THOMPSON

Harvard University

CAMBRIDGE
UNIVERSITY PRESS

PUBLISHED BY THE PRESS SYNDICATE OF THE UNIVERSITY OF CAMBRIDGE
The Pitt Building, Trumpington Street, Cambridge, United Kingdom

CAMBRIDGE UNIVERSITY PRESS
The Edinburgh Building, Cambridge CB2 2RU, UK
40 West 20th Street, New York, NY 10011-4211, USA
477 Williamstown Road, Port Melbourne, VIC 3207, Australia
Ruiz de Alarcón 13, 28014 Madrid, Spain
Dock House, The Waterfront, Cape Town 8001, South Africa

http://www.cambridge.org

© Dennis F. Thompson 2005

First published 2005

Printed in the United States of America

Typeface ITC New Baskerville 10.5/13.7 pt.   *System* LATEX 2$_\varepsilon$ [TB]

A catalog record for this book is available from the British Library.

Library of Congress Cataloging in Publication Data

Thompson, Dennis F. (Dennis Frank), 1940–
Restoring responsibility : ethics in government, business, and healthcare /
Dennis F. Thompson.
p. cm.
Includes bibliographical references and index.
ISBN 0-521-83830-4 – ISBN 0-521-54722-9 (pb.)
1. Political ethics. 2. Medical ethics. 3. Business ethics. 4. Responsibility. I. Title.
JA79.T575 2004
174–dc22   2004040654

ISBN 0 521 83830 4 hardback
ISBN 0 521 54722 9 paperback

Contents

Acknowledgments

These essays are contributions to a relatively new field of inquiry, variously called practical ethics or institutional political theory. Working in a nascent field can often be a lonely endeavor, but I am fortunate to have been joined by other pioneers, a group of talented junior and senior scholars from many different disciplines and professions, who recognize the importance of undertaking interdisciplinary and cross-professional study of fundamental values at issue in public life. Many of these scholars have given me advice on the manuscripts that have become the essays in this volume. Their names are mentioned at the beginning of the notes to the relevant essays. Less directly but no less significantly, I have benefited from informal comments and criticisms from the many faculty members and graduate students who have been Fellows in the Center for Ethics and the Professions at Harvard. I would not have written many of these essays without their intellectual stimulation. On some views of responsibility – you are responsible for an outcome if it would not have happened but for your actions – they might be blamed for my errors. But following the more robust view described in Chapter 1, I take full responsibility for this outcome. I know that I can count on my critics to make sure that this taking of responsibility is not a mere ritual.

I have resisted the temptation to revise the essays in light of subsequent historical events and scholarly debate. Except for some editorial changes, they remain mostly as originally published or written. Although there are a number of particular claims I would now wish to qualify and a few I might even abandon, I am encouraged by the four anonymous readers for the Press to believe that the basic arguments are no more misguided, and perhaps even more relevant, than when they were originally made. My fundamental positions on most of the questions addressed in the essays have been constant, but close readers will notice some changes in terminology and even a few in substantive argument and methodological approach as they proceed from the earlier to the later essays.

Two of the essays have not been previously published, and one has appeared before only in Spanish. The publishers of the essays in their original forms are acknowledged in the Credits.

In preparing the essays for publication, I have been aided by a highly capable and dedicated team of assistants in the Ethics Center at Harvard. Simone Sandy and Jean McVeigh applied their sharp-eyed editing skills to the entire manuscript. Maria Catoline and Jaime Muehl provided first-class research assistance throughout the process. Jean McVeigh and Mandy Osborne managed the rest of my professional life with efficiency and intelligence. At Cambridge University Press, Terence Moore, Stephanie Achard, and Sally Nicholls provided superior editorial guidance. Joan Green prepared the index. My greatest debt is to my wife Carol, whose loving support has been essential in my life from the first of these essays to the last, and who will, if I am fortunate, be there for all the rest that I may write.

Restoring Responsibility

Ethics in Government, Business, and Healthcare

Introduction

The Need for Institutional Responsibility

Ethics scandals have proliferated in the worlds of government, business, medicine, and on the sites of many other professions, even the clergy. In the United States more members of Congress have been investigated and sanctioned for misconduct in recent decades than in all of its previous 200-year history. Some 500 officials in the executive branch have been charged with misconduct since 1970. The top executives of Enron, once the world's seventh largest corporation, perpetrated fraudulent schemes that brought about the company's collapse in 2001. The ensuing inquiries exposed ethical failures in other corporations and in the institutions that are supposed to oversee them. Accountants, lawyers, bankers, security analysts, and brokers were implicated. The Catholic Church in the United States has yet to recover from the most devastating scandal in its modern history – the failure to deal early and properly with the hundreds of priests who abused young children. Less dramatic but no less significant lapses occurred in the healthcare system, philanthropic organizations, universities, the legal profession, and the media.

Are public officials, corporate executives, and other leaders becoming more corrupt? Are we in the midst of a "corruption crisis" as some have declared? There is no good reason to believe that our leaders in general are more corrupt than they used to be. In some respects, they may be less corrupt. Conduct that was widely ignored in previous eras (petty graft, nepotism, payola, drunkenness, and physical violence in Congress) would be grounds for prosecution today. Despite prominent exceptions, the moral and intellectual quality of public officials in many governments is no lower and arguably higher than it has ever

been. Most corporate leaders are more public spirited than their predecessors, or at least act in ways that are more socially responsible. It is
less likely that human nature has changed than that the environment
in which human nature shows itself has shifted.

Why then are there so many ethics charges and ethics violations?
Reformers have been more zealous in recent years, and the media
have been more aggressive, both for good and for ill. But there are
other more systematic causes that are probably more important and
merit more attention than they have received. First, there are more
violations simply because there are more rules to violate. Governments
at both federal and state levels have responded to public demands
for new rules to limit campaign contributions, require disclosure of
financial interests, restrict the gifts officials may accept, and regulate
the types of jobs they may take after they leave office. New investigative
bodies, such as public integrity agencies and special prosecutors, have
been established. Two dozen state legislatures now have independent
ethics commissions, many of which regulate the conduct of legislators
as well as campaign practices and lobbyists.

Beyond government, many institutions and professions have
strengthened both their ethics procedures and expanded their ethics
training. In 1982 less than 1 percent of American hospitals had ethics
committees; today more than 90 percent of large hospitals have them.
After years of ignoring the problem, the American Medical Association is finally addressing the conflicts of interest that physicians
frequently face. In most large scientific laboratories that receive federal support, scientists are now expected to undergo ethics training.
Corporations are hiring ethics consultants, promulgating codes of
ethics, and providing ethics workshops for their employees. After
Enron and the other corporate scandals, boards of directors, the accounting profession, and other "gatekeepers" of the corporate world
are coming under greater scrutiny. The legal profession, subject to
increasing criticism for a wide range of deficiencies in ethics, is considering new approaches to professional discipline. Accountants, architects, clergy, computer programmers, engineers, social workers,
veterinarians, among others, have turned their attention to formulating or strengthening the standards of conduct in their professions.

The second cause of the escalation of ethical scrutiny has a deeper
source. It arises from a growing movement calling for greater moral
responsibility on the part of the leaders of the large institutions
that govern our daily lives. The movement expresses a dispersed but

widespread insistence that those who exercise power over us and in our name should answer to us, and a discontent with the traditional means of calling them to account. As voters, customers, employees, patients, or clients, we find our lives affected more and more often by decisions made by others – by politicians, managers, doctors, lawyers, or others who exercise authority in today's society. Their decisions have become not only more complex but also more contentious; increasingly, they involve disagreements about fundamental moral values. At the same time, more people from different backgrounds and with different perspectives are seeking a voice in making the decisions and in influencing the institutions that affect their lives. As the participants in ethics debates become more diverse, the ethical differences become sharper and the ethical scrutiny more salient.

In these circumstances it should not be surprising that charges of unethical conduct have proliferated. But it should also be clear that the usual responses – more (or fewer) prosecutions, more (or fewer) rules, more (or fewer) media investigations – are at best inadequate. What is required is a more direct response to the movement for greater accountability – a more cogent answer to the challenge directed against the traditional forms of responsibility.

We cannot ourselves make many of the decisions in the institutions that govern our lives, but we can try to shape the conditions under which the decisions are made. Those conditions critically implicate the principles and practices by which leaders are held responsible for the decisions. We can and should develop principles and practices of responsibility that are more appropriate to the institutions that now dominate our social and political world.

The essays in this collection, written over a period of twenty-five years, are themselves part of the movement that has sought greater responsibility in institutional life. They are the products of their circumstances, and naturally reflect the concerns of the times in which they were written. But they express a common and consistent theme – the need to develop a more robust concept of individual responsibility for social and political institutions. That theme is now more relevant than ever – not only in the general approach it suggests but also in the specific arguments it supports.

The essays seek to reorient our thinking about ethics in public life toward a more institutional approach to individual moral responsibility. Restoring responsibility, they suggest, will require revising responsibility. In many different ways and in several different contexts, the essays suggest that we should stop thinking about ethics so much in terms of individual vices (bribery, extortion, greed, personal gain, sexual misconduct) and start thinking about it more in terms of institutional vices (abuse of power, improper disclosure, excessive secrecy, lack of accountability). We have been paying too much attention to individual, and too little to institutional, vice.

These mistakes are connected. The preoccupation with individual vices sometimes causes, sometimes even contributes to, the neglect of institutional vices. The obsession with individual vices rests on a misconception. It fails to appreciate the difference between individual and institutional ethics. Although they share a common moral foundation, these two kinds of ethics are quite different, both in their origins and in their purposes. Individual ethics originates in face-to-face relations among individuals, and it aims to make people morally better. Institutional ethics arises from the need to set standards for impersonal relations among people who may never meet, and it seeks to make institutions better by making their leaders more accountable.

Institutional ethics does not reject the possibility of holding the institutions themselves accountable. In the case of legal liability, the organization may be the only feasible defendant. Suing the corporation, or threatening to do so, may also be a necessary complement to holding its officers liable. But by blocking one of the most common ways that officials try to avoid taking responsibility – blaming the organization or the system (Chapter 1) – institutional ethics focuses on the individuals who run the organization and those who have the power to change it.

Adopting an institutional approach (Chapter 12), the essays shed light on a wide variety of ethical questions in public life. How can we hold officials in large organizations accountable for policies that many different people had a hand in making (Chapter 1)? Are advisers responsible for the consequences of the advice they give (Chapter 2)? How can the conflict between secrecy and accountability be resolved (Chapter 6)? Why do campaigns corrupt even honest legislators, and what can be done about it (Chapters 7 and 9)? Can elections make representatives accountable (Chapter 8)? The approach also illuminates problems beyond politics by showing, for example, why the ethical principles we should emphasize in hospital decision making are different from those we should apply in doctor-patient relations (Chapter 13); and why good character is neither necessary nor sufficient for ethical management in corporations (Chapter 15).

The institutional approach has three general implications for the project of restoring responsibility. First, the approach supports a concept of responsibility that is best understood as democratic. Although the concept takes several different forms in these essays (sometimes because the contexts are different, sometimes merely because the essays were written at different times), its essential core is constant. Democratic responsibility requires that officials and others who exercise power (1) acknowledge their agency in making decisions for the institution; and (2) provide a justification for their decisions.

The acknowledgment is what is usually called "taking responsibility." When this is not merely a ritual (Chapter 1), it results in sanctions (informal praise and blame, or more systematic rewards and punishments), which are imposed by citizens or others to whom the agent is accountable. Without rejecting the possibility that institutions themselves may be responsible agents, democratic responsibility, like most conceptions of democracy, respects persons as the fundamental moral agents. It is individuals who are ultimately held accountable. Because officials are regarded as responsible agents when they do not act under coercion or in ignorance, democratic responsibility tracks the traditional criteria of moral responsibility. It transposes the criteria of individual moral responsibility into an institutional key. The project of restoring responsibility is in this way an effort to strengthen individual responsibility in institutional life.

The second requirement – the demand for justification – captures part of what is usually meant by "exercising responsibility." It expresses the idea that people who have power must justify their decisions to those who are significantly affected by those decisions. Yet because the number of people affected is greater in institutional than in private life, so is the likelihood that they will disagree about the principles that should apply, and how they should apply. These disagreements are often reasonable, and cannot be resolved by an appeal to any simple set of rules, whether it be the law or the Constitution. Even judges, as Chapter 4 shows, should be subject to the demands of certain kinds of democratic responsibility.

To deal with such disagreements, citizens need to deliberate together, seeking to reach moral agreement when they can, and to find constructive ways to live with it when they cannot. Democratic responsibility therefore often needs the institutions of deliberative democracy, not only within but also outside government – for example, in ethics committees in hospitals (Chapter 13) and lay councils in the Church (Chapter 11). In the international sphere, the disagreement may go even deeper, and the need for deliberation may even prove greater (Chapter 16). These institutions fall short of the ideal of deliberative democracy, not only because people are imperfect and circumstances intractable, but also because the ideal is not always appropriate for all institutions at all times. Several of these essays explore the various forms the reason-giving requirement of democratic responsibility takes in different institutions – including the various standards for what should count as a reason.

A second implication of the institutional approach is that the focus of responsibility should be widened. The standard questions in practical and professional ethics typically take this form: What should I do? or What ought to be done? But equally important is a kind of question that is less often asked: What ought to be done when others do not do what they ought to do? Many of the essays in various ways address the responsibility for seeing that other people do the right thing, and, if they do not, for doing the right thing to correct the problem. The errors of some of the leaders in Enron, the Church and the FBI (Chapter 11) were failures in the ethics of oversight, an important form of moral responsibility in organizations.

More generally, an institutional approach implies that officials are responsible not only for the institutional decisions they make but also for the institutional conditions in which they make them. Institutional reform therefore must be part of the continuing agenda of any project to restore responsibility. The essays mention some possible reforms, but these should be seen less as proposals than as illustrations intended to clarify concepts and principles that could be useful in identifying the need for institutional change and evaluating its success or failure.

A third implication of an institutional approach concerns method – the level of analysis we should use for examining democratic responsibility. An institutional approach operates most fruitfully in a midrange of inquiry between abstract theory and concrete practice where principles and institutions meet. Institutional ethics is informed by philosophy. It favors a concept of responsibility that pays less attention to rules and regulations (such as those in codes of ethics) and more to the broader moral principles that underlie the processes that the rules and regulations govern. If we take institutional ethics seriously, we would for example view the responsibilities of bureaucrats more broadly and less negatively (Chapter 3). In an official manual for the training of U.S. civil servants entitled *How To Keep Out of Trouble*, one section addresses the question: "Can You Gamble While on Duty?" The answer – in case anyone is in doubt – is "No." This kind of handbook may be necessary, but ethics education and principles for bureaucrats (as well as for other officials) should of course go further. They should be about not only how to stay out of trouble but also how to take and exercise responsibility. Even in the case of a practice that necessarily involves rules – such as the prohibition of conflicts of interest – we should attend more to the moral purposes of the rules (Chapter 14).

Yet institutional ethics does not aspire to be a branch of philosophy. It counsels theoretical modesty: concentrate on institutional norms rather than philosophical doctrines. It does not take a stand on the question of free will versus determinism. Nor does it seek to resolve controversies about individual responsibility in general – whether, for example, one is responsible only for choices as distinct from circumstances. However such disputes may be resolved, the distinctive problems on which institutional ethics concentrates remain – and in much the same form.

Even in political philosophy, the most fruitful arguments about institutional responsibility rarely turn on choices between grand theoretical alternatives – liberalism or conservatism, utilitarianism and Kantianism, or other competing "isms." Many of the debates about responsibility evoke elements of these theories, and are easily turned into battles between ideologies or comprehensive philosophies. But the deliberation that responsibility requires is more likely to be productive in the midrange of controversy, where more citizens can express their disagreements and accommodate their differences without abandoning their comprehensive conceptions of morality and politics. This midrange method also offers the prospect of a more meaningful engagement with the actual views of members and leaders of organizations, and the actual arguments of citizens and representatives in government and other institutions.

The essays in this collection are arranged in three sections, each of which explores a different aspect of the project of restoring moral responsibility in social and political institutions. The first section develops the concept of responsibility needed for making ethical judgments about leaders in public institutions. Although the basic concept remains the same across a wide range of contexts, the various roles in public institutions – executive, adviser, judge, legislator – create different obligations and raise different issues even in the same context.

The second section turns to some of the particular vices for which public officials should be held responsible: secrecy in government, corruption in office and campaigns, and immorality in private life. The third section takes the discussion beyond government to issues of moral responsibility in corporations, hospitals, and religious organizations. It concludes with an essay that shows the need for extending deliberation about responsibility across national boundaries.

Restoring responsibility in our institutions may require modifying our attitudes toward ethics itself. We need to resist the popular notion that ethics is only what you do, not also what you talk about. We should not be satisfied with any version of what some would call the John Wayne theory of ethics: stand up for what you think is right, but never say why. If we are to hold our leaders responsible, we ourselves must become more comfortable with articulating ethical principles in institutional forums and in terms that others can appreciate, if not accept. We must be prepared to justify our own decisions to others as we ask others to justify their decisions to us.

In the increasingly complex and contentious democracies in which we live, these justifications – even while addressed to individuals – must go beyond the familiar territory of individual morality. The reasons we ask for, and the reasons we give, should be firmly rooted in the circumstances of institutional life. Although the basic values on which individual and institutional ethics rest and the agents to which they apply are often the same, the interpretations, implications, and applications of the principles of each are often significantly different. The theory and practice of responsibility in democratic societies should respect these differences. Those who exercise power in these societies, whether in government, business, or other pursuits, must accept responsibility not only for their own character but for the character of the institutions they govern.

PART I

DEMANDS OF INSTITUTIONAL POLITICS

1

The Problem of Many Hands

Philosophers and political scientists in recent years have begun to apply moral principles to public policy and to public officials.[1] None of these scholars supposes that moral principles can, without modification, be directly deployed in politics. Indeed, one of their preoccupations is the possibility that public life may require officials to act in ways that would be wrong in private life, raising the classic problem of "dirty hands" (Walzer 1973). But in a significant respect, their analyses are often apolitical: the official they portray agonizing over a moral dilemma seems a solitary figure, single-handedly gathering information and implementing decisions. This paradigm of the lonely leader obscures a pervasive feature of modern government – a feature that stands in the way of applying moral principles, whatever their content, to individual officials. Because many different officials contribute in many ways to decisions and policies of government, it is difficult even in principle to identify who is morally responsible for political outcomes. This is what I call the problem of many hands.

The two most common ways of ascribing responsibility to officials – the hierarchical and the collective models – do not adequately respond to this problem; and personal responsibility, suitably interpreted, can be imputed to officials more often than these models suggest. The criteria for personal responsibility I adopt are common to a wide range of moral theories; they hold us responsible for outcomes insofar as we cause them and do not act in ignorance or under compulsion. On these criteria we can say that one official is more or less responsible than another official without implying, as in the law, that degrees of fault correspond to proportionate shares of compensation or match the standard categories of criminal liability. Legal responsibility, though suggestive, is not a reliable guide to moral responsibility (see Hart 1968, 211–30; Feinberg 1970, 24–54).

Corresponding to each of the criteria of personal responsibility are types of excuses officials use to eliminate or mitigate their responsibility for political outcomes.[2] Drawing examples from episodes in contemporary American government (chiefly the executive branch), I shall outline some of the conditions under which the excuses seem to be acceptable or unacceptable.

From such an outline, we should not expect to derive anything so systematic as a general theory of excuses, but we should be able to develop a set of considerations based on a body of cases, more like traditional moral casuistry than modern ethical and political theory. In most political contexts, this set of considerations will have to be supplemented by substantive principles of political ethics grounded in concepts such as justice and the public interest. But even by itself an analysis of excuses can serve to inform our judgments about those who govern us, and thus enrich our understanding of political responsibility.[3] Its use might even influence the conduct of public officials. Those who took the idea of personal responsibility seriously would perhaps make decisions with greater care, and if they did not, citizens or other officials could reinforce ascriptions of responsibility with sanctions, such as public criticism, dismissal from office, or exclusion from public office in the future. Whether personal responsibility could actually support democratic accountability in this way depends partly on the nature of the social and political structure in which citizens and officials act. But as important as it is to analyze this structure, the prior task, and the one on which I concentrate here, is to establish a framework for the discourse of responsibility.

HIERARCHICAL RESPONSIBILITY

According to the hierarchical model, responsibility for political outcomes falls on the person who stands highest in the (formal or informal) chain of authority. Weber provides the classic statement of the model. He holds, first, that modern government recognizes "fixed jurisdictional areas" and "office hierarchy" in which "there is a supervision of the lower offices by the higher ones" (Gerth and Mills 1958, 196–7). Second, he sharply distinguishes between administration and politics: administrators merely execute the policies set by politicians

(95, 214–16). Finally, the administrator and the politician are therefore subject to "exactly the opposite principle of responsibility":

> The honor of the civil servant is vested in his ability to execute conscientiously the order of the superior authority, exactly as if the order agreed with his own conviction.... The honor of the political leader ... however, lies precisely in an exclusive personal responsibility for what he does, a responsibility he cannot and must not reject or transfer.[4]

Weber's model vastly simplifies the task of ascribing responsibility to public officials since it places most public officials most of the time beyond the province of moral responsibility. As long as they follow the orders of their superiors and the procedures of the organization, they are not responsible for any harmful results of their actions. We are of course still left with the chore of sorting out the responsibility of the various politicians who have a hand in making the policies that the administrators carry out, but because the hands are fewer and because the jurisdictions are well defined, the problem is much more tractable.

Weber's model, however, does not correspond to the portrait of politics that emerges from modern studies of the making of public policy. Instead of functioning within well-defined jurisdictions and settled lines of authority, officials act within overlapping "issue networks" whose membership is shifting and partially drawn from outside government (Heclo 1978, 87–124); they engage in a "bargaining game" where victory depends more on "skill and will in using [other] bargaining advantages" and "other players' perceptions" than on positions in a hierarchy (Allison 1971, 144–84). Instead of respecting a clear distinction between politics and administration, bureaucrats exercise discretionary authority, either delegated to them or simply assumed by them, to shape and often to make policy; meanwhile, elected politicians concern themselves with the details of implementation (Altshuler 1977, 2–17; Lowi 1979, 92–126; Rourke 1978, 253).

The empirical deficiencies of the hierarchical model do not necessarily defeat it as a normative standard. Weber himself anticipated some of the developments that impugn the model (Gerth and Mills 1958, 232–3), and later writers continue to commend the model in spite of – or perhaps because of – the growth of administrative discretion and the dispersion of authority in the modern state (e.g., Lowi 1979, 295–313; and Krasner 1972, 160).

But even if a more hierarchical structure of government is desirable, the hierarchical model is not a satisfactory basis on which to ascribe responsibility in the structure of government that now prevails – at least not where discretion and dispersion abound. Insofar as officials holding the top positions in a hierarchy cannot be expected to have control over political outcomes, hierarchical responsibility does not coincide with moral responsibility. To try to impute moral responsibility according to hierarchical position would in these circumstances violate a fundamental presupposition of morality, namely, that a person should be blamed only if he or she could have acted otherwise.

The difficulty is not that it would be unfair to hold top officials responsible for failures beyond their control. Officials know in advance that they may lose their jobs because of events over which they could have had little or no influence, and they thus tacitly consent to the risk of this kind of political punishment. Such risk, moreover, may be a useful feature in the design of political institutions, encouraging officials to take every possible precaution to avoid mistakes. But these considerations show only that strict liability in politics may be morally justifiable; they do not establish that such liability is equivalent to moral responsibility. Even when we hold officials strictly accountable in this way, we usually do not condemn them morally.

That hierarchical responsibility imparts scarcely any moral force explains why political leaders are often quite ready to declare themselves fully responsible for some pernicious decision or policy. Taking responsibility becomes a kind of political ritual that has no negative effect on a leader. Indeed, leaders can often turn this ritual to their advantage (cf. V. Thompson 1961, 129–37; and Edelman 1964, 79). With regular incantations of "I accept full responsibility," an official strengthens his or her own political standing – by reassuring the public that someone is in charge and by projecting an image of a courageous leader who does not pass the buck. Also, as one becomes known as a leader who takes the blame for subordinates, one gains gratitude and thus greater obedience from those subordinates in the future. Most significantly, the ritual often quells public debate about a controversial decision or policy, effectively blocking further inquiry into the genuine moral responsibility of all of the officials involved, especially that of the leader. After the failure of the Bay of Pigs invasion, President Kennedy privately blamed the CIA, the Joint Chiefs, and just about everyone who knew about the invasion in advance. But publicly he accepted the "sole responsibility" and objected to anyone's "attempting to shift responsibility" away from him (Schlesinger 1965, 289–90). The hierarchical model, reinforcing this ritual taking of responsibility, in this case not only cut short public inquiry into other officials' responsibility for the failure of the invasion, but, more importantly, also forestalled public debate about each official's failure to consider whether subversion of this kind is morally justified at all.

It seems, further, that the more personally blameworthy an official, the more strenuously the official is likely to insist on accepting hierarchical responsibility. In the spring of 1973, as Watergate intruded more and more into the office of the president itself, Nixon invoked the ritualistic formula of responsibility in almost its pure form:

> Who is to blame for what happened in this case? . . . The easiest course would be for me to blame those to whom I delegated the responsibility to run the campaign. But that would be a cowardly thing to do. . . . In any organization, the man at the top must bear the responsibility. That responsibility, therefore, belongs here in this office. I accept it (transcribed from tape of the CBS broadcast of Nixon's address to the nation, April 30, 1973).

COLLECTIVE RESPONSIBILITY

The argument underlying the collective model begins by posing a version of the problem of many hands: many political outcomes are the product of the actions of many different people whose individual contributions may not be identifiable at all, and certainly cannot be distinguished significantly from other people's contributions. The second step is the claim that no one individual, therefore, can be morally blamed for these outcomes. At the final stage of the argument, its proponents reach two seemingly contradictory conclusions: one stating that every individual associated with the collectivity should be charged with moral responsibility, the other holding that only the collectivity can be so charged. But the conclusions are not so different since neither ascribes responsibility to persons on the basis of their specific and distinct connections to the outcome in question.

The first version of the collective model can be illustrated by Herbert Kaufman's effort to pin the blame for the (immoral as well as inefficient) consequences of bureaucratic "red tape":

> It would not surprise me . . . if [public officers and employees] are merely scapegoats. . . . We may accuse them because, intuitively, we want to divert the

guilt from the real cause: ourselves. No one element of the population is responsible for all red tape or even for most of it . . . we all have a hand in it.[5]

W. H. Walsh has offered a general theoretical defense for this sort of dispersion of responsibility. Walsh rejects noncollective ideas of moral responsibility because they incorrectly assume that the individual is "self-contained and self-subsistent" (Walsh 1970, 4). We are morally responsible for the actions of people with whom we have any "special relationship" (5). That includes all our fellow citizens, and even earlier generations, but fortunately does not encompass all humanity since we are not, Walsh concedes, culpable for the actions of Genghis Khan. While Walsh thus radically expands the responsibility of citizens, he drastically diminishes the responsibility of public officials. Because officials act as representatives, limited by the demands of citizens and bound by longstanding commitments their predecessors have made, their decisions are not fully voluntary, and, Walsh concludes, they are therefore not fully responsible for the decisions.

This version of the collective model, however, cannot account for many distinctions that we intuitively wish to draw in apportioning blame. We normally distinguish degrees of responsibility that citizens and officials bear for policies of the government or of the groups with which they are associated. For example, those who do not protest against an unjust policy are usually thought to be more responsible for it than those who do protest. Among those who do not protest, those who have greater resources with which to influence the policy are more responsible than those with fewer such resources. These and many other similar distinctions presuppose some form of the principle Walsh must reject (at least for citizens), namely, that responsibility for a policy depends in part on the contribution an individual actually made, or could have made, to the policy.

The second version of the collective model – blaming the collectivity rather than any specific member of it – is sometimes represented by the hypothetical example of the old-time train robbery (Feinberg 1970, 248). An armed bandit holds up a carload of passengers and escapes with all their money. All of the passengers, or even a few of them, could have prevented the robbery had they coordinated their actions. In this way the passengers were collectively responsible for their own losses, but since no passenger was obligated to resist the bandit, none was individually responsible. The fault lay not in individual actions or omissions, but in the structure of the group.[6]

Similarly, a political system may suffer from structural faults that block the efforts of all but the heroic bureaucrat or politician to accomplish morally respectable ends. An example appears in "The Blast in Centralia No. 5," the introductory case in a widely used casebook in public administration:

> Responsibility [for the mine disaster that killed 111 men] here transcends individuals. The miners at Centralia, seeking somebody who would heed their conviction that their lives were in danger, found themselves confronted with officialdom, a huge organism scarcely mortal. . . . As one strives to fix responsibility for the disaster, again and again one is confronted, as were the miners, not with any individual but with a host of individuals fused into a vast, unapproachable, insensate organism. Perhaps this immovable juggernaut is the true villain in the piece.[7]

However, the responsibility of the private and public officials in this case differs from that of the passengers in the train robbery example. Officials act in the context of an ongoing institution, not an isolated incident, and they or other officials therefore may be culpable for creating the structural faults of the institution, or for neglecting to notice them, or for making inadequate efforts to correct them. The responsibility of officials is no more temporally bounded than is the existence of the institutions in which they act.

Because both versions of the collective model distort the idea of responsibility, neither can serve as the foundation for judgments we wish to make about public officials. The first version blurs moral distinctions not only among various officials but also between officials and citizens. The second version recognizes no connection between structural faults and individual responsibility for making structural criticisms or changes.

The hierarchical model has the advantage of locating responsibility in determinate positions, but it neglects the problem of many hands. Proponents of the collective model take that problem all too seriously, reproducing it in the model itself and, as a result, weakening democratic accountability. I do not want to deny that hierarchical position is relevant in imputing responsibility, or that collective responsibility sometimes makes sense. But I do wish to suggest that an approach that preserves a traditional notion of personal responsibility – with its advantages for democratic accountability – can accommodate many of the complexities of a political process in which many different officials contribute to policies and decisions.

PERSONAL RESPONSIBILITY

Ascribing responsibility to officials as persons rather than simply as occupants of certain offices or as members of a collectivity relies on two criteria of moral responsibility. An official is morally responsible for an outcome insofar as (1) the official's actions or omissions are a cause of the outcome; and (2) these actions or omissions are not done in ignorance or under compulsion. These are notoriously difficult ideas, and I can provide only a few general comments about them before turning to the excuses they underlie.

The criterion of causal responsibility, as I interpret it, is quite weak. It requires only that one be a cause of an outcome in the sense that the outcome would not have happened but for one's act or omission.[8] To say that a person is a cause merely connects his or her action with an outcome – along with the action of many other hands and the influence of many other forces. It does not establish that the person is the most important cause or even an agent on whom we should pin responsibility at all. If we wish to select an individual from among all the other causal factors in this cone of causation, we have to invoke other moral and political considerations, chiefly the importance of the outcome in question and the formal and informal expectations of the individual's official role.

It might be objected that we should not use the causal criterion at all. Ladd argues that the part played by any single official is neither necessary nor sufficient to bring about an organizational decision. Therefore, to require, as a necessary condition of responsibility, that an official be a cause of the decision is to "give aid and comfort to officials who want to avoid responsibility" (Ladd 1970, 513–15). Ladd is surely correct in refusing to assimilate moral responsibility to causal responsibility. We should not want to say that an official is less responsible to the degree that he or she is less causally effective. But the weak causal criterion does not have this implication since it is not sufficient to determine moral responsibility, let alone degrees of moral responsibility. Yet unless an official's action is at least a causal factor of an outcome, it is hard to see why the question should arise of holding that official, rather than anyone or everyone else, responsible for it.

The second criterion – volitional responsibility – in its most general form stipulates that a person is responsible for an action insofar as he or she could have done otherwise.[9] Inability to act otherwise takes many different forms, ranging from general incapacity (such as insanity) to specific defects in particular actions (such as inadvertence). Most relevant for assessing the actions of public officials are these specific faults, which may be considered under the traditional Aristotelian categories of ignorance and compulsion (Aristotle 1963, 1109b–1111b; cf. Glover 1970, esp. 60–1; Donagan 1977, 112–42).

Ignorance of what one does (not knowing that a certain description applies to one's action) counts as an excuse only if the ignorance is not negligent. In the case of public officials, the standards of negligence depend on moral and political considerations, such as an assessment of the outcomes in question and the nature of the role of the official. So does the question of whether compulsion should count as an excuse. The compulsion that public officials cite to excuse their conduct is rarely the extreme physical and psychological kind that philosophers and lawyers usually discuss. When officials proclaim, "I had no choice," we seldom take them literally. They can usually be understood as implying that they did not choose the *range* of alternatives within which they made some decision. Like Aristotle's sea captain (1110a 8–15), they confront two undesirable options (jettisoning the cargo or sinking the ship). The duties of office conspire with the forces of nature to pose a choice between disagreeable alternatives. Limitations on the range of alternatives do not eliminate an official's responsibility, but they do warrant our specifying, in any ascription of praise or blame, what alternatives were realistically accessible.

CAUSAL EXCUSES

In "Centralia No. 5," one of the persons blamed for the deaths of the miners was Inspector Scanlan, who had the authority to close the mine he knew to be unsafe but failed to do so. Scanlan's defense (in part) was that "had he closed the Centralia mine, Medill [the Director of the Illinois Department of Mines and Minerals] simply would have fired him and appointed a more tractable inspector" (Stillman 1976, 33). This is an example of the excuse from alternative cause: "If I hadn't done it, someone else would have," or "If I don't do it, someone else will." The excuse is more common in official than in personal life because in organizations the empirical assumption on which it depends is more likely to be true. In organizations persons often are fungible.

In a general and unqualified form, the excuse seems incoherent. To relieve one person of responsibility, the excuse asserts that other people (the alternative causal agents) would be responsible for the action. But if the excuse is valid, each of the other people would be exonerated, seriatim, just as the first person was. In other words, if the excuse is valid, no one is responsible. In any case, the excuse has not been accepted in civil or criminal law (Hart and Honoré 1959, 225–6), and moral judgment agrees with the law in this regard.

Nevertheless, the excuse may sometimes be acceptable in a modified form. One such form is as a criterion of causal relevance. Here an official claims not that someone else would have made the same mistake, but rather that someone else would have made a different mistake that would have been sufficient to cause the harmful outcome. The excuse is thus used to show that the respect in which the official's action is faulty is not a cause of the outcome.[10]

In the political process, however, judgments about causal connections or their absence are often uncertain. Consider the case of an FDA official who permits a drug, which subsequently turns out to be unsafe, to be placed on the agency's list of substances "generally recognized as safe" – without ordering certain standard laboratory tests on the drug. We might perhaps not blame this official for any harm suffered by users of the drug if we believe that the technicians charged with performing the tests would have approved the drug anyhow. But to the extent that the causal relevance remains uncertain (e.g., we doubt that the technicians would have approved the drug), then other factors will influence our judgment about the validity of the excuse. Specifically, we will be more likely to accept the excuse if the fault is relatively minor (e.g., failing to order the tests because of overlooking some technicality rather than because of accepting a bribe), or if the consequences to which the fault allegedly contributed are relatively harmless. It is perhaps odd that these factors should affect our judgment at all, since in principle officials should be blamed only if their fault was a cause of the outcome. But given the inevitable uncertainty of causal connections in organizations, we may be justified, as a practical matter, in considering these other factors when assessing even causal excuses.

The excuse from alternative cause is also acceptable if it is combined with certain kinds of justifications. To the plea that someone else would have committed the wrong is added the claim that he or she would have committed a worse wrong, or in some other way would have made the consequences worse. This excuse comes most naturally to officials who do not resign from a government that is pursuing an admittedly wrong policy. During the Vietnam War, many officials, including Hubert Humphrey and Robert McNamara, privately told friends that they were staying on to keep the escalation from getting worse; others, like Charles Frankel (Assistant Secretary of State for Educational and Cultural Affairs) pointed to benefits they could accomplish that in their judgment outweighed any effect their resignations might have on the war (Weisband and Franck 1976, 92–3).

We are right to be suspicious of such pleas. The heady mixture of exercising power while believing oneself to be doing good can easily forestall a sober assessment of the consequences of alternative courses of action. Still, the plea is sometimes surely acceptable. Even when the government an official serves is utterly evil, resignation may not be the most appropriate course. It has been argued that the S.S. Officer Kurt Gerstein, by continuing in his post during the Second World War, "prevented worse things from happening" (Friedlander 1969, 199). In less extreme circumstances, the range of choice is usually greater, but an argument based on the worse alternative may still seem plausible. After Attorney General Elliot Richardson and then his deputy resigned rather than carry out Nixon's order to fire the Watergate Special Prosecutor Archibald Cox, the Solicitor General Robert Bork decided to stay on the job and dismiss Cox. Bork argued that he would be more likely to protect the integrity of the Justice Department and the independence of any future Special Prosecutor than anyone Nixon would appoint as his replacement (Lukas 1977, 592). In this way, the justifiability of Bork's use of the argument from the worse alternative comes to depend on his subsequent conduct.

It might be argued that the validity of this sort of excuse-cum-justification should not turn simply on a comparison of the consequences of an official's actions and the consequences of the actions of alternative causal agents. Bernard Williams maintains that this way of ascribing responsibility (which he associates with utilitarianism) ignores the value of personal integrity (Williams 1973, 97–8). He argues that a young scientist who opposes research on chemical and biological warfare should not take a job in a government laboratory engaged in such research, even if as a result another scientist will take the job and pursue the research much more zealously. Agents should be primarily responsible for their own "projects" (actions based on commitments that form part of their personal character) and should not abandon them simply because the calculation of general social utility dictates that they should (116).

While Williams may be correct in criticizing utilitarianism for permitting an impersonal perspective to dominate a personal one, his own account of personal integrity remains insufficiently developed to support the radically circumscribed responsibility he evidently favors. Acting to protect one's personal integrity, at the expense of avoidable and serious harm to other people, seems too close to moral self-indulgence. It could represent an effort to keep one's hands clean no matter what happens to the rest of society.

A second category of causal excuses comprises those pleas that would disconnect an official completely from the chain of events leading to a harmful outcome. These may be called excuses from null cause. Since it is often possible to cite as a cause almost any act or omission by an official in the organization that brings about the outcome, an official who uses the excuse must distinguish his or her act or omission from that of others. One way to do this is the familiar plea, "It's not my job." In this form the excuse is usually intended to cut short any argument about whether the official could have made any difference, or could make any difference in the future. Because the duties of the official's role do not concern the policy in question, failure to oppose the policy or to resign from the government that pursues it should not be considered a cause of its perpetuation. As George Ball said in an interview in 1973, "Why *should* I have resigned in protest over Vietnam policy just because I disagreed with it? My main responsibility...was Western Europe. Perhaps five per cent of my time was spent on Vietnam. It simply wasn't my responsibility;...it wasn't as if I were the Honduras desk officer being put in the position of having to approve a U.S. military action in Honduras" (quoted in Weisband and Franck 1976, 139).

Ball is surely right to suppose that the nature of an office circumscribes an official's responsibility to some extent. One cannot be culpable for all the policies on which one could have had any influence. That Ball's "main responsibility" did not concern Vietnam at least counts as a reason for ascribing less responsibility to him than to those officials whose main duties did concern Vietnam. By the same token, as a high-ranking State Department official, Ball shares more blame than (say) an official in the Department of Health, Education and Welfare. The nature of the role or office, however, should not be understood rigidly. Contrary to the implication of Ball's reference to the Honduras desk officer, it is not enough to claim that one's role does not require specific positive decisions in the area in question. Omissions, acquiescence, tacit approval, even ritualized opposition – all may gain one a place in the causal chain.

Similarly, a narrowly technical definition of an office does not necessarily exonerate the person who holds that office. Scientific personnel, for example, may be responsible for the uses others make of their work, especially if the risks of harm from these uses are great. The case for ascribing responsibility to scientists for their discoveries increases if, like J. Robert Oppenheimer, they continue to have influence on how politicians use their discoveries. Defending himself in 1954, Oppenheimer disclaimed any such responsibility: "I did my job . . . I was not in a policy-making position . . . " (U.S. Atomic Energy Commission 1971, 236). But earlier he evidently accepted a rather extreme form of such responsibility. According to Truman, Oppenheimer in 1946 "came into my office . . . and spent most of his time wringing his hands and telling me that they had blood on them because of the discovery of atomic energy" (Donovan 1977, 97). To say that scientists or other officials who are engaged in technical work may be morally responsible for the consequences of their work is not necessarily to claim that they should not perform the work when its use offends their conscience (they may have an overriding duty to contribute their talents and skills to society in some circumstances). But it does imply that their choice of whether to perform the work is a moral one, and that they have a continuing obligation to consider and question the uses to which their contributions are put.

Even if the duties of office do not require (or perhaps do not permit) an official to do anything about an immoral policy, we may wish to criticize the official for remaining in office as part of an immoral regime. But this would be an accusation of complicity (claiming that one's association with this regime is itself immoral or dishonorable), rather than an ascription of responsibility (asserting that by some act or omission, one actually furthered specific immoral politics) (see Hill 1979).

VOLITIONAL EXCUSES

Some theories of responsibility would obviate the problem of many hands by making officials responsible only for what they intend, and not at all (or at least never as much) for what anyone else does as a result of their decisions. Kant expresses this view in its most absolute form. He insists, for example, that you must tell the truth even to a murderer who asks where your friend, his intended victim, is hiding (Kant 1949, 346–50). You are responsible for your own intentional act (truth-telling or lying), and if you tell the truth you cannot be blamed for what other people do as a result of your honesty. The implausibility of this view in ordinary moral life is magnified in public life. Even if we deny that a public official should let utilitarian calculation determine whether he or she lies or commits other acts that are absolutely wrong on a Kantian view, we would surely hold the official morally responsible for failing to take precautions to avoid harmful consequences of others' responses to his or her decisions. Even a traditional morality, which otherwise disregards consequences, "commands" that we carefully consider "what bad consequences flow from abiding by it" and "what dispositions [we] can make to avoid them . . . " (Donagan 1977, 206–7).

To say that intention is not a necessary condition for charging an official with responsibility is not inevitably to embrace a consequentialism that holds that we are all "equally morally responsible for all consequences."[11] It is simply to recognize that, at least for public officials, the contours of responsibility are likely to be more irregular than the criterion of intention would draw. In tracing the bounds of responsibility, we shall also have to pay attention to other criteria, specifically those of ignorance and compulsion.

If ignorance in general were a valid excuse, the innocence of some public officials would be irreproachable. But the kind of ignorance relevant to the problem of many hands concerns an official's lack of specific knowledge about the actions of other officials. An official who admittedly contributes to an objectionable outcome may seek to excuse the contribution by claiming that he or she did not know, and should not have been expected to know, that other officials had acted wrongly or would act wrongly. When as UN Ambassador in 1961 Adlai Stevenson stated that the United States did not have anything to do with the invasion of Cuba, he could not have been expected to realize that his statement was false, and therefore escapes responsibility for any wrong that was committed (Muller 1967, 283–4). Whether Stevenson should have been told is another matter, but ambassadors, spokespersons, and others in similar roles have to trust that they are being told the truth, or at least that they are being told everything they need to know about governmental activities within their purview.

At the other end of the causal chain, an official may sometimes be excused for consequences of a decision when he or she could not be expected to foresee the wrongs that other officials would commit in implementing the decision. After the surrender of Germany, President Truman signed an order terminating the shipment of food, clothing, and other goods that our allies had been receiving under Lend-Lease. The abrupt disruption of these supplies threatened significant hardship for many citizens in these countries until Truman rescinded the order. Truman defended himself by claiming that his aides had executed the order too literally (Truman 1955, 227–8).

Such an excuse will not work when officials are the instruments of their own ignorance. They may, for example, encourage subordinates not to tell them about certain possibly objectionable plans so that they can deny knowledge of the plans if they go awry. Or officials may elicit misleading information from subordinates by indicating, sometimes unwittingly, what kind of conclusions they wish to hear, as when Rusk and McNamara, considering an American intervention in the Dominican Republic in 1965, asked the acting U.S. Ambassador to the Dominican Republic if "he agreed with their view that a rebel victory would probably lead to a pro-Communist government" (Martin 1966, 659). Not surprisingly, the acting ambassador agreed.

To reject a plea of ignorance, we do not have to show that an official should have foreseen the specific act of some particular official (for example, that an aide would misinterpret an order in exactly this way). It is sufficient that the official should have realized that mistakes of the kind that occurred were likely. In bureaucracies, certain patterns of fault are common enough that we should expect any competent official to anticipate them and to take reasonable precautions to avoid them or at least to minimize their harmful consequences.

During the early months of the Peace Corps, Sargent Shriver, disappointed in the small number of requests foreign governments had submitted for Corps programs, urged his "programmers" to seek out more requests. According to one account, those who failed to come back with programs "in their pockets" were fired or fell into disfavor; consequently, some programmers created fictitious programs. It has been argued that Shriver should bear some responsibility for these consequences since he should have foreseen that his own injunction could induce such behavior by some of his staff (Peters 1973, 22; for a different account, see Ashabranner 1971, 19–42). When a superior puts great pressure on subordinates to produce results and gives the impression that questionable practices to achieve these results will be condoned – as allegedly occurred in the army recruiting scandals reported in the fall of 1979 – then the blame falls at least equally on the superior. Ignorance ceases even to mitigate responsibility.

But that an official apply pressure, even of the mild sort Shriver evidently exerted, is not a necessary condition for making an official responsible for the subsequent actions of others. An official who sets in motion bureaucratic routines cannot escape culpability for the consequences even if he or she is no longer involved in the process when the consequences occur. The system of double-bookkeeping that Henry Kissinger approved in 1969, supposedly to conceal a single bombing attack on Cambodia, persisted "by rote and without a special new decision" and led other officials in 1973 to give Congress false information (Kissinger 1979a, 7; 1979b, 239–54). Even if the initial bombing and secrecy could somehow be justified, Kissinger would not escape blame for the subsequent deception. Whether the bureaucratic routines are pathological or conventional (or both), the fact that they have a life of their own, often roaming beyond their original purpose, is a feature of organizational behavior that officials should be expected to appreciate. The more that the consequences of a decision fit such bureaucratic patterns, the less an official can plausibly appeal to the excuse from ignorance.

Yet an official may still have an escape. Some of the most normal and expected patterns of behavior in bureaucracies are also the most difficult for anyone to change, and some of these may obligate officials to act in certain ways despite harmful consequences they may be able to foresee. Thus, just as the excuse from ignorance begins to falter, the excuse from compulsion comes to the rescue. Of the many kinds of constraints that officials cite to reduce their responsibility for decisions, those that derive from other officials' actions, rather than from forces of nature or reactions of the public, most directly bear on the problem of many hands.

The question of responsibility certainly arises when an official issues an explicit order to carry out some morally objectionable policy, but I set aside such cases because they are extensively discussed in the literature on war crimes (Walzer 1977, 287–327), and also because they are less prevalent in the workaday life of administrators in modern bureaucracies. More common are cases where no explicit order has been given but a subordinate believes that a superior expects him or her to pursue what is seen as a morally dubious course of action. This is the gray area between command and discretion. When a superior relies on subordinates to know what to do without being told, the superior can no more escape responsibility for the subordinates' actions than they can. No one ordered FBI Director L. Patrick Gray to destroy the incriminating files from E. Howard Hunt's safe, but, as Gray later testified, "The clear implication . . . was that these two files were to be destroyed . . ." (Congressional Quarterly 1975, 226).

But an even more common constraint than orders from a superior, however implicit, is the persistence of various practices established by other officials, who may not be identifiable. Such practices circumscribe a current official's range of choices, and thus may mitigate his or her responsibility. Consider Mayor Beame's dilemma during the New York City fiscal crisis before the market for city securities collapsed in the spring of 1975 (D.Thompson 1981). Among other charges, critics accused Beame of misleading the public by failing to disclose the true state of the city's finances. Beame insisted that it was not his fault if the budget misrepresented the city's financial condition. He had inherited the questionable accounting practices ("gimmicks," the critics called them) that gave rise to any misrepresentation. Those practices that he knew about, he could neither change nor even publicize without risking the bankruptcy of the city, thereby jeopardizing the welfare of millions of the city's residents and employees. For example, the budget overstated the amount of federal and state aid the city expected to receive because city officials recorded, as receivable, funds that federal and state authorities did not intend to allocate. Beame argued that if he had removed the disputed receivables from the books, or even had conceded that they were in dispute, he would have significantly reduced the chances for collecting these funds from the federal and state governments. There were other such "gimmicks" – nearly all difficult to change and none of them of the mayor's making.

We may be prepared to excuse Beame as mayor for the existence of these practices, and blame him less for any decisions constrained by these practices. We would normally impute more responsibility to the mayor's predecessors. But in this case there is a twist: among his predecessors were Abe Beame, Controller, 1969–73, 1962–65; Abe Beame, Budget Director, 1952–61; and Abe Beame, Assistant Budget Director, 1946–52. Personal responsibility, unlike role responsibility, pursues officials through time.

Some bureaucratic practices, unobjectionable in intent, turn out to constrain the performances of officials in harmful ways. Such constraints particularly affect those officials who have been called "street-level bureaucrats" – social workers, police officers, and the like, who deal frequently with citizens, and exercise considerable discretion in an uncertain environment (Lipsky 1980, 81–156). Because these officials face demanding standards of job performance and rarely have sufficient resources to meet them, they develop "bureaucratic mechanisms" to evade responsibility for their failures. For example, because the performance of officials in the Job Corps program was measured by the number of trainees who received a job after completing the program, officials tended to recruit those youths who already seemed disposed to succeed in a job; these turned out to be youths with more middle-class than lower-class orientations (Sjoberg et al. 1978, 42–3). A seemingly neutral procedure of evaluation thus gave rise to discriminatory bureaucratic conduct. In these circumstances, we would want to impute major responsibility to the higher-level officials who set up the procedures – if we can locate these officials.

But street-level bureaucrats themselves cannot be considered blameless no matter what they do. Even within the constraints of fixed routines, some officials perform worse than others, and these variations open some space for ascribing responsibility. A measure of actual variation – for example, an average performance – would not serve as a satisfactory base line from which to assess responsibility since all officials may be doing less well than they could, even given the constraints. We would need some criterion based on a hypothetical average performance – what the average official could reasonably be expected to do under the circumstances (a "reasonable bureaucrat" test). Moreover, when these lower-level officials come to recognize how certain bureaucratic routines cause them to perform in morally questionable ways, they acquire, as do other officials who work within defective structures, a special responsibility to call attention to the defects, even if they cannot correct them.

CONCLUSION

The conditions under which excuses eliminate or mitigate the responsibility of a public official depend not only on factors to which the excuses refer directly (causality and volition) but also on factors that help interpret the excuses (the nature of the policy in question and the role the official holds). The interaction of these factors is best captured not by a general theory of responsibility but by a casuistic analysis of a range of exemplary cases. We should reject the simpler approaches favored by the hierarchical and collective models, and avoid formulas (such as alternative cause) that would simplify the ascription of personal responsibility itself.

Insofar as we can locate those officials who are personally responsible and thus most closely connected with the policies and decisions that governments promulgate, we can refine and fortify the praise and blame that, as democratic citizens, we direct toward public officials. Personal responsibility can in this way lay a foundation for democratic accountability of the officials who make objectionable decisions and policies.

But it can also support accountability for harmful policies and decisions that are less attributable to any current officials as moral agents than to bureaucratic routines and structural defects of the organization in which the officials act. Because personal responsibility attaches to persons, not to offices or collectivities, it follows officials wherever they go. We can trace it through time – to the past when the mayor was the controller, or to the future when the solicitor general makes good on his claim that he was the least bad alternative.

Moreover, we can hold officials responsible for harmful decisions made within a defective structure if they fail to make adequate efforts to criticize and change that structure, even if they made the best decision possible within the constraints they faced. The grounds for this extension of responsibility derive from the volitional criteria. Officials who operate within faulty machinery of government may be presumed to know more than others about its faults; the excuse of ignorance is usually less accessible to them. They are also often in the best position to refute or to fulfill the claim that they cannot do anything about the defects; the excuse from compulsion becomes less plausible to the extent that an official fails to make efforts toward criticism or reform.

We can hardly expect to identify officials who are responsible for all, or perhaps even the worst, evils that governments visit upon their citizens. Nor for that matter can we always identify officials who deserve credit for the good that governments occasionally accomplish. But the pursuit of personal responsibility provides the best foundation for understanding the role that human agency plays in good and bad government, and therefore establishes some basis for initiating whatever political change may be necessary.

Notes

I am grateful to Joel Feinberg, Amy Gutmann, Geoffrey Hawthorn, Albert Hirschman, Marion Smiley, and Michael Walzer for advice on earlier versions of this chapter. I am also indebted to the Institute for Advanced Study in Princeton, which provided a congenial environment in which to work on this project.

1. For example, Anderson 1979; Bok 1978; Hampshire 1978; Rohr 1978; and Walzer 1973. For a survey of the growing literature in this field, see Fleishman and Payne 1980.
2. Austin's classic essay (1956–57) is a valuable source on this topic, but more directly relevant are Hart and Honoré 1959; and Feinberg 1970.
3. Generally on the concept of political responsibility, see Pennock 1979, 260–308.
4. Gerth and Mills 1958, 95. This distinction does not depend on accepting Weber's further claim that the political leader should act on an "ethic of responsibility" rather than an "ethic of ultimate ends" (120–8).
5. Kaufman 1977, 27–8. For discussion of similar arguments in the context of war crimes, see French 1972.
6. I put aside the question of whether it makes sense to hold a collectivity morally responsible. Even if it does, individual responsibility for collective faults is not necessarily or usually extinguished.
7. Stillman 1976, 34. For some other examples (drawn from the Vietnam War), see Weisband and Franck 1976, 79–80.
8. The interpretation of this statement is not only much more complex than I can indicate here, but also a chief point of controversy between the two best works in the theory of responsibility. Cf. Hart and Honoré 1959, 61–2, 103–22; and Feinberg 1970, 201–7, 184. My interpretation more closely follows Feinberg.
9. I hope that I will be excused for disregarding the relevant but complex metaphysical problems raised by this criterion. Two of the best contemporary discussions are: Frankfurt 1971; and Strawson 1968.
10. Feinberg 1970, 196, 207–12. In this form, then, the excuse from alternative cause becomes the basis of what I call the excuse from null cause. Both kinds of excuse should be distinguished from the excuse from additional cause (see Hart and Honoré 1959, 216–25).
11. Fried 1978, 34–5. Fried himself defends a qualified version of the Kantian theory, conceding that we are morally responsible for some of the unintended consequences of our actions but insisting that we are "primarily" responsible for only what we intend in the sense that we may never do intentional harm in order to avoid greater unintended harm (21–2, 26, 28, 42, 168).

References

Allison, Graham. 1971. *Essence of Decision*. Boston: Little, Brown.

Altshuler, Alan A. 1977. "The Study of American Public Administration." In *The Politics of the Federal Bureaucracy*, edited by Alan A. Altshuler and Norman C. Thomas. New York: Harper & Row.

Anderson, Charles W. 1979. "The Place of Principles in Policy Analysis." *American Political Science Review* 73: 711–23.

Aristotle. 1963. "Ethica Nicomachea." In *The Works of Aristotle,* edited by W. D. Ross. Oxford: Oxford University Press.

Ashabranner, Brent. 1971. *A Moment in History.* Garden City, NY: Doubleday.

Austin, J. L. 1956–57. "A Plea for Excuses." *Proceedings of the Aristotelian Society* 57: 1–30.

Bok, Sissela. 1978. *Lying.* New York: Pantheon.

Congressional Quarterly. 1975. *Watergate.* Washington, DC: Congressional Quarterly.

Donagan, Alan. 1977. *The Theory of Morality.* Chicago: University of Chicago Press.

Donovan, Robert J. 1977. *Conflict and Crisis.* New York: Norton.

Edelman, Murray. 1964. *The Symbolic Uses of Politics.* Urbana: University of Illinois Press.

Feinberg, Joel. 1970. *Doing and Deserving.* Princeton, NJ: Princeton University Press.

Fleishman, Joel, and Bruce Payne. 1980. *Ethical Dilemmas and the Education of Policymakers.* Hastings-on-Hudson, NY: Hastings Center.

Frankfurt, Harry G. 1971. "Freedom of the Will and the Concept of a Person." *Journal of Philosophy* 68: 5–20.

French, Peter A., ed. 1972. *Individual and Collective Responsibility.* Cambridge, Mass.: Schenkman.

Fried, Charles. 1978. *Right and Wrong.* Cambridge, Mass.: Harvard University Press.

Friedlander, Saul. 1969. *Kurt Gerstein.* New York: Knopf.

Gerth, H. H., and C. Wright Mills. 1958. *From Max Weber.* Oxford/New York: Oxford University Press.

Glover, Jonathan. 1970. *Responsibility.* London: Routledge & Kegan Paul.

Hampshire, Stuart, ed. 1978. *Public and Private Morality.* Cambridge: Cambridge University Press.

Hart, H. L. A. 1968. *Punishment and Responsibility.* New York and Oxford: Oxford University Press.

Hart, H. L. A., and A. M. Honoré 1959. *Causation in the Law.* Oxford: Clarendon Press.

Heclo, Hugh. 1978. "Issue Networks and the Executive Establishment." In *The New American Political System,* edited by Anthony King. Washington, DC: American Enterprise Institute.

Hill, Thomas E., Jr. 1979. "Symbolic Protest and Calculated Silence." *Philosophy and Public Affairs* 9: 83–102.

Kant, Immanuel. 1949. "On a Supposed Right to Lie from Altruistic Motives." In *Critique of Practical Reason,* edited by L. W. Beck. Chicago: University of Chicago Press.

Kaufman, Herbert. 1977. *Red Tape.* Washington, DC: Brookings.

Kissinger, Henry. 1979a. "Letters." *Economist* 272: 6–7.

———. 1979b. *The White House Years.* Boston: Little, Brown.

Krasner, Stephen D. 1972. "Are Bureaucracies Important? (Or Allison in Wonderland)." *Foreign Policy* 7: 159–79.

Ladd, John. 1970. "Morality and the Ideal of Rationality in Formal Organizations." *Monist* 54: 488–516.

Lipsky, Michael. 1980. *Street-Level Bureaucracy.* New York: Russell Sage.

Lowi, Theodore J. 1979. *The End of Liberalism,* 2d ed. New York: Norton.

Lukas, J. Anthony. 1977. *Nightmare.* New York: Bantam.

Martin, John Bartlow. 1966. *Overtaken by Events.* Garden City, NY: Doubleday.

Muller, Robert J. 1967. *Adlai Stevenson.* New York: Harper & Row.

Pennock, J. Roland. 1979. *Democratic Political Theory.* Princeton, NJ: Princeton University Press.

Peters, Charles. 1973. "The Culture of Bureaucracy." *Washington Monthly* 5: 22–4.

Rohr, John A. 1978. *Ethics for Bureaucrats.* New York and Basel: Dekker.

Rourke, Francis E., ed. 1978. *Bureaucratic Power in National Politics,* 3rd ed. Boston: Little, Brown.

Schlesinger, Arthur M., Jr. 1965. *A Thousand Days.* Boston: Houghton Mifflin.

Sjoberg, Gideon et al. 1978. "Bureaucracy and the Lower Class." In *Bureaucratic Power in National Politics,* edited by Francis E. Rourke. Boston: Little, Brown.

Stillman, Richard J. 1976. *Public Administration: Concepts and Cases,* 2d ed. Boston: Houghton Mifflin.

Strawson, P. F. 1968. "Freedom and Resentment." In *Studies in the Philosophy of Thought and Action,* edited by P. F. Strawson. Oxford: Oxford University Press.

Thompson, Dennis. 1981. "Excuses Officials Use: Moral Responsibility and the New York City Fiscal Crisis." In *Public Duties: The Moral Obligations of Government Officials,* edited by Joel Fleishman, Lance Liebman, and Mark H. Moore. Cambridge, Mass.: Harvard University Press.

Thompson, Victor. 1961. *Modern Organizations.* New York: Random House.

Truman, Harry. 1955. *Memoirs,* vol. 1, *Years of Decisions.* New York: Doubleday.

U.S. Atomic Energy Commission. 1971. *In the Matter of J. Robert Oppenheimer.* Cambridge, Mass.: MIT Press.

Walsh, W. H. 1970. "Pride, Shame and Responsibility." *Philosophical Quarterly* 20: 1–13.

Walzer, Michael. 1973. "Political Action: The Problem of Dirty Hands." *Philosophy and Public Affairs* 2: 160–80.

———. 1977. *Just and Unjust Wars.* New York: Basic Books.

Weisband, Edward, and Thomas M. Franck. 1976. *Resignation in Protest.* New York: Penguin Books.

Williams, Bernard. 1973. "A Critique of Utilitarianism." In J. J. C. Smart and Bernard Williams, *Utilitarianism For and Against.* Cambridge: Cambridge University Press.

2

The Responsibility of Advisers

In other times and other places, counselors often bore the responsibility for the consequences of their rulers' decisions – and with a vengeance. When for whatever reason the decisions of the Chinese emperors went awry, their ministers, it is said, could expect to have their hearts cut open, their feet cut off, or to be pickled in brine.[1] Today, advisers to government officials have less cause to worry. Rather than strict liability for the advice they give, advisers are commonly assumed to have no responsibility at all for the consequences of decisions made on the basis of their advice.[2] If anyone is to blame when decisions turn out badly, it is usually the official who made the decision, not the adviser who counseled the official (unless of course the adviser deceives the official or otherwise acts wrongly in ways the official could not be expected to take into account).

I want to criticize the three most important claims that are put forward to absolve advisers of specifically moral responsibility: the first refers to causal criteria; the second, to the concept of intention; and the third, to role.[3] Each claim in effect takes one feature of the relationship between advisers and the people they advise and turns it into the exclusive test for responsibility. None of these shortcuts will do, although each, substantially modified, may contribute something to a full account of the responsibility of advisers.[4]

I concentrate on only one kind of adviser since I suspect that any general theory of responsibility for advice will have to be constructed piecemeal from analyses of various particular kinds of advising. A good place to begin is the world of governmental advisers, whose influence in public life has expanded greatly in recent years.[5] Because these advisers work in institutional contexts, we are more likely to discover generalizations about their responsibility than if we were to consider (say) people who give occasional advice in everyday life. Because governmental advisers must sometimes decide whom their advice should serve (for example, their immediate superior or the public), we are also more likely to notice problems in the definition of the role of adviser itself than if we were to consider (say) lawyers or doctors.

CAUSES

The basic commonsense notion of responsibility derives from the idea of making something happen. Applied to relations between persons, the idea is that one person is responsible for what someone else does only if the first person causes the second to do it. On this view, as long as an adviser merely advises, we would not normally say that the adviser causes an advisee to decide one way rather than another. Since advisees remain free to accept or reject advice, we would not blame advisers for anything their advisees did. Just as in the law a voluntary intervention by another agent – a *novus actus interveniens* – breaks the chain of responsibility,[6] so in morality a subsequent voluntary decision shifts the entire responsibility to the official who made it. Such a view may be appropriate for ascribing responsibility to agents who act independently in causal chains that produce physical effects. However, it fails completely to capture the complexities of the process of advising, which involves interaction among agents and influence that differs from causing physical events.

The key assumption of this version of the causal view – that causing advisees to act is incompatible with their acting voluntarily – seems plausible only if one concentrates on instances in which an adviser makes an advisee do something, and ignores the great variety of other ways advisers may influence advisees. Advisers often contribute significantly to the final decision advisees make. The way advisers frame the alternatives, the weight they give to various arguments, the language and the illustrations they use (often chosen perhaps to appeal especially to the advisees) – all these forms of influence may make the final decision different from what it would otherwise have been. On the causal view, such influences should count as causes of the outcome and therefore warrant ascribing some responsibility to advisers. But at the same time, none of these forms of influence necessarily undermines the voluntariness of the advisees' decisions. The nature of the process of advising itself, as a form of deliberation, requires that advisees both make decisions voluntarily and respond to the influence of advisers. Rather than causal influence being incompatible with voluntary decision making, the presence of both is what characterizes proper relationships between advisers and advisees.

An adviser's influence, moreover, need not always take the form of giving explicit reasons or arguments. When an official accepts advice more because of whom it comes from than because of what it says (as Roosevelt sometimes accepted Louis Howe's counsel; or as Kennedy often followed his brother's or Ted Sorensen's),[7] we would want to impute some responsibility to the advisers and to do so without necessarily canceling or even reducing the responsibility of the official who made the decision. Stronger kinds of influence (such as advice accompanied by offers of support or threats of resignation), which even more clearly implicate the adviser in the consequences of an advisee's decision, would still allow us to call the decision voluntary.

More sophisticated proponents of the causal view, such as Hart and Honoré, recognize that "interpersonal transactions" (which include advising) constitute exceptions to their general principle that a subsequent voluntary intervention "negatives" causal connection and responsibility.[8] But Hart and Honoré still want to insist that (at least in legal theory) an adviser is not responsible for an advisee's actions based on the advice. They must therefore find some way to distinguish advice from other forms of influence that in their view do warrant the ascription of responsibility. In the law, a person who "merely advises" others is generally not liable for any harm the others commit; but a person who in some way "induces" others to act is generally liable.[9] To account for this distinction between inducing and advising (neither of which "negative" causal connection), Hart and Honoré suggest but do not develop two different criteria: a person is responsible for another's action (1) insofar as the second person acted in the way the first person intended; or (2) insofar as the first person advises the second person to follow a certain course of action rather than merely giving advice about the course of action.[10]

Both of these criteria have problems of their own that I discuss later, but the significant point to notice here is that by introducing the criteria, Hart and Honoré have not only abandoned the principle that voluntary intervention breaks the causal chain but have moved well beyond the idea of one person's making another do something. All that remains of causal responsibility is the idea of one person's acting "in consequence" of another's influence, and, to decide whether this is so in any particular instance, Hart and Honoré are forced to invoke what would normally be regarded as noncausal considerations (the intention of the adviser or the kind of advice given).

A similar problem confronts any attempt to determine responsibility exclusively according to the degrees of causal influence – for example, by stipulating that advisers are more responsible to the degree that they have more influence over the people they advise. The problem is that an adviser who fails to discourage an official from pursuing a certain course of action may be just as culpable as one who encourages the official to follow it. To discriminate among the indefinite number of such omissions that influence a decision, we would have to invoke noncausal considerations, such as the expectations that attach to the role a particular adviser holds.[11] From among the many equally influential advisers who failed to try to prevent an official from implementing a harmful policy, we single out for blame those whose office should normally deal with the policy in question. The nature of the official role may be even more significant than potential causal influence in determining how much responsibility to impute to an adviser. A press secretary might have more potential influence over all the decisions a president makes than does the secretary of state, but if both failed to try to dissuade the president from undertaking a disastrous diplomatic initiative, we would usually blame the secretary of state more than the press secretary. We might not even blame the press secretary at all (although the requirements of an adviser's role are not always sufficient grounds for absolving the adviser from blame).

A causal criterion, then, does not get us very far in determining the responsibility of advisers. The most that we can coherently include in such a criterion would be the requirement that an adviser is responsible only if the advisee would not have decided the way he or she did but for the advice (or the omission of the advice).[12] This requirement exonerates advisers who, either by giving or refraining from giving advice, could have no influence on a decision maker (unless the advisers through negligence or some other act placed themselves in a position where they could have no such influence). The requirement would cancel or mitigate the responsibility of advisers whose counsel was solicited after a decision maker had already made up his or her mind. Responding to the crisis in the Dominican Republic in 1965, Rusk and McNamara probably had already decided to order an American intervention when they asked the acting United States ambassador there if "he agreed with their view that a rebel victory would probably lead to a pro-Communist government."[13] Given the ambassador's well-known anti-Communist views and the form and timing of the request for the advice, we should not be inclined to impute much, if any, responsibility to the ambassador in this episode.

No doubt the causal criterion will give rise to some difficult cases as we try to determine whether a decision would have been made but for some piece of advice (for example, was a decision maker encouraged to act more vigorously because of the advice?). But the critical questions of responsibility more often turn on other criteria. Even if advisers are causally responsible (in the weak sense I have indicated) for harmful consequences of decisions based on their advice, they are far from being morally responsible. Advice (or its omission) may be misinterpreted. It may, for example, set off in the advisee's mind an entirely unexpected or unrelated chain of thought without which the advisee would not have made a particular decision but for which we could hardly blame the adviser.

INTENTIONS

Since the causal criterion by itself seems to spread responsibility too widely and indiscriminately, many theorists understandably look for a more restrictive criterion. Some notion of intention, drawn from a long and respectable philosophical tradition, has seemed the obvious candidate. Charles Fried presents a version of the criterion explicitly as a way of limiting moral responsibility: you are "personally" responsible only for what you intend. What you intend is to be understood as what you do, as distinguished from what you allow to happen.[14]

Using this notion of intention certainly would shrink the scope of responsibility defined by the consequentialists against whom Fried explicitly develops his own theory. But where consequentialism (at least in unqualified form) places no limits on the harms that officials are responsible for preventing, theories like Fried's seem to insulate officials from responsibility for some harms for which we would intuitively want to blame them. On Fried's view, public officials who negligently or even corruptly divert money that should be spent for police protection are not morally responsible for any criminal assaults that occur as a result of the reduced protection, even when the officials could have anticipated that the assaults would occur.[15] By the same token, an adviser (like a lawyer) presumably is not culpable for harmful decisions made on the basis of his or her advice, as long as the adviser does not intend harm and as long as the adviser does not violate any duties of office in giving the advice (for example, by lying to the advisee).[16]

Yet Fried evidently does not want to deny that sometimes we may morally criticize advisers for failing to anticipate the uses others make of their advice or that we may morally condemn officials for even remote consequences of their negligence or corruption. Thus it appears that, in some broader sense, Fried would hold officials responsible for consequences they do not intend.[17]

But then we must wonder what is the force of holding someone personally responsible rather than merely morally responsible in this broader sense? Fried's answer seems to be that consequences for which we are personally responsible take precedence over other consequences in the sense that no remote consequences, side effects, or omissions can ever justify our intentionally doing wrong ("a person may not do wrong, even to prevent a greater wrong by others"). Fried therefore would have to hold that when an adviser's position requires giving a certain kind of advice (such as merely technical analysis), the adviser may be violating a trust (committing a wrong) by refusing to provide that analysis or trying to offer some other kind of advice, even if the intention is to prevent the official from committing a greater wrong.[18] Here a consequentialist response, which would compare the harm of violating the trust with the harm of fulfilling it, seems more plausible. We not only would want to justify a Defense Department analyst's refusal to provide superiors with targeting plans for bombing medical facilities or civilian residences but also would hold an analyst who provided such plans partly responsible for the bombing.

Even if theories like Fried's could coherently find a place for moral criticism of unintended consequences, the priority these theories give to intention distorts the nature of responsibility in bureaucratic and other governmental institutions, where unintended consequences are so rife they might well be regarded as an occupational hazard. The standard counterexamples to such theories call into question the distinction between consequences that are means to one's end and consequences that are merely side effects.[19] In these examples the agent achieves the intended end, and the issue is whether the agent is responsible for certain foreseeable consequences: are they "means" or "side effects"?

No doubt there are cases of this sort involving advisers: consider an adviser who in helping pass a beneficial law knowingly ruins the reputation and destroys the career of the official to whom the advice is given. But more common are instances where advisers do not achieve the end they intend and indeed may intend just the opposite end to that which results from the advice. Such cases are instructive because at first glance they seem to support the use of the criterion of intention. Advisers to President Johnson who consistently opposed expansion of the Vietnam War and urged the withdrawal of American forces certainly did not intend their advice to have the effect of strengthening Johnson's resolve to continue the war. Yet dissenters such as George Ball became "domesticated," and their participation in the advisory process helped to legitimize the decisions they opposed.[20] They were welcomed as devil's advocates, their presence reassuring the President and others that the major objections to the Administration's policy were being fully considered. To this extent, these dissenters, contrary to their own intentions, became part of the set of causes that sustained this policy.

It is of course difficult to know at what point one's objections serve mainly to further purposes one opposes, but at the point we could expect any reasonable person to recognize that dissent has become counterproductive in this way, we should consider a dissenting adviser at least a moral accessory.[21] Good intentions may make us think less badly of the adviser than of the advisee, but they cannot, at this point, absolve the adviser of responsibility for all the consequences. Insofar as we are inclined to cancel or mitigate responsibility, we would do so, not by citing an absence of intention, but by accepting either a plea that under the circumstances advisers should not be expected to realize that they are promoting results they oppose, or a plea that they could not have done anything to prevent that result.

Notice, however, that even if we accept the latter plea (which in effect asserts that an official is not a cause even in the weak sense mentioned above), we might still want to criticize the official for continuing to serve as a member of a government pursuing immoral policies. Such criticism seems better framed in the language of complicity than of responsibility, however.[22] We would condemn an adviser for his or her continued association with an immoral regime, without purporting to be able to show that this association actually helps perpetuate the regime or any of its policies. In any case, intention does not appear to be the exclusive or even the chief factor in our assessment of the adviser's connection with the policies in question.

Another illustration of why intention is insufficient is the problem that sometimes confronts experts who serve on part-time advisory panels to various government agencies. It has been claimed that a series of advisory panels to the Food and Drug Administration provided advice that was intended, or at least should have been interpreted, as grounds for banning cyclamates, but FDA officials, allegedly for political reasons, presented the advice as being consistent with their decisions not to ban cyclamates completely.[23] Whatever the advisers intended, some of them – at least those who took part in the later phases of a process that went on for more than a decade – could have foreseen that the conclusions of the panels would be misinterpreted. Insofar as these advisers did not try to prevent their advice from being misused in this way, or did not dissociate themselves from its misuse, we should say that they too became partly responsible for the consequences of the failure to proscribe cyclamates.

Foreseeability, then, needs to be considered in ascribing responsibility, especially in the context of the organizations in which public officials and their advisers work. Many patterns of bureaucratic behavior, including practices that social scientists call pathological, are quite common in government and often could be anticipated by officials within these organizations, even if no one intends that the practices should exist, or that any harmful consequences they produce should occur.[24] Furthermore, some of these practices and consequences are avoidable. Yet with a theory of responsibility that relies only on the criterion of intention, or that always gives intended consequences moral precedence over merely foreseen consequences, we are less likely to hold officials responsible for doing something about these defective organizational practices and the harmful consequences that flow from them. Moreover, committing some lesser intentional wrong (breaking a promise to one's superior) may sometimes be necessary to prevent some greater wrong that would result from permitting the bureaucratic process to proceed as usual.

A criterion of foreseeability places some limitations on the scope of an adviser's responsibility: the less an adviser can reasonably be expected to anticipate the harmful consequences that result from advice, the less responsible the adviser is for a failure to prevent them.[25] But, to say that an adviser is more responsible because he or she could have foreseen the effects of the advice is not to imply that the advisee is any less responsible for those effects. There is no fixed pool of responsibility such that when one person's share goes up, another's must go down (as with certain kinds of compensation in the law of torts). The advisee's responsibility must be appraised from the perspective of his or her own place in the process: in light of the advice received and the options faced, what could the advisee have anticipated and controlled in the stream of consequences that flowed from his or her decision? The answer to such a question will not necessarily ascribe responsibility to an advisee directly or inversely in proportion to the responsibility ascribed to the adviser.

ROLES

A third way to limit the responsibility of an adviser is to invoke the requirements of an official role.[26] Advisers may claim that by the formal or informal expectations of their office they are bound to give advice in certain specific ways (such as providing merely technical analysis), and as long as they do so properly, they cannot be held responsible for anything other officials do with their advice.

The classic source of a definition of the responsibility of advisers based on the requirements of their role is (or should be) Chapter 25 of *Leviathan*.[27] There Hobbes clearly recognizes the special conditions that must obtain if a role is to shield an adviser from responsibility for the consequences of advice. Hobbes distinguishes command, which purports to be directed to the benefit of the commander, from counsel, which purports to be directed only to the benefit of the person to whom it is given. No one may be "obliged to do as he is counseled, because the hurt of not following it, is his own," and therefore no one should be blamed (accused or punished) for the counsel. Up to this point, Hobbes's argument would appear to yield much the same conclusions as does the doctrine of *novus actus interveniens*. But then Hobbes introduces a further distinction: counsel that is consistent with, and counsel that is contrary to, the duty of a counselor. The latter consists of counsel that is "vehemently pressed," in which the adviser "urges action, appeals to common passions and opinions" instead of "true reasoning," and hence may be supposed to be acting with regard to his or her own benefit rather than that of the person being advised.[28] A counselor who in this way acts contrary to the duty of an office may be accused and punished and presumably may also be blamed for consequences that follow from the advice.

This sharp distinction between two kinds of counsel is intelligible within the bounds of *Leviathan,* where shared standards of objective reasoning prevail in politics and where advisers speak to a single sovereign who authoritatively determines the public good. In modern democracies where these conditions do not exist, such a distinction, as a basis for insulating advisers, will be difficult to maintain, even with respect to scientific advisers, whose role most closely approximates that of Hobbes's dutiful counselors.

The view nevertheless persists that some advisers can completely escape responsibility if they confine themselves to giving merely technical analysis (advice about means) and, conversely, that they risk blame if they overstep this role by recommending one public policy over another (advice about ends). In a report on the role of scientific advisers in the controversy in the late 1960s over the Anti-Ballistic Missile System (ABM), the Operations Research Society distinguished between analysts and advocates in a manner that recalls Hobbes's contrast between two kinds of counselors. Analysts restrict themselves to the "quantifiable and logically structured aspects of the problem only," while advocates need not admit the weaknesses of their positions and may put forward "unsupported allegations."[29] The report sharply criticized those scientific advisers who became advocates in the ABM debate. However, even on the highly technical questions in this debate, the kind of questions on which advisers on both sides chose to focus betrayed their partisanship and became a form of advocacy. Pro-ABM scientists concentrated on an analysis of the need for an ABM system, while the anti-ABM scientists stressed the evidence showing the inadequacy of an ABM system to meet this alleged need.[30] If on scientific questions such as this advisers are not able to purge their analyses of partisanship, we can hardly expect advisers on issues with even more economic and political content to sustain the role of Hobbesian analyst.[31]

It of course may be possible for an adviser only to analyze, not advocate. But even an adviser who presents a completely neutral analysis does not thereby escape moral responsibility for the consequences of that analysis. Under non-Hobbesian conditions, what the role of an adviser should be will often be contestable – morally so. A procedural controversy over the proper role of an adviser often simply reflects the substantive controversy in which the various advisers are engaged. The reaction to the ORS report, and its criticism of the scientists who advocated instead of analyzed, followed the divisions of the ABM controversy itself, pro-ABM scientists favoring the report and anti-ABM scientists disapproving of it.[32] When the nature of the role remains in such serious dispute, advisers are responsible for the consequences of their choice of which role to play in the controversy.

To be sure, there must be a place in government for advisers who provide mainly technical analysis. The Commissioner of the Food and Drug Administration, for example, should be able to insist that technical analysis of the safety and efficacy of drugs be given as impartially as possible and without any bias for or against regulation. The scientific personnel who provide such analysis should then not be held responsible for the consequences of some higher official's decision to ban, or not to ban, the drug. But to account for the limitation of responsibility of persons in technical or other similarly circumscribed roles, we do not have to attribute any intrinsic moral significance to the distinction between analysis and advocacy. The general utility of a division of labor in government, plus the obligation to fulfill one's freely assumed duties of office, are sufficient bases for excusing a technical adviser whose properly provided analysis leads to harmful consequences, or for accusing a technical adviser whose unauthorized advocacy contributes to such consequences.

These same kinds of considerations may also be reasons for overriding the requirements of role. Technical advisers may be blameworthy for failing to offer more than mere analysis – for example, when they realize that unless they strongly oppose a particular policy serious and irreversible harm will ensue, worse on balance than the harm of disturbing the normal practices of an advisory system. The advisers on the Pesticides Panel of the President's Science Advisory Committee in 1962 normally might have merely analyzed the scientific evidence of the effects of pesticides such as DDT, but instead they advocated steps to end their widespread use. Had they played their usual role, they would have been partially culpable for a significant delay in imposing the ban and hence for any irreversible harm to human health that occurred as a result of the delay.[33]

Beyond the realm of technical and scientific analysis, advisers are not likely to deny that advice almost inevitably involves advocacy and are not likely to rely on the distinction between analysis and advocacy to limit their responsibility. Instead, advocacy itself becomes a duty of counselors, and the more advocates, the better. We leave the territory of *Leviathan* and enter the world of *On Liberty*. Advice to public officials becomes a kind of microcosm of Mill's vision of a liberal society, where the free expression of many different perspectives is supposed to offer the best chance for arriving at policies that promote the public interest. An advisory system based on this model would populate government with advisers of diverse views and encourage each to advocate his or her particular and partial perspective. The official charged with making a decision would presumably be less likely to neglect any important consideration and therefore more likely to discover the general interest (at whatever level of government the decision is made).[34] Given such a system, advisers may well claim that they should not be held responsible for the decision an official makes after listening to their advice, even if the official happens to follow the advice. Advisers themselves may not subscribe to the position they are advocating but may be merely putting forward the partial point of view required by the role they play in the advisory system.

If such a system exists and is understood to exist by advisers and the officials they counsel, any particular adviser's responsibility might be plausibly limited in this way. But no system of this kind is likely to be so well tuned that it will always produce an optimal balance of advice (let alone decisions in the public interest). Alexander George, who presents the most compelling design for such a system, specifies an elaborate set of structural conditions that would be necessary to make it function properly.[35] We should therefore say that, when an adviser has good reason to believe that the advisory system is not yielding a reasonable balance of opinions or is otherwise distorting decisions, and the adviser's own expected role as advocate of a particular point of view is contributing to that distortion, the adviser should abandon the normal role and seek to remedy the distortion in the process. If the adviser fails to do so, he or she cannot, simply by appealing to the requirements of the role, disclaim any responsibility for the harmful decisions that the system produces.

It might be objected that to permit (or require) an adviser to transcend a role in this way is to create an advisory system that is self-defeating. One adviser decides that other advisers collectively are not providing balanced advice at a particular time, and she corrects her own advice to restore a proper balance. But in the meantime each of the other advisers, seeing the same original imbalance, acts to try to restore the balance. The result at best will be a return to the original imbalance and at worst, chaos. This objection, and the model of inherent disequilibrium on which it is based, must assume that the advisers act independently and simultaneously, and that none can inform the officials whom they are advising that their counsel takes into account certain faults in the advisory system. Since these assumptions do not usually hold in real systems, an adviser cannot readily appeal to the model to excuse a failure to compensate for defects in a system, even if the specific role would dictate that the adviser ignore such defects.

A general problem with appeals to role, as ways to limit the responsibility of an adviser, is that they tend to confuse the responsibility of persons and the responsibilities of a role, permitting the latter to absorb the former. At the extreme, this predominance of role produces what has been called Pooh-Bahism, after the Emperor's "Lord High Everything Else" in the *Mikado*.[36] When the Emperor asks for advice about how much to spend on his wedding, Pooh-Bah in one short scene gives ten different answers, each from the perspective of one of the various official roles he holds. As Private Secretary, Pooh-Bah says, "Don't stint." But as Chancellor of the Exchequer he counsels frugality. Finally, even Pooh-Bah realizes that he must have a personal view that is not simply the sum of all the views given in the various roles he occupies. As it turns out, he thinks that the views of "all these distinguished people" can be "squared" if the Emperor gives him "a very considerable bribe," which he will accept not in any particular role but simply as Pooh-Bah.

To be sure, advisers seldom let their personal responsibility be so completely absorbed by their role. More often advisers will simply claim that, as long as they stay in office, they are bound to provide counsel according to the requirements of their role, and if (as a person) they can no longer abide by these requirements, they will resign. Resignation thus becomes the last refuge of personal responsibility.[37] But this is surely too rigid a conception of the role of adviser. In most circumstances an adviser enjoys a great deal of discretion in fulfilling the expectations of a role. This discretion involves not only shaping advice according to different conceptions of the role (for example, in deciding whether to analyze or advocate) but also varying the advice, within a particular conception of the role, according to general moral standards (for example, in deciding what to include or exclude when engaging in advocacy).

Moreover, an adviser trapped in a role that contributes to harmful policies often has many other options besides resigning or carrying on as usual – including private and public criticism of the system of advising and the policies that it occasions. Given such discretion, an adviser's responsibility can hardly be said to be limited to the consequences of a choice of whether to resign or to continue in office acting strictly in accord with the normal requirements of the particular role. How advisers exercise the discretion – including whether they create whatever discretion is morally necessary – may often be an even more important factor in morally assessing their conduct and in ascribing responsibility to them for the consequences of their advice.

CONCLUSION

None of the shortcuts I have considered for ascribing responsibility to advisers seems adequate to account for the variety of relationships between advisers and the officials they advise, or the occasions on which advice is given. To hold that advisers escape responsibility if another person voluntarily intervenes after they present their advice, or if they do not intend the foreseeable consequences of the advice, or if they merely analyze the pros and cons of a policy, or if they only play their part in an advisory system that requires making recommendations that they do not necessarily favor – to accept any of these formulas or variations on them is to neglect important aspects of moral responsibility and produce counterintuitive results in some critical cases.

The analysis of each of these formulas, however, suggested some criteria that, taken together, could form a set of necessary and jointly sufficient conditions for ascribing responsibility to advisers. From the idea of causal responsibility comes a criterion that holds an adviser responsible only if the advisee would not have made the decision in question but for the advice (or its omission). That an adviser intended a certain result may be a further reason to criticize him or her, but such intent is not necessary to blame the adviser for the result. Advisers are responsible for the consequences of decisions based on their advice insofar as they could reasonably be expected to foresee that the consequences would follow from the advice. Finally, although the requirements of role can create a prima facie excuse, an adviser is responsible for any foreseeable harm the role-bound advice causes when that harm is greater than the harm that would result from breaching the requirements of the role.

Although these criteria remain schematic it should be clear that the scope of responsibility they define is likely to be more extensive than that found in everyday moral life. This expanded responsibility seems appropriate for public life not only because advisers to public officials can have great influence over the welfare of many people, but also because advisers voluntarily accept these positions of influence and therefore the greater risk of moral criticism that they invite. To expand the responsibility of advisers, however, is not to diminish the responsibility of the persons they advise. Often it is reasonable to assume that officials who make a decision are more responsible than their advisers. The officials are usually "closer" to the consequences in the sense that we have stronger grounds for believing that they satisfy the criteria of responsibility. The consequences would not have occurred but for their decision, they could anticipate that the decision would produce these consequences, and their role provided a clear opportunity or imposed a duty to prevent them. But however we apportion blame or praise among advisers and advisees, we are likely to find that the contours of responsibility of each are more complex than most general theories of moral responsibility and the pleas of most public officials would lead us to believe.

Notes

I am grateful to Joel Feinberg, Amy Gutmann, Albert Hirschman, and Marion Smiley for advice on problems discussed in this article. Since they could hardly have foreseen what I would do with their advice, they escape any blame for what I have written here.

1. Han Fei Tzŭ, *The Complete Works* (London: Probsthain, 1939), vol. 1, 113–33, cited by Herbert Goldhamer, *The Adviser* (New York: Elsevier/North-Holland Publishing, 1978), 118.

2. William R. Nelson, ed., *The Politics of Science* (New York: Oxford University Press, 1968), 119; and Lyman Bryson, "Notes on a Theory of Advice," in *Reader in Bureaucracy*, ed. Robert K. Merton et al. (New York: Free Press, 1952), 203.

3. The responsibility is moral in two senses: *what* an adviser is responsible for is assessed according to substantive principles of morality; and the extent to which *the adviser* is responsible is determined by criteria of moral agency. This paper concentrates on the second aspect of moral responsibility – what J. L. Austin calls excuses rather than justifications ("A Plea for Excuses," *Proceedings of the Aristotelian Society* 57 [1956–57]: 1–30, at 1–2). For another distinction between first- and second-order principles, see Alan Donagan, *The Theory of Morality* (Chicago: University of Chicago Press, 1977), 52–7.

4. This account would have to be situated in a general framework for ascribing responsibility to public officials. See Chapter 1, where I describe such a framework in a way that accommodates, at least in a rough form, the chief features of the responsibility of advisers that I analyze in this essay.

5. For an indication of the growth and variety of advising of governmental agencies in recent years, see Thomas E. Cronin and Norman C. Thomas, "Federal Advisory Processes: Advice and Discontent," *Science* 171 (February 26, 1971): 771–9.

6. H. L. A. Hart and A. M. Honoré, *Causation in the Law* (Oxford: Clarendon Press, 1959), 69ff., 94, 295.

7. Arthur M. Schlesinger, Jr., *The Coming of the New Deal* (Boston: Houghton Mifflin, 1959), 514–15; and Graham Allison, *Essence of Decision* (Boston: Little, Brown, 1971), 203–4.

8. Hart and Honoré, 48ff., 171–2.

9. This is so even in many systems of criminal law: see Hart and Honoré, 338–9. Cf. Glanville Williams, *Criminal Law*, 2d ed. (London: Stevens & Sons, 1961), 353–60, 38–83, 404–9; and George Fletcher, *Rethinking Criminal Law* (Boston: Little, Brown, 1978), 755.

10. Hart and Honoré, 51, 78, 338–40.

11. See Joel Feinberg, *Doing and Deserving* (Princeton, NJ: Princeton University Press, 1970), esp. 200–4; and John Casey, "Actions and Consequences," in *Morality and Moral Reasoning*, ed. John Casey (London: Methuen, 1971), 185–6. For a criticism of this view, see Eric Mack, "Bad Samaritanism and the Causation of Harm," *Philosophy and Public Affairs* 9 (1980): 230–59, at 235–41.

12. The advice must thus in Feinberg's sense be a "causal factor": "A member of a set of jointly sufficient conditions whose presence was necessary to the sufficiency of the set" (202n.). Although my interpretation of the causal criterion more closely follows Feinberg's analysis than that of Hart and Honoré, I am indebted to the latter authors' discussion of "causally relevant factors" and "conditions sine qua non" (103–22).

13. John Bartlow Martin, *Overtaken by Events* (Garden City, NY: Doubleday, 1966), 659.

14. Charles Fried, *Right and Wrong* (Cambridge, Mass.: Harvard University Press, 1978), 1–2, 20–8. For criticism of Fried's theory (specifically discussing responsibility for advice), see Brian Barry, "And Who Is My Neighbor?" *Yale Law Journal* 88 (1979): 629–58, at 647–9.

15. Fried, 160, 22n.

16. Ibid., 182–3.

17. Ibid., 28, 41–2, 162–3.

18. Ibid., 162, 167–8.

19. Fried himself presents two such examples, as well as an annotated bibliography on "intention" (23–4, 202–5).

20. James C. Thomson, "How Could Vietnam Happen? An Autopsy," *Atlantic Monthly* (April 1968), 47–53; and George Reedy, *The Twilight of the Presidency* (New York: World Publishing, 1970), 11. Cf. Albert O. Hirschman, *Exit, Voice and Loyalty* (Cambridge, Mass.: Harvard University Press, 1970), 115–19.

21. William Safire reminds us about "the Rejected Counsel": "The White House staffer whose job it is to go into the Oval Office in times of crisis and say 'Mr. President – do the popular thing! Take the easy way!' The President can then say: 'Some of my advisers have suggested that I do what is politically popular. I have rejected such counsel'" ("Rejected Counsel's Return," *New York Times* [December 31, 1979], 15).

22. See Thomas E. Hill, Jr., "Symbolic Protest and Calculated Silence," *Philosophy and Public Affairs* 9 (1979): 83–102.

23. Joel Primak and Frank von Hippel, *Advice and Dissent* (New York: New American Library, 1976), 87ff., 34–5, 101.

24. For some examples, see Francis E. Rourke, *Bureaucracy, Politics and Public Policy*, 2d ed. (Boston: Little, Brown, 1976), 26–32, 154. Also see Michael Lipsky, "Toward a Theory of Street-Level Bureaucracy," in *Theoretical Perspectives on Urban Politics*, ed. Willis D. Hawley et al. (Englewood Cliffs, NJ: Prentice-Hall, 1976), 196–213.

25. For an analysis of the general relation of foresight and intention, see Thomas Baldwin, "Foresight and Responsibility," *Philosophy* 54 (1979): 247–60. For an account of traditional morality that gives both intention and foreseeability important roles, see Donagan, esp. 122–7.

26. Generally, on role responsibility, see Gerald Cohen, "Beliefs and Roles," *Proceedings of the Aristotelian Society* 67 (1966–67): 17–34; H. L. A. Hart, *Punishment and Responsibility* (New York and Oxford: Oxford University Press, 1968), 212–14; and R. S. Downie, *Roles and Values* (London: Methuen, 1971), 121–45.

27. Thomas Hobbes, *Leviathan*, ed. M. Oakeshott (New York/London: Macmillan, 1962), 191–7.

28. Ibid., 192–3. Machiavelli also warns advisers not to "advocate any enterprise with too much zeal" and to give their advice "calmly and modestly." But he does so because he sees this as the only way counselors can cope with a common dilemma in their role: if they "do not advise what seems to them for the good of the republic or the prince . . . then they fail of their duty; and if they do advise it, then it is at the risk of their position and their lives" (Niccolò Machiavelli, *The Discourses*, bk. 3, ch. 35, in *The Prince and the Discourses*, trans. C. Detmold [New York: Random House, 1950], 514).

29. Operations Research Society of America, "Guidelines for the Practice of Operations Research," *Operations Research* 19 (1971): 1123–58, at 1134–5, 1144–8. Also see the "Reactions to the Guidelines . . . ," *Operations Research* 20 (1972): 205–44.

30. Paul Doty, "Can Investigations Improve Scientific Advice? The Case of the ABM," *Minerva* 10 (1972): 280–94, at 282–7. For another example, see Robert Gilpin, *American Scientists and Nuclear Weapons Policy* (Princeton, NJ: Princeton University Press, 1962), 262–98.

31. See, e.g., Edward S. Flash, Jr., *Economic Advice and Presidential Leadership* (New York: Columbia University Press, 1965), 276–325; T. E. Cronin and S. D. Greenberg, eds., *The Presidential Advisory System* (New York: Harper & Row, 1969); and Morton H. Halperin, *Bureaucratic Politics and Foreign Policy* (Washington, DC: Brookings Institution, 1974), 158–72.

32. Doty, 281.

33. Primak and von Hippel, 43–5.

34. Alexander George, "The Case for Multiple Advocacy in Making Foreign Policy," *American Political Science Review* 66 (1972): 751–85; Aaron Wildavsky, *The Politics of the Budgetary Process*, 2d. ed. (Boston: Little, Brown, 1974), 166–7; and Charles E. Lindblom, "Policy Analysis," *American Economic Review* 48 (1958): 298–312, 306.

35. George, 784–5.

36. W. S. Gilbert, *The Savoy Operas* (London: Macmillan, 1926), 325–6. This scene is cited and discussed by Cohen, 19–20.

37. Edward Weisband and Thomas M. Franck, *Resignation in Protest* (New York: Penguin Books, 1976), esp. 181–92.

3

Bureaucracy and Democracy

Democracy does not suffer bureaucracy gladly. Many of the values we associate with democracy – equality, participation and individuality – stand sharply opposed to the hierarchy, specialization, and impersonality we ascribe to modern bureaucracy. Yet for a long time political theorists did not see bureaucracy as a threat to democracy, and democratic theorists still have not formulated a satisfactory response to the challenge bureaucratic power poses to democratic government.

One response to this challenge denies bureaucracy any place at all in a genuine democracy. Theorists who take this approach usually realize that they must show that bureaucracy does not inevitably appear in every modern society, but only in those societies they consider nondemocratic. Thus, nineteenth-century British writers often referred to bureaucracy as the "Continental nuisance," from which their democracy was immune.[1] Marx and other socialist writers agreed that France and Germany had the most highly developed bureaucracies, but they insisted that, as merely one manifestation of the bourgeois state, bureaucracy would disappear with the capitalism that gave rise to that state.[2] Yet socialist societies (admittedly not yet the democracies Marx had in mind) turned out to be more bureaucratic than the governments they replaced. Similarly, the belief that bureaucracy inheres in only socialist government could hardly be sustained once capitalist societies created the administrative structures necessary to maintain their large welfare states.

Still, from time to time, voices on both the left and the right revive the hope that bureaucracy might be abolished. Many have called for decentralization to eradicate bureaucracy. But smaller political jurisdictions develop petty bureaucracies of their own that usually are no more responsive than those of larger states. Other writers (and many politicians) insist that bureaucracy could be reduced if government simply did less. But even if government could do less, administrative power would simply shift to private bureaucracies, which may be more efficient but are hardly any more accessible to citizens. No one has yet shown that the quality of life that citizens in modern democracies demand can be sustained without bureaucracy, or a form of organization very much like it. Weber's prognosis – that the further advance of bureaucracy is inevitable – has stood the test of time.[3] Rather than confining itself to certain kinds of societies, bureaucracy has become ubiquitous. The twentieth century witnessed "the bureaucratization of the world."[4]

The other response to the conflict between democracy and bureaucracy – and the one on which this essay concentrates – assumes, with Weber, that bureaucracy is here to stay. The "great question," Weber wrote, is "what we can set against this mechanization to preserve a section of humanity from . . . this complete ascendancy of the bureaucratic ideal of life."[5] Those who take this approach seek in various ways to tame bureaucracy through democratic controls. That these controls have proved insufficient has often been noticed.[6] But that this failure in the practice of democratic control might indicate the inadequacy of its theory has not been so often considered. I shall examine four models according to which theorists suppose that bureaucrats may be held responsible in a democracy. None of these models of administrative responsibility provides a proper place for bureaucracy in a democracy because each misconceives or misapplies the idea of democratic responsibility. However, one of the models – one that stresses citizen participation – is less deficient than the others.

Democratic responsibility refers both to a process of deliberation (giving reasons for policies of government) and to a process of accountability (identifying the agents of those policies, and punishing or rewarding them). An adequate concept of democratic responsibility must include a wide range of reasons that officials may give for their decisions. It should not, for example, limit deliberation to only technical issues, but should promote discussion of the values underlying the policies officials pursue. An adequate concept must also provide a basis for identifying which officials actually make specific policies. The model should not, for example, confine accountability to formal lines of authority, but should call for identification of officials who actually influence particular decisions. The problem of responsibility is of course only one of the many problems that bureaucracy poses for democracy, but it is a fundamental one.

HIERARCHY

The first and still most influential idea of administrative responsibility – what I call the hierarchical model – arose at a time when the power of bureaucracy seemed negligible. Even as the scope of government grew and bureaucracies burgeoned, theorists could presume that administrators posed no threat to political leaders. They understood the role of bureaucrats much as Hobbes had explained the role of public ministers: they resemble "the nerves and tendons that move the several limbs of a body natural."[7] Because nerves and tendons of the body politic do not initiate anything on their own, political theory could safely ignore them. "Of the ministerial and subordinate powers," Locke commented, "we need not speak" because they are all accountable to some other power in the commonwealth.[8] While the nerves and tendons might from time to time twitch on their own, none would show political will of its own. When democratic theorists later began to write seriously about administration, they worried that politicians might constrain bureaucrats too much, not that bureaucrats would ever challenge their "political masters."[9]

It was Max Weber who turned the Hobbesian metaphor into a systematic theory of bureaucracy.[10] The hierarchical model that appears in his theory states, first, that administration follows "fixed jurisdictional areas" and "office hierarchy" in which there is "a supervision of lower offices by the higher ones." Second, it sharply distinguishes between administration and politics: administrators merely execute the policies set by politicians. Finally, the administrator and politician are subject to exactly the opposite principle of responsibility. The "honor of the civil servant" consists in his executing the orders of his superiors, unlike the politician who must take "personal responsibility" for his decisions. Although the model originally referred to a parliamentary form of government, it is compatible with a presidential form (and also with proposals for more presidential control or for more congressional control).

Empirical studies of modern bureaucracies present a picture of policymaking that departs drastically from the hierarchical model. In place of well-defined jurisdictions and settled lines of authority, we find overlapping "issue networks," with decision makers drawn from various agencies and various levels of government (and often also from outside government).[11] Instead of a clear distinction between politics and administration, we see bureaucrats exercising substantial discretion in defining the goals of policies, and bargaining with one another, politicians, and citizens to win acceptance of these goals.[12] This discretion goes well beyond the traditional role of filling in the "details" or the "gaps" in legislation. It often involves mobilizing public support for or opposition to programs, determining priorities, choosing among possible beneficiaries, and evaluating the success or failure of programs.[13] Instead of standing at the end of the hierarchical chain, bureaucrats initiate a process in which they encourage citizens to ask their elected representatives to make certain policies, which bureaucrats then implement and finally assess.

Elected officials can, and do, review some of this political activity, especially controversial issues, but much of the public policy of the modern state results from the cumulative effect of many small, barely noticeable decisions that middle- and low-level officials make.[14] It is true that bureaucratic decisions frequently anticipate what legislators want, but this is a distortion of the hierarchical model. Bureaucrats are responding neither to the instructions of their superiors nor to the will of the legislature, but to the political clout of certain influential legislators, or members of their staffs.[15]

The discrepancies between the hierarchical model and actual bureaucratic behavior have been most clearly documented in American government but they appear in other industrial democracies too.[16] This is so even in Britain, where in the form of the doctrine of ministerial responsibility the model has probably come closer to realization than anywhere else.[17] As the size and complexity of administration have grown, so have the influence and the independence of British civil servants; it is estimated, for example, that only about 2 percent of all delegated rules are ever examined.[18] Few ministers hold a particular portfolio long enough to learn enough to master their departments. Neither are the lines of jurisdiction as clear as they once were. Civil servants formulate many policies and settle disputes as much in consultation with groups outside government as with other officials inside government.

That modern bureaucracies do not follow the hierarchical model that some democratic theorists favor, need not entail that we abandon the model as a normative standard or ideal. Weber himself recognized that bureaucrats could very well act independently, and were already beginning to dominate elected officials.[19] But this development did not discourage him, or a succession of other theorists, from insisting on the hierarchical model as the standard for judging the place of bureaucracy in a democracy.[20] In one of the most influential cases for the hierarchical model, Theodore Lowi proposes a package of reforms that would move American government toward what he calls juridical democracy – no delegation of legislative power without clear standards, more formal and explicit administrative rules, legal codification, and sunset laws.[21] Juridical democracy could promote democratic deliberation by discouraging the cozy clientelism that develops when bureaucrats associate mainly with the corporate executives they are assigned to regulate, or even with the beneficiaries of the programs they are supposed to administer. It could also enhance democratic accountability, Lowi implies, by pushing political disputes to the highest levels of responsibility and thus subjecting them to greater public scrutiny.

Should the hierarchical model ever be realized, it may offer democracy these and other benefits. It may also create problems of its own. Even in the best circumstances in a complex society, the whole legislature or even its committees and subcommittees can hardly be expected to formulate all the specific provisions of law and oversee their execution. Much of this business would almost certainly fall to the staffs of legislative committees, those usually anonymous but already influential actors in legislative politics (particularly in the United States Congress). The hierarchical model in this way could very well abolish administrative independence in the executive only to see it rise again in a legislative bureaucracy. As the experience of the growing power of legislative staffs suggests, the creation of a legislative bureaucracy would not represent an advance in democratic deliberation or accountability.

The most pressing objection against the model turns not on the desirability of the system it proposes, but on the desirability of the process of change it encourages in any present system. That current practice departs from the model casts doubt on the use of the model, even as an ideal, to direct change in modern democracies. We should distinguish between the use of a model to recommend a state of affairs in the future, and its use to advocate criticism and reform under current conditions. A model that defines a perfectly acceptable ideal may not be the best guide to political practice under nonideal conditions.

It may cause criticisms to miss their target, and it may urge reforms that, though they approximate the ideal, make the present system worse. Such consequences follow for democratic responsibility when we use the hierarchical model in conditions where it falls so far short of being realized.

Although the hierarchical model does not adequately represent bureaucratic practice in most democracies, it does shape political deliberation about administration. Its most general effect is to turn moral and political issues into technical and procedural ones. If bureaucrats simply implement the policies set by elected officials, the only serious criticism we can make of bureaucrats is that they fail to carry out their duties efficiently. The most common complaints about bureaucracies in fact center on the consequences of their inefficiency, such as the "red tape" citizens encounter when they deal with government agencies.[22] Official inquiries also stress questions of efficiency. All of the major studies of the civil service that the British government has conducted since 1850 have concentrated almost wholly on matters of effective management and personnel policy.[23] As governments have turned over more and more economic planning and control to administrators, the criticism and the reform of this process have increasingly focused on technical questions of budgeting and forecasting. These techniques of course embody moral and political choices, but since bureaucrats are not supposed to make such choices, critics do not challenge the choices; they merely question the techniques.[24]

The hierarchical model also directs attention more to whether bureaucrats follow prescribed procedures than to whether they make proper substantive judgments. When the special counsel to the U.S. Energy Department in 1981 gave $4 million of government funds to four national charities, critics focused on the procedural propriety of his action, charging for example that he failed to clear his action with his superiors. The money had come from a government settlement with oil companies that had allegedly overcharged consumers for fuel. The specific consumers could not be identified, and the charities agreed to distribute the money to poor people for their fuel bills. Almost no one addressed the question of the criteria the government should apply in distributing funds of this kind, let alone the larger question of the role of government in the regulation of energy.

Similarly in Britain, the concern for procedure often predominates. Only great reverence for the hierarchical model could account for the preoccupation with the protocol of civil servants that often marks

British political deliberation. The Select Committee on Parliamentary Questions in England in 1971 exhaustively examined the question, "Should Ministers be permitted to ask civil servants to prepare questions for tabling by friendly MPs?" The committee scarcely discussed the content of the questions, or how such a practice might affect the policies that civil servants formulated.[25]

The hierarchical model, applied under present conditions, also tends to weaken democratic accountability. By locating responsibility at the highest levels of government, the model neglects accountability not only for the many decisions made by lower- and middle-level officials, but also for some of the decisions made by higher-level officials as well. In general, the higher the level of government, the less significant is any particular decision in our overall appraisal of the performance of an official. We may, for example, ignore a president's objectionable position on health policy if we approve of his stand on other issues. But we would be less tolerant of the official whose principal job was to formulate and advocate this policy.

Because the hierarchical model directs our criticism upward and away from many of the actual decision makers in government, it encourages a ritualistic taking of responsibility: high officials regularly accept "full responsibility" for decisions of their subordinates, whether or not the superiors had anything to do with the decisions.[26] This ritual depreciates the democratic value of ascriptions of responsibility because the persons who actually made the decisions escape scrutiny, and the officials who "take responsibility" often suffer no political punishment (and sometimes may reap political rewards for seeming to be courageous leaders who do not pass the buck). When formal responsibility diverges radically from actual responsibility, even this ritualistic responsibility begins to disappear, and genuine accountability of lower-level officials rarely takes its place. In the Canadian system, for example, the principle that ministers are strictly responsible for the conduct of civil servants is increasingly ignored. But the other part of the doctrine of ministerial responsibility – the principle that ministers should not publicly blame individual civil servants – remains very much in force.[27]

The hierarchical model also discourages – and may even prevent – reforms that would strengthen the influence of citizens over the bureaucrats who actually make decisions and policies. In the absence of an effective hierarchical system, such reforms may be the only hope of establishing any accountability in the administrative process. If we assume, with the hierarchical model, that citizens through their elected representatives hold bureaucrats accountable, then we will discount changes that would bring citizens directly into the administrative process. Indeed, many reforms, such as requiring bureaucrats to consult with citizens or even to publicize their proceedings more extensively, would on the hierarchical model distort the democratic process by permitting particular groups to try to influence policy after the general interest had already been determined by the legislators and elected executives.

But if we recognize that in any current system, this process is flawed in various ways at almost every stage, we are less likely to rely exclusively on the hierarchical model to ensure the accountability of administrators. The inequalities in the electoral process, the distortions in the legislative process, the diffusion of executive authority – these all give ample reason to seek alternatives to the hierarchical model. Other models cannot completely dispense with hierarchy since it is an essential feature of bureaucracy, but they may moderate hierarchy by emphasizing other foundations for responsibility.

PROFESSIONALISM

A second approach to reconciling bureaucracy and democracy relies on the professionalism of a civil service. This professionalist model first appears in systematic form in Hegel's theory of the state. Detached from the personal ties of family and friendship and educated in "ethical conduct," Hegel's civil servants express the universal interest of the state.[28] Although embracing very different conceptions of the general good, many democratic theorists adopt some form of the professionalist model to locate the proper place of administrators in a democracy.[29] Proponents of the model hold, first, that a substantial amount of administrative discretion is inevitable in the modern state; second, that this discretion is also desirable if bureaucrats exercise it according to the principles of their profession; and third, that in order to enforce these principles, administrators should have professional education and be responsive to the professional opinion of their colleagues. This model may be compatible with the hierarchical model – some theorists explicitly combine them – but those who stress professionalism must grant administrators considerable independence from their political superiors. The professionalist model therefore must find its democratic legitimacy not only or mainly in the hierarchical chain leading back to the electorate, but in the content of the norms establishing the claims to expertise of the profession.

Whether professionalism encourages democratic deliberation, then, depends in part on what kind of expertise or special competence we attribute to the profession of public administration. If, as in some interpretations of the model, the expertise consists in a kind of technical knowledge, such as policy analysis, the model tends to insulate bureaucrats from substantive moral and political criticism in the same way that the hierarchical model does. The techniques of policy analysis, like the methods of utilitarianism and welfare economics from which they originate, are hardly morally and politically neutral.[30] Insofar as policy analysts persuade politicians and citizens to accept their conclusions as completely objective, they use their professional standing to conceal the moral and political choices inherent in their methods of analysis. They thereby stifle the process of deliberation about these choices in a wider public forum.

More recently, however, administrators and politicians have begun to dispute about the use of the technique itself. Analysts who oppose much government regulation of occupational health and safety in the United States insist that every rule be justified by cost-benefit analysis. Their critics argue that such analysis tends to ignore the long-term benefits of regulation.[31] Insofar as the method of analysis becomes a point of political contention in this way, administrators and their academic consultants cannot stand aloof from the political fray. A dispute, even among professionals, about the basis of professional expertise may contribute to democratic deliberation. But if it does so, it also exposes the weakness of any interpretation of the professionalist model that rests on technical competence. Such disputes transcend disagreement about technique. They turn on differences about the content of policy, and in resolving these differences technical experts can claim no special authority.

Other versions of the model locate the expertise of the profession in a more general competence – a cultivated ability to apply to public policy the fundamental values of a society. On its face, these interpretations of the model seem more democratic: bureaucrats appeal to values that all citizens share, and therefore engage in deliberation in which all citizens may take part. But, we must ask, what gives bureaucrats any special standing in this deliberation (as the claim of professionalism would require)?

One answer cites the institutional position of bureaucrats: because they hold permanent appointments and are not subject to direct political pressures, they are less likely to act on their political biases and therefore are more likely to formulate and implement policy in an impartial manner. That institutional position overcomes biases of class and ideology – particularly the antisocialism ascribed to top civil servants in some governments – has often been doubted, most notably in Australian political debates. But even if civil servants do not succumb to such biases, they may use their institutional position to pursue the interests of the profession itself in maintaining and enlarging its influence within government. Many policies in the modern state now affect the employment and compensation of civil servants, and public employee unions increasingly have pressed for pay increases and job protections that the politicians and other citizens deem contrary to the public interest. Also, civil servants may resist governmental reforms that appear to threaten their own influence, particularly on economic policy. Such resistance evidently played a part in Britain in the dispute about the Expenditure Committee's recommendation to return the management functions of the Civil Service Department to the Treasury.[32]

The other response to the question of the special competence of civil servants appeals to professional education. Through a broadened curriculum in schools of public policy, persons destined for careers in government would acquire the sensitivity and skills to shape public policy according to democratic values. This response offers a more promising basis for a professionalism that could be compatible with democracy, but advocates of this approach have barely begun to think about what would constitute the content of such a professional education in social values.[33] It cannot be sufficient for future bureaucrats even to learn how to translate the fundamental values of a society into public policy, since they will often have to choose among values about which citizens fundamentally disagree.

The distinctive form of accountability in the professions is collegial. Individual professionals (in principle) answer to their colleagues through the licensing and disciplinary procedures of professional associations or through the less formal peer review as in the scientific community. This kind of professional accountability is not without problems. Even when effective, it perpetuates a kind of paternalism in the professions that ill serves democracy.[34] Public administration may escape such problems, but only because it is not fully a profession. If public administrators have not agreed upon the standards and established the organizations that would call errant members to account, then the professionalist model, applied to bureaucrats, lacks any adequate basis for accountability.

Neither has the search for other forms of accountability been notably successful. Some theorists have urged "representative bureaucracy," which would recruit and promote public employees so that the ethnic, class, and sexual composition of the civil service would approximate that of society as a whole.[35] While a representative bureaucracy might contribute to a more just policy of employment, it is not likely to reconcile professionalism and democracy. The social and ethnic origins of bureaucrats evidently affect very little the decisions and policies they make. Whatever their background, most civil servants quickly adapt to the expectations of their office and the prevailing culture of the bureaucracy.

More recently, other theorists have attempted to democratize the profession of public administration more directly. This "new public administration" bids bureaucrats to serve the interests of the disadvantaged members of society.[36] This role will usually put administrators in confrontation with elected officials, who speak for majorities and privileged minorities in society. The new public administrators are to be "strong on personal commitment to justice for the poor, rather than on hierarchical obedience and professional neutralism."[37] This new breed of bureaucrat may (or may not) strike us as a more virtuous public servant, but the new public administration offers no reason to suppose that its practitioners would be any more democratic than the old-style administrators. In face of the inevitable and legitimate disagreements about what justice requires in any policy, the new bureaucrats can look only to their own moral sense and that of their like-minded colleagues. Without abandoning their professionalism, they cannot permit other citizens – not even the poor themselves – to dictate the moral content of their decisions.

Despite its radical tone, the new public administration solves the problem of democratic accountability no better than the other versions of the professionalist model. The idea of a profession – whatever particular content we give it – implies exclusion and self-regulation that do not comport well with control by those who are not members of the profession. We may soften this tension in various ways, as proponents of the professionalist model do, but insofar as we do so, we supplant the model with other forms of democratic responsibility.

PARTICIPATION

The remaining models I examine prescribe that citizens take part in the administrative process, but they conceive this participation in quite different ways. What I call the pluralist model would provide opportunities ("multiple points of access") for individuals and groups to petition, advise and in other ways influence administrative agencies.[38] Bureaucrats would then aggregate the claims of the individuals and groups who happen to take advantage of these opportunities. The other model – which may more justly claim the title of participatory – would expand the opportunities for participation by citizens whose voices the political process otherwise neglects.[39] On this view, bureaucrats would not simply adjudicate among contending groups who appear before them, but would encourage other groups and individuals to come forward. Bureaucrats themselves would bear some responsibility for making participation more egalitarian.

Traditional democratic theorists – even those who favor greater participation in other spheres of political life – have generally opposed any active involvement of citizens in the administration of government. Rousseau forbids citizens to take part in the making of executive decisions, which require judgments about particular individuals and would therefore corrupt the universality of the general will.[40] Similarly, Mill fears that partiality and incompetence result if private citizens have much to do with administration; he also cautions that responsibility becomes diffused when many people are charged with making executive decisions.[41] These warnings anticipate in a general way the major problems that both the pluralist and the participatory models have encountered in recent times (though the pluralist approach seems less capable of overcoming them).

The pluralist model comes closer to describing the pattern of administrative politics that prevails in modern democracies. By far the most active participants in national administration in recent years are interest groups, chiefly composed not of ordinary citizens but of highly organized elites who represent various (predominantly economic) sectors of society.[42] These groups influence administrators in a variety of ways – ranging from informal personal contacts and exchanges of information to legally required consultation as in the *remiss* system in the Scandinavian governments or the group representation on official advisory boards of ministries in Germany. In some countries (for example, the Netherlands) interest groups actually administer much of the complex system of economic regulation of industry. Because the interactions between administrators and these groups are so intimate, and their joint decisions so independent of electoral and legislative control, administrators – ensconced in "captive agencies" – often serve only the interests of the dominant groups in the society.

This kind of politics, it has often been observed, creates many problems for democracy. My concern is with the less noticed difficulties it presents for a democratic concept of administrative responsibility. The pluralist model, applied in current systems, focuses political deliberation on how well bureaucrats manage to aggregate the various demands that interest groups put forward. It permits bureaucrats to justify their decisions by claiming that they are merely arbitrating among groups, not making policy. When bureaucrats cannot maintain the pose of neutral arbiter, they may claim that they can take account of only those interests expressed by groups that actually participate in administrative proceedings. The pluralist model does not encourage us to ask them to justify why they choose to listen to only those groups, or why they do not attempt to bring other groups into the process. The model does not necessarily assume that all interests in society are represented in this process, but if they are not, administrators are not responsible for compensating for the misrepresentation. Yet administrators can, and often do, use their discretion to influence what groups come forward and can also contribute to changing the structure of opportunities and incentives for participation. The pluralist model exempts bureaucrats from any praise or blame for using, or failing to use, their discretion in these ways.

The pluralist model also confounds the process of accountability. When bureaucrats and interest groups interact so closely, we may not be able to discover who actually contributed to a particular policy or decision, and to what extent, even when the participants make no effort to conceal their contributions. Moreover, the sheer number and variety of organizations that have a hand in the administrative process frustrate efforts to trace their role in the making of policies. It is doubtful that anyone can accurately identify all of the enormous number of quasi-nongovernmental organizations ("quangos") that carry on much governmental business in Britain.[43] Even if we can identify these and other organizations as agents of certain policies, we usually have no way to punish (or reward) them, except in the most flagrant cases. They stand outside government, yet they govern.

More recently, some governments have sought to expand the number and kinds of groups that take part in the administrative process.[44] In the United States, some public interest groups now have legal standing before administrative agencies, and may initiate challenges rather than merely respond to decisions. Some agencies pay the expenses of groups that wish to participate in rule-making proceedings. These reforms no doubt mitigate the unfairness in the administrative process, and are for this reason to be welcomed. They also encourage more groups to take part in the process and in this respect tilt the pluralist politics in the direction of the participatory model.

But these reforms remain well within the bounds of the pluralist model, and do not overcome the deficiencies of that model. Bureaucrats still pose as mere adjudicators of the claims of contending groups. They need not take any responsibility for bringing more citizens into the administrative process as the participatory model urges, or even for maintaining a fair balance of representation in the process. Moreover, by multiplying the number and kinds of groups in the process, the reforms may actually further erode accountability. Faced with so many competing groups, bureaucrats can easily play them off one against another, blaming all or any of them for whatever policies are adopted, or – what is more likely – for the stalemates that produce no policy at all.

Proponents of the participatory model go beyond pluralist reforms by seeking to make participation more egalitarian. To pursue this aim, they usually turn their attention to local government because there the structures of power seem more accessible and the patterns of decision making more comprehensible to ordinary citizens. Local bureaucracies that act on behalf of the central government have been the chief targets of reform. Early efforts proceeded fitfully in isolated localities in various countries, but a sustained nationwide movement began with the passage of the Economic Opportunity Act of 1964 in the United States. The Act called for "maximum feasible participation" of the poor in the planning and conduct of programs designed to reduce poverty.[45]

The ill-fated War on Poverty has been exhaustively examined by social scientists, who generally agree that the programs the Act created did not have much effect on poverty. But it is by no means certain that the participation mandated by the Act contributed to this failure, as some analysts suggest. Nor is it clear that the participation itself had little value for citizens, as others charge. The kind and extent of participation varied greatly from city to city, and often when a community action agency threatened to become effective in mobilizing the poor, the established local authorities cut off their funds or reorganized the agencies. In any event, the Act spawned demands for increased citizen participation in many other areas of public life. Since 1964, Congress has required citizen participation in the administration of policies for urban renewal, community development, revenue sharing, flood control and healthcare, among others.

Even many years later, the evidence remains inconclusive. Both those who oppose and those who favor the participatory model can find support for their views. Its critics contend that these reforms brought into the political process not the poor and alienated but mostly the middle class and politically sophisticated. Although representation of minorities (especially blacks) increased, the reforms simply added another group to the competition among elites. The participatory model would thus revert to the pluralist model, giving administrators yet another reason to conceive of their role as neutral arbiters: how can administrators dare speak for the poor when the poor now have their own spokespersons? Furthermore, since the jurisdiction of the representative bodies strictly follows the boundaries of policy areas, political deliberation disregards such important questions as the priorities among policies in the various areas.

Proponents of the participatory model could reply that the addition of new elites, especially from groups that previously did not take part, at the least has increased the attention that administrators and citizens give to the question of who participates. The issue of racial representation has won a more prominent place on the agenda of administrative politics, and administrative structures are now more often examined for their effects on the political power of various other disadvantaged groups.

It is true that most of the new participatory boards, councils, and the like tend to specialize in particular policy areas. But the participatory model itself does not require such specialization. It is possible to imagine a system of participatory bodies, structured so that at each higher level the body would take a more general perspective, progressively integrating more policy areas. The recommendations of the board that oversees the administration of healthcare, for example, might be reviewed by a board that examines healthcare in the context of mass transit plans, community development, and welfare policy. Such a system could be extended to provide geographical as well as functional coordination, and in principle could be applied at the national as well as the local level. In its more elaborate forms, such a system would put hierarchy back into the participatory model, but it would be a hierarchy of citizens instead of bureaucrats and politicians.

Critics of the participatory model also worry about its effects on accountability. As more citizens take part in administration, they are less likely to be informed and skillful in politics, and more likely to be vulnerable to the blandishments of bureaucrats. In place of the captive agencies of pluralist administration, we find captive citizens, co-opted to legitimize decisions that bureaucrats want made. Co-optative participation obscures the identity of the agents of policy, making accountability more difficult. When citizens do manage to control the bureaucrats through the institutions proposed by the participatory model, they usually act on their own, free from any further requirement to answer to other citizens. The Health Systems Agencies in the United States, and the Health Council System in Scotland, for example, both lacked adequate procedures for communicating with constituents, let alone for giving constituents power to influence their representatives on the board.[46]

To avoid co-optative participation, defenders of the participatory model urge that governments provide programs to educate citizens who assume positions on the various boards and councils that control administrators. Some "participatory experiments" in Sweden, Austria, and the Netherlands suggest that even in science policy, citizen advisory councils can be effective (though controversial) if their members have the benefit of educational programs.[47]

The problem of the accountability of the citizens who serve as representatives could be partly overcome by increasing the publicity about the proceedings in which they take part. The Swedish practice of maintaining written records of administrative deliberations and permitting citizens (including the press) to inspect them at any time could encourage not only bureaucrats but also citizen representatives to be more responsible.[48] The flaws in accountability would not be so troublesome if the citizens who participate in administration did not come disproportionately from certain classes and groups. Most recent reforms favor those citizens who already have the time and interest to participate; for example, in the community action agencies in the poverty program the routine clerical positions were salaried but the more influential policymaking positions were not. While proponents of the participatory model would not, like an Aristotelian democrat, replace administrators with citizens chosen by lot, they would select by lot at least some of the citizens who serve on boards or in other ways participate in administration. Like citizens who take their turn on juries, these citizens would be paid.

The movement toward greater participation in administration has fallen far short of the goals of the participatory model. But the difficulties we have noticed in the participatory reforms are not so much failures of the model as failures to apply the model consistently and comprehensively. Unlike the effects of incompletely applying the hierarchical model, those of the participatory model do not typically worsen the condition of democratic responsibility. The changes the participatory model prescribes usually improve deliberation and accountability. When they do not, the model itself provides the basis for criticism and further reform. Unlike the professionalist model, the participatory model does not contain any principles, such as claims to special competence, that may inherently constrain democratic responsibility. And, unlike the pluralist model, the participatory model does not relieve bureaucrats of the responsibility to consider the views and encourage the involvement of citizens beyond those who happen to take part in the administrative process at any particular time.

If the participatory model is in these respects superior to the others, it may be the best starting point from which to continue a search for the place of bureaucracy in a democracy. But the model bristles with problems of its own, and though some may be overcome through further exploration of the ideas and institutions mentioned earlier, others seem more intractable. Perhaps the most troublesome is the accountability of the citizens who participate in the administrative process to the citizens who do not participate.

Even if we were to accept the participatory model, we would need to find a way to combine with it the indispensable features of the other models. We cannot completely do without hierarchy in administration: when the legislative will is clear and proper, bureaucrats should not obstruct it. Moreover, legislators (and elected officials more generally) should have the authority to tell bureaucrats how to organize administrative processes. On a participatory model, legislators would still be the principal architects even of structures that encourage citizens to take part in administration. They would devote more time to making the administrative process more democratic than to eliminating administrative discretion.

Professionalism, too, must have a place in any effective bureaucracy. The participatory model may encourage us to take a more favorable view of rotation of office, and perhaps even political patronage. But we can hardly neglect the need for expertise and political independence in modern government – a need that a professional civil service may not always fulfill but for which it is essential. The various boards of citizen representatives that the model recommends would not preclude the exercise of considerable discretion by professionals in administration. Many of these boards would stand ready to intervene, but only if administrators consistently reached decisions that citizens deemed wrong.

Finally, we should wish to preserve some of the procedures that the pluralist model prescribes, such as representation of public interest groups before administrative agencies. If the participatory model provides a promising approach to the problem of the place of bureaucracy in a democracy, it is at best an incomplete approach. Apart from its inherent difficulties, the model has so far failed to accommodate adequately the legitimate claims of the other models.

Neither democratic theory nor democratic practice has yet discovered a form of administrative responsibility that would let democrats comfortably consort with bureaucrats in the governing of society. To appreciate the extent of the failure of democracy to come to terms with the problem of bureaucracy is not to show where success might lie. But it is to take a necessary step in the pursuit of democratic ways to subdue bureaucratic power in the modern state.

Notes

1. Thomas Carlyle, "The New Downing Street," in *Works of Thomas Carlyle* (30 vols., New York: Scribner, 1898), vol. xx, 143.
2. Karl Marx and Friedrich Engels, *The Marx–Engels Reader*, 2d ed., edited by R. Tucker (New York: Norton, 1978), 23–5, 607, 614.
3. Max Weber, *Gesammelte Aufsätze zur Soziologie und Sozialpolitik* (Tübingen: Mohr, 1942), 413; see also Weber, "Bureaucracy," in *From Max Weber*, ed. H. H. Gerth and C. W. Mills (Oxford / New York: Oxford University Press, 1958), 196–244.
4. Henry Jacoby, *The Bureaucratization of the World* (Berkeley: University of California Press, 1973).
5. Weber, *Gesammelte*, 414. *Pace* Weber, democrats seek to preserve more than a "section" of humanity from bureaucracy.
6. B. Guy Peters, *The Politics of Bureaucracy* (London: Longman, 1978), 229–36.

7. Thomas Hobbes, *Leviathan*, ed. M. Oakeshott (London/New York: Macmillan, 1962), 180–1.

8. John Locke, *Two Treatises of Government*, ed. P. Laslett (New York: New American Library, 1965), 415.

9. *The Federalist Papers*, ed. C. Rossiter (New York: New American Library, 1961), 423–5, 435–6, 447; and John Stuart Mill, *Considerations on Representative Government*, in *Collected Works*, ed. J. M. Robson (Toronto, University of Toronto Press, 1977), vol. 19, 435–7, 520–33. For a "Madisonian" defense of administrative agencies, see James O. Freedman, *Crisis and Legitimacy* (Cambridge: Cambridge University Press, 1978), 260–1.

10. Weber, "Bureaucracy," 196–7, 214–16; and "Politics as a Vocation," in *From Max Weber*, 95.

11. Hugh Heclo, "Issue Networks and the Executive Establishment," in *The New American Political System*, ed. A. King (Washington, DC: American Enterprise Institute, 1978), pp. 87–124.

12. Graham Allison, *Essence of Decision* (Boston: Little, Brown, 1971), 144–84.

13. Donald P. Warwick, "The Ethics of Administrative Discretion," in *Public Duties*, ed. J. Fleishman et al. (Cambridge: Harvard University Press, 1981), 93–127.

14. Michael Lipsky, *Street-Level Bureaucracy* (New York: Russell Sage, 1980), 81–156.

15. R. Douglas Arnold, *Congress and the Bureaucracy* (New Haven, Conn.: Yale University Press, 1979), 207–16.

16. Arnold Heidenheimer and Donald P. Kommers, *The Governments of Germany* (New York: Crowell, 1975), 238–51; Ezra Suleiman, *Politics, Power and Bureaucracy in France* (Princeton: Princeton University Press, 1974), 155–80; H. Bakkerode et al., "The Responsibility of the Civil Servant in the Netherlands," *Administration* 23 (1975), 400, 408–9; and Kenneth Kernaghan, "Politics, Policy and Public Servants," *Canadian Public Administration* 19 (1976), 432–56.

17. Maurice Wright, "The Responsibility of the Civil Servant," *Administration* 23 (1975), 374–9; F. F. Ridley, "Responsibility and the Official," *Government and Opposition* 10 (1975), 444–72; Douglas E. Ashford, *Policy and Politics in Britain* (Philadelphia: Temple University Press, 1981), 31–43.

18. H. W. R. Wade, *Administrative Law* (4th ed., Oxford: Clarendon Press, 1977), 735.

19. Weber, "Bureaucracy," 232–42.

20. Woodrow Wilson, "The Study of Administration," *Political Science Quarterly* 2 (1887), 197–222; Herman Finer, "Administrative Responsibility in Democratic Government," *Public Administration Review* 1 (1941), 335–50; Herbert Simon, *Administrative Behavior* (3rd ed., New York: Macmillan, 1976), 57–8; and R. J. S. Baker, *Administrative Theory and Public Administration* (London: Hutchinson, 1972), 94, 130–6.

21. Theodore J. Lowi, *The End of Liberalism* (2d ed., New York: Norton, 1979), 93–127.

22. Herbert Kaufman, *Red Tape* (Washington, DC: Brookings, 1977).

23. Ashford, *Policy and Politics in Britain*, 69, 73.

24. Peters, *The Politics of Bureaucracy*, 178–89.

25. *Report from the Select Committee on Parliamentary Questions*, 1971–72, H.C. 393 (London: HMSO, 1972).

26. See Chapter 1.

27. "Kernaghan, Politics, Policy and Public Servants," 451–4.

28. G. W. F. Hegel, *Philosophy of Right*, trans. T. M. Knox (Oxford: Oxford University Press, 1967), 192–3, 291.

29. Jeremy Bentham, *Works*, ed. J. Browring (11 vols., New York: Russell & Russell, 1962), vol. II, 195, V, 448, X, 337; J. S. Mill, *Considerations on Representative Government*, 520–33; Carl J. Friedrich, "Public Policy and the Nature of Administrative Responsibility," *Public Policy* 1 (1940), 3–24; Joseph Schumpeter, *Capitalism, Socialism and Democracy* (4th ed., London, Allen & Unwin, 1961), 293–4; and Frederick Mosher, *Democracy and the Public Service* (Oxford: Oxford University Press, 1968), 99–133.

30. Peter Self, *Econocrats and the Policy Process* (London: Macmillan, 1975) and Robert A. Goldwin, ed., *Bureaucrats, Policy Analysts, Statesmen* (Washington, DC: American Enterprise Institute, 1980).

31. Martin J. Bailey, *Reducing Risks to Life* (Washington, DC: American Enterprise Institute, 1980); and U.S. Senate, Committee on Governmental Affairs, 96th Congress, 2d session, *Benefits of Environmental, Health and Safety Regulation* (Washington, DC: Government Printing Office, 1980).

32. Ashford, *Policy and Politics in Britain*, 84–5.

33. Joel L. Fleishman and Bruce L. Payne, *Ethical Dilemmas and the Education of Policymakers* (Hastings-on-Hudson, NY: Hastings Center, 1980).

34. Dennis F. Thompson, "Paternalism in Medicine, Law and Public Policy," in *Ethics Teaching in Higher Education*, ed. D. Callahan and S. Bok (Hastings-on-Hudson, NY: Hastings Center, 1980), 256–61.

35. Samuel Krislov, *Representative Bureaucracy* (Englewood Cliffs, NJ: Prentice-Hall, 1974). The best general critique is: Kenneth John Meier, "Representative Bureaucracy," *American Political Science Review* 69 (1975), 526–42.

36. H. George Frederickson, "Toward a New Public Administration," in *Toward a New Public Administration*, ed. F. Marini (Scranton, PA: Chandler, 1971), 309–31.

37. Lewis C. Mainzer, *Political Bureaucracy* (Glenview, IL: Scott Foresman, 1973), 135.

38. Emmette S. Redford, *Democracy in the Administrative State* (Oxford: Oxford University Press, 1969), 106. Cf. Paul H. Appleby, *Morality and Administration in Democratic Government* (Baton Rouge: Louisiana State University Press, 1952), 251; Norton Long, *The Polity* (Chicago: Rand McNally, 1962), 50ff.; and Victor A. Thompson, "Bureaucracy in a Democratic Society," in *Public Administration and Democracy*, ed. R. Martin (Syracuse, NY: Syracuse University Press, 1965), 210–12.

39. For a brief discussion and a bibliography, see Mainzer, *Political Bureaucracy*, 135–48, 181–2.

40. Jean-Jacques Rousseau, *The Social Contract*, trans. M. Cranston (Harmondsworth, England: Penguin, 1968), 101–7, 112–16.

41. Mill, *Considerations on Representative Government*, 528–33.

42. Peters, *The Politics of Bureaucracy*, 141–59; Suleiman, *Politics, Power and Bureaucracy in France*, 316–51; Wright, "The Responsibility of the Civil Servant," 382; and Lowi, *The End of Liberalism*, 50–63, 295–8, 311–12.

43. Outer Circle Policy Group, *What's Wrong with Quangos?* (London: Outer Circle Policy Unit, 1979).

44. Richard B. Stewart, "The Reformation of American Administrative Law," *Harvard Law Review* 88 (1975), 1709–90.
45. John H. Strange, "Citizen Participation in Community Action and Model Cities Programs," *Public Administration Review* 32 (1972), 655–9; J. David Greenstone and Paul F. Peterson, *Race and Authority in Urban Politics* (New York: Russell Sage, 1973); Lowi, *The End of Liberalism*, 223–6; and Howard I. Kalodner, "Citizen Participation in Emerging Social Institutions," in *Participation in Politics*, ed. J. R. Pennock and J. W. Chapman (New York: Lieber-Atherton, 1975), 161–85.
46. James A. Morone and Theodore R. Marmor, "Representing Consumer Interests," *Ethics* 91 (1981), 440–2; and Dorothy Bochel and Morag MacLaran, "Representing the Interest of the Public," *Journal of Social Policy* 8 (1979), 449–72.
47. Dorothy Nelkin, *Technological Decisions and Democracy* (Beverly Hills, CA: Sage, 1977).
48. Roger Choate, "The Public's Right to Know," *Current Sweden* 93 (Stockholm, Swedish Institute, 1975), 4.

4

Judicial Responsibility

Judges are not responsible to citizens in ways that most other officials are. Judges are supposed to protect basic values of justice from infringement by citizens and other officials, and are therefore supposed to act independently of any political influence. On this view, judges exercise responsibility simply by preserving their independence. Yet judges often make decisions that are, in effect, no different from the policies that other officials make. In such cases, democracy would seem to require that judges be held accountable by citizens and their representatives. On this view, we need a more politically robust concept of responsibility – one that would require judges to interact with citizens more than they do now. This kind of judicial responsibility may conflict with judicial independence as usually understood.

The tension between the more democratic forms of responsibility and the standard types of judicial independence cannot be so easily resolved as the conventional approaches to the problem assume. The most common way that theorists deal with the tension is to accept the idea that judges should be independent so that they can protect basic values of justice, but then to seek a foundation for those values that would obviate the need for the responsibility that democracy requires of other officials. The Constitution, substantive justice, and the democratic process are the most prominent foundations offered. The objections to these approaches are well known and need not be repeated here.[1] Although the objections cannot be expected to settle the question on such a longstanding dispute, they provide a reason to consider a different approach – one that tilts more toward democratic responsibility than judicial independence. This approach faces up to a problem that the conventional ones tend to neglect – what may be called the problem of many minds.

The root of the problem is that reasonable persons – judges, citizens, and other officials – disagree on questions of fundamental values. They disagree about what values the Constitution, substantive justice, and the democratic process require. Some of the disagreements fall within the range of differences that neither party to the disagreement has good and sufficient reason to reject. Yet adjudicating such disagreements involves choosing for the whole society one set of values and rejecting others. In the face of reasonable disagreement, judges who are not accountable to citizens do not have good grounds for imposing their choice on citizens. But neither do citizens acting through the democratic process have any better grounds for imposing their choice on society. To argue as do the critics of judicial policymaking that the democratic majority should determine which values to enforce is to assume that the value of a certain kind of democracy takes priority over the other values that independent judges might enforce. Reasonable persons may disagree about that choice, too.

The problem of many minds does not presuppose moral skepticism. On the contrary, the problem arises only if we take seriously the idea that there are values that are valid independently of any political process, and that there are better and worse ways to reason about those values.[2] Simple disagreement is not sufficient to create the problem. The persons who disagree must at least be engaging in a moral discussion.

It is not easy to say exactly what should characterize such a discussion, but in most political contexts we can usually distinguish a moral claim from a mere expression of preference or assertion of self-interest. Making a moral claim involves taking a disinterested perspective and proposing a principle that could be accepted by others whose preferences and interests may otherwise differ from yours.[3] It is quite possible that persons engaged in a moral discussion may rightly come to different conclusions about particular policies even if they share common principles. They may, for example, weigh the principles differently, as in a conflict between free speech and personal privacy. But more significantly, there may be irresolvable moral disagreement at an even more fundamental level, as in the controversy over abortion, in which the most reasonable assessments conclude that moral principles yield conflicting conclusions.[4]

That a society is of many minds does not disprove the validity of moral values even for that society, but it does cause problems for the making up of the collective mind. If neither citizens nor judges can finally justify making the authoritative choice of fundamental values for society, we must preserve the possibility of continual moral challenge to the choices of values that public officials inevitably make for us. A necessary condition for justifying these choices as binding on all citizens is that they are made in a process of deliberation, understood as an interaction in which citizens and their representatives offer moral justifications for their actions and respond to the moral criticisms of those actions. The values chosen by officials cannot be said to be our values – they have no moral claim on us as citizens in this society – unless they are chosen through a process of deliberation of this kind.

To sustain the possibility of deliberation, officials must act so that citizens can respond to their decisions about fundamental values. Citizens can respond only if officials take moral responsibility for their actions. Officials accept moral responsibility if they (1) acknowledge a decision as their own (agency); (2) give public reasons for the decision (justification); and (3) provide occasions for reasoned challenges to the decision (interlocution). These requirements are the political manifestation or institutional expression of standard criteria of moral responsibility: an agent is responsible for an action if the action is his or her own in the sense that it is not coerced; not done in ignorance; and is subject to responses such as praise or blame.[5]

In their political form, the three requirements manifest a concept of responsibility that captures the features of its etymological parent, the idea of response. Responsibility involves an interaction between agents and principals – or, more specifically, in politics between officials and citizens. Responsibility is not the same as responsiveness in the sense of a reaction to a stimulus or to political pressure as such.[6] It implies a reciprocal relationship in which an agent acts in such a way that principals have the opportunity to respond. Responsible officials encourage responses to their decisions.

Why should judges have any duty to encourage a response to their decisions? Introducing what is still one of the most powerful arguments for judicial restraint, James Bradley Thayer more than a century ago asserted that judicial review "tends to dwarf the political capacity of the people and to deaden its sense of moral responsibility."[7] When judges correct the mistakes of legislators, they deprive citizens of "political experience and moral education" and deflect attention of citizens from "the spot where responsibility lies."[8]

Stripped of its excessive judicial modesty, Thayer's argument points toward a concept of judicial responsibility that would require judges to encourage citizens to react to their decisions. Judges would be responsible only if they sought to make their decisions enhance the capacity of citizens to choose collectively whether to accept those decisions. The concept does not imply, as Thayer probably intended it should, that citizens or their representatives should, if possible, always decide questions that involve fundamental values. But the concept does suggest that whoever makes these decisions should make them in a way that permits citizens to challenge the decisions they oppose. In deciding whether to make such a decision, as well as how to make it, a judge would ask: does my making this decision now encourage citizens to respond in ways that enable them to decide the question for themselves in the future? The responsible judge is one who helps citizens to be responsible.

The requirements of responsibility serve this general purpose. Citizens are better able to respond to a judicial decision if the judge acknowledges it as his or her own; gives reasons for it that citizens can understand; and supports practices that permit challenges to it. The judicial process has three features that may be seen as ways of implementing, respectively, each of these requirements. But as traditionally understood each actually creates obstacles to realizing judicial responsibility.

First, judicial passivity: judges decide only issues in particular cases that others initiate. This may seem to limit their independence and thus minimize their interference with democratic decision making. But it can also provide an excuse for not recognizing the discretion that they actually have, and therefore not fully acknowledging the decision as their own. Second, judicial rationality: judges give reasons based on neutral principles after hearing all the parties to the case. To the extent that the reasons are truly neutral, the judges may seem to be above politics. But as is now generally recognized, judicial reasoning is rarely neutral in the required sense, and justifications that only purport to be neutral obviously do not satisfy the requirement of responsibility. Third, judicial discipline: judges are subject to sanctions if they violate their duties of office. This seems to provide a way for citizens to respond to judicial decisions, but it is limited in its scope. We need to revise the standard ways of understanding these characteristics if we are to develop a satisfactory concept of judicial responsibility.

THE ACTIVITY OF PASSIVITY

"An American judge," Tocqueville wrote, "can only pronounce a decision when litigation has arisen, he is only conversant with special cases, and he can not act until the cause has been duly brought before the court."[9] This judicial passivity embodies one of the cardinal rules of what used to be called natural justice – a rule ancient and important enough to have its very own Latin couplet: *ubi non est actio, ibi non est jurisdictio.*[10] Because the judge is "brought into the political arena independently of his own will," he is less likely to act out of partisan fear or favor.[11] He will be free to decide in accordance with law, and forced to leave democratic officials to themselves most of the time. In this way, it seems that the responsibility of judges is limited because they do not choose the cases they decide. They do not have to take responsibility for that choice because it is not their own.

As a limit on judicial responsibility, this passivity does not seem very potent. It applies only to the decision to decide the case, not to the decision in the case. Some courts exercise enormous discretion in their choice of cases; the Supreme Court chooses to decide on the merits less than a tenth of the cases on its docket.[12] Lower courts that do not have such discretion nevertheless do enjoy considerable freedom in defining the issues in a case. The political significance of a case may vary greatly depending on how its issues are defined and even the form the judgment takes (for example, a decree rather than a verdict). Judicial passivity thus would not prevent judges from refusing on partisan grounds to dismiss a case, or deciding it on partisan grounds if they chose to hear it.

Since Tocqueville's time, judicial policymaking has not only become more active but also more visible. The passivity has not kept courts from making political decisions. But while allowing courts to have political influence on others, passivity may still be performing its original function of protecting the courts from political influence from others. Because judges can plead that they are only deciding the instant case, they can escape responsibility for the wider political consequences of their decisions. They are not answerable, according to the traditional requirements of judicial passivity, for their decisions to hear a case nor for the effects of their decision beyond the case. As often happens in the design of institutions, a virtue that fails to achieve its purposes may become a vice. Passivity may now serve mainly to insulate judges from accountability commensurate with their political power.

Many of the important cases decided by the federal courts in recent years do not conform to the traditional model of a lawsuit. Instead of a process initiated and controlled by the parties to a dispute, and a result focused on the resolution of the particular dispute between the parties, these cases give judges discretion to determine who should be a party to the dispute, and to fashion results that affect public policy.[13] This trend began with the school desegregation cases in which courts imposed specific goals for integration and detailed plans for achieving them.[14] It has spread to other governmental agencies – not only the federal bureaucracy but also state prisons and mental hospitals, juvenile detention facilities, and public housing authorities.[15]

The job of the judge in these cases – often involving continual adjudication over many years and day-to-day administration of the institutions by court-appointed "special masters" – hardly resembles the passive role that Tocqueville described. Indeed, as Tocqueville would have expected, activist judges have come under criticism as they have come into the political arena.[16] But whether this criticism is warranted from the perspective of judicial responsibility does not turn on whether they are active or passive as such. It depends on whether they acknowledge their agency. More specifically, it depends on whether they take responsibility for their decision to act by considering whether it furthers the responsibility of citizens.

Applying this criterion, we ask whether judges acknowledge their responsibility for the consequences of their inaction as well as their action insofar as it affects the responsibility of citizens. To illustrate the implications of this criterion, consider a set of cases in which activist judges satisfied the criterion, and another in which nonactivist judges failed to satisfy it.

In a series of cases in several states, federal judges have issued decrees calling for extensive reform in prisons. In Arkansas, they demanded massive changes in the entire state prison system. The prisons were overcrowded, understaffed, and unsanitary; prisoners were brutalized by inmate guards and generally subjected to inhumane conditions. In most states, the problems had persisted for many years, and though some officials had called for reform, most legislators and most citizens ignored them. Judges did not simply issue decrees; they became actively and continually involved in implementing them. In some cases they asked the defendants to fashion the remedies, and in some cases they appointed special masters. But in all the cases they watched the process closely themselves.

The result of all this judicial activity, according to a careful study of reform in four cases (including the Arkansas system), was a dramatic change in public attitudes toward prison reform. Before litigation, most citizens and many officials, mainly out of ignorance, had been "largely apathetic and unconcerned about jail and prison matters."[17] After judicial intervention, public attitudes toward reform began to change, which in turn affected officials who shared responsibility for operations of the facilities, particularly appropriating bodies. Corrections achieved a higher ranking among governmental priorities as a result of changing public opinion. Public administrators were more receptive to the idea of correctional reform.[18] If we assume that judges could have reasonably foreseen these effects, we may conclude that they were acting responsibly. By taking an active role, they may have temporarily usurped what would normally be legislative authority, but in doing so they encouraged citizens and legislators to take responsibility for reform themselves.

Conversely, judges following the dictates of judicial modesty can discourage citizens from taking responsibility. The clearest examples are cases where higher courts have overturned the activist decisions of lower courts. Under the pressure of a federal district judge, Philadelphia police officials devised a complaint procedure to deal with widespread allegations of police brutality. The Supreme Court struck down the decree of the lower court, holding that it infringed the "latitude" that the local administration needs in the "dispatch of its own internal affairs."[19] Further reflecting the traditional understanding of judicial passivity, the Court also seemed to imply that the lower court should have treated the case not as a matter of policy concerning the police department as a whole but as nineteen separate claims of individual victims against individual police officers.[20] Although the Supreme Court's action did not bring reform of the police department to a halt, it gave greater legitimacy to the opponents of reform. The complaint procedure brought about by the district judge's pressure had been widely praised,[21] but the efforts to build on this first step became mired in legal wrangling about its constitutionality. Instead of debating on their own terms the conflict between the principles of liberty and order and how they might be reasonably

balanced in law enforcement in Philadelphia, citizens found themselves worrying more about how the courts might view any solution
they chose.

From the general principle that judges should encourage citizens
and their representatives to make their own decisions, it does not
follow, as some theorists suggest it does, that the judges should never
initiate a process in which citizens and their representatives make their
own decisions.[22] On the contrary, the principle has just the opposite
implication in many circumstances, as we have just seen. If judicial
activity promotes democratic activity, judicial responsibility favors it.
To meet the challenge of the first requirement of responsibility –
agency – judges thus must recognize that they are accountable for
inaction as well as for action. They must acknowledge that even in
passivity there is agency.

THE LIMITS OF RATIONALITY

Judges are supposed to give reasons for their decisions – the second
requirement of judicial responsibility. This simple demand was the
main claim of an important group of legal theorists who, beginning in
the 1950s in reaction to the legal realists, emphasized the necessity of
"reasoned elaboration" in judicial decision making.[23] Giving reasons,
they suggested, is part of the definition of judicial office. If judges
have to give reasons, they cannot so easily make policy on the basis of
their own will, and they cannot so easily deny citizens the chance to
criticize the policy on a basis other than mere will.

But not any kind of reason will do. The "reasons" the legal realists
attributed to judges – personal and ideological preferences – do not
qualify. Such reasons are at best explanations, not justifications, and
therefore do not even begin to make a rational argument or to invite
a rational reply. If judges justified their decisions by saying simply that
they liked the defendants or their case, they would be exercising mere
power – a kind of verbal force – instead of the rational persuasion that
the judicial process is supposed to exemplify. The right kind of reason
therefore must appeal not to preferences or to desires, but to general
principles.

A general principle is one that is universalizable in the sense that
if it applies to one case, it applies to all cases that are similar in the
relevant respects.[24] The philosophical foundation of this idea owes
most to Kant, whose various versions of the categorical imperative

serve as criteria for what is to count as an acceptable moral principle. If a principle cannot "stand the test of the form of a general law of nature," Kant writes, "then it is morally inadmissible."[25] But as the Kantian criteria have often been criticized for being only formal, so their legal analogues have been dismissed for being mostly empty. To say that a decision is based on neutral or general principles, even if we can discover such principles in controversial cases, is to say little about the rightness of the decision, or even the right of the court to make the decision. It is harmless enough if it means that "a principle, once promulgated, is to be applied to all cases it controls and not just when one is in the mood."[26] The test of generality, legal theorists now commonly conclude, is necessary but not sufficient to justify judicial decisions.[27] What has not been recognized, however, is that the test as usually interpreted may actually make judicial decisions less justifiable and thereby judges less responsible.

The problem is that the quest for generality banishes from judicial opinions some of the particular considerations that judges take into account, or should take into account, in reaching a decision. Intent on formulating the most general principle under which to bring a decision, a judge may be reluctant to mention and perhaps even to consider particular political factors that motivated the decision itself. Such factors seem too specific to the case in question or too contingent on the partisan forces to belong in a justification that purports to be general.

No doubt some of these factors should be banished – but for the same reason they should not influence the decision at all. Personal prejudice, professional rivalry, partisan favor, and their ilk do not belong in the opinion because they do not belong in the reasoning that leads to the decision. They do not address ends to which the judge or any public official should be committed. But other political factors – legislative coalitions that prevent certain reforms, or tactical compromises necessary to form a majority on a court – may be a perfectly appropriate part of a justification. They are appropriate if they are among the reasons that a judge reasonably believes enable the decision to achieve a just result in current political circumstances.

One of the few judges to acknowledge, at least in public, that political considerations of this sort played a role in his decisions is Richard Neely, a former justice of the West Virginia Supreme Court. Neely wrote his court's opinion striking down the state's juvenile detention laws, which permitted children to be sent to reform school for

offenses, such as truancy, that are not crimes for adults. The opinion
took the classic form of an argument from general principle, in effect denying that the state had offered an adequate reason to justify
treating children differently from adults. In the familiar language of
substantive due process, the opinion held that there is no rational relationship between the legitimate state interest (protecting children)
and the means intended to accomplish it (sending children to reform
school, which increases their chances of becoming criminals). Whatever one may think of the reasoning in the opinion, it was not the
actual reasoning that led Justice Neely to his decision:

> What I reasoned about the case myself and what I wrote in the court's opinion
> were two entirely different things . . . Many legislators had a concern for juveniles,
> but there was not enough interest among enough members to appropriate the
> money necessary to treat different types of juveniles more appropriately. The
> force of inertia was so great that without court intervention the legislature would
> pursue agendas made compelling by organized constituencies and pay no at-
> tention to the problems of the poor, often retarded, children. When my court
> held the existing structure of juvenile control unconstitutional, the whole issue
> was suddenly up for grabs again, and the legislator was forced to rethink the
> problem.[28]

Neely does not explain why he could not put such thoughts into
his opinion. Perhaps he calculated that voicing these political calculations would defeat his political purposes. Judges simply do not say
these sorts of things. But his political reasoning – at least as a supplement to the constitutional and other arguments – may be a necessary
part of the justification. Although claims about defects in the democratic process do not provide the sole or general basis for judicial
authority, they may count as part of a justification for a particular decision. Judges sometimes discuss political factors in their decisions,
most notably in cases raising the doctrine of "political questions."[29]
It is, however, one thing to concede one's own limitations and quite
another to criticize the limitations of others. Judges have a long way to
go before they develop a satisfactory principled mode for presenting
such criticisms.

Regardless of whether an appeal to political factors is warranted
in a particular case or whether it is warranted in general, citizens
deserve to know when judges decide partly on the basis of such claims.
Judges evade responsibility if they do not state their reasons for a
decision. If the judicial norm of rationality is interpreted as it usually is
to exclude political calculations of this kind, then the judicial process

itself contributes to judicial irresponsibility. We need a more refined test of what should count as a principle in legal reasoning – one that rejects reasons that assert mere preferences or prejudices, but admits reasons that express relevant political factors.

For a start, we should look less to Kant the moral philosopher, and more to Kant the political philosopher.[30] Instead of Kant's test for a moral principle,[31] we should consider his test for a legal principle – the criterion of publicity. No rule can be an acceptable principle of public law unless it can be publicly stated without defeating its own purpose.[32] This criterion could encourage judges to consider the public to whom their principles are addressed as much as the principles themselves. Applied to the principles themselves, the publicity criterion may not yield results that differ from the more familiar test. On either, we would have to assume that the audience is composed of – if not Kantians, then – people who are in some sense reasonable.

But the criterion poses a question to judges they might not otherwise face: can you justify omitting from your opinion any of the significant reasons that led to your decision? If the argument for withholding some reasons could not in itself be presented to a (reasonable) public without defeating the purpose of the decision, then the argument should be rejected. The judge should either make the reasons public, or reconsider the decision itself. This test would require further refinement, but its potential should be clear. It would encourage judges to pay as much attention to what they exclude from their opinions as to what they include – more fundamentally, to what they tell their publics. The norm of rationality is a worthy one but only if it is understood as a test of the reasons that produce an opinion as well as the reasons that happen to be included in it.

THE SIGNIFICANCE OF SANCTIONS

When modern legal writers refer to methods to enforce judicial responsibility, they most often have in mind one of two general kinds of sanctions: subjecting judges to disciplinary control (as in impeachment) or to political control (as in elections). The first seeks to control the misconduct of judges who act contrary to the duties of office; the second attempts to influence the decisions of judges who, consistent with their office, make policy. Both of these are misconceived as solutions to the problem of many minds, but for opposite reasons. Appreciating why can point to a better way of thinking about the third requirement of judicial responsibility – the kind of response that interlocution calls for.

The attraction of disciplinary control is its apparent neutrality. Judges are held strictly accountable but to standards that anyone would accept, whatever his or her policy views. Typically, such standards demand that judges avoid conflicts of interest, as described in the Code of Judicial Conduct of the American Bar Association.[33] Furthermore, the standards are usually enforced by independent commissions, professional associations, or courts themselves, thus further protecting judges from direct political influence. This kind of responsibility, then, seems to preserve judicial independence.

But it does so at a price. The range of conduct for which judges must answer on this view is narrow. They are responsible only for meeting the minimum standards of office – simply for being a judge, not for being a good judge. The problem is not simply that the disciplinary system manifests an incomplete conception of responsibility. The system carries the further implication that the conduct not covered by its standards is conduct for which judges are not answerable. It does this in two ways. First, the system conveys an implicit promise to the judge: if you do not violate these minimum standards of judicial conduct, you are free from public criticism. You are answerable only for your opinions and decisions, and then only through the usual processes of legal appeal and legislative revision.

Second, the disciplinary system impoverishes the language of responsibility. Its categories of criticism, designed to deal with the deviant judge, fit awkwardly the activities of the normal judge. It is a vocabulary suited for asserting that this judge should not judge this case, or should not judge any case, rather than for arguing that no judge should judge in this way in any case or in cases like this. It thus encourages the belief that responsibility mainly refers to judges when they step outside their office – to judges who do not act like judges at all.

Relying on discipline to make judges responsible thus neglects a large part of judicial life. It ignores the routine decision, which in itself lacks the salience to command the attention or the energy of the other branches but which multiplied many times throughout the judicial system amounts to a significant exercise of political power. Disciplinary responsibility neglects the use of power, which, though exercised within the legitimate limits of office, is nonetheless irresponsible.

A court that declares a city ordinance unconstitutional may be acting within its authority, but if the court refuses to hear the city council's justification for the ordinance it may be acting irresponsibly. Disciplinary responsibility in these various ways encourages the wider debate about judicial responsibility to focus on the worst case and drive out discussion of the merely questionable or even the simply bad case.

The second kind of sanction – political control – reaches more broadly. It applies to all judges, not only judges who commit an injudicious act. It is also meant to influence the decisions of judges, not only the circumstances in which judges make decisions. The various forms of political control – appointment by elected officials, periodic elections, recall, impeachment – are seen as necessary means for making judges responsible. The view of responsibility presupposed by this kind of control assumes that for all of their decisions (or for the general trend of all of their decisions) judges should be responsible to the democratic will, however that will is taken to be expressed, or however indirectly it is expressed.

But this assumption begs the question with which we began: it ignores the claims of judicial independence entirely. Even if we are committed to a democratic process, we should not take it for granted that judicial authority should always defer to the popular will, whether expressed in elections or legislation.

The preoccupation with political controls is misplaced for another reason. Political sanctions are only symptoms of responsibility. They do not reveal much about the underlying practice of responsibility – how much and what kind of independence judges actually enjoy. Electoral control itself does not seem to make a great deal of difference in the decisions that judges make. It is not necessary for popular control since, in the absence of elections, judicial policy often follows public opinion if citizens have other channels by which to communicate to judges.[34] It is not sufficient because even elected judges usually do not respond to public opinion or act as politicians typically do.[35] Part of the reason undoubtedly is that many judicial elections are by custom or by law nonpartisan, and some are "unopposed candidate" elections in which the incumbent runs against his or her record.[36] If elections and similar controls do not matter as much as their proponents or their critics believe, then we should be looking elsewhere for ways to promote responsibility consistent with judicial independence.

Where we should look is the judicial culture – the set of attitudes and beliefs that define the role of the judge in our society. Insofar as judges resist political control, it is because of norms of judicial independence – a whole set of informal rules and practices that encourage officials and citizens to see the judicial role as requiring judges to answer only for their opinions and decisions and to answer only by publishing them. Judges are expected to avoid speaking publicly in any detail about cases before or after deciding them (at least while in office). They are not supposed to try to win support for their judicial positions by lobbying other officials or organizing citizens. Judges of course have often engaged in political activity, but the fact that they have almost always kept such activity secret suggests that they believe that it violates widely held norms.[37]

Undoubtedly, this culture of independence has its benefits – among them the support of the traditional judicial virtues of passivity and impartiality. But a judicial culture that exaggerates these virtues is not conducive to judicial responsibility. It indiscriminately insulates judges from every kind of responsibility, not only direct political accountability. Responsibility requires more than the disciplinary approach permits but less than the political approach demands.

THE AGORA OF PRINCIPLE

If we move away from the orthodox ideas of independence and the emphasis on sanctions that accompany them, we can begin to formulate a richer conception of the interaction between judges and citizens. We can appreciate (as the third requirement suggests) that judicial responsibility demands interlocution – genuine opportunities for citizens to respond to the decisions judges make. The requirement focuses on how the judicial process recognizes respondents: it directs attention to the question of whom the judges listen to before they decide, and whom they encourage to speak after they decide. In the spirit of Thayer's principle, the responsible judge seeks to encourage as many citizens as possible to participate in the discussion of these issues.

Some legal theorists portray judges as engaged in a "dialogue" with society.[38] In society as in the courtroom, judges listen to all sides of a controversy and speak to principles that all members of society could share. Insofar as such a dialogue takes place, it would go some way toward making judges responsible. When judges give reasons for their decisions (at least when they give reasons of the kind we have seen are necessary), they fulfill part of the requirements of responsibility.

But the dialogue, as it is conceived and as it occurs, is distinctly one-sided. In the wider political arena, it is more of a monologue. Judges listen only to citizens who happen to appear as parties in the cases before them. They do not, except incidentally, seek parties who might better speak to the political issues that the cases raise. They are not supposed to listen to voices beyond the instant case because their office seems to require a kind of independence that prevents them from taking into account much of the normal controversy of political life. They are not encouraged to listen because the judicial office protects their judgments from many of the normal challenges of political action. Only with a different and genuinely two-sided conception of dialogue can we define a judicial role that will begin to meet the requirements of democratic responsibility.

There must of course be constraints on who participates – not only within the halls of justice but also outside of them. Some kinds or some degrees of participation could defeat the purpose for which we seek participation in the first place – the securing of responsibility. If we think of the purpose of responsibility in this context as developing the common moral principles by which citizens can collectively accept or reject decisions and policies, we would not welcome all kinds of participation. Mass demonstrations in the courtroom or referendums on constitutional cases hardly seem conducive to principled deliberation that the idea of responsibility assumes. But if the constraints are based on the purpose of the responsibility, they are likely to imply significantly more participation, or at least different forms of it, than prevail at present. Many of the limitations on who is heard and who may speak on constitutional questions – the debate about fundamental values – bear no relation to this purpose, or any other purpose of comparable significance. Customs of confirmation, rules of standing, and doctrines of judicial supremacy are three such limitations.

By relaxing or eliminating some of these artificial constraints, we can begin to develop the other side of the conversation – the aspect neglected by the legal theorists who extol the dialogic character of the judicial process. Instead of the "forum of principle,"[39] we should think of the judicial process as the "agora of principle." In the Greek agora in its earliest periods, citizens conducted public business of all kinds in this space that symbolized their common life. The judiciary did not stand apart, architecturally or politically. Later, most clearly in the Roman Forum, the judiciary acquired its own building, imposingly looking down on the public space where ordinary citizens gathered.[40] In a more open judicial process – an agora of principle – we stand a better chance of resolving the problem of many minds. If judges must bring others into the discussion of fundamental values, the judicial mind would not finally determine the values by which the society is governed. The way to manage the problem of many minds is to accept the problem as permanent – to let many minds deliberate.

The Customs of Confirmation

If judges are not subject to election and especially if they hold office for life, the appointments process should play a critical role in promoting judicial responsibility. Confirmation of federal judges by the Senate is the last chance for any direct political control. Yet a custom has developed that impedes this control and inhibits deliberation. Nominees are expected to decline to answer questions that probe their moral and political views in ways that might reveal how they would decide future cases. In her confirmation hearings, Sandra Day O'Connor testified:

I do not believe that as a nominee I can tell you how I might vote on a particular issue which may come before the Court, or endorse or criticize specific Supreme Court decisions presenting issues which may well come before the Court again. To do so would mean that I have prejudged the matter or have morally committed myself to a certain position.[41]

O'Connor was willing to endorse decisions such as *Brown v. Board of Education* that are unlikely to be challenged in the future.[42] And she revealed her views on a wide variety of issues (as distinct from cases), including abortion.[43] Yet she refused to indicate in any way how her views could influence her judgments about the law as it might develop in the future. Her stance was widely praised by editorialists, politicians, legal figures, and other public leaders, especially those who had been critical of President Reagan's campaign promise to appoint judges who would "respect traditional family values and the sanctity of innocent life."[44] The assumption underlying this praise is evidently that character and competence should be the main considerations in the appointment of judges, and that nominees' discussions of how their moral and political views might influence their conduct on the bench is either irrelevant or improper.

It is difficult to maintain that moral and political views are not relevant to many of the decisions judges make. Most observers of the judiciary now recognize that even in many lower courts moral and political views cannot be entirely excluded from the reasoning or justification of decisions. Even on a view of constitutional interpretation that favors strict construction, the potential influence of moral and political views should not be regarded as irrelevant. Interpretation can rarely proceed in a moral vacuum. Senators may reasonably need to assess to what extent a nominee's moral views might unconsciously or indirectly influence future decisions.

O'Connor made a further argument: it would be improper to reveal her views in a way that might have implications for future cases because she would risk the possibility of having to disqualify herself in those cases.[45] It would be a violation of the obligation of impartiality required by judicial ethics, she suggested, to decide a case on which one had previously expressed an opinion (outside of one's judicial role). O'Connor's sensitivity here deserves respect, but she carries it too far. As her future colleague, Justice Rehnquist, wrote in explaining why he would not disqualify himself in a case about which he had earlier expressed a view: "Proof that a Justice's mind at the time he joined the Court was a complete *tabula rasa* in the area of constitutional adjudication would be evidence of lack of qualification, not lack of bias."[46]

It may not be necessary for judicial responsibility that a prospective judge respond to questions about how he or she would actually vote on future cases (certainly not those that are pending). But without some discussion about how one's moral and political principles relate to real cases, those representatives who are charged with assessing nominees cannot exercise their own responsibility adequately. It is not possible to adequately understand how nominees will approach questions of law, without seeing how they apply their principles or methods to specific facts of a case. As one commentator observed about O'Connor's testimony, "Since the universe consists entirely of those fact situations that have come before the Court and of those that have not but might someday, Justice O'Connor's exclusionary rule ensured that the Senators would learn next to nothing about the principles and methods she would apply on the bench."[47]

A nominee who refuses to respond to questions about the application of principles to cases, then, is not only undermining the responsibility of these representatives but is also in effect disclaiming his or her responsibility for future decisions. This kind of responsibility is prospective – giving some account of the reasons the nominee is likely to employ in cases that will come before the court. But given the limitations of retrospective responsibility (for officials who are appointed without term), the prospective kind may be the best hope for maintaining any effective responsibility at all.

The Standing of Citizens

Who is heard in the halls of justice depends partly on who can pay the price of admission. This fact has been often noted, and proposals to improve the "access to justice" now abound.[48] Less emphasized are the obstacles over which the judges themselves have more direct control, and that fall more distinctly within the sphere of judicial responsibility. Judges determine who is heard when they decide who is to count as a party in a case, and on what issues the parties may speak. Some examples of each show how judges could admit more citizens to the judicial agora where public policy is made.

Who is a party in a case is partly determined by how judges interpret the rules of standing. The rules are usually interpreted as requiring that a citizen have a "personal stake" in the outcome; suffering "an injury in fact, economic or otherwise" is a necessary condition.[49] "To entitle a private individual to invoke the judicial power," the Court declared in an early case, "he must show a direct injury . . . and it is not sufficient that he has merely a general interest common to all members of the public."[50] The heavy hand of individualism inherent in these rules places sharp limits on the access to the courtroom by citizens who would challenge government on the basis of commonly shared principles rather than particular interests. Standing as a citizen is not sufficient to challenge, for example, the appointment of a member of the Supreme Court, the qualification of a member of Congress, or the failure of a governmental agency to give a public account of its receipts and expenditures.[51]

Neither of the two most important arguments the Court has offered for these constraints on standing is compelling. The first argument is that only complainants with a "personal stake" in the outcome are able "authoritatively to present to a court a complete perspective upon the adverse consequences flowing from the specific set of facts undergirding [the] grievance."[52] One problem with this argument is that the "adverse consequences" may appear trivial if ascribed to single individuals or a group of individuals, but would be seen to constitute substantial harm if placed in the context of the polity as a whole. The perspective of the "personal stake" does not lend itself to considerations of such values as the integrity of government. Furthermore, to require a "personal stake" may detract from the principle at issue even where there is such a stake. If only persons actually charged with a criminal violation can raise the claim of discriminatory enforcement of the criminal laws,[53] the concern about their guilt or innocence is likely to take precedence over the allegation of unfair patterns of law enforcement in the community. The issue surely could be more "authoritatively" presented by law-abiding citizens who are part of the same racial or social group against which the discrimination is alleged to be directed.

The second argument for requiring a personal stake is that it keeps the courts from intruding into the sphere of authority of the legislature and the executive. To grant standing to citizens as citizens would "distort the role of the Judiciary in its relationship to the Executive and the Legislature and open the Judiciary to an arguable charge of providing 'government by injunction.'"[54] The distortion against which this argument warns assumes a separation of powers more rigid than that envisaged by the framers in their time and more strict than that practiced by the courts in our time. If judges make general policy on the occasion of deciding particular cases, they can hardly deny citizens the chance to raise issues of general policy on the same occasions. Nor should the existence of other forums for raising these issues necessarily preclude the citizens from choosing to raise them in court. Even if we agree their "subject matter is committed . . . ultimately to the political process," as the court has insisted,[55] we should remember that the court is part of that same political process.

Congress has already gone some distance toward providing a statutory basis for citizens to raise such issues. This is part of the effect of recognizing legal rights to clean air and water, governmental information, occupational health and safety, and other such interests.[56] The courts did not always in the past wait for the legislature to incorporate such rights into law before hearing claims based on some of them, and courts need not wait in the future.[57]

When citizens seek a hearing before governmental agencies, the courts are less reluctant to relax the traditional rules of standing and to permit appeals to principles based on public values rather than simply private interests. In the regulation of the environment, courts have begun to create what has been called "a right of initiation" by granting citizens who have no personal stake in an issue the right to a hearing before the relevant administrative agency, and sometimes even the right to force the agency to take action to protect some public value.[58] Judicial review of agencies is necessary in these circumstances, the court said, to "help ensure that the agency gives due consideration to citizen participation."[59]

Relaxing the rules of standing before an administrative agency is of course not the same as relaxing the rules of standing in court. But if courts often make public policy as they decide particular cases, the justification for their adopting completely different rules of standing from those that they impose on administrative agencies begins to seem less compelling. Agencies and courts begin with much the same traditional rules of standing (for example, the test of "injury in fact"), and if the judges force administrators to change their rules, judges should have to consider why they should not change their own rules. There may be cogent reasons in many kinds of cases for courts to adopt different rules, but these reasons should be presented, not assumed on the basis of some formal and increasingly artificial distinction between the kinds of adjudication in which each institution is supposed to engage.

It may not yet be possible to prescribe specific content for the rules of standing that responsible judges should adopt when making public policy. But it should be clear that they can no longer automatically invoke the traditional criteria for who is to count as a party. These criteria can exclude citizens from the judicial process for reasons that bear no relation to the decision a judge is actually making in a particular case. Judges should have to account for the representational basis of their decisions about standing. They should have to explain why the parties they choose are more appropriate representatives for the interests in question than other citizens who could claim to speak for these interests.[60] Judges should also have to explain how the whole set of parties they choose should constitute the best representatives for a deliberation about the common interest. Trying to provide these explanations, judges are likely to find that they must open their proceedings to more, or at least to different, voices than they have heard in the past. But whether or not they adopt more inclusive rules of standing, judges control the channels of challenge to the actions of government. Even when restricting standing (and thereby limiting their own power to make policy choices), judges are still deciding who can hold government responsible. For this, no less than for making policy, they should be accountable.

Judicial Supremacy

"Marbury v. Madison . . . declared the basic principle that the federal judiciary is supreme in the exposition of the law of the constitution, and that principle has ever since been respected by this Court and the Country as a permanent and indispensable feature of our constitutional system."[61] This basic principle has often been interpreted by judges and other officials as granting the federal courts a monopoly on the making of constitutional judgments. Because the Constitution, however ambiguous and incomplete in itself, comprises the framework of so much of our public deliberation about fundamental values, such a monopoly significantly restricts the opportunity of citizens to join in that deliberation. To be sure, no one is denied the chance to offer an interpretation of the Constitution and to try to persuade others to act on it. But no one but a federal judge is permitted to speak and act with the seriousness that the power of authoritative decision can stimulate.

Judicial responsibility requires judges to relinquish part of this monopoly so that citizens and other officials have the incentive and the authority to take part in making judgments about fundamental values for society. To promote judicial responsibility, we need to qualify the doctrine of judicial supremacy. We need to understand the doctrine in a way that could achieve this goal without abandoning the idea of judicial review.

The doctrine works its spell more through subtle discouragements than outright prohibitions, but it does occasionally show its face in actual decisions of courts. Reversing a judgment of the Oregon Supreme Court, which invoked the Fifth Amendment to exclude from trial a defendant's statement to police, the U.S. Supreme Court concluded that "a State may not impose . . . greater restrictions as a matter of federal constitutional law when this Court specifically refrains from imposing them."[62] Notice that Oregon was not violating anyone's constitutional rights by imposing this additional restriction on its police. Nor was the state acting, or permitting any of its citizens to act, contrary to a ruling of the Supreme Court. The state's alleged error was simply that it had interpreted the Fifth Amendment's prohibition against self-incrimination in a more demanding way than the Supreme Court had done.

The unspoken theory of law that underlies this assumption of judicial monopoly is a form of positivism that owes most to Hobbes and Austin. On this view, no rule or interpretation of a rule is law unless it is commanded by the sovereign. It is not necessary that the sovereign be one person (as Hobbes preferred) or that it be Parliament (as Austin assumed), but it is necessary that the sovereign speak with one voice.[63] Otherwise, there would be "contradiction in the laws,"[64] and no way to tell lawful judgments from mere private opinions. This is so, a fortiori, in a system of divided powers where, if the fundamental law can be interpreted by any power, that law can no longer serve its essential function of limiting that power.

But this fear of contradiction – and the legal if not social "war of all against all" it evokes – is misplaced. It results from confusing consistency in the law with consistency in the commands of the law. We certainly should not want the law to issue contradictory commands. The law would defeat one of its basic purposes – providing standards to regulate social conduct – if, with respect to the same action, it required performance and nonperformance by the same individuals. But other kinds of inconsistency in the law seem to be acceptable as long as they are not discriminatory. The law may require an action of some individuals but not of others, or it may require different actions of the same individual at different times. Such inconsistencies may result from the law itself or from different interpretations by different authorities. Citizens and officials could have no reason to wonder what the law requires, as long as some authority gives an authoritative interpretation in the case that affects them.

Abandoning judicial supremacy may make less difference in the way that judges decide cases than in the way that other officials and citizens think about the choice of fundamental values. If constitutional judgments are not the exclusive province of judges, legislators can take more seriously their own responsibility to consider fundamental values when they make law. They would be less inclined to act on the common assumption that their job is to make policy and let the Court decide later on its constitutionality.[65] They would be more inclined to act on the principle that their duty is to make policy consistent with the constitutional values as best they can interpret them.[66]

To act on this principle a legislator does not have to deny that the Court's interpretation carries special weight. On the contrary, a legislator who believes that the Supreme Court's interpretation of the Constitution is authoritative may be obligated in some cases to act on a more demanding reading of the Constitution than the Court has given. The weak "rational relation test" that the Court has generally used since 1937 to review most social and economic legislation may itself presuppose that legislators act on a stronger standard.[67] The Court will accept, as consistent with the equal protection clause, legislative classifications if they bear a rational relation to some conceivable purpose of government and if they do not use racial or certain other "suspect" grounds or affect certain other fundamental interests. The Court grants the benefit of the doubt to the legislature not only on the question of the purpose of the classifications, but sometimes even on the question of the nature of a fundamental interest. Why should judges defer to legislators on such questions? The most plausible answer is that judges assume that legislators are deciding on the basis of their own view of a substantive standard of equal protection. They are acting in good faith on their own interpretation of the Constitution.

In a case in which the Court upheld Texas's system of school finance that resulted in great inequalities among districts,[68] Justice Powell for the majority of the Court held that the classification met the rational relation test, and that the Court could not declare any fundamental interest to be involved that would call for a stricter test. If the justices were to declare education to be a fundamental interest, Justice Powell feared, it would turn the Court into a "super-legislature." The Court would be "assuming a legislative role and one for which [it] lacks both authority and competence."[69]

We should interpret Justice Powell as claiming only that the Court is not competent to decide what is to count as a fundamental interest in this case, not that no one else can reasonably decide that the Constitution or the values on which it is based make education a fundamental interest. The latter claim would again establish a judicial monopoly and in a form particularly subversive of responsibility. While seeming modestly to withdraw from making fundamental value judgments, the Court actually would be arrogantly denying others the opportunity to make them. The Court would be creating a responsibility gap – a sphere where no one has the duty to consider the fundamental values expressed in the Constitution.

To be responsible, the Court need not confine itself to a role as deferential as implied by the rational relation test. A judgment striking down the Texas school financing system might very well have stimulated legislatures to take greater responsibility for considering fundamental values in reforming these systems. Responsibility does not necessarily demand deference, but when judges (for whatever reason) adopt a deferential standard, responsibility requires that they also recognize the right of the bodies to whom they defer to make constitutional judgments. Otherwise, they create a circle of deference – judges deferring to legislators deferring to judges. In such a circle, no one is responsible. But, irrespective of the standards judges adopt, they must renounce any claim of judicial supremacy that would discourage citizens and their representatives from making their own judgments about the Constitution and the values that it expresses.

CONCLUSION

Restoring a more robust form of responsibility in the judicial process requires that we abandon or at least revise some of our traditional ways of thinking about adjudication. It demands that judges develop new practices and new habits of mind that encourage citizens to challenge the policies the judiciary makes. This kind of responsibility may draw on older but half-forgotten attitudes (such as the assumption that all citizens should have a voice in what the Constitution says). It may be already emerging in some parts of the judicial world (as in the changing attitudes toward the rules of standing). But in other parts (such as the customs of confirmation) it will have to be more actively pursued.

If judges are to be responsible in a democracy, they must act so that citizens can share in the making of collective decisions about fundamental values. We have seen various ways in which judges could succeed or fail in any of the three dimensions that define democratic responsibility – agency, justification, and interlocution. Because reasonable people disagree about questions of fundamental values, judges cannot claim, any more than can any official, the authority to make final decisions about these values. In this sense, there is no solution to the problem of many minds, except to let many minds deliberate. But judges have a responsibility to ensure that the deliberation actually takes place in their own agora.

Notes

1. These approaches are discussed in the longer version of this essay: "Judicial Responsibility: The Problem of Many Minds," Working Paper, Center for Advanced Study in the Behavioral Sciences, Stanford, CA, 1985.

2. As Thomas Nagel has pointed out, "no one, whatever his views about the proper role of the Court, is a complete skeptic about ethics" – "The Supreme Court and Political Philosophy," *New York University Law Review* 56 (1981), 519–20. Michael Perry cites Justices Rehnquist and Bork as counterexamples to Nagel's assertion, since these justices deny that individual value judgments have any "moral claim" upon us as a society except insofar as they are enacted into law or the Constitution: see *The Constitution, The Courts, and Human Rights* (New Haven, Conn.: Yale University Press, 1982), 103–5. But then for a moral skeptic why should the law or the Constitution have any moral claim upon us? According to Perry, these justices take the principle of electorally accountable policymaking as "axiomatic in our political-legal culture." If so, they purchase their philosophical consistency at the price of abandoning any reasoned basis for politics. They have no principled answer to someone who would by force of arms or any other means seek to substitute a new axiom for the one we now happen to hold.

3. One of the reasons it is difficult to specify what should count as a moral position is that the specification should be powerful enough to exclude some principles but not so powerful as to favor one particular moral position over others. For some of the more satisfactory efforts to resolve this problem, see John Rawls, *A Theory of Justice* (Cambridge, Mass: Harvard University Press, 1971), 130–6; Kurt Baier, *The Moral Point of View* (Ithaca, NY: Cornell University Press, 1958), 187–213; and Ronald Dworkin, *Taking Rights Seriously* (Cambridge, Mass.: Harvard University Press, 1977), 248–53.

4. See L. W. Sumner, *Abortion and Moral Theory* (Princeton, NJ: Princeton University Press, 1981); and Marshall Cohen et al., eds., *The Rights and Wrongs of Abortion* (Princeton, NJ: Princeton University Press, 1974).

5. The first two criteria correspond to Aristotle's requirements that an action or omission not be done under compulsion or in ignorance. See Aristotle, *Ethica Nicomachea, The Works of Aristotle*, ed., W. D. Ross (Oxford: Oxford University Press, 1963), Bk. III, 1–5. See Chapter 1 in this volume.

6. See J. Roland Pennock, *Democratic Political Theory* (Princeton, NJ: Princeton University Press, 1979), 261, 266–8.

7. James Bradley Thayer, *John Marshall* (Boston: Houghton Mifflin, 1901), 107.

8. Ibid., 106, 109.

9. Alexis de Tocqueville, *Democracy in America*, trans. Henry Reeve (New York: Appleton, 1904), vol. I, ch. VI, 92. Modern theorists of the judicial process who emphasize this and related characteristics include: Benjamin N. Cardozo, *The Nature of the Judicial Process* (New Haven: Yale University Press, 1929), 98–141; Lon L. Fuller, "The Forms and Limits of Adjudication," *Harvard Law Review* 92 (1978), 385–6; Owen Fiss, "Foreword: The Forms of Justice," *Harvard Law Review* 93 (1979), 12–13; and Mauro Cappelletti, "The Law-Making Power of the Judge and Its Limits: A Comparative Analysis," *Monash University Law Review* 8 (1981), 43–4.

10. "If no action is brought to court, the judicial function cannot be exercised." More generally on the rules of natural justice and their extensive appeal

in many different cultures, see Suranjan Chakraverti, *Natural Justice, or Fundamental Principles of Judicial Procedure* (Lucknow and Delhi: Eastern Book, 1967), esp. chs. II–III, VII–VIII; and Martin Shapiro, *Courts: A Comparative Analysis* (Chicago: University of Chicago Press, 1981), 114–16.

11. Tocqueville, *Democracy in America*, 95–6.

12. Henry J. Abraham, *The Judiciary* (Boston: Allyn & Bacon, 1983), 31.

13. Abram Chayes, "Foreword: Public Law Litigation and the Burger Court," *Harvard Law Review* 96 (1982), 4–60; Abram Chayes, "The Role of the Judge in Public Law Litigation," *Harvard Law Review* 89 (1976), 1281–316; and Fiss, "Foreword: The Forms of Justice," 1–58.

14. Jennifer Hochschild, *The New American Dilemma: Liberal Democracy and School Desegregation* (New Haven, Conn.: Yale University Press, 1984).

15. See Gerald Frug, "The Judicial Power of the Purse," *University of Pennsylvania Law Review* 126 (1978); and Special Project, "The Remedial Process in Institutional Reform Litigation," *Columbia Law Review* 78 (1978).

16. See, for example, Donald L. Horowitz, *The Courts and Social Policy* (Washington, DC: Brookings Institution, 1977); and Nathan Glazer, "The Judiciary and Social Policy," in *The Judiciary in a Democratic Society*, ed. L. Theberge (Lexington, Mass.: Lexington Books, 1979).

17. M. Kay Harris and Dudley P. Spiller, Jr., *After Decision: Implementation of Judicial Decrees in Correctional Settings* (Washington, DC: Government Printing Office National Institute of Law Enforcement and Criminal Justice, October 1977), 8.

18. Ibid., 11.

19. *Rizzo v. Goode*, 96 S. Ct. 608 (1976).

20. Ibid., at 605–7.

21. Ibid., at 610 (Blackmun, H., dissenting).

22. Alexander Bickel, *The Least Dangerous Branch* (Indianapolis, Ind.: Bobbs-Merrill, 1962), 143–56.

23. The pioneers were Hart and Sacks, but the work that generated the most scholarly literature was that of Wechsler. For a general survey that places the movement in historical perspective, see G. Edward White, "The Evolution of Reasoned Elaboration," *Virginia Law Review* 59 (1973), 279–302.

24. For a discussion of universalizability see J. L. Mackie, *Ethics: Inventing Right and Wrong* (New York: Penguin, 1977), 102.

25. Immanuel Kant, *Critique of Practical Reason*, in *The Philosophy of Kant*, ed. C. J. Friedrich (New York: Random House, 1949), 259.

26. John Hart Ely, *Democracy and Distrust* (Cambridge, Mass.: Harvard University Press, 1980), 55.

27. Ibid., 25–7.

28. Richard Neely, *How Courts Govern America* (New Haven, Conn.: Yale University Press, 1981), 15.

29. Laurence H. Tribe, *American Constitutional Law* (Mineola, NY: Foundation Press, 1978), 71–9.

30. When legal theorists invoke Kant, they typically refer to his moral philosophy: see for example M. P. Golding, "Principled Decision-Making and the Supreme Court," *Columbia Law Review* 63 (1963), 35.

31. Immanuel Kant, *Foundations of the Metaphysics of Morals*, ed. L. W. Beck, (Indianapolis, Ind.: Bobbs-Merrill, 1959), 18, 39.

32. Kant, *Eternal Peace*, in *The Philosophy of Kant*, ed. Friedrich, 469–70.
33. John Henry Merryman, "Judicial Responsibility in the United States," *Rabels Zeitschrift* 41 (1971), 339–40. Generally, see Mauro Cappelletti, "'Who Watches the Watchman?' A Comparative Study on Judicial Responsibility," *American Journal of Comparative Law* 31 (1983), 1–62.
34. See James H. Kuklinski and John E. Stanga, "Political Participation and Government Responsiveness: The Behavior of California Superior Courts," *American Political Science Review* 73 (1979), 1090–9.
35. For a near exception that we might say proves the rule, see the discussion of the 1964–65 elections for the Wisconsin Supreme Court in Jack Ladinsky and Allan Silver, "Popular Democracy and Judicial Independence: Electorate and Elite Reactions to Two Wisconsin Supreme Court Elections," *Wisconsin Law Review* (1967), 147–65.
36. Merryman, "Judicial Responsibility," 342–3.
37. The reaction to the revelations about political activity of Supreme Court justices such as Abe Fortas' relations with Lyndon Johnson tends to confirm that belief. See, generally, Bruce A. Murphy, *The Brandeis/Frankfurter Connection* (New York: Oxford, 1982), 3–8, passim.
38. Fiss, "Foreword: The Forms of Justice," 12–13; Chayes, "The Role of the Judge," 1315–16; Perry, *The Constitution*, 25; Ronald Dworkin, "The Forum of Principle," *New York University Law Review* 56 (1981), 472–3; Bickel, *The Least Dangerous Branch*, 26, 156; Harry Wellington, "Common Law Rules and Constitutional Double Standards: Some Notes on Adjudication," *Yale Law Journal* 83 (1973), 246–9; and Bruce Ackerman, *Reconstructing American Law* (Cambridge, Mass.: Harvard University Press, 1984), 96–101.
39. Dworkin, "The Forum of Principle."
40. Homer A. Thompson and R. E. Wycherley, *The Athenian Agora* (Princeton, NJ: The American School of Classical Studies at Athens, 1972), 52–72; and Michael Grant, *The Roman Forum* (London: Weidenfeld & Nicolson, 1970), 144–53. At times the civil courts attracted enormous crowds, including professional applauders ("supper-praisers") employed to cheer for one side or the other. Such "signs of enthusiasm," according to some contemporary accounts were necessary to "palliate the boredom of the speeches" (Grant, 149).
41. *Nomination of Sandra O'Connor: Hearings Before the Senate Comm. on the Judiciary on the Nomination of the Judge Sandra Day O'Connor of Arizona...*, 97th cong., 1st sess. 1–414 (1981), at 57–8.
42. Ibid., at 253.
43. Ibid., at 61–3, 79, 98, 125.
44. Grover Rees, "Questions for Supreme Court Nominees at Confirmation Hearings: Excluding the Constitution," *Georgia Law Review* 17 (1983), 922.
45. *Nomination of Sandra O'Connor*, 253.
46. *Laird v. Tatum*, 409 U.S. 824 (1972).
47. Rees, "Questions," 949.
48. Mauro Cappelletti, ed., *Access to Justice*, 4. vols. (Milan: Dott. A. Giuffre Editore, 1978).
49. See *Association of Data Processing Service Organizations v. Camp*, 397 U.S. 150, 152–3 (1970); *Flast v. Cohen*, 392 U.S. 83 (1968), at 99; and *Baker v. Carr*, 369 U.S. 186 (1962), at 204. Also see Louis L. Jaffe, "Standing Again," *Harvard*

Law Review 84 (1971). Generally, on the development of the doctrine of standing, see Joseph Vining, *Legal Identity: The Coming of Age of Public Law* (New Haven, Conn.: Yale University Press, 1978).

50. *Ex Parte Levitt*, 302 U.S. 633 (1937), at 634.

51. *Ex Parte Levitt*, 302 U.S. 633 (1937); *Schlesinger v. Reservists Committee to Stop the War*, 418 U.S. 208 (1974); and *U.S. v. Richardson*, 418 U.S. 166 (1974).

52. *Schlesinger v. Reservists Committee to Stop the War*, at 221.

53. *O'Shea v. Littleton*, 414 U.S. 488 (1974).

54. *Schlesinger v. Reservists Committee to Stop the War*, at 222.

55. *U.S. v. Richardson*, at 166.

56. 42 U.S.C. secs. 7401–642 (Supp. IV 1980); 33 U.S.C. secs. 1251–376 (1976 & Supp. IV 1980); 5 U.S.C. sec. 552 (1976); and 29 U.S.C. secs. 651–78 (1988).

57. The need to rethink the basis of standing is especially clear in class action suits. Stephen C. Yeazell, "From Group Litigation to Class Action, Part II: Interest, Class and Representation," *UCLA Law Review* 27 (1980), 1107–20.

58. Richard B. Stewart and Cass R. Sunstein, "Public Programs and Private Rights," *Harvard Law Review* 95 (1982), 1204–6, 1278–89.

59. *Natural Resources Defense Council, Inc. v. SEC*, 606 F. 2d 1031 (D.C. Cir. 1979).

60. Chayes, "Foreword: Public Law Litigation," 25–6.

61. *Cooper v. Aaron*, 358 U.S. 18 (1958).

62. *Oregon v. Hass*, 420 U.S. 719 (1975).

63. Thomas Hobbes, *Leviathan*, ed. M. Oakeshott (London/New York: Macmillian, 1962) ch. 26; and John Austin, *The Province of Jurisprudence Determined* (London: J. Murray, 1832).

64. Hobbes, *Leviathan*, ch. 26, 201.

65. For example, D. Morgan, *Congress and the Constitution: A Study of Responsibility* (Cambridge, Mass.: Harvard University Press, 1966); and Abner J. Mikva and Joseph R. Lundy, "The 91st Congress and the Constitution," *University of Chicago Law Review* 38 (1971), 449.

66. See Paul Brest, "The Conscientious Legislator's Guide to Constitutional Interpretation," *Stanford Law Review* 27 (1975), 587–8.

67. Ibid., 594–9.

68. *San Antonio School District v. Rodriguez*, 411 U.S. 1 (1973).

69. Ibid., at 31.

5

Representatives in the Welfare State

If the welfare state is to be democratic, the legislators who make its policies must be responsible to the citizens who are affected by them. Responsibility requires that legislators explain their actions to the citizens they represent. Giving reasons is part of what being responsible means, and part of what being reelected requires.[1] But the nature of welfare itself poses a dilemma for democratic responsibility. To justify decisions about welfare, representatives must consider the preferences of citizens. But those preferences at any particular time are not adequate grounds for a justification of welfare policy. Orthodox theories of representation provide no way to cope with this problem; a satisfactory theory must take a different approach. Instead of looking for justifications solely in the preferences of citizens at a particular time, we should look at the legislative process in which the justifications are made.

Welfare policy, more than most other kinds, is grounded in the preferences of citizens. The reasons that representatives give for other kinds of policies, such as civil rights or cultural development, should not follow preferences so closely. When justifying these policies, representatives might not count some preferences as reasons at all (those based on racial prejudice, for example), and might regard other reasons as decisive (those based on individual rights or ideals of excellence). But when welfare is in question, what citizens say should count for more. Citizens may be mistaken about their own welfare, but at some point they must be taken as competent judges of it. A welfare policy that makes citizens better off without their ever knowing it is a logical, but neither a feasible nor a desirable, possibility

99

in a democracy. To justify disregarding the preferences of citizens in the area of welfare policy, representatives usually appeal to other preferences – either the preferences of the same citizens in the future or the preferences of other citizens now.

But welfare policy is not adequately grounded in the preferences of citizens at any particular time. Its effects are more temporally extensive than those of most other kinds of policies. It directly affects more people for a longer period (from cradle to grave). It comprises many different programs, which begin and end at different times. Welfare policy is more likely to consist of what Madison called a "train of measures," which have "gradual and perhaps unobserved" instead of "immediate and sensible" consequences.[2]

Because the policies that promote welfare are multiple and because their effects extend over time, the citizens who judge the policies now may not be in the best position to assess the policies fully and fairly. They may not be the citizens who benefit from or pay for them later. Federal policy on unemployment, for example, cannot be identified with a single bill adopted at one time; its effects must be assessed and reassessed over time. Even comprehensive legislation such as the Social Security Act of 1935 or the Economic Opportunity Act of 1964 cannot be appraised within a single electoral cycle or in isolation from prior and subsequent measures.[3] Representatives thus seem to be justified not only in disregarding the present preferences of citizens in favor of their future preferences, but also in disregarding preferences altogether in favor of principles that do not depend so much on time.

DELEGATES AND TRUSTEES

The conflict between these demands – that representatives should and should not consider the preferences of citizens – recalls the opposition between the two traditional theories of representation. A delegate considers the preferences as expressed at some particular time, whereas a trustee refers to the principles to which preferences should conform. But this contrast is too simple. Delegates are not strictly bound to consider preferences expressed at any particular time, and trustees are not completely free to ignore even momentary preferences. In their more plausible forms, both theories recognize both demands, but in doing so they undermine democratic responsibility. Neither provides a coherent basis on which representatives can justify their actions to citizens. If we understand how even the modified versions of these theories fail, we can begin to appreciate the need for a different approach.[4] Although welfare policy stands most clearly in need of a new approach, other kinds of policies to some degree raise the same problem.

Most delegate theorists would not bind a representative in advance to a specific mandate or set of policies. Rather, they would make a representative responsible for policies after they had been adopted. The reasons that representatives give for policies at any particular time relate to the preferences that citizens can be expected to have at the next election. That familiar creature of contemporary political science – the retrospective voter – makes this modification of delegate theory possible.[5] Whether voters look at past performance as such or at past performance as a basis for future actions, they do not commit representatives in advance to any particular policies or results of policies.[6] This modification thus allows representatives more room for leadership and innovation than does pure delegation theory, but they are still assumed to be delegates because they follow the ends set by constituents. Political scientists who espouse this theory typically assume that the ends and means of policy can be distinguished, and that representatives are free to choose the means but not the ends of policy.[7] Delegates choose the means that will best satisfy the preferences that citizens will come to have at some time in the future.

But even this small modification regarding the preferences of citizens subverts the democratic basis of delegate theory. The distinction between ends and means cannot limit the discretion of representatives in the way that delegate theorists wish. The means that representatives choose now shape the ends that citizens can choose in the future. Once the welfare programs of the New Deal were in place, citizens could no longer so easily choose policies based on laissez-faire principles. By the time these welfare programs were ready to be evaluated retrospectively, citizens could not readily dismantle them, and most did not want to.[8] Whether citizens developed this satisfaction with the programs on their own or as a result of the persuasion of their representatives, they were surely influenced by their experience of the programs. If choosing the means of policy can in this way help create the desire for new ends of policy, then representatives create the preferences of citizens as much as they anticipate them. Yet delegates are not accountable for this creation of preferences. They do not have to refer to the principles guiding the change of preferences, because their role presumes that they are merely giving effect to preferences that citizens already have.

Trustee theory does require representatives to invoke principles to justify their actions. Trustees appeal to principles of justice, which are independent of the preferences citizens have at any time, even their hypothetical preferences. The difficulty is that representatives and citizens reasonably disagree about what those principles should be. We are no longer as confident as Burke was that there are objective principles on which citizens and representatives should agree.[9] Even within the liberal tradition, the principles that philosophers urge upon representatives conflict in fundamental ways. Utilitarians tell representatives to maximize the social welfare, or at least the welfare of their constituents.[10] Their representatives would not necessarily act in accordance with the expressed preferences of citizens, but they would not give any independent weight to justice. Theorists of justice instruct representatives to vote on the basis of their "opinion as to which laws and policies best conform to principles of justice."[11] According to which principles, then, should trustees act?

It will not do to say that each representative should act on the basis of the principles he or she believes to be right, and then let citizens choose at the next election. This would turn trustees into delegates – delegates of principle, to be sure, but no less vulnerable to the objection already raised to delegate theory. It is true that trustees (and their theorists) assume that citizens will eventually come to accept the principles on which the trustees act, or at least the policies based on those principles. Even that arch trustee Burke believed that in time his constituents would agree with him: "I aim to look, indeed, to your opinions; but such opinions as you and I must have five years hence."[12]

But the validity of the principles does not depend on the concurrence of citizens. The justification of a principle is not that citizens will accept it, but that it is the right principle to accept, now as well as in the future. The point of trustee theory is not simply that representatives should act independently of citizens, but that they should act rightly. Any particular trustee theory offers substantive principles that representatives are supposed to follow. To accept a trustee theory is to accept one set of substantive principles, and to reject competing sets of principles. By the terms of their trust, representatives are bound to act on the basis of certain principles, and exclusively those principles, when they conflict with principles that other theories uphold.

Building consideration of substantive principles into the role of the representative, though necessary in any trustee theory, undermines the democratic legitimacy of trustees. Trustee theory in effect places the choice of fundamental principles outside the political process. Representatives are to obtain their principles from some other source – typically, a philosophical theory. Even if we could show that one set of principles is philosophically superior to others, we would not be warranted in concluding that representatives should act exclusively on the basis of those principles. The principles must actually be accepted at some time by citizens. If the acceptance is to involve a genuine choice, citizens or at least their representatives must have the option of choosing other principles. The other principles cannot be excluded either from the deliberation in the legislature or from the menu of principles on the basis of which responsible representatives can act. Without such a process of choice, there is no ground for saying that they are the principles that should bind all citizens in a particular society. To settle such questions in advance in defining the duties of the trustee is to make political choices by philosophical fiat.

This is so even if trustee theory does not require representatives to adopt a complete set of principles but only places certain principled constraints on their conduct. A theory might, for example, hold only that representatives should not violate any rights of citizens.[13] The problem is that the definition of what is to count as a right in the society is itself a question that, to some extent, should be determined in the political process, including the deliberations and votes in the legislature. A principle that tells legislators not to violate certain existing rights is not much help when they are considering whether to support legislation that would establish new rights. The growth of the welfare state has often been explained and defended as a progressive recognition that the government should provide certain benefits (positive rights) in order to prevent harm being done to citizens (negative rights). But its opponents claim that the welfare state violates the negative rights of some citizens (property owners, for example). We expect legislators, among others, to resolve such disputes. In doing so they do not merely observe, but sometimes change, the prevailing boundaries between positive and negative rights.

These objections to trustee theory are quite general in their implications. They apply to any theory that attempts to limit the role of a representative to acting in accordance with the dictates of any single substantive theory of fundamental values, such as a theory of liberty, equality, or the common good. The choices among these values are among the most important decisions that legislatures make, and the choices should not be predetermined by the role of the representative. There must be some moral constraints on that role, but they must not prevent representatives (and ultimately citizens) from choosing from a range of substantive theories.

Neither delegate theory nor trustee theory succeeds in resolving the problem that welfare policy poses for the role of the representative. Delegate theory takes account of the need to hold representatives responsible for complex policies that reach into the future, but at the price of severing the connection with the preferences of citizens in the present. Trustee theory tries to escape the conflict between present and future preferences by relying instead on principles, but at the cost of giving citizens less choice about the principles.

THE SIGNIFICANCE OF PROCESS

The root of the problem is that conventional theories of representation misconceive the nature of political time. In all of them, whether pure or modified, time is divided into discrete units – isolated moments of responsibility when representatives stand accountable for their actions. Representatives give reasons at particular times, and the reasons they give connect their actions to the attitudes of their constituents at particular times. Delegate theory provides no way to reconcile the conflicts that inevitably occur at different times. Trustee theory either assumes that citizens will accept representatives' choice of principles at some future time or removes the choice of principles from political time completely.

Missing is a recognition of the continuous nature of representation. Representation takes time. What representatives do during that time is an important part of what citizens should hold them responsible for. To avoid the conflict in the role of the representative, we must understand representation not as a relationship between constituents and representatives at particular political moments, but as a *process* in which the relationship between citizens and representatives continues over time.[14]

Representation can involve changes not only in the preferences of constituents (as trustee theorists appreciate), but also in the principles acted upon by representatives. The process is also affected by interactions among representatives in the legislature, which in turn affect the roles that representatives adopt in relation to their constituents. The concept of process thus allows for change not only in preferences and principles but also in the identities of constituents and their representatives. The concept therefore provides a more satisfactory way of confronting the temporal problems that welfare policy and similar issues pose for representation.

The process that most continuously affects representation is the legislative process (understood broadly to include not only lawmaking but the wide range of political activities in which legislators typically engage). Accordingly, the requirements of responsibility – the constraints we impose on the reasons representatives give to justify their choices – should refer to the legislative process. The most promising sources of such requirements are the criteria that philosophers have suggested to define moral discourse. Because a principal purpose of democratic responsibility is to hold officials accountable for choosing fundamental values for society, the reasons that officials give to justify these choices should be judged according to standards of moral deliberation. The legislative process should facilitate discussion of such values, and the explanations of legislators should qualify as contributions to that discussion. The problem is to find criteria that do not build into the process of deliberation a bias in favor of the fundamental values of an exclusive philosophical theory.

Three constraints on what should count as a reason in moral discourse can, with some modification, serve as the criteria for what should count as a reason in political discourse designed to promote democratic responsibility. The criteria are drawn from what some moral philosophers call the conditions of the "moral point of view" or the "formal constraints of the concept of right."[15] They require that a reason be general, public, and autonomous.[16] Together, the criteria are meant to define a discourse that does not exclude claims that express any genuine moral perspective (at least any held in modern liberal democracies), but does exclude claims that express only self-interests or group interests.

It may not be possible, even theoretically, to specify necessary and sufficient criteria for a moral reason, but it ought to be possible, even with a less systematic set of criteria, to establish the contrast we need to make between kinds of reasons that representatives should give in political practice. The difference should be clear between reasons based solely on political power and reasons based on moral principle, even if the philosophical nuances of the distinction remain controversial, and even if the actual motives of the persons who give the reasons remain questionable.

The contrast will become clearer as we trace the implications of the criteria for the legislative process. As usually stated in moral philosophy, the criteria are excessively formal. They refer to the form of reasons or principles, not to the conditions in which persons present them. Yet in the context of political judgment, each of the criteria presupposes the existence of certain institutional structures. The process itself is supposed to structure political discussion to make possible moral deliberation about the fundamental values that citizens and their representatives share or come to share while participating in the process.

THE PARTICULARS OF GENERALITY

A general reason is one that is universalizable: if it applies to one case, it applies to all cases that are similar in relevant respects.[17] The philosophical foundation of this idea owes most to Kant, whose various versions of the categorical imperative determine what is to count as an acceptable moral principle. If a principle cannot "stand the test of the form of a general law of nature," Kant writes, "then it is morally inadmissible."[18] Kant thought that this test would rule out the basic principles of many other moral theories, including utilitarianism, but most modern philosophers reinterpret it as a necessary condition that any moral principle, including the principle of utility, can satisfy.[19] In this form, the test provides an approximate criterion for generality in a theory of responsible representation.

Although the requirement of generality by itself does not exclude very much from legislative deliberation, it does exclude enough to create a problem for representation. By its nature, representation presupposes that representatives have some special responsibility to a particular group of citizens – their constituents.[20] This responsibility need not be as specific as delegate theory implies, but it must be specific enough to distinguish those whom a legislator represents from those whom the legislator does not. Even Burke recognized that he owed more to the electors of Bristol than to the electors of Warwick or Stafford.[21] Some special relationship between legislators and constituents must be assumed in any theory of representation in which a legislator stands for election by district, and by any theory that permits a legislator to speak for or answer to a particular group of citizens rather than to all citizens. Even in a legislature that seeks to ensure the general welfare through moral deliberation, the common good does not result from a sudden, simultaneous insight of all the legislators. It emerges only as each legislator expresses the views of particular groups within society (usually those to whom the legislator is electorally accountable), and it must be defended to particular groups by the legislators who represent them.

If a representative may legitimately act for particular citizens, how can we insist that the representative give reasons that are general? The natural answer is that reasons that refer to the welfare of constituents *are* general in the sense that we can universalize the principle that each representative has a special responsibility for the welfare of his or her constituents. No representative claims any special privilege not granted to other representatives. But the appeal of this answer lies not so much in the formal test it satisfies as in the substantive assumption it makes: that a process in which representatives primarily act for parts of the whole functions to the benefit of the whole. The particular is thus justified by its consequences for the general.

What can justify this assumption? Neither of the familiar justifications seems plausible, though legislators seem to act (and theorists seem to write) as if one or the other were true. The first is the claim that there is an objective common good, on the definition of which the judgments of representatives and citizens will, in due time, converge. This we have already rejected in criticizing trustee theory. The second justification is that the common good is the sum of particular interests. Even if this were an adequate conception of the common good, it would not provide the link we need to move from the particular to the general. The most single-minded advocate of this conception himself recognizes this problem. According to Bentham, the only way to determine what is in the public interest is for each representative to express the views of his constituents. But since these views may be mistaken, representatives must also be able to express their own view of the public interest. Bentham resolves these contradictory demands on the representative by means of one of his characteristically mechanical devices: The representative is to speak for what he views as the public interest but to vote in accordance with the views of his constituents.[22]

Despite its obvious inadequacy, Bentham's proposal contains an important insight – one that does not depend on his assumption that the public interest is simply the sum of particular interests. Speaking for the public interest is not just a way of fulfilling the duty to the public; it can also "have the effect of working a change in . . . [the] opinion" of constituents, and "on a later occasion causing them to concur with" their representative.[23] The public interest does not emerge either from the discovery of an objective good or from the aggregation of subjective preferences; it must be created in the legislative process. We can think of this creation as occurring in an iterated, four-step process: representatives express particular views, modify their own views in light of what other representatives say, act on the modified views, and then seek to justify them to constituents. The process begins again with the new views of the constituents if they have been persuaded, or their original views if they have not.

In this kind of legislative process, we could count as a reason a particular claim of an individual representative, provided that it can be justified as consistent with a legislative process that seeks a common good. There are, of course, many notions of the common good, and many ways the process can fail to pursue it. With respect to the criterion of generality, however, the most fundamental problem concerns the nature of the legislation. The more general the legislation, the more legislators may be encouraged to give general reasons to justify their views of it.

The requirement resembles Rousseau's stipulation that the general will should consider "all subjects collectively and all actions in the abstract; it does not consider any individual man or any specific action."[24] But it differs from Rousseau's by permitting legislation to use concrete terms to describe particular categories when they can be shown to be necessary to formulate a policy that promotes the general goals. The point is not that the language of the legislation or even its topics should be perfectly general, but rather that legislators can justify the purpose of the policy, as reflected in the legislation, from a general perspective. The legislation might be replete with particular categories, as were most of the eleven titles of the original Social Security Act (the categories included old-age and survivors, unemployed, dependent children, blind). But the legislation can still be said to satisfy the criterion of generality because it, or its legislative history, demonstrates a substantial relation of these categories to the general purposes of the legislation.

Even this modest requirement is more controversial than might at first appear, however. Some political scientists have argued that if we take any such requirement seriously, we should reject many of the policies of the modern welfare state. Consider the claim that whereas the "old welfare" (instituted in the New Deal) meets the requirement, the "new welfare" (established by the New Frontier and Great Society Programs) does not.[25] For Theodore Lowi, the most vigorous proponent of this claim, the Social Security Act of 1935 and the Economic Opportunity Act of 1964, respectively, exemplify these two kinds of welfare policy. "In contrast to the Social Security statute," he writes, the Economic Opportunity statute avoids "the identification and definition of categories and . . . cumulation of these into some kind of interrelated package. The most important sources of standards in old welfare – definitions, lists of examples, exceptions, exclusions, prerequisites – are almost absent here."[26] Instead of the explicit attention that the old welfare gives to the relation between particular categories and general rules, the new welfare employs open-ended categories; they are almost always introduced with "not limited to" or "such as."[27]

These differences in the language of the statutes reflect different conceptions of the role of the legislature. In the old welfare, Congress decided the main elements of the policies in advance. Although the legislature allowed administrators and the states considerable discretion, it did not leave open many important political questions, such as the level and kinds of aid or the qualifications necessary for receiving it. In the new welfare, Congress deliberately left key elements of the policy to be decided by local authorities, including some of the recipients themselves in the Community Action Programs. The new welfare assumed that the poor should have a say about the causes and cures of their poverty; it mandated "maximum feasible participation" of the poor in the planning and conduct of the programs designed to reduce poverty.

The War on Poverty, declared by the 1964 act, had neither defeated poverty nor improved participation by the time it officially ended three years later.[28] Lowi and other critics of that war blame its failures partly on the delegation of power – which they see as equivalent to the refusal of Congress to state general standards for the policies. In their view, Congress abdicated its responsibility to identify the causes of poverty and to establish general programs to attack those causes directly. Legislators refused "to make moral choices and set clear legislative standards."[29] By delegating the authority to make policy, Congress encouraged battles over control of the local programs instead of attacks on poverty itself.

It is by no means clear that the delegation of power and the provisions for more popular participation contributed to the failure of the poverty programs. The kind and extent of participation varied greatly from city to city, and often, when a community action agency threatened to become effective in mobilizing the poor, the established local authorities reorganized the agency or cut off its funds.[30] The relatively modest sums of money appropriated in the three years of the program could hardly have had a major effect on either participation or poverty. But even if the critics are correct that the delegation of power as practiced under these programs contributed to the failure of the War on Poverty, they are not necessarily correct that delegation as practiced in any form cannot serve to promote welfare.

Lowi and his fellow critics seem to assume that delegation and generality are incompatible.[31] But they are not. If the legislature can justify delegation as the best means to promote the general purposes of welfare, then delegation not only satisfies the criterion of generality but may do so to a greater extent than does nondelegation. The justification itself can be perfectly general even if the reasons express the needs of the particular groups in society who are granted more political power.

Both the critics and the defenders of the new welfare, however, neglect the temporal dimension of representation. Any justification of programs of this kind must be part of a continuing process of deliberation. The process should not be conceived of as a one-time decision, which initiates or terminates the delegated authority. Arguably, the problem of the War on Poverty was not that Congress delegated authority to local groups, but that it did not regularly review and revise the terms of the delegation in light of the responses of the participants and the deliberations of representatives. The justifications that generality requires cannot be accepted or rejected once and for all. They call for continual consideration of the relation between the general purposes of legislation and the exercise of power by particular representatives – whether that power is delegated or not.

From this perspective, the legislative process that sustained the old welfare does not necessarily look better than the one that supported the new welfare. For more than thirty years, the policies of the old welfare (and many of its administrators) remained unchanged and mostly unreviewed.[32] The aid to dependent children title of the 1935 act (now the AFDC Program) granted states wide discretion to set the levels of support, and some states have set the levels so low that they may undermine the general purposes of welfare policy.[33] There may be good reasons to allow some differences among states, but democratic responsibility, even according to a loose interpretation of the criterion of generality, requires legislators to present and discuss the reasons in a national forum. Neither the old nor the new welfare should escape the requirement of continuing deliberation about the general purposes of legislation, and the fundamental values that support those purposes.

THE AUTONOMOUS LEGISLATOR

When representatives legislate, they should consider the legislation on its merits. This principle seems simple enough, and most legislators (at least in public) claim to act on it. The reasons they give to justify their actions generally refer to the welfare or the rights of citizens, not to the pressures of lobbyists or the influence of campaign contributors. The principle plainly excludes bribery and extortion, in which legislators act on the basis of reasons related more to the money they receive than to the purposes of the legislation they support. But extended beyond such clear cases, the principle creates some puzzles.

Like most people, members of Congress often rationalize their conduct; the reasons they give may not be their real reasons. Their rationalizations are rarely the crude kind popularly ascribed to politicians. Members do not typically keep their true reasons to themselves and give another set of reasons to the public. Nor are they inclined to fool themselves by accepting reasons that are not their real reasons for taking a position. Based on careful interviews with many members, John Kingdon concluded that most

like to believe that they are going through some sort of rational consideration which is connected to the issue of public policy they are deciding. They do not enjoy seeing themselves as being manipulated or pushed and pulled by forces beyond their control.... [The member] must seize on some sort of argument that will justify his vote to himself and to others. For some congressmen, this is reinforcement; for others, persuasion.[34]

Even when this search for reasons takes place and affects the votes of representatives, it can hardly allay all our suspicions about the nature of the reasons that representatives give. One of Kingdon's examples shows why. Members from tobacco-growing districts, he suggests, could not have brought themselves to vote against the cigarette advertising bill if they believed that smoking caused cancer. They

arranged lengthy hearings to try to refute the evidence presented
in the Surgeon General's Report. They finally gathered enough
seemingly respectable testimony to convince themselves that a causal
link between smoking and cancer had not been established, and
thus enough to allow themselves in good conscience to vote against
the bill.[35]

These members may have been sincere, though under the circumstances citizens might have had reasonable doubts. But it is not the
sincerity of representatives or even their conscious motives that should
be at issue. Both are difficult enough to appraise in personal interactions. In the distant and mediated relations of political life, they
can hardly be the basis for reliable judgments of responsibility. If we
are trying to establish whether reasons are relevant to the merits of
legislation, we should focus on the conditions under which representatives give reasons, rather than on the connection between the
reasons that representatives give and their motives in particular cases.
We should judge differently the legislative conduct of those Congress
members who depend on tobacco interests for most of their campaign contributions and those who do not. The more independent
members may still vote for tobacco subsidies – perhaps to protect the
jobs of workers in their district. But their voting decision could be understood as a choice between the values of health and employment,
because they might be less influenced by pressures unrelated to these
values.

More generally, a theory of responsibility should focus on the conditions under which representatives give reasons because this approach
constitutes the most reliable basis on which citizens can continually
assess the actions of their representatives. Representatives must enjoy
discretion, not only in their choice of policies but also in their choice
of roles, and citizens may not be able to judge the results of these
choices for many years, if ever. What citizens are in a better position
to assess are the circumstances in which the representatives make the
choices. Citizens can reasonably assume that some circumstances will
prevent genuine deliberation and will produce undesirable legislation. Among the circumstances that bear directly on the reasons that
responsible representatives should give are those in which there is improper influence. The criterion of autonomy is intended to preclude
such influence.

Representation does not readily accommodate autonomy, however.
The tension between the two would be impossibly acute if we were

to adopt any of the leading philosophical standards of autonomy. If autonomy were thought to rule out, as Kant argued it should, any kind of desire as a basis for action, it would have little relevance to political life.[36] Even Rawls's concept ("acting from principles that we would consent to as free and equal rational beings") seems an inappropriate standard for representatives. It would "force [representatives] to consider the choice of principles unencumbered by the singularities of the circumstances in which [they] find themselves."[37] Some special obligation to a constituency is one singularity of circumstance that representatives cannot fail to consider; they must, after all, stand for reelection. Nearly as inescapable in modern politics is the obligation to a political party.[38]

The criterion of autonomy therefore cannot demand, even as an ideal, a wholly unencumbered legislator, one who acts utterly unswayed by political pressures and partisan loyalties. It can, however, place some constraints on the kinds of reasons that representatives give to justify their conduct. Such a criterion would require that a representative's reasons for acting be relevant to either the merits of the legislation or the means necessary for adopting the legislation, where the means are consistent with a legislative process in which representatives generally consider legislation on its merits.

According to this criterion, legislators may still trade votes on measures they think less important in order to win passage of measures that are more important, but not if such logrolling prevents consideration of the most important measures on their merits. Reelection and party loyalty can also count as reasons when they do not impair the process of deliberation. In the case of reelection, what the criterion of autonomy demands should be clear in principle. It urges us to resist the tendency of the electoral connection to become a pecuniary connection. The most pressing problem is the influence of private money, and one of the most promising solutions is the public financing of campaigns. Although laden with practical difficulties, this reform presents fewer theoretical problems for the criterion of autonomy than does the role of political parties.

THE PLACE OF PARTY

Can loyalty to party be a reason that responsible representatives give to justify their actions? Such a reason seems on its face to abandon autonomy. Rather than acknowledging responsibility, this reason seems to shift responsibility to others. The party, not the representative, is to blame. The appeal to party, furthermore, seems even less general than a reference to constituency. A political party may be just another particular group within society. Constituents at least have some claim on a representative because they elected him or her (often with little regard to the program of the national party).[39] William Graham Sumner expressed the doubts of several generations of American observers of the party system: "I cannot trust a party. I can trust a man. I cannot hold a party responsible. I can hold a man responsible. I cannot get an expression of opinion which is single and simple from a party; I can get that only from a man."[40]

Behind these doubts about party lies a worthy conception of the legislative process. The connection between the doubts and that conception can be seen most clearly in the work of a more systematic theorist who opposed party government. Writing even before party discipline had become firmly established in Britain, John Stuart Mill objected to party government because it constrains deliberation in the legislature. It does so in two ways. First, it artificially reduces the number of voices in the legislature. It is wrong that "all the opinions, feelings and interests of all members of the community should be merged in the single consideration of which party shall predominate."[41] Second, party government arbitrarily restricts the possibility of change. It keeps those voices that do gain a hearing in the legislature from changing their tune. With highly disciplined parties, no amount of discussion could normally convince legislators to alter their views, and no independent representative (or the legislative leader) can have much influence.[42]

A conception of the legislative process that emphasizes diversity and change certainly supports autonomy. But accepting this conception does not entail rejecting party government. We should be able to find a place for party while preserving the virtues of diversity and change in the legislature. It is certainly worth trying because, contrary to what their critics claim, parties can promote responsibility.

Party loyalty may qualify, under the proper conditions, as a reason that a responsible representative can give. Representatives act autonomously if they acknowledge personal responsibility for choosing a party, and explain their actions in relation to what the party has accomplished. Autonomy is the opposite of the individualistic behavior that many members of Congress now display. When members "run *for* Congress by running *against* Congress," they do not give reasons that connect their actions to the legislative process of which they are a part.[43]

Party loyalty, furthermore, may count as a general reason if the policies of the party express a more general perspective than that of individual legislators. A party can serve as an instrument to help a representative take into account the views of other similarly situated representatives – a step toward fulfilling the more difficult duty of taking into account the views of all representatives, however differently situated they may be.

Furthermore, the party provides a way of locating responsibility for the Madisonian "train of measures." A party manifests greater temporal continuity than does any individual representative or even the legislature itself, whose programmatic identity changes as its membership changes. In this sense, the appeal to party generalizes a reason not only with respect to constituencies and policies at any particular time but also with respect to both over time.

To satisfy the requirements of responsibility, therefore, a party system should promote two different practices in the legislature. It should encourage representatives to relate their own actions to those of their party and to engage in legislative deliberation. These two practices usually conflict; thus any party system that seeks to maximize one is likely to sacrifice the other.

The proposal for a "more responsible two-party system" illustrates the first practice.[44] It encourages representatives to take responsibility for the collective actions of the party, but it would make deliberation more difficult. Because the party is committed to programmatic coherence and electoral victory, sustained discussion and persistent dissent are not likely to be welcomed. In the legislature, there would be little scope for members to change their minds, and little room for independent legislators to play a prominent role.[45]

A party system such as that imagined by Ostrogorski illustrates the second practice. He believed that the "party as a wholesale contractor for the numerous and varied problems, present and to come, should give place to special organizations, limited to particular objects and forming and reforming spontaneously, so to speak, according to the changing problems of life and the play of opinion brought about thereby."[46] In a system of this kind, citizens would find it difficult to call representatives to account for comprehensive programs such as welfare policy. There is no reason to suppose that the shifting coalitions within parties would produce the set of interrelated policies that citizens should reasonably expect from any group that claims to govern. If a party happened to succeed in formulating a comprehensive program, its coalitions probably could not hold together long enough for the necessary legislation to be passed in both houses, especially if legislative discussion extended over several sessions. The "train of measures" might never leave the station. The parties themselves may not even form in the first place without some strong leadership in the legislature, and they would not be likely to persist without some incentives for members who dissent from parts of the party's program.

Neither of these concepts of a party system satisfies the requirements of responsibility. A truly responsible party system would combine aspects of both. Following the first concept, a responsible party would stand for a general program, a comprehensive set of measures. In accordance with the second, the party would not be an organization dedicated to winning power regardless of the issues its legislative members favored. Representatives would stand for election on the party's record, but through discussion in legislative caucuses they could substantially modify the party's program. Legislative leaders would have considerable power to reward party loyalists, but legislators could change parties with less cost than at present. Party voting would be more regular than it has been in recent Congresses, but party membership would be more fluid. The party leadership would have greater authority over what are called "control" committees (such as Appropriations and Ways and Means), but would grant considerable freedom to other committees and subcommittees so that individual members could more readily challenge the dominant opinion in the party.

A complete model of a party system of this kind calls for an empirical analysis better conducted by political scientists than by political theorists. But the approach suggested here – combining in one party system aspects of the two conflicting practices – provides a framework for the empirical analysis, as well as for formulation of an ideal party system that favors legislative responsibility. Such a system would support a legislative process in which representatives give general and autonomous reasons for the comprehensive and long-term measures that constitute welfare programs and many similar policies. This system would be more likely to sustain the kind of political parties to which representatives could responsibly pledge their loyalty.

THE NECESSITY FOR PUBLICITY

It was Kant who first emphasized the deep connection between morality and publicity. He presented the criterion of publicity as a fundamental test of morality, equivalent to one version of the categorical imperative. "All actions which relate to the right of other men are contrary to right and law, the maxim of which does not permit publicity."[47] That a reason can be made public is not sufficient to make the reason moral, but it is necessary. If a reason must be kept secret, it is because the reason cannot be generally and freely accepted. In this sense, publicity is a test of the other requirements of responsibility – generality and autonomy. Representatives cannot publicly justify a lie by invoking the principle that they will tell the truth except when they believe it will jeopardize their reelection. Making that justification public would defeat its purpose. That the reason must be kept secret shows that it is not general enough (it favors the representative), and that it would not be chosen freely by others (the representative presumes their ignorance).

Because Kant considered the criterion of publicity to be an "experiment of pure reason," abstracted from all actual conditions, he did not insist that justifications in fact be made public.[48] This formality prevents his criterion, in its original form, from serving as a requirement of political responsibility. Especially in politics, the actual process of publicizing reasons differs significantly from the hypothetical process. Facing an audience, politicians are more likely to take into account arguments they have not previously considered; they also are more likely to change their minds if they cannot answer those arguments. Moreover, before an audience, they have the opportunity to change the minds of other people. As Mill stressed, publicity can "compel deliberation and force everyone to determine, before he acts, what he shall say if called to account for his actions."[49]

Unlike the other two criteria of responsibility, the requirement of publicity does not directly conflict with representation. The practice of representation does not license secrecy as it legitimizes particularity and dependency. On the contrary, representation seems to require that citizens know as much as possible about the conduct of their representatives. This is all the more true if we accept the earlier argument that representatives must have considerable discretion in deciding how to interpret their role. The more discretion they have, the more citizens must know about their decisions.

The problems that publicity creates come instead from conflicts with generality and autonomy. The more public the activities of legislators, the more pressure the legislators may face to support particular interests, and the more dependence they may develop on outside groups. We do not have to assume that legislators are political cowards who give in to pressures whenever they have to make decisions in the open. The problems of publicity persist even if legislators act conscientiously; indeed, they result partly from the legislators' effort to observe the other two criteria of responsibility. When legislators must always act in the glare of publicity, they are forced to justify their conduct continually. They enjoy no escape from the demand for explanation. Consequently, in giving justifications, legislators focus more on immediate issues and on more momentary audiences. Legislators are less likely to consider the "train of measures" that Madison saw as essential to responsible government, and they are more likely to respond to the citizens who have the most direct access to their attention. Both tendencies run counter to the criterion of generality (which considers the legislative process as a whole continuing over time), and to the criterion of autonomy (which prescribes deliberation on the merits of the issues).

That publicity sometimes conflicts with these criteria, however, does not justify rejecting it as a requirement of responsibility. The existence of conflict itself provides a reason not only for preserving publicity but also for granting it status equal to the other criteria. The conflicts among the criteria reflect disagreements about the relative importance of the fundamental values presupposed by both processes and policies. Is it more important to let citizens know what is happening in the conference committee, or to leave the members free to deliberate without citizens looking over their shoulders?

Even if legislators rightly choose secrecy over publicity in certain circumstances, they should make that choice openly. The decision must be justified to citizens, and that can only be done in public. To be sure, it can only be done by giving reasons that are also general and autonomous. But to judge whether the reasons are general and autonomous, citizens must know what they are. No less than the other criteria, publicity is a necessary condition for deciding how much weight we should assign to each criterion – including publicity itself – and for deciding whether in certain circumstances we should disregard any criterion, also including publicity.

It may hardly seem necessary to urge the importance of publicity in the U.S. Congress, generally regarded as the most open legislature in the world. Indeed, the problem of publicity, in the judgment of some observers, is that there is too much of it. In the early 1970s, as part of a general effort of self-reform, the House opened all committee meetings to the public (including television audiences), and decided that names and votes should be recorded in virtually all voting. The House Select Committee on Committees later criticized these "sunshine" provisions, complaining that they inhibit candid discussion of controversial issues, discourage changes of opinion, hamper efforts to reach compromises, and subject members to greater pressures from lobbyists.[50]

Some of these effects could subvert responsibility, and could indeed provide justifications for limiting publicity. But such justifications, tailored to fit each case or type of case, can be presented and debated in open session. This is an approach that neither the Select Committee nor most other critics of publicity seriously consider. In justifying secrecy, moreover, its advocates would have to distinguish between the need to keep the proceedings closed and the need to keep the records of the proceedings confidential. The argument for closed sessions is more compelling than the argument for confidential records. But the former argument is often mistakenly assumed to establish the conclusion of the latter argument, thereby extending indefinitely into the future the secrecy that may be warranted only in the present. Citizens may reasonably refuse to accept a justification for closed sessions unless they can inspect records of the sessions at some future time. Even if secrecy is warranted now, the further question should always be asked: When may citizens learn what happened? If the temporal nature of responsibility implies that citizens should in some cases wait to judge what their representatives have done, it also requires that representatives should not fail to provide citizens with the information they need when the time comes to judge.

Secrecy does not always take the form of closed meetings or concealed records, however. Even in the legislative sessions of so open an institution as the Congress, public policy can be made without the public knowing much about it. Sometimes the ignorance is the fault of citizens themselves, who do not demand to know. Their representatives are only accessories, guilty of failing to enlighten their constituents. But at other times legislators, out of perfectly benign motives, deliberately prevent an issue from receiving wide public discussion, and pass laws without the benefit of the reactions that such discussion might bring. This strategy is especially tempting when the welfare of citizens is at stake, and the motives of representatives are genuinely benevolent.

A case in point is the policy on public financing of treatment for kidney disease. According to one observer, the debate on this policy in the early 1970s was conducted sotto voce. It was "carried out mainly within the inner councils of the medical-scientific community and the political-governmental system.... Both opponents and proponents were reluctant to have this issue fully considered in public debate, fearing that it was too divisive for the polity to handle."[51] Some political scientists would endorse this reluctance, arguing that policies that put a price on human life, such as those that allocate scarce medical resources, should not be the subject of open discussion. One can imagine the "perfectly 'rational' congressman" trying to justify the legislature's decision to limit expenditures for medical care: "Mrs. Jones, I share your grief about the plight of your husband, but we simply cannot afford to spend $30,000 per year to keep him alive when people are dying elsewhere who could be saved for much less." Such candor threatens the "life-preserving norm that decent societies should respect."[52] Similarly, one scholar would encourage policymakers to pretend that they are not putting a price on human life even though they are in fact doing so: "the polite fiction might just be enough to protect people's self-respect."[53]

These arguments posit a gap between representatives and citizens that is neither plausible nor desirable. Why should we assume that representatives are any more capable than their constituents of rationally considering questions about the value of life? In allocating funds for the treatment of kidney disease, legislators did not in fact act like rational economists. Congress committed far too many financial resources to one disease and one group of victims, thus diverting funds from programs that could help a larger number of people who suffered from other diseases.

But even if legislators could in secret strike the right balance between efficient allocation of resources and respect for the "life-preserving norm," they would have to make sure that citizens did not understand their real reasons for the balance they struck. Perhaps Mrs. Jones does not at this moment want to hear a cost-benefit analysis of her dying husband's treatment, but neither would she want to hear lies from her representative.

The rational representative may exhibit a lack of sensitivity, but the benevolent representative exhibits a fault much more dangerous in the character of a public official in a democracy – a lack of candor. If citizens cannot know the reasons for the actions of representatives, they cannot judge the way in which representatives act. Judging the way that representatives act may be the only way that citizens can hold representatives accountable for many policies, especially policies intended to promote the welfare of citizens.

No less troublesome is the argument that representatives should quietly suppress consideration of some controversial questions. Some political scientists look back nostalgically to the late nineteenth century, when congressional leaders "put the lid on" discussion of many issues of intense concern to their constituents, such as the controversial issue of bilingual education. Similarly, they praise the House Rules Committee for keeping the question of aid to parochial schools off the congressional agenda in 1961, and wish legislative leaders now would do the same with the question of abortion funding.[54]

There may be good reasons for legislatures to avoid such issues, but they are not reasons of responsibility. More precisely, responsibility requires that legislators give reasons for refusing to consider these issues. Nothing in the legislative process is more important than the agenda; nothing, therefore, is more important in the explanations that representatives give than the reasons for setting that agenda. If leaders can keep the agenda clear of questions that should not be discussed, they can also keep it clear of questions that should be discussed. The leaders of the Democratic Party have abused the power to control the agenda; for more than a century, they kept Congress from seriously confronting the question of racism.[55] Legislators stand guilty of similar abuses insofar as they refuse to consider, or to explain why they refuse to consider, pressing questions of welfare policy, however divisive such questions may be.

Publicity, like generality and autonomy, focuses our attention on the conditions under which representatives make decisions for citizens. All the requirements of responsibility emphasize the temporal dimension of those conditions. Representation takes place in a legislative process that takes time, and citizens need to judge what representatives do during that time.

This need is all the more critical because none of the standard theories of the role of the representative can serve as a foundation for the responsibility of representatives. They are not adequate because none encourages citizens to judge the part that representatives play in the legislative process as a whole. A theory that emphasizes the legislative process does not necessarily place a higher value on the process than on its results. Nor does it make the rightness of a process a sufficient test of the rightness of policy. We judge representatives by the process they maintain because that is the best way to hold them accountable for fundamental choices of value about which we disagree. At least, it is the best way if the choices involve consideration of a "train of measures" that, like welfare policy, join many different issues and stretch many years into the future.

Responsibility requires that representatives justify their conduct to citizens now but also that their justifications speak to citizens in the future. Welfare policy poses the dilemma in an acute form since its justifications refer directly to the preferences of citizens now but its effects extend into the distant future. Democratic representatives are supposed to defer to the preferences of citizens at some point in time, but at any moment in political time they may have good reason to disregard those preferences. This conflict has no final resolution. But we stand a better chance of coping with its consequences if we adopt a theory of responsible representation that emphasizes, as most such theories do not, the significance of the legislative process.

Notes

1. On the concept of political responsibility, see John Plamenatz, *Democracy and Illusion* (London: Longman, 1973), 80–1, 87, 98, 110, 114, 177–8, 199; and J. Roland Pennock, *Democratic Political Theory* (Princeton, NJ: Princeton University Press, 1979), 260–308. On the political significance of giving reasons, see John W. Kingdon, *Congressmen's Voting Decisions*, 2d ed. (New York: Harper and Row, 1981), 47–54; and Richard F. Fenno, *Home Style: House Members in Their Districts* (Boston: Little, Brown, 1978), 136–70.

2. *The Federalist Papers*, ed. C. Rossiter (New York: New American Library, 1961), no. 63, 383–4; no. 52, 327–8; and no. 57, 353. Madison is credited with introducing the term "responsibility" into political theory – see Douglass Adair, *Fame and the Founding Fathers* (New York: Norton, 1974), 257n; his analysis of the concept, though brief, recognizes a form of the tension (he calls it a paradox) that I discuss here. In a discussion of the optimal lengths of terms for representatives, Madison suggests that shorter terms strengthen responsibility (by binding representatives more closely to their constituents), but that longer terms also strengthen responsibility (by holding representatives accountable for the "train of measures").

3. See National Conference on Social Welfare, *Report of the Committee on the Economic Security of 1935* (Washington, DC: National Conference on Social Welfare, 1985).

4. We would miss this implication if, following Hanna Pitkin, we were to treat the concepts of delegate and trustee as polar opposites. See *The Concept of Representation* (Berkeley: University of California Press, 1967), 166.

5. Morris Fiorina, *Retrospective Voting in American National Elections* (New Haven, Conn.: Yale University Press, 1981), 193–211; V. O. Key, *The Responsible Electorate* (New York: Vintage Books, 1966); and Anthony Downs, *An Economic Theory of Democracy* (New York: Harper & Row, 1957).

6. Fiorina, *Retrospective Voting*, 201.

7. See, for example, ibid., 197–8.

8. See Stanley Kelley, Jr., Chapter 8 in *Democracy and the Welfare State*, ed. A. Gutmann (Princeton, N.J.: Princeton University Press, 1988), 185–206.

9. On Burke's assumption about objective interests, see Pitkin, *The Concept of Representation*, 180, 189.

10. J. J. C. Smart and Bernard Williams, *Utilitarianism For and Against* (Cambridge: Cambridge University Press, 1973), esp. 67–74, 135–50; and Amartya Sen and Bernard Williams, *Beyond Utilitarianism* (Cambridge: Cambridge University Press, 1982).

11. John Rawls, *A Theory of Justice* (Cambridge, Mass.: Harvard University Press, 1971), 361.

12. Edmund Burke, "Speech at the Conclusion of the Poll," cited in James Hogan, *Election and Representation* (Cork, Ireland: Cork University Press, 1945), 189.

13. For an example of such a theory, see Alan H. Goldman, *The Moral Foundations of Professional Ethics* (Totowa, NJ: Rowman & Littlefield, 1980), 24, 76, 88–9.

14. Fenno (*Home Style*) is one of the few political scientists who emphasize the idea of representation as process. But he concentrates on what occurs in the constituency more than on what happens in the legislature. Pitkin (*The Concept of Representation*, 221–2) is one of the few contemporary political theorists to notice the significance of process, but she never specifies any standards by which we might assess its patterns, and scarcely discusses the legislative process itself.

15. Rawls, *A Theory of Justice*, 130–6; and Kurt Baier, *The Moral Point of View* (Ithaca, NY: Cornell University Press, 1958), 187–213. For further references, see W. K. Frankena, "Recent Conceptions of Morality," in *Morality and the Language of Conduct*, ed. H. N. Castaeda and George Nakhnikian (Detroit: Wayne State University Press, 1965), 1–24.

16. The criteria correspond roughly to four of Rawls's five formal constraints (*A Theory of Justice*, 131–5). My use of "generality" could be understood as combining and simplifying his conditions of generality and universality. "Publicity" follows closely his condition of the same name, and "autonomy" is meant to capture the most relevant political element in his requirement of "ordering" (that the ordering of conflicting claims be independent of the capacity to intimidate and coerce). His condition of "finality" does not seem necessary for or appropriate to the legislative process.

17. One of the most lucid discussions of universalizability in the vast literature on the subject is that of J. L. Mackie, *Ethics: Inventing Right and Wrong* (New York: Penguin, 1977), 83–102.

18. Immanuel Kant, "Critique of Practical Reason," in *The Philosophy of Kant*, ed. C. J. Friedrich (New York: Random House, 1949), ch. 2, 259.

19. See, for example, R. M. Hare, *Freedom and Reason* (Oxford: Clarendon Press, 1963), 7–50.

20. Even at-large representatives elected nationally stand in a special relationship to those who voted for them, as John Stuart Mill imagined they would. See Mill, "Considerations on Representative Government," in *Essays on Politics and Society*, vol. 19 of *Collected Works*, ed. J. M. Robson (Toronto: University of Toronto Press, 1977), ch. 7.

21. "Speech on the State of the Representation," in *Burke's Politics*, ed. Ross J. S. Hoffman and Paul Levack (New York: Knopf, 1959), 229. But Burke also assumes that a representative owes some special obligation to those districts such as Birmingham, which do not yet have members of Parliament but whose citizens share some "interests" with those of Bristol.

22. Jeremy Bentham, *Constitutional Code*, ed. Frederick Rosen and J. H. Burns (Oxford: Oxford University Press, 1983), vol. 1, VI.1.A11, 44.

23. Ibid.

24. Jean-Jacques Rousseau, *The Social Contract*, ed. M. Cranston (New York: Penguin, 1968), bk. 2, ch. 6, 80–1.

25. The argument is made most forcefully and influentially by Theodore Lowi in *The End of Liberalism*, 2d ed. (New York: Norton, 1979), esp. 198–236. For a more dispassionate discussion of the distinction between the two kinds of welfare, see Charles E. Gilbert, "Welfare Policy," in *Policies and Policymaking*, vol. 6 of *Handbook of Political Science*, ed. Fred I. Greenstein and Nelson W. Polsby (Reading, Mass.: Addison-Wesley, 1975), 157–73.

26. Lowi, *The End of Liberalism*, 213.

27. Ibid., 214.

28. For sympathetic critiques of the War on Poverty, see John H. Strange, "Citizen Participation in Community Action and Model Cities Programs," *Public Administration Review* 32 (1972): 655–9; and J. David Greenstone and Paul F. Peterson, *Race and Authority in Urban Politics* (New York: Russell Sage, 1973).

29. Lowi, *The End of Liberalism*, 216.

30. See Strange, "Citizen Participation," 655ff.

31. When Lowi writes that the "principle of representation" on which delegation is based is "antithetical to the principle of administration" (212), he implies that representation is inconsistent with responsible legislation that establishes the rules for administration.

32. Gilbert, 159–60.

33. The differences between states have ranged from about $30 to $170 per month per person (1981 figures). Variations in cost of living in different regions account for only a part of these differences in levels of support. See James E. Anderson, David W. Brady, Charles Bullock III, and Joseph Stewart, Jr., *Public Policy and Politics in America*, 2d ed. (Monterey, Calif.: Brooks-Cole, 1984), 138–9.

34. Kingdon, *Congressmen's Voting Decisions*, 266–7.

35. Ibid., 267.

36. Kant, *The Metaphysical Elements of Justice*, trans. John Ladd (Indianapolis, Ind.: Bobbs-Merrill, 1965), 15–16.

37. Rawls, *A Theory of Justice*, 516.

38. Even Burke recognizes a special duty to one's party. He condemns any representative who "abandons the party in which he has long acted, and tells you it is because he proceeds upon his own judgment; and that he acts on the merits of the several measures as they arise; and that he is obliged to follow his own conscience" (*Burke's Politics*, ed. Hoffman and Levack, 42). To accomplish anything in politics, Burke reminds us, representatives must act in concert, and that means they must be open to influence from members of their party.

39. Gary C. Jacobson, *The Politics of Congressional Elections* (Boston: Little, Brown, 1983), 81–6.

40. William Graham Sumner, *The Challenge of Facts and Other Essays*, ed. A. G. Keller (New Haven, Conn.: Yale University Press, 1914), 367.

41. J. S. Mill, *Speech on Personal Representation*, speech delivered in the House of Commons, May 29, 1867 (London: Henderson, Rait, and Fenton, 1867), 12.

42. Mill, "Considerations on Representative Government," ch. 6.

43. Fenno, *Home Style*, 167–8. The condemnation of this kind of conduct is the closest that contemporary political scientists come to affirming a normative canon on political representation. See also Fiorina, *Retrospective Voting*, 210–11; Fiorina, "The Decline of Collective Responsibility," *Daedalus* 109 (Summer 1980): 26, 39, 40; Kingdon, *Congressmen's Voting Decisions*, 51–3; David Mayhew, *Congress: The Electoral Connection* (New Haven, Conn.: Yale University Press, 1974), 114–22; and James L. Sundquist, *The Decline and Resurgence of Congress* (Washington, DC: Brookings Institution, 1981), 451, 455. For earlier statements, see Woodrow Wilson, *Congressional Government* (Boston: Houghton Mifflin, 1885), 318; and James Bryce, *Modern Democracies*, vol. 2 (New York: Macmillan, 1921), 494–5.

44. Committee on Political Parties, American Political Science Association, "Toward a More Responsible Two-Party System," *American Political Science Review* 44 (September 1950), supplement. See also Gerald M. Pomper, "Toward a More Responsible Two-Party System? What Again?" *Journal of Politics* 33 (November 1971): 916–40; and J. Harry Wray, "Rethinking Responsible Parties," *Western Political Quarterly* 34 (December 1981): 510–27. The call for "collective responsibility" also usually includes a plea for strong "responsible" parties (see, for example, Fiorina, "Decline of Collective Responsibility," 28–39). Also, see David E. Price, *Bringing Back the Parties* (Washington, DC: Congressional Quarterly Press, 1984), 104–16.

45. For criticisms of the idea of a responsible party system, see Charles Lindblom, *The Intelligence of Democracy* (New York: Collier-Macmillan, 1965), 318–19.

46. M. Ostrogorski, *Democracy and the Party System in the United States* (New York: Macmillan, 1926), 441.

47. Immanuel Kant, "Eternal Peace," in *The Philosophy of Kant*, ed. C. J. Friedrich, 470.

48. Ibid. Rawls's interpretation of the condition of publicity is also hypothetical in the sense that it is meant to constrain choices in an "original position," in which the agents do not know their particular circumstances. But part of his rationale for the condition refers to its consequences for actual political

life: publicly known principles "support the stability of social cooperation" (Rawls, *A Theory of Justice*, 133).

49. Mill, "Considerations on Representative Government," 214. Sissela Bok emphasizes the importance of actual publicity as a criterion of morality: see Bok, *Lying* (New York: Random House, 1979), 99–108; and Bok, *Secrets: On the Ethics of Concealment and Revelation* (New York: Pantheon, 1982), 112–15.

50. Arthur Maass, *Congress and the Common Good* (New York: Basic Books, 1983), 62–6.

51. Richard Rettig, "The Policy Debate on Patient Care Financing for Victims of End-Stage Renal Disease," *Law and Contemporary Problems* 40 (Autumn 1976): 212–30.

52. Steven E. Rhoads, "How Much Should We Spend to Save a Life?" in *Valuing Life: Public Policy Dilemmas*, ed. Steven E. Rhoads (Boulder, Colo.: Westview Press, 1980), 304.

53. Robert Goodin, *Political Theory and Public Policy* (Chicago: University of Chicago Press, 1982), 120–1.

54. Fiorina, "Decline of Collective Responsibility," 41.

55. Ibid., 44. Since Fiorina himself considers this an abuse, he clearly does not favor letting legislators "put the lid on" all controversial issues. But he does not indicate how we should distinguish the issues that should be suppressed from those that should not; nor does he suggest that such distinctions should be discussed in the legislature.

PART II

VARIETIES OF INSTITUTIONAL FAILURE

6

Democratic Secrecy

Sunshine laws, the Freedom of Information Act, investigative journalism, and a robust First Amendment ensure that U.S. citizens have access to more information about public officials and public agencies than ever before in history. Yet even in what may be the most open national government in the world, secrecy persists. According to the Information Security Oversight Office, which keeps watch over the U.S. government's secrets, more than three and a half million new secrets are created each year.[1] That works out to almost ten thousand new secrets a day. No doubt many more secrets were not even recorded. Until recently, even the rules and criteria for classifying and declassifying secret information were themselves secret. There are now two million officials in government and another one million in private industry with the authority to classify documents. Many of these are what are called derivative classifiers, who without signing their own names can declare their own document classified just because it quotes from another, originally classified, document.[2]

Government secrecy certainly has not been ignored. Many scholars and reformers have examined it critically, and government bodies have investigated the problem. A bipartisan national Commission on Government Secrecy headed by Senator Daniel Patrick Moynihan concluded that a massive "culture of secrecy" has spread with little oversight throughout the government during the past eighty years, and has now seriously eroded our democratic process.[3] Nevertheless, most of the literature on government secrecy neglects the fundamental democratic values underlying the problem and focuses instead on the laws and policies that regulate secrecy, patterns of abuses by individual officials, or particular practices such as executive privilege and national security.[4] When writers examine fundamental values, they usually pose the problem as a conflict between secrecy and democracy.[5]

For a limited but significant class of public policies there is a fundamental conflict of values that is not readily resolvable and that creates a continuing problem for government secrecy in a democracy. The conflict is not primarily between secrecy and democracy but arises within the idea of the democratic process itself. Some of the best reasons for secrecy rest on the very same democratic values that argue against secrecy. The democratic presumption against secrecy (and in favor of publicity) can be defended, but not as simply as is usually supposed.

The conflict involves this basic dilemma of accountability: democracy requires publicity, but some democratic policies require secrecy. The first horn of the dilemma is familiar enough: the policies and processes of government must be public in order to secure the consent of the governed. At a minimum, democracy requires that citizens be able to hold officials accountable, and to do that citizens must know what officials are doing, and why. The second horn points to the fact that some policies and processes, if they were made public, could not be carried out as effectively or at all. These policies and processes may well be ones to which citizens would consent if they had the opportunity. The most familiar examples are in foreign policy and law enforcement. If the Dayton negotiations on Bosnia had been open to the press and all the terms of the final agreement fully disclosed, the leaders almost certainly would not have been able to reach an agreement. Or if the plans for a sting operation to catch drug dealers were revealed even after it took place, the safety of informers and future operations of a similar kind would be jeopardized.

The dilemma of accountability may be thought of as a political version of the Heisenberg uncertainty principle. Just as physicists cannot measure a particle's position and momentum at the same time (because the process of measuring the position disturbs the momentum), so citizens cannot evaluate some policies and processes because the act of evaluating defeats the policy or undermines the process.

Faced with this dilemma, democrats might seem to have only two alternatives: abandon the policy or sacrifice democratic accountability. The first alternative is sometimes the right one. In the Iran-Contra affair during the mid-1980s, Lieutenant Colonel Oliver North kept his actions and the policy of trading arms for hostages secret by giving misleading answers to Congress. A congressional counsel later challenged him by asking, "But these operations were designed to be secrets from the American people?" North responded: "I'm at a loss as to how we could announce it to the American people and not have the Soviets know about it."[6] But the trouble was that it was not only the Soviets who would have undermined the policy but also many Americans, including a majority in Congress. If one of the reasons that a policy cannot be made public is that it would be defeated in the democratic process, then the policy should be abandoned.

Even the second alternative – sacrificing accountability – may be appropriate in exceptional circumstances. President John Kennedy did not tell the American people during the Cuban missile crisis that in order to get Nikita Khrushchev to withdraw Soviet missiles from Cuba, he agreed to remove American missiles from Turkey.[7] Nor through most of the nuclear era did most Americans, including most members of Congress, know much about critical elements of nuclear strategy. Moral, not only technical, choices were made without public accountability.

But many policies that require secrecy to be effective do not lend themselves to either of these alternative strategies. We usually do not want to give up either the policy or the accountability. So, in practice, we try to compromise by moderating the secrecy – by lifting the veil of secrecy just enough to allow for some degree of democratic accountability. In general, this strategy is more difficult and should be employed with more caution than is usually practiced. The dilemma of accountability is often inescapable, and in any choice between secrecy and publicity, publicity should have ultimate priority. The basic reason is that in any balancing of these values, there should be enough publicity about the policy in question so that citizens can judge whether the right balance has been struck. Publicity is the precondition of deciding democratically to what extent (if at all) publicity itself should be sacrificed.[8]

This dilemma can be seen more clearly by considering two general ways in which secrecy may be moderated – ways in which the veil of secrecy may be penetrated. In each case we need to ask what kind of democratic accountability this makes possible and whether it is sufficient. This approach is intended to broaden the discussion of government secrecy to include some forms that are common enough in the life of public officials but neglected in the literature.

TEMPORALITY: WHEN IS THE VEIL LIFTED?

The first way in which secrecy may be moderated involves its temporal dimension. We moderate the secrecy by making it temporary: lift the veil in time for citizens to judge the policy or process. The main question we should ask is: What if any democratic accountability is lost by the delay?

Consider the case of the Clinton administration's ill-fated Task Force on National Health Care Reform, which in early 1993 brought some five hundred experts together in four months of meetings to design a comprehensive plan to guarantee healthcare. For much of that time, the meetings were closed, and even the identities of the experts were kept secret. The administration argued that this kind of process allowed participants to take more risks at the earlier stages of the formulation of policy and that it reduced the chance that a well-grounded policy (which could later win public approval) would be rejected early simply because it was unpopular with special interests.[9] The courts eventually disallowed the secrecy.[10]

But the administration did not ask citizens or their representatives to consider whether the secrecy was justified for this purpose. It is difficult to argue that secrecy served the overall cause of healthcare reform very well. In the end, the healthcare plan failed – no doubt for many reasons. But it should have been clear that public support for any plan ultimately would be harder to achieve if the policymakers did not show that they were responding to criticisms and taking into account diverse interests in the process of formulating the plan.

This is not only a political but also a moral point: the less that citizens know about a policy, the less accountable the government is for the policy. Further, the less meaningful the consent citizens give to the policy, the less justifiable is the use of state power to enforce it. Thus even temporary secrecy can block citizens from knowing about critical phases of the process in which the policy is adopted and thereby diminish both accountability and consent.

Temporary secrecy does not of course always diminish accountability. Sometimes it can enhance the democratic process, and there is even some information that is made public but that should be kept temporarily secret. For example, the exit polls conducted by the news media during an election reveal the likely results before some citizens have had a chance to vote and thereby may influence their decisions in ways that seem inappropriate. This kind of publicity distorts the process of accountability.

So how should we decide whether temporary secrecy is justified? Is there a general principle that might help officials and citizens focus their inevitable arguments about particular cases? Any such principle should have two parts: a secret is justified only if it promotes the democratic discussion of the merits of a public policy; and only if citizens and their accountable representatives are able to deliberate about whether it does so.

The first part of the principle is simply a restatement of the value of accountability. The second part is more likely to be overlooked but is no less essential. Secrecy is justifiable only if it is actually justified in a process that itself is not secret. First-order secrecy (in a process or about a policy) requires second-order publicity (about the decision to make the process or policy secret).

The requirement of second-order publicity is a sensible resolution of the dilemma of accountability for many cases, but there are some kinds of cases it does not handle well. The first are policies or practices in which the accountability is essentially context-sensitive. These are cases in which the controversial element of the policy is specific to the case, cannot be revealed without undermining the policy, and has irreversible effects. In such cases, giving advance approval of the general type of the policy or counting on retrospective review are not adequate forms of accountability.[11]

It seems perfectly acceptable for a city council to approve the use of unmarked police cars while keeping the specific times and locations secret. But consider the case of a covert operation run by the Drug Enforcement Administration (DEA) in Texas in the late 1980s. The DEA routinely allowed local police officials to claim that they had seized illegal drug shipments, even though the shipments were brought into the United States by the DEA's own undercover agents.[12] The practice was designed not only to stop the drugs from reaching distributors in the United States but also to protect the identity of the agents who were acting as middlemen for South American drug traffickers so that the investigations could continue. The practice was evidently effective and became public only after reporters began to have suspicions that the numbers of drug arrests were inflated. DEA officials argued that the practice was carefully limited and had been effective in serving an important goal that Congress had approved in general terms. But the absence of any prospective accountability for the method (as distinct from the goal) of the policy is still troubling. If we believe that this and similar undercover operations are necessary, we have an unresolved conflict between secrecy and accountability in all cases of this kind.

TRANSPARENCY: HOW THICK IS THE VEIL?

The other type of case that the proviso requiring second-order publicity does not handle brings us to another way in which secrecy may be moderated – transparency (how thick the veil is). Here the problem is that publicizing the practice or policy, making it explicit even in general terms, tends to undermine it. These are cases in which second-order publicity about a policy would destroy its first-order efficacy. Democratic accountability requires transparency, but some policies and processes require obscurity.

The form of secrecy at issue here, rarely discussed in the literature, is partial: it lies somewhere between deep concealment and full disclosure. Such secrets are not completely concealed because their content may be widely known or could be widely known. But their content is not made explicit, and its not being made explicit is necessary for the policy's being effective. We might think of such partial secrets as tacit silences: things that are better left unsaid.

Excuses and Nonenforcement

The first kind of partial secret or tacit silence can be illustrated by a feature of the administration of the criminal law. Jeremy Bentham once proposed a scheme that he thought would maximize both the deterrence and the humanitarian aims of the criminal justice system.[13] As a good utilitarian, he did not like capital punishment, but he thought that the threat of capital punishment was sometimes necessary to deter serious crimes. His solution: the law should prescribe death by poison for certain crimes; the poison would be given to the convicted criminal in public, and after he collapsed and was carried away, he would be given an antidote. The criminal would of course have to be told that the penalty for revealing this secret was death by poison – without any antidote. The same would go for the officials who were in on the secret.

Like many of Bentham's schemes, this is not the most sensible so-lution to the problem, but it reveals, in an only slightly more extreme form, some features in the administration of our contemporary crim-inal justice system that many scholars and jurists defend. This is the phenomenon of what is called "acoustic separation" (or in terms of the metaphor here it could be called "differential transparency").[14]

On this view, most particular laws imply two kinds of rules: conduct rules, which tell citizens that if they engage in certain conduct, they will be punished in certain ways; and decision rules, which tell officials how to apply the conduct rules. In a system that is purely transparent, one that completely satisfies the publicity principle, the decision rules as well as the conduct rules would be known to all citizens. But in our current system, there is an acoustic separation between the citizens and officials: citizens hear only the conduct rules, not the decision rules. Following the metaphor of transparency, we could say that they can see through only the part of the veil that covers the conduct rules.

An example comes from the law of excuse – the excusing or mit-igating factors that are considered in applying a law to a particular individual. "Ignorance of the law is no excuse." Most people (and many officials) evidently believe that this is a prevailing rule in our legal system. They believe that the court decisions and statutes do not allow ignorance of the law as an excuse for breaking the law. But that does not seem to be the case. According to certain authoritative (though not widely publicized) commentaries, there are so many ex-ceptions to the excuse that it hardly expresses a rule at all. Ignorance of the law is in fact quite often accepted as a legitimate excuse. You may be excused, for example, if the charge is based on a regulation in-stead of a statute, if the charge is based on an omission rather than an action, or if you relied on an authoritative source for your information even if the source was mistaken.[15]

These exceptions have developed because in many cases it is clearly unfair to punish someone who really did not know that he or she was breaking a law. We usually hold people morally responsible only for their intentional actions and therefore think that punishment is justi-fied only if they knowingly or at least negligently commit an offense. But if it were generally known that one could avoid punishment by claiming ignorance of the law, not only would some people try to feign ignorance of the law, but also there would be an incentive to cultivate legal ignorance.

Similar considerations apply to imposing penalties of many different kinds in administrative proceedings, whether the parties are citizens outside government or civil servants inside the agency. The Environmental Protection Agency (EPA) and the Internal Revenue Service (IRS) do not reveal specifically what kinds of excuses have been accepted in the past. In many cases, the agencies simply do not enforce the rules when the violations fall beyond a certain (unpublicized) threshold. Complete transparency would require publicizing these thresholds and other facts, such as that the agency usually gives a warning, perhaps even two warnings, to violators of a particular rule before taking any further action. But both citizens and employees would be less likely to violate the rules in the first place if this fact were left somewhat unspecified.

Thus, publicizing the stricter conduct rule while obscuring the more lenient decision rule resolves what would otherwise be a difficult dilemma. It mitigates the conflict between two important values – deterrence and fairness. Although the acoustic separation is not complete – the veil does not totally obscure the decision rules to citizens – we should be glad (the proponents of acoustic separation say) that the decision rule is not more generally known. It is fortunate that the exceptions to the conduct rule that ignorance of the law is no excuse are not more widely publicized.

But if this concession to obscurity – this sacrifice of transparency – mitigates this conflict in the law, it exacerbates the more general democratic conflict in the dilemma of accountability. Differential transparency is not a desirable practice in a democracy, and should not be encouraged even if it is to some extent inescapable. It is undesirable for at least three reasons.

One problem with acoustic separation is that it tends to be self-defeating over time. The rationale for the exceptions to general rules (like "ignorance of the law is no excuse") is that they make the law conform more closely to our ordinary notions of morality (in this case the principle that people should be punished only for intentional wrongdoing). But if the exceptions are developed over time by administrators and judges in unpublicized cases, the law may begin to diverge from common morality, or at least citizens can have no assurance that they conform to it. Public deliberation seems to be a precondition for keeping the exceptions secret in the first place.

A second problem with acoustic separation is that because in practice it can never be complete, some citizens can penetrate the barrier and use the information while other citizens cannot. Large corporations and individuals who can afford regularly to consult lawyers can use their inside knowledge of the decision rules to their advantage. The unfairness of this advantage is especially evident in the areas of tax and environmental law. The internal enforcement guidelines of the IRS or the EPA (what excuses are accepted, what levels of violation are ignored, what conduct triggers investigations) may not always be publicized, but some corporations and individuals can still find out what they are and use their knowledge to their own advantage.

Finally and more generally, any attempt in a democracy to send differential messages to different publics about general policies as fundamental as criminal justice is likely to miscarry. The audience with the most to lose or the most to gain usually gets the real message first, and the general public is the last to know. The American criminal justice system sends a different message to the public than it does to criminals, but with just the opposite effect from what Bentham or the advocates of acoustic separation intend. Similarly, the administrative law system may send a different message to well-financed and well-connected lobbyists than it does to ordinary citizens.

To convince the public that they are vigorously fighting crime, politicians enact popular get-tough measures on crime – longer prison terms, mandatory sentences, and capital punishment for more crimes. But without adequate institutional support for these measures (police and prosecutors to enforce the laws, judges and juries prepared to impose the sentences, and prisons to house adequately the convicted criminals), the measures are not likely to reduce crime and may merely result in more plea bargains, more parole, and fewer convictions. The system tells the criminal on the street that, despite the public rhetoric, the actual risk of getting caught, let alone serving a long term, is not high. Acoustic separation – differential transparency – in these circumstances not only fails to promote genuine accountability but also defeats its own policy aims.

COMPELLED SILENCE

The second kind of case in which transparency is transgressed carries the partial secrecy of excuses and non-enforcement a step further. Here the law explicitly requires that conduct be kept secret; the conduct becomes illegal only if it is revealed. An instructive example is the controversial policy on gays in the military: the "don't ask – don't tell" regulations proposed by the Clinton administration in 1993, endorsed by Congress, and upheld by the courts.[16] The military is no longer permitted to ask applicants for military service their sexual orientation and cannot investigate their sexual orientation unless they receive "credible information" about it from other sources. At the same time, individuals who are gay are not permitted to disclose their orientation. They may go to gay bars, designate their partners on insurance forms, and take other similar actions; but they may not announce to anyone that they are gay. If they do, they are subject to discharge and other penalties.

Notice that this is different from laws that protect rights of privacy. In the policy on gays, the conduct is prohibited even if it takes place in private and even off-duty. To make clear that the law is not neutral on the question of the legitimacy of the conduct itself, the House added to the Pentagon order the statement "homosexual conduct in the military is unacceptable."[17]

Defenders of the policy describe it as a compromise between the needs of the military and the rights of a disadvantaged minority. Most if not all of the dangers that the military says homosexuality causes can be avoided if gays keep their orientation secret. The military presumably is worried that the presence of openly gay soldiers will make close-quarter living, as on shipboard, more difficult and create some ambivalence in the camaraderie that fighting units require. The rights of gay individuals are also partially protected: they can serve in the military if they are discreet in what they say and what they do. Gay individuals now serving in the military are better off than they were under the previous policy; according to one report, most welcomed the new policy, though of course "their joy [had to be] savored quietly" in private.[18]

But, as with many compromises, this one does not please most people on either side of the controversy. Those sympathetic to the military think that it undermines combat readiness, and those sympathetic to gays still find it discriminatory. Much could be said against the policy, but the relevant points here relate specifically to its lack of transparency.

Notice first that the policy is not vulnerable to the objection that it breaches democratic accountability in the way that some similar policies might. For example, many government-financed hospitals and HMOs implicitly allow physician-assisted suicide, presumably with the tacit approval of their doctors and most citizens of the community but contrary to existing law. The practice is tacitly permitted as long as no one talks about it openly, which means that most citizens or their representatives have not had a chance to vote for or against permitting the practice. In contrast, the "don't ask – don't tell" policy on gays in the military has been the subject of ample deliberation and has been openly endorsed in a democratic process. This was possible because the policy itself is public. The policy does not require that any of its essential features be secret, only the specific conduct of certain individuals. The policy thus seems to be an instance of partial secrecy or nontransparency that is consistent with democratic accountability.

But the lack of transparency still creates problems for accountability. The policy inevitably leaves a great deal to the discretion of individual military officers to decide what is to count as "telling" and what is to count as "credible information" sufficient to launch an investigation. Given the nature of the policy, this discretion is likely to be exercised in private at least in the initial stages. There have been accusations that some officers have abused this discretion by undertaking investigations without sufficient evidence. It would seem then that greater accountability, a degree of publicity at least within the government, is necessary. Yet the more public this process becomes (even within the military), the more the effect is the same as if the accused themselves did in fact "tell." They would now be revealed as gay. But avoiding this consequence means granting some officers considerable discretion that cannot be effectively monitored. The lack of transparency brings about a deficiency in accountability – not for the policy itself but for its application.

The policy has further problems of accountability. The pressure toward silence drives not only homosexual activity underground but also activities and discussion about the effects of the policy. The secrecy the policy requires makes it harder to find out how the policy is actually working – to learn to what extent it is discouraging gay individuals from entering the military and making their life difficult once in service, and whether the suppression of gay identity is worse for military effectiveness than open toleration would be. Much of what citizens and legislators need to know in order to judge whether to continue the policy or to change it over time is not easily accessible, because so much of the operation of the policy lies behind a less than transparent veil.[19]

CONCLUSION

Democratic accountability does not require unconditional publicity in the conduct of democratic government. Secrecy of various kinds is sometimes justified and even desirable in a democracy. But it is justified only under carefully specified conditions, which ensure that the secrecy itself is subject to democratic accountability.

The first part of any justification requires second-order publicity: the decision to keep a decision or policy secret should be made publicly. Further, it may not be sufficient to have procedures for deciding whether particular decisions or practices should be public. It may also be necessary to design procedures for deciding whether decisions about these decisions should be public. (It is usually not necessary or desirable to carry this logic to some nth-order publicity.)

The requirement of second-order publicity takes care of most cases of temporary secrecy, but it does not handle so well the important but neglected cases of partial secrecy. The challenge here is to provide procedures for acknowledging partial secrets without undermining the policies they support. The only feasible solutions seem to be either to rely on representatives who can be trusted to review in private the policy and its application, or to conduct public debates in general terms without revealing the specific nature of the policy. That neither of these alternatives usually provides adequate democratic accountability is a further reason to seek ways to promote transparency in the design of government institutions and the making of public policies.

The dilemma of accountability poses a choice between either abandoning a policy or weakening responsibility for it. The dilemma cannot always be resolved because it is inherent in the theory and practice of democratic government itself, or at least in any democratic government in which citizens would wish to adopt policies that cannot be promptly disclosed or processes that are not fully transparent. But public officials and political institutions can diminish the damage to democratic accountability by making sure that temporary secrets do not become permanent, and that partial secrets do not become total.

Notes

An earlier version of this chapter was presented at Rice University in April 1997, and I am grateful to Larry Temkin and his colleagues there for their valuable comments. I have also benefited from discussion of some of the arguments in this paper with Arthur Applbaum, Amy Gutmann, Lawrence Lessig, and the late Judith Shklar.

1. Information Security Oversight Office, *Report to the President,* 1995 (Washington, DC: U.S. Government Printing Office, 1996), ii.

2. *Report of the Commission on Protecting and Reducing Government Secrecy,* Pursuant to Public Law 236, 103rd Congress (Washington, DC: Government Printing Office, 1997).

3. Ibid.

4. Itzhak Galnoor, ed., *Government Secrecy in Democracies* (New York: Harper & Row, 1977); Donald C. Rowat, ed., *Administrative Secrecy in Developed Countries* (New York: Columbia University Press, 1979); Kenneth G. Robertson, *Public Secrets: A Study of the Development of Government Secrecy* (New York: St. Martin's Press, 1982); Mark J. Rozell, *Executive Privilege: The Dilemma of Secrecy and Democratic Accountability* (Baltimore: Johns Hopkins Press, 1994); Daniel P. Moynihan, *Secrecy: The American Experience* (New Haven: Yale University Press, 1998); and David Vincent, *The Culture of Secrecy in Britain, 1832–1998* (New York: Oxford University Press, 1998).

5. Francis E. Rourke, *Secrecy and Publicity: Dilemmas of Democracy* (Baltimore: Johns Hopkins Press, 1966). But see Sissela Bok, *Secrets: On the Ethics of Concealment and Revelation* (New York: Pantheon Books, 1982), 102–15, 171–90.

6. David Nacht, "The Iran-Contra Affair," in Amy Gutmann and Dennis Thompson, eds., *Ethics and Politics,* 3rd ed. (Chicago: Nelson-Hall, 1997), 57–66.

7. Graham T. Allison and Lance M. Liebman, "Lying in Office," in ibid., 49–53.

8. For discussions of the publicity principle, see Amy Gutmann and Dennis Thompson, *Democracy and Disagreement* (Cambridge, Mass.: Harvard University Press, 1996), 95–127; and David Luban, "The Publicity Principle," in Robert E. Goodin, ed., *The Theory of Institutional Design* (Cambridge: Cambridge University Press, 1996), 154–98.

9. For contemporaneous editorial comments on the secret deliberations, see "Health Team Needs Breathing Room," *St. Louis Post-Dispatch,* 31 March 1993; and "Let's All Be Health Care Insiders," *New York Times,* 13 March 1993.

10. The first federal court ruling was *American Association of Physicians and Surgeons, Inc., v. Clinton.* Civil Action No. 93–0399, 11 March 1993, 813 F. Supp. 82, 1993 U.S. Dist.

11. On the difficulties with these forms of accountability, see Dennis F. Thompson, *Political Ethics and Public Office* (Cambridge, Mass.: Harvard University Press, 1987), 22–31.

12. Associated Press, "U.S. Looking Into Undercover Drug Manipulation," *New York Times,* 29 November 1988.

13. Shirley Letwin, *The Pursuit of Certainty* (Cambridge: Cambridge University Press, 1965), 173.

14. Meir Dan-Cohen, "Decision Rules and Conduct Rules: On Acoustic Separation in Criminal Law," *Harvard Law Review* 97 (January 1984): 625–77.

15. Ibid., 645–8.

16. "Gay Rights in the Military: The Pentagon's New Policy Guidelines on Homosexuals in the Military," *New York Times,* 20 July 1993.

17. Clifford Krauss, "With Caveat, House Approves Gay-Troops Policy," *New York Times*, 29 September 1993.

18. Thomas L. Friedman, "Gay Rights in the Military," *New York Times*, 21 July 1993.

19. A section on political hypocrisy in the original article is omitted here. See Chapter 9 for discussion of the issue.

7

Mediated Corruption

The case of the "Keating Five" – featuring five prominent U.S. Senators and Charles Keating, Jr., a savings and loan financier who contributed to their campaigns – has "come to symbolize public distrust of elected officials" and has reinforced the widespread view that many members of Congress and the institution itself are corrupt.[1] The nine months of investigation and seven weeks of hearings conducted by the Senate Ethics Committee that concluded in January 1992 revealed an underside of the system of representation in the United States to a depth and at a level of detail rarely seen before or since.

The broad shape of this underside is familiar enough: politicians take money from contributors to get elected, then do favors for them. But the deeper significance, theoretical and practical, is to be found in the details and in the relation of those details to principles of democratic representation. Although the case reveals a darker side of our politics, we can still try to recognize degrees of darkness. We should aim for a kind of moral chiaroscuro. More generally, the case can help us to better understand a more subtle form of political corruption that is becoming increasingly common but has not received the attention it deserves from political scientists or political theorists.

This form of corruption involves the use of public office for private purposes in a manner that subverts the democratic process. It may be called mediated corruption because the corrupt acts are mediated by the political process. The public official's contribution to the corruption is filtered through various practices that are otherwise legitimate and may even be duties of office. As a result, both the official and citizens are less likely to recognize that the official has done anything wrong or that any serious harm has been done.

Mediated corruption is still a form of corruption. It includes the three main elements of the general concept of corruption: a public official gains, a private citizen receives a benefit, and the connection between the gain and the benefit is improper.[2] But mediated corruption differs from conventional corruption with respect to each of these three elements: (1) the gain that the politician receives is political, not personal, and is not illegitimate in itself, as in conventional corruption; (2) the way the public official provides the benefit is improper, not necessarily the benefit itself, or the fact that a particular citizen receives the benefit; (3) the connection between the gain and the benefit is improper because it damages the democratic process, not because the public official provides the benefit with a corrupt motive. In each of these elements, the concept of mediated corruption links the acts of individual officials to qualities of the democratic process. The concept provides a partial synthesis of conventional corruption (familiar in contemporary political science) and systematic corruption (found in traditional political theory).

To show the value of the concept of mediated corruption, I criticize two interpretations of the Keating Five case that assume a conventional concept of corruption. A concept of mediated corruption provides a better characterization of this case and, by implication, of the many similar cases that have occurred and are likely to occur. The characterization is intended to identify more coherently the aspects of actions and practices that we regard, or should regard, as wrong. The concept of mediated corruption helps bring our considered judgments about corruption in particular cases into "reflective equilibrium" with our moral and political principles.[3]

WHAT THE KEATING FIVE GAVE
AND WHAT THEY GOT

A brief summary of the events in this case will set the stage for examining the competing interpretations.[4] The senators who are forever joined together by the name "the Keating Five" had never worked together as a group before, and will (it is safe to assume) never work together again. Four are Democrats – Dennis DeConcini (Arizona), Alan Cranston (California), John Glenn (Ohio), and Donald Riegle (Michigan) – and one is a Republican, John McCain (Arizona).

All were influential in the Senate; Riegle was chair of the Banking Committee.

They were brought together by Charles Keating, Jr., who was later convicted on charges of fraud and racketeering. As chairman of a home construction company in Phoenix, he bought Lincoln Savings and Loan in California in 1984 and began to shift its assets from home loans to high-risk projects, violating a wide variety of state and federal regulations in the process. In 1989, Lincoln collapsed, wiping out the savings of twenty-three thousand (mostly elderly) uninsured customers and costing taxpayers over two billion dollars. It was the biggest failure in what came to be the most costly financial scandal in American history. Lincoln came to symbolize the savings and loan crisis.

But to many in the financial community during the years before the collapse, Keating was a model of the financial entrepreneur that the Republican administration wished to encourage through its policy of deregulation. His most visible political lobbying was directed against the new rule prohibiting direct investment by savings and loans, which many legitimate financial institutions and many members of Congress also opposed. His most prominent and persistent target was Edwin Gray, the head of the three-member bank board that regulated the industry, himself a controversial figure.

The fateful meeting that would link the Keating Five took place on April 2, 1987, in the early evening in DeConcini's office. The senators asked Gray why the investigation of Lincoln and their "friend" Keating was taking so long. Gray said later that he was intimidated by this "show of force." Toward the end of the meeting, he suggested that the senators talk directly to the San Francisco examiners who were handling the Lincoln case. And so they did, a week later, in what was to become the most scrutinized meeting in the hearings. The senators told the examiners that they believed that the government was harassing a constituent. After the regulators reported that they were about to make a "criminal referral" against Lincoln, the senators seemed to back off.

After that meeting, McCain, Riegle, and Glenn had no further dealings of significance with Keating. Glenn arranged a lunch for Keating and House Speaker Jim Wright the following January, but the committee concluded that although this showed "poor judgment," Glenn's actions were not "improper" (U.S. Senate 1991b, 18). McCain had already broken off relations with Keating, who had called him a "wimp" for refusing to put pressure on the bank board. Cranston and DeConcini continued to act on Keating's behalf.

The Keating Five, particularly DeConcini and Cranston, certainly provided this constituent with good service. Since an act of corruption typically involves exchange of some kind, we have to ask: What did the Senators get in return? The answer is $1.3 million, all within legal limits.[5] But this figure and this fact, handy for headline writers, obscures important details (especially the timing and uses of the funds) that should affect our assessment of corruption.

In February 1991, the Ethics Committee rebuked four of the Senators – DeConcini and Riegle more severely, McCain and Glenn less so – and concluded that further action was warranted only against Cranston. Then in November, after much behind-the-scenes political negotiation, the committee reported to the full Senate that Cranston had "violated established norms of behavior in the Senate." To avoid a stronger resolution by the committee (which would have required a Senate vote), Cranston formally accepted the reprimand. In a dramatic speech on the floor, he also claimed that he had done nothing worse than had most of his colleagues in the Senate.

COMPETITION OR CORRUPTION?

Cranston's own defense exemplifies, in a cynical form, one of the two standard interpretations of the conduct of the Keating Five. This interpretation holds that the conduct was part of a normal competitive process, in which politicians are encouraged by the political system to solicit support and bestow favors in order to win elections. We may call this the competitive politics theory.[6] On this view, most politicians are not corrupt; nor is the system – even if some citizens like Keating happen to have corrupt designs. The quest for campaign contributions and the provision of service to influential contributors are necessary features of a healthy competitive politics.

The second interpretation also holds that what the Keating Five did is not significantly different from what other members have done but concludes that it is corrupt. On this view (call it the pervasive corruption theory), most politicians are corrupt or (more sympathetically) are forced by the system to act in corrupt ways even if they begin with honest intentions.[7] This interpretation is more popular among the press, the public, and academics than it is among politicians. It is consistent with the views of both those who urge radical reforms in the political system (such as abolishing campaign contributions completely) and those who believe that corruption is unavoidable in government. The latter either accept it or advocate reducing the scope of government to reduce it.

These two common interpretations seem to be different. Indeed, they seem to be opposites: one finds corruption where the other does not. But on closer inspection, their concepts of corruption turn out to be fundamentally similar. We can begin to see the similarity in the fact that they both conclude that the conduct of the Keating Five is not morally distinguishable from that of most other politicians.[8] On both accounts, the Keating Five were simply intervening with administrators on behalf of a campaign contributor, a common practice. The competitive politics theory accepts the practice, the pervasive corruption theory condemns it. But on neither theory do the details of the case (such as the nature of the intervention) make any difference in the moral assessment.

The reason that both theories take this view is that they agree in their fundamental assumptions. The analysis that follows focuses on three of these assumptions (each corresponding to an element in the general concept of corruption) and argues that each is mistaken. Understanding why they are mistaken points toward the need for a concept of mediated corruption.

First, both interpretations assume that corruption requires that the public official receive a personal gain, either directly or indirectly in the form of an advantage that is not distinguished from personal gain. They disagree about whether a campaign contribution should count as personal gain in the required sense, but they agree that some such gain or its moral equivalent is necessary. The image of the self-serving politician acting on base motives contrary to the public interest supplies much of the force of the moralistic reactions to corruption, both the defensiveness of the competitive politics view, and the censoriousness of the pervasive corruption view. This is also the image that most public officials themselves evidently have of the corrupt official: the more personal and larger the payoff and the less the favor seems part of the job, the more likely is the conduct to be regarded as corrupt (Peters and Welch 1978, 980–1).

Second, both interpretations assume that corruption requires that the citizen receive a benefit that is not deserved, or be threatened with not receiving one that is deserved. More generally, the justice of the constituent's claim is the only aspect of the benefit that is relevant to the determination of corruption.

Third, both interpretations assume that corruption requires a corrupt motive. The personal or political gain and the citizen's benefit are connected in the mind of the public official. The official knowingly acts for the contributor in exchange for gain to himself or herself.

PERSONAL GAIN: THE AMBIGUITY OF SELF-INTEREST

Is personal gain by an official a necessary element of corruption? Only one of the Keating Five – McCain – ever received anything from Keating for his own personal use, and he (along with Glenn) is generally considered to have been the least guilty of the group. (The McCain family took some vacation trips to Keating's Bahamas home in the early 1980s, for which McCain eventually paid when notified by the company in 1989.) If personal gain is an element of the corruption in the Keating Five case, it must be found in the campaign contributions. Should campaign contributions count as the personal gain that the conventional concept of corruption requires?

This case suggests a negative answer. Cranston received no personal financial benefit; yet his conduct was reasonably regarded as the most flagrant of the Five. He was the only one ultimately reprimanded by the Senate. Most of the $850,000 Keating gave to Cranston went to voter registration groups, which had public-spirited names such as Center for the Participation in Democracy, and had the purpose of trying to increase turnout in several different states. One of Cranston's main defenses was that he did not gain personally from these contributions.

But he did gain politically, or at least he thought he would.[9] Why not count this political advantage as the element of personal gain? This is a tempting move and is commonly made, but it should be avoided. It is a mistake to try to force contributions into the category of personal gain. Doing so obscures a moral difference between personal and political gain. These should be distinguished even if one insists on treating both as forms of self-interest. "Personal gain" refers to goods that are usable generally in pursuit of one's own interest (including that of one's family) and are not necessary by-products of political activity. "Political gain" (which may also be a kind of self-interest) involves goods that are usable primarily in the political process, and are necessary byproducts of this process.

The distinction is important because in our political system (and any democracy based on elections) the pursuit of political profit is a necessary element in the structure of incentives in a way that the pursuit of personal profit is not.[10] Our system depends on politicians seeking political advantage: we count on their wanting to be elected or reelected. Among the advantages that they must seek are campaign contributions. If political gain were part of what makes a contribution corrupt, it would also discredit many other kinds of political support, such as organizational efforts on behalf of a candidate, on which a robust democratic politics depends. This is part of the truth in the competitive politics theory.

Some political scientists would offer a more sophisticated rationale for regarding contributions as just another form of personal gain. They begin with the methodological assumption that politicians act only on self-interest, seeking to maximize their chances of reelection or in other ways to advance their careers. They could then argue that contributions, to the extent that they help achieve these goals, constitute personal gain no less than do other goods that further the self-interest of politicians.

The trouble with this expansive concept of personal gain is that it does not help identify which contributions should be permitted and which should not. As far as the personal gain is concerned, all contributions are created equal: they are either all proper or all corrupt. If self-interest is viewed favorably (as in some competitive politics theories), the expansive concept would not require that any contributions be prohibited, even those involving what would normally be considered bribery or extortion. If self-interest is viewed unfavorably (as in some pervasive corruption theories), the concept would imply that no contribution should be permitted, even those serving what would normally be regarded as the public interest. In either case, the self-interest assumption does not itself supply any way to distinguish legitimate from illegitimate pursuit of personal gain.

Neither could we get much help with this difficulty from a more refined model based on principal-agent theory, which is sometimes used to analyze corruption.[11] On this model, the politician acts as an agent for constituents, the principals. Because of the costs of monitoring and similar factors, the principals cannot reliably control the agent's actions. In the absence of other constraints, the resulting "slack" allows the agent to act on his or her own interest contrary to the interest of the principals. The model could help us see that corruption may be partly the result of the structure of incentives in the system: agent-principal slack creates moral hazards that permit corruption.

But a principal-agent model is neutral between proper and improper behavior. It is as applicable to corrupt principals and agents as to honest ones. It could treat the Keating Five as agents of Keating in carrying out corrupt purposes. It does not explain why we should have a system that allows some kinds of incentives (contributions) and not other kinds (bribes). It might be said, of course, that taking bribes has more socially harmful consequences than accepting campaign contributions. But if this is the claim, then what is wrong is no longer the personal gain, but a certain kind of personal gain; and it is wrong not because it is a personal gain at all but because of its effects on the system.

If the presence of personal gain is not necessary to make a contribution corrupt, neither is its absence sufficient to make a contribution correct. Consider this hypothetical example. Suppose that after Keating meets with Mother Teresa (which in fact he did), he decides in a fit of saintly fervor that a portion of his campaign contributions and those of others he solicits for the Keating Five should go secretly to a government trust fund to support new programs to help the poor. Suppose, further, that the Keating Five, respecting this act of charity by a constituent, work together behind the scenes to establish the Mother Teresa Fund for this purpose. (To add a further touch of irony, let the fund be administered, at Keating's request, by Ed Gray.) None of the senators would have gained personally, and a good cause would have been served.[12] Would there be any grounds for concern about corruption?

There surely would be some. Keating would have managed to promote a private project with the aid of public officials but without the warrant of the democratic process. The cause, however noble, was not one that citizens or their representatives had chosen through legitimate procedures. Acting on principle for higher causes can be no less corrupt – and may be even more dangerous – than acting for personal gain because the perpetrators are more likely to be able to enlist others in their schemes. Oliver North would have not been able to mobilize so much support for his projects in the Iran-Contra affair had he been acting mainly for personal gain.

OFFICIAL FAVORS: THE PERILS OF
CONSTITUENT SERVICE

Consider now the second element of corruption – the official favors that the senators provided. The Keating Five claimed that there was nothing improper about the help they gave Keating. The benefits that Keating received were all provided in the name of "constituent service," a normal practice in a political system in which representatives have to compete for the support of voters and campaign contributors.

The senators – and even sometimes the Ethics Committee – seemed to assume that if what a member does is constituent service and breaks no law, it is never improper. If the conduct does not involve bribery, extortion, or an illegal campaign contribution, it is not only acceptable but admirable.[13] This is the competitive politics theory in its purest form. But as the hearings progressed, some of the senators came to accept a slightly more moderate view. In effect, they allowed that otherwise proper constituent service could become improper if it were provided unfairly. It would be wrong (and perhaps evidence of corruption) if it were provided only to big contributors.[14] The senators seemed to accept as a reasonable test the question: Does the member typically intervene in this way for other constituents?

DeConcini made it a major part of his defense to show that he responded to virtually any constituent who asked for help. (He brandished a list of 75,000 constituents who could be called to testify, though to everyone's relief he settled for inviting only three – a social worker for Hispanics, a drug-busting sheriff, and a handicapped veteran.)[15] Despite these heroic efforts, the answer to the question in this case is still probably negative: what the Keating Five provided was not typical constituent service. Five senators meeting in private with regulators on a specific case is unusual. During the hearings, no one could cite a sufficiently close precedent.[16]

But even if we were to accept that the senators would do for other constituents what they did for Keating, we should still be concerned about another feature of this case, what may be called the problem of too many representatives. Only DeConcini and McCain could claim Keating as a constituent in the conventional (electoral) sense. The other three count as his representatives mainly by virtue of his business interests in their states.[17] It is true that business interests, like other interests, may deserve representation, and geographical districts need not define the limits of representation, even of constituency service.

However, we should criticize multiple representation if, in practice (as this case suggests), the extra representatives tend to go disproportionately to those with greater financial resources. That this tendency is undesirable is part of the truth in the pervasive corruption theory. A fair system of democratic representation does not grant more representatives to some citizens just because they have more financial resources.

So far, these criticisms could be consistent with the concept of conventional corruption, which assesses the benefit only in relation to the justice of the constituent's claims. Mediated corruption goes further and considers the effects on the policymaking process – most importantly, the foreseeable reactions of other officials (in this case, the regulators, staff, and other members). Instead of asking whether a member would provide this benefit equally for any constituent, mediated corruption asks whether the benefit should be provided in this way at all.

Unmentioned in the Constitution, unimagined by the founders, and until recently unanalyzed by journalists, constituent service has become a major part of the job of most members of Congress (Cain, Ferejohn, and Fiorina 1987, 50–76; and Fenno 1978, 101). It serves some valuable functions, the most important of which, perhaps, is to provide a check on abuse of power by executive agencies in individual cases – in effect, fulfilling the role played by an ombudsman in some other political systems.[18] If administrators are "harassing a constituent," as some of the senators said they suspected in this case, members may be obligated to intervene not only to protect the constituent but also to correct administrative procedures.

Yet, as political scientists have shown, constituent service is not a wholly beneficial practice even when legitimately performed (Cain, Ferejohn, and Fiorina 1987, 197–229). Even if the casework done by each individual member is perfectly proper, the collective consequences may not be beneficial for the system as a whole. One danger is that as constituent service becomes such a prominent part of the job, legislative duties suffer. Voters tend to pay more attention to personalized service than to legislative records, and political responsibility for these records withers. Another danger is that by concentrating on righting wrongs against individual citizens, constituent service can favor particular remedies over general reforms. Ad hoc and local solutions do not necessarily produce changes in procedures or policies that benefit the public as a whole. Yet another danger is that to the extent that incumbents gain electoral advantage through constituent service, new members who might bring fresh policy views or offer new criticisms of government performance are less likely to make their way into the legislature.

Once we accept that constituent service, quite independently of campaign contributions, is a mixed blessing for democracy, we can see that to justify any act of constituent service, it is not sufficient to point to the benefit to particular constituents or even to the value of the practice for the system in general. Standards to assess constituent service are best derived from principles of legislative ethics, which identify the general characteristics that a system of representation should have in order to provide conditions for making morally justifiable decisions (Thompson 1987, ch. 4). Three principles – generality, autonomy, and publicity – yield three sets of standards.

Generality

Standards of generality require that legislative actions be justifiable in terms that apply to all citizens equally. These standards refer most directly to legislation itself, where they favor actions that provide public goods for a broad class of citizens over those that confer private advantage on individual citizens. They also have institutional implications, one of the most important of which is the separation of powers, a chief purpose of which is to maintain the appropriate level of generality by assigning to branches other than the legislative the role of applying the laws. Legislative actions that are appropriate in the process of making laws may not always be appropriate in the process of administering them. Some of the most important standards of legislative ethics in various ways prescribe that any legislative intervention should be appropriate to the administrative proceeding in question.

In the Keating case, the senators evidently did not recognize any difference between what would be an appropriate intervention in rule-making proceedings and what would be appropriate in quasi-adjudicatory proceedings. In the latter kind of proceeding (which the Lincoln case resembled), there is generally more procedural protection for constituents and less legitimate scope for disputes about policy.[19] Political intervention is less appropriate. Some political bargaining, of course, is necessary in the administrative process. But at

least some of the senators in this case went beyond what we might
call the normal range of acceptable political pressure. They did more
than make status inquiries (which are perfectly proper even in quasi-
adjudicatory proceedings). To the regulators, their conduct looked
more like a threat – specifically, a threat to oppose a pending bill to
fund the savings and loan bailouts, which nearly everyone believed
was urgently needed.

Autonomy

Standards of autonomy prescribe that representatives act on relevant
reasons (Thompson 1987, 111–14). They require that any intervention be appropriate to the substantive merits of the constituent's case.
Such standards would not prohibit members from acting aggressively
on behalf of constituents, but they would clearly direct members to
consider the substance of constituents' claims in deciding whether
and how to intervene. Members may have a duty to support meritori-
ous claims, but they should not press claims that they have, or should
have, reason to believe are without merit. Furthermore, the higher
the stakes, the greater the responsibility to investigate the merits of
a claim. More generally, to simply press claims without any regard to
their merits is to promote a policymaking process moved more by
considerations of power than of purpose.[20]

Many members may not recognize an ethical problem in intervention because they take their roles to be like that of a lawyer, whose duty
is assumed to be to press a client's case without regard to merits. They
may consider that the only alternative is to play a judge's role, which
would allow no scope for partiality toward their constituents. But the
role of the representative differs from both. It permits members to
give special consideration to their own constituents provided that
they take into account the effect on other citizens and on the public
generally.

It is now known (and could have been known then) that Keating's
case lacked merit. Glenn and McCain made some effort to find out
about the case before they went to the meetings with Gray and the
regulators. Giving the senators the benefit of the doubt, we might
say that under the pressure of time they took all the steps one
could reasonably expect before they intervened with the regulators.
The senators did, after all, have some evidence at the time (a letter from Alan Greenspan and a statement from the firm of Arthur

Young) that appeared to lend credibility to Keating's complaints. But once the senators heard about the regulators' intention to make a criminal referral, they had adequate notice that his aims were questionable. Although criminal referrals are not unusual and are not clear evidence of wrongdoing, a conscientious senator (indeed, even a prudent one) would have looked more closely into the merits of Keating's case before continuing to assist him. The only two who continued to press his case, DeConcini and Cranston, did not. This is partly why their conduct could be criticized more severely, as the special counsel (and, less clearly, the Ethics Committee) concluded.

Publicity

Standards of publicity require that an intervention take place in ways that could be justified publicly. It is, of course, neither practical nor desirable that all interventions be formally on the record and made public at the time. But the intervention should not be so clandestine that the member and the agency cannot be held accountable should the action later be called into question.[21] This is why some members put in writing their inquiries to administrative agencies and keep a record of other similar contacts.

The interventions for Keating, though not strictly secret, fell short of meeting the publicity principle. The pattern of the interventions – after-hours meetings, the absence of aides, early morning phone calls to regulators at home, the vagueness of records (except for the much discussed "transcript" of the April 9 meeting) – made it difficult to reconstruct the events. They create a reasonable suspicion that the discussions were never intended to be accessible for public review.

The constituent service that the senators provided Keating, as measured by these standards, did not serve the democratic process well. To this extent – and in varying degrees in the case of each senator – the benefits that Keating received qualify as improperly provided. They count as fulfilling the second element of mediated corruption. With the concept of mediated corruption, we can criticize some forms of constituent service for contributors without rejecting all forms, as does the pervasive theory, or accepting all forms, as does the competitive theory.

CORRUPT CONNECTIONS: THE SIGNIFICANCE
OF MIXED MOTIVES

In any form of corruption, there must be an improper connection between the benefit granted and the gain received. Otherwise, there would be only simple bias or simple malfeasance. With conventional corruption, we look for the link in the guilty mind of the public official – a corrupt motive. But a question immediately arises: How can we distinguish corrupt motives from other kinds? We have already seen that personal gain is neither a necessary nor a sufficient condition. Nor is the impropriety of the benefit. The corruption, therefore, has to be found partly in the nature of the exchange.

The difficulty is that corrupt exchanges do not seem obviously different from many of the other kinds of deals that go on in politics – exchanges of support of various kinds, without which political life could not go on at all. Politics is replete with quid pro quos: you vote for my bill, and I'll support yours; you raise funds for my primary campaign, and I'll endorse you in the next election. What is so corrupt about the exchange of campaign contributions for constituent service? Without an answer to this question, we would be forced either to brand nearly all ordinary politics as corrupt or to excuse much political corruption as just ordinary politics.

The competitive politics theory, fearing a purification of the process that might enervate political life, attempts to contain the concept of corruption. It insists on narrow criteria for what counts as a corrupt link. The connection between the contribution and the service must be close in two senses: proximate in time and explicit in word or deed. In the case of several of the Keating Five, the connection between the contributions and the service were, by these standards, close. The connection was especially close in the case of Cranston – one reason that the committee singled him out for special criticism. He solicited contributions from Keating while he was also working to help Lincoln with its problems. His chief fundraiser combined discussions about regulations and contributions. Favors and contributions were also linked in memos and informal comments. He made the connection explicit in a memorable line delivered at a dinner at the Belair Hotel, where he "came up and patted Mr. Keating on the back and said, 'Ah, the mutual aid society.'"[22]

The committee found the contributions and services to be "substantially linked" through an "impermissible pattern of conduct," but they stopped short of finding "corrupt intent" (U.S. Senate 1991b, 36). Why did the committee decline to find corruption here? The connection, it would seem, could hardly have been closer. For that matter, we might also wonder why the committee did not find the pattern impermissible in the case of Riegle and DeConcini. Part of the answer probably is that "corrupt intent" is the language of the bribery statutes, and the committee did not dare suggest that campaign contributions could be bribes. The line between contributions and bribes must be kept bright.

But is the line so bright? "Almost a hair's line difference" separates bribes and contributions, Russell Long once testified (Noonan 1984, 801). Courts have not been able to provide a principled way of distinguishing the two.[23] There is, furthermore, no good reason to believe that connections between contributions and benefits that are proximate and explicit are any more corrupt than connections that are indirect and implicit. The former may be only the more detectable form of corruption – not necessarily the more deliberate or damaging.

Are we driven, then, to accept the conclusion of the pervasive corruption theory that virtually all contributions are corrupt? This theory is right to insist that corruption should be viewed in the context of the political system, that it can work through patterns of conduct, institutional routines, and informal norms. But the theory does not encourage the distinctions that are necessary in the kind of politics we actually have and are likely to have in the foreseeable future. It treats, for example, the explicit, proximate bribe as categorically equivalent to the routine thousand-dollar campaign contribution to one's longtime party favorite.

Both the competitive politics and pervasive corruption theories assume the criterion of the corrupt connection to be the actual motives of the citizens and politicians. This assumption is mistaken because it ignores an important structural feature of representative government. Any electorally based representative system permits – indeed, requires – representatives to act on mixed motives. They act for the benefit of particular constituents, for the good of the whole district or state, for the good of the nation, and for their own interest in reelection or future political ambitions. Some of these motives may be more admirable than others, but none is illegitimate in itself, and all are necessary in some measure in our system.

Under the circumstances of mixed motives, it is hard enough for any official, however conscientious, to separate proper from improper motives and, more generally, to find the right balance of motives in making any particular decision (see Douglas 1952, 44, 85–92). It is harder still for citizens – even well-informed and nonpartisan ones – to judge at a distance whether the official has really found that balance. In the design of a representative system or in the practice of judging representatives, we cannot in general count on being able to evaluate motives in individual cases.

What we need, instead, is a standard that assesses an individual official's action in the context of the system as whole. The standard should identify systematic tendencies that we know from past experience are likely to lead to corruption. It would then refer to the motives on which any official in the circumstances may be presumed to act, instead of the motives on which a particular official actually acts. It is this kind of logic that underlies the so-called appearance standard, at least when properly interpreted.

In a plethora of codes, rules, and statutes that regulate the ethics of government, public officials are now enjoined to avoid the appearance of impropriety (U.S. Senate 1991b, *Additional Views*, 14–16). The term appearance is unfortunate, however, as it encourages misinterpretations of the standard.[24] The mere appearance of an ethical wrong is contrasted with a real wrong, and the violation of the appearance standard is taken to be a minor, lesser offense, a sort of pale reflection of the real offense. The standard then comes to be regarded as merely prudential, a piece of political advice, which, if not followed, is seen as grounds for a charge of mistaken judgment, rather than an ethical wrong. The Ethics Committee found that DeConcini and Riegle, whom they charged with creating an appearance of impropriety, showed only "insensitivity and poor judgment" (U.S. Senate 1991b, 17, 19).

Properly interpreted, the appearance standard identifies a distinct wrong, quite independent of – and potentially no less serious than – the wrong of which it is an appearance. The standard would be more appropriately called a "tendency" standard because it presumes that under certain conditions the connection between a contribution and a benefit tends to be improper. The standard seeks, first, to reduce the occasions on which the connection is improper in the conventional sense. These are the occasions on which the provision of the benefit is actually motivated primarily by the contribution.

The second, more distinctive, aim of the standard is to decrease the occasions on which the connection is reasonably perceived to be improper. This perception is grounded on our general knowledge of the conditions that tend to produce actual improper connections. But the wrong is based on a different kind of moral failure. When an official accepts large contributions from interested individuals under certain conditions, whether or not the official's judgment is actually influenced, citizens are morally justified in believing the official's judgment has been so influenced and in acting on that belief themselves. The official is guilty of failing to take into account the reasonable reactions of citizens.[25]

The justification for this kind of standard should be distinguished from the type of argument (common in discussions of rule utilitarianism) that justifies particular acts by appeals to general rules or policies. In the rule utilitarian argument, an overly broad rule is justified by showing that the costs of deciding each case are greater than the costs of wrongly deciding some cases. The argument for the appearance standard differs in two respects. First, it counts as a cost not simply the risk that a case might be wrongly decided but also the likelihood that the public will perceive the case to have been wrongly decided. Public confidence could be undermined, and misconduct by others encouraged, even if a case were rightly decided but were not perceived to have been so decided. Second, the rationale for the appearance standard rests in part on a publicity principle, which holds that the reasons on which public officials may be presumed to act should be accessible to citizens. Appearances, then, are in these ways valuable beyond their role as evidence for corrupt motives.

Because appearances are often the only window that citizens have on official conduct, rejecting the appearance standard is tantamount to denying democratic accountability. This was dramatically demonstrated in the objections frequently raised during the hearings by several of the senators and their attorneys. Cranston, most notably, kept objecting to the idea that his conduct should be judged by how it appears to a reasonable person. That is a "mythical person," he said. The only real person who can judge is the senator himself. "You were not there. *I* was there. And I know that what I knew at the time convinced me that my [actions] were appropriate" (U.S. Senate 1991a, pt. 1, November 16, 1990, 121–2).

The appearance standard does not itself identify the kinds of conditions that would warrant a conclusion of mediated corruption. But

it points in the right direction – away from actual motives to presumed motives and objective intentions and to the tendencies or conditions that create corrupt connections in democratic systems. We
still need some basis on which to distinguish corrupt from noncor-
rupt contributions.

We can begin to see the basis for such a distinction in the common
reaction that there was something peculiar about Keating's lavishing
support on senators whose political views he so strongly opposed.
Keating and Cranston were an odd couple: an arch-conservative
Arizona businessman devoted to the free market and opposed to
pornography and abortion teamed up with one of the leading liberals in the Senate, a former candidate for president who had called
for a nuclear freeze and higher social spending. The two differed even
on government policy toward the financial services industry.

This ideological incongruence is significant not because it exposes
cynical or self-interested motives but because it reveals apolitical practices. Specifically, it identifies a type of contribution that serves no
public political function. A contribution given without regard to the
political positions of the candidate only incidentally provides political
support. Its aim is primarily to influence the candidate when in office.
In its pure form, it has no function other than to translate the desires
of a contributor directly into governmental action. In effect, it short-
circuits the democratic process. Contrast this kind of contribution
with one given to support a candidate with whom one shares a general political orientation or agrees on issues that one thinks salient.[26]
A contribution of this kind directly serves a political function: its aim
is to help a candidate get elected, and it works through the political process.[27] Rather than bypassing the process, the contribution
animates it.

Neither the pervasive corruption nor the competitive politics view
can easily distinguish these types of contributions (though the competitive politics view could recognize an analogous distinction between contributions that further the competitive process and those
that do not). The basis of the distinction is the principle that citizens
should influence their representatives – and representatives should
influence policy – only in ways that can be contested through public
discussion in a democratic political process. This principle is consistent with a wide range of conceptions of representation. The problem
with the first kind of contribution – the Keating type – is not that it
turns representatives into agents of individual constituents but that
it makes them apolitical agents. The objection is not only that the

contributions come with strings attached but also (even more insidiously) that the strings have no political substance.[28]

Ideological incongruence – common enough in the current regime of campaign finance as big contributors hedge their electoral bets – is not itself a necessary or sufficient condition of corruption. Neither does its absence make an otherwise questionable practice acceptable. However, its presence is a strong indication in any particular case that corruption may also be present. More generally, the phenomenon reveals the need for a more comprehensive criterion for identifying corrupt connections.

The connection between contributions and benefits is corrupt if it bypasses the democratic process. The corruption here is twofold. It consists, first, in the actual and presumed tendency of certain kinds of contributions to influence the actions of representatives without regard to the substantive merits of issues. This is the corruption of the representative's judgment. The corruption also shows itself in broader effects on the democratic process – in the actual and presumed tendency of the contributions to undermine political competition and deliberation. This is the corruption of the representative system.

There are, of course, many different ways in which contributions might be regarded as undermining the democratic process; which ways we build into the concept of corruption will depend on what conceptions of democracy we accept. The principles of legislative ethics invoked earlier to assess forms of constituency service could be used again here to generate some criteria for identifying corrupt connections. We could then hold that a connection is more likely to be corrupt (1) the more particular the aim of the contributor; (2) the less closely connected the contribution is to the merits of conduct it is intended to influence; and (3) the less accessible the exchange is to publicity. Each of these criteria would have to be specified more fully and translated into enforceable standards before we could conclude that we have a satisfactory test for the corrupt connection in mediated corruption.[29] But it should already be clear that the criteria presuppose an approach that makes the relationship to democratic processes more fundamental than do conventional approaches to corruption.

CONCLUSION

Mediated corruption is not new, but it is newly prospering. It thrives in the world of large, multinational financial institutions that increasingly interact, in closed and complex ways, with governments. Many of the major governmental scandals in recent years have involved a large measure of mediated corruption – the affairs involving Iran-Contra, Housing and Urban Development (under Samuel Pierce), the Bank of Credit and Commerce International, and the Banca Nazionale del Lavoro's Atlanta branch, among others. Where private greed mixes easily with the public good, where the difference between serving citizens and serving supporters blurs, where secret funds lubricate the schemes of public officials, there mediated corruption is likely to flourish.

We can better understand the cunning ways of this growing form of corruption if we keep in mind its distinctive characteristics. The concept of mediated corruption serves this purpose. Each of its three elements differs from those of conventional corruption, the kind assumed by the competitive politics and pervasive corruption theories.

First, in mediated corruption a public official typically receives a political gain. But, as the pervasive corruption mistakenly denies and the competitive politics theory rightly implies, there is nothing wrong with this gain itself. Mediated corruption, furthermore, does not require that the public official personally gain or otherwise serve a narrow self-interest, as conventional corruption typically assumes. The gain contributes to mediated corruption insofar as it damages the democratic process – for example, by influencing a representative to serve private purposes without regard to their substantive merits.

Second, the public official provides a benefit, typically as an intermediary attempting to influence other officials to serve a constituent's private ends.[30] Contrary to both the competitive politics and the pervasive corruption views, the benefit itself may be deserved and may even be something that the official would provide for any constituent. But if the way in which the official provides the benefit damages the democratic process, it still counts as a contribution to the corruption. The way in which the member presses the constituent's claim, not simply the justice of the claim, is relevant to the assessment of the corruption.

Third, the connection between the gain and the benefit is corrupt if it would lead a reasonable citizen to believe that an exchange has taken place that damages the democratic process in specified ways (typically in ways that bypass the process). Mediated corruption thus adds an appearance standard to the corrupt-motive test of conventional corruption. It goes further, and, like the pervasive corruption theory, relates the corruption in any particular case to corruption of the system as a whole. But the standards for determining whether the connection is corrupt are more fine-grained than that theory allows. They permit some connections that might otherwise seem corrupt (for example, money is not necessarily corrupting) and condemn some connections that otherwise seem legitimate (money can be corrupting independently of the inequalities it perpetuates). The standards ultimately depend on what kind of democratic process we wish to maintain.

The concept of mediated corruption is consistent with a wide range of theories of democracy but is probably best justified from the perspective of a theory that prescribes that officials act on considerations of moral principle, rather than only on calculations of political power. This is sometimes called the deliberative conception of democracy.[31] As we have seen, mediated corruption characteristically attempts to translate private interest directly into public policy, bypassing the democratic processes of political discussion and competition. It thereby blocks citizens from considering the substantive reasons for and against a policy. Mediated corruption also prevents deliberately adopting a policy even without considering substantive reasons: it precludes deliberation about whether to deliberate.

If we accept the concept of mediated corruption (as a supplement to the concept of conventional corruption), at least three implications follow. First, cases like the Keating Five would look different in the future. It would be easier to justify making finer distinctions of kind and degree in judging misconduct. The kind of conduct in which McCain and Glenn engaged, for example, would be more clearly distinguishable from that of the other three; and the kind of conduct in which all five engaged would be more clearly set apart from that of most other senators. More generally, we would hear less talk of motives (whether honest or rationalized), fewer appeals to constituent service (as if it excused all sins), and fewer attacks on the appearance standard. We would see more concern about the mixing of private profit and public service, more attention to the merits of constituents' claims, and more worry about the effects of practices of individual representatives on the broader process of democratic representation. This shift of attention from the individual to the system (or, more precisely, to the effects of individual behavior on the system) would require not only new ways of thinking but also new standards of ethics.

The practical change most emphasized by the committee and most often mentioned by observers is campaign finance reform. Reducing the importance of money in campaigns (and politics more generally) is certainly desirable and could be seen as one of the implications of the concept of mediated corruption. But since the dominating role of money in politics is objectionable from the perspective of many different theories, it is worth emphasizing an implication that points toward a different dimension of reform. The concept of mediated corruption helps bring out the fact that money is not the only important source of corruption. Some of the kinds of misconduct to which mediated corruption calls attention depend less on money than do the kinds condemned by conventional corruption. As far as public officials are concerned, mediated corruption works its wiles less through greed than through ambition and even a misplaced sense of duty. Even some quite radical campaign finance reforms would not completely eliminate some forms of mediated corruption. Recall that political action committees, the bêtes noires of many progressive reformers, played almost no role in the case of the Keating Five.

A second implication of adopting the concept of mediated corruption concerns the process by which charges of unethical conduct should be heard and decided. In the Keating Five case, the process was directed by the Senate Ethics Committee. Legislatures have traditionally insisted on exclusive authority to discipline their own members, and the ethics committees of both houses have in the past managed to bring some tough judgments against some of their colleagues. But these have almost always been in flagrant cases of wrongdoing, closer to clear violations of rules that resembled the criminal law. It is difficult enough for colleagues who have worked together for years and may have to work together again to bring themselves to judge one another harshly in these cases. It may be almost impossible in cases involving mediated corruption. The less the charge is like conventional corruption, the harder it is to reach a severe judgment. The members implicated in mediated corruption, showing no obvious signs of a guilty mind or especially selfish motives, are often seen as simply doing their job. Under such circumstances, the sympathy of colleagues is maximized, and their capacity for objectivity minimized.

Furthermore, the legislature is, in a sense, also judging itself – specifically, its own practices and procedures, through which the corruption is mediated. In these circumstances, we might reasonably wonder whether any body, including a legislative body, should be a judge in its own case. The clear implication of these considerations, suggested in part by the concept of mediated corruption, is that we should consider establishing an outside body to judge cases of ethics violations. To overcome possible constitutional objections, Congress could ultimately control the body. But it should be established so that it would have at least the independence and respect of an institution like the Congressional Budget Office.

The third implication is methodological in character and is perhaps the most significant for the study of corruption and democracy. The concept of mediated corruption has the potential to integrate the very different approaches to corruption that prevail in political theory and in social science. The difference was strikingly illustrated some years ago when the *American Political Science Review* published a pair of articles on corruption, one by a political theorist and one by two political scientists (Dobel 1978; Peters and Welch 1978). The editor perhaps intended to take a step toward unifying the discipline by putting the articles together in the same section. Yet the articles had little in common except the word "corruption" in their titles; the authors might as well have been writing about different subjects.

The political theorist faithfully followed his tradition, invoking Machiavelli, Rousseau, Montesequieu, and Madison (among others), and presented corruption as a characteristic of a political system as a whole. He saw it as a sickness of the body politic, a turning away from civic virtue toward private interests. It may afflict individual citizens and their rulers, but it can only be fully understood from the perspective of the whole society.[32] The political scientists described corruption in terms of transactions between individuals. The transactions, of course, take place within a system; and the system may be called corrupt when its structures and incentives encourage corruption. But the basic unit of analysis remains an exchange between individual officials and individual citizens.

Mediated corruption holds the promise of putting back together the structuralist and the individualist conceptions of corruption that these intellectual traditions have split apart. The integrating instrument is the idea of the democratic process. With mediated corruption, we cannot decide whether corruption exists, let alone how serious it is, without paying attention to its effects on the democratic process and therefore without making moral judgments about the kind of democratic process we wish to encourage. The concept of mediated corruption permits a conclusion that corruption is pervasive and the system needs radical reform; but the grounds of the conclusion, as well as the nature of the reform, would be guided by a conception of the democratic process. Mediated corruption also supports judgments about individuals competing within the existing system; these, too, are to be shaped by a view of the democratic process. We cannot assess either patterns of systematic corruption or instances of individual corruption without presupposing a theory of democracy.

Because the concept of mediated corruption is theory dependent in this way, we should not suppose that we can understand corruption without making value judgments about politics. In this respect, those social scientists who try to justify corruption in some societies as necessary to achieve certain political values (such as efficiency or social integration) are right about the structure of the argument required to assess corruption.[33] Whether certain kinds of conduct should count as corrupt depends in part on their net effects on the political system as a whole. However, in making their calculations, these social scientists tend to give too much weight to outcome values relative to process values, a mistake that an approach using the concept of mediated corruption avoids.

The social scientists who find corruption functional also tend to assume that their methods are objective and realistic while the methods of those who criticize corruption are subjective and moralistic. But even if we were to accept certain kinds of corruption as functional, we would still be making a moral judgment. As this search for the meaning of corruption in the case of the Keating Five should make clear, on the subject of corruption we are all moralists. The only question is what kind of moralists we want to be. Unlike the Keating Five, their apologists, and even most of their critics, we should try to be democratic moralists.

Notes

During part of the investigation and hearings in this case, I served as a consultant to the special counsel to the Senate Ethics Committee, Robert S. Bennett. I am grateful to him and members of his staff, especially Benjamin Klubes, for helpful advice and convenient access to public documents. I have also learned from discussion with Senator Cranston's attorney, William W. Taylor III (although, he may believe, not enough). I have benefited from valuable comments on various versions of this article from Ted Aaberg, Arthur Applbaum, Charles Beitz, Morris Fiorina, Charles Fried, Amy Gutmann, Sanford Levinson, Thomas Scanlon, Judith Shklar, Alan Wertheimer, David Wilkins, and Kenneth Winston. An earlier version of this article was presented at Princeton University under the auspices of the University Center for Human Values.

1. Berke 1991. Although other factors no doubt contributed to the low public regard for Congress in this period, the percentage of respondents who rated the honesty and ethical standards of senators "very high" or "high" declined by five points between 1990 and 1991; and the rating of Congress itself fell to an all-time low (Hugick 1991; Hugick and Hueber 1991). Other surveys found that a majority of respondents believed that at least half the members of Congress are "corrupt" and that the institution itself is "corrupt" (CBS News/*New York Times* 1991; NBC News/*Wall Street Journal* 1992). The latter survey found that of the "scandals and controversies that have taken place during the past few years in Washington," the handling of problems with the savings and loan industry "most bothered" more respondents.

2. This general concept is meant to be consistent with a wide variety of definitions in the social science literature. However, further specification of the concept beyond this level of generality remains controversial (mostly with regard to what should count as "improper"). It should also be noted that in some forms of conventional corruption, the "public official" and "private citizen" may be the same person. For a review of various approaches, see Heidenheimer, Johnston, and LeVine 1989, 7–14; Peters and Welch 1978, 974–8.

3. The most influential explanation of reflective equilibrium is Rawls 1971, 48–51. A more recent systematic account is Richardson 1990.

4. No one is likely to mistake this summary for authoritative history. It is intended to serve only as a simplified reminder of some of the highlights of the case. The summary (as well as subsequent comments about the case) relies primarily on the evidence presented during the hearings and in the reports of the special counsel and the Ethics Committee. See U.S. Senate, Select Committee on Ethics 1991a, 1991b. Two readable accounts of the affair, including some useful background material, are Adams 1990, pt. 4; Pizzo, Fricker and Moulo 1989, 263–97.

5. Keating acted often as a broker for others, sometimes as a "bundler," taking "the separate individual contributions and bundling them together . . . claiming credit for the harvest" (Sorauf 1992, 54). This is yet another way in which the corruption in this case could be regarded as mediated.

6. Examples of this interpretation, typical of many public comments on the affair, are Yoder 1991 and testimony by Senator Daniel Inouye (U.S. Senate, Select Committee on Ethics 1991a, pt. 3, December 3, 1990, 2–50). Similar views can be found in court opinions and in more general discussions of campaign reform (for example, *McCormick v. U.S.* 1991, 1825; Gottlieb 1989). The competitive politics view is also consistent with a number of well-known analyses of corruption (for example, Banfield 1975; Wilson 1974, 29–38). Although the view might be supported by various democratic theories, the version of pluralist theory (sometimes called the competitive theory of democracy) is its most natural ally. The classic statements are those of Schumpeter 1962, and Downs 1957.

7. Typical examples of this interpretation from public comment on the case are Abramson and Rogers 1991, Etzioni 1990/91, and Wilkinson 1991. Also see the affidavit of Senator Ernest Hollings (U.S. Senate, Select Committee on

Ethics 1991a, Exhibits of Senator DeConcini, 493–5). In the literature on campaign reform and political corruption more generally, the interpretation would find support in several different analyses (for example, Etzioni 1984; Lowenstein 1985, 826–8; Lowenstein 1989, 301–35; Noonan 1984, 621–51). For discussions of democratic theory that could be used to support this view, see Cohen and Rogers 1983; Dahl 1989, ch. 9; Lindblom 1977, pt. 5.

8. This conclusion is evidently widely accepted by the public. Asked in an NBC/*Wall Street Journal* poll whether they thought that the ethical violations of which the Keating Five were accused are "typical" of the behavior of Senators and members of Congress, 71 percent of the respondents agreed that they were; 19 percent disagreed.

9. The conventional wisdom that higher turnout helps the Democrats has been challenged. See DeNardo 1980; and Tucker, Vedlitz, and DeNardo 1986.

10. Compare Madison's observation in *Federalist* 51: "Ambition must be made to counteract ambition ... This policy of supplying, by opposite and rival interests, the defect of better motives, might be traced through the whole system of human affairs" (Hamilton, Madison, and Jay 1961, 349).

11. A pioneering work that exemplifies both the strengths and weaknesses of this approach is Rose-Ackerman 1978, 6–10.

12. A variation on this hypothetical example actually took place. According to the testimony of James Grogan, a Keating aide, Senator DeConcini's wife at times solicited contributions from Keating for her favorite charities in the community (U.S. Senate, Select Committe on Ethics 1991a, pt. 4, December 14, 1990, 248–9).

13. U.S. Senate, Select Committee on Ethics 1991b, 14–16; 1991a, pt. 1, November 16, 1990, 126–32 and November 19, 1990, 91–2.

14. U.S. Senate, Select Committee on Ethics 1991a, pt. 1, November 16, 1990, 111, and November 19, 1990, 23.

15. Ibid., pt. 4, December 10, 1990, 58–94.

16. Lobbying the Defense Department to support Apache helicopters, asking the Customs Service for an exception to trade restrictions, questioning the Justice Department about a potential indictment of a shipyard company (U.S. Senate, Select Committee on Ethics 1991a, pt. 1, November 19, 1990, 14–17; pt. 4, December 10, 1990, 9–12; pt. 6, January 10, 1991, 137–40) – these examples and all the others paraded before the committee lacked some critical feature of the Keating case. None involved pressure on independent regulators to give special treatment to a particular company in a quasi-adjudicatory process; and in none did the intervention continue after the member could reasonably have been expected to know that company's intentions were questionable, if not illegal.

17. Admittedly, the three senators not from Arizona could claim that they were acting for the constituents in their own states who would benefit from Keating's businesses. But this ceases to be constituent service and should, like legislative activity, be evaluated from a broader perspective that takes into account all of a representative's constituents. From this perspective, the benefits that these senators were providing to some of their constituents arguably did not serve most others well, specifically taxpayers and depositors.

18. Relying on constituents to call attention to administrative abuses (what has been called "fire alarm" oversight) is said to be more common and more

efficient than direct and continuous monitoring by Congress, called "police patrol" oversight (McCubbins and Schwartz 1984). But on the limitations of this and other forms of retrospective monitoring, see McCubbins, Noll, and Weingast 1987.

19. Cf. Kappel 1989; Rosenberg and Maskell 1990.

20. Consider the standards practiced in Cranston's office, as described in the testimony of his aide, Carolyn Jordan: "Unless you have a complete kook . . . the number one rule of this game is you never kiss a constituent off. That's the rule in our office. And you never tell them, no, unless they're asking you to do something that is just so far from the beaten path" (U.S. Senate, Select Committee on Ethics 1991b, *Additional Views*, 84).

21. Many of the opinions in the line of cases interpreting the Administrative Procedures Act (*Pillsbury* and its progeny) are especially critical of secret congressional interventions, even when the courts do not invalidate the agency results. See Kappel 1989, 144–7.

22. U.S. Senate, Select Committee on Ethics 1991a, pt. 4, December 14, 1990, 178.

23. Generally, see Lowenstein 1985, 808–9, esp. nn. 86, 87; Noonan 1984, 621–51, 687–90, 696–7. See also the opinions of Justices Brennan and White in *U.S. v. Brewster* 1977, 558. In the most recent case dealing with public corruption, the best that the Supreme Court could do to justify sustaining a narrow standard requiring explicit promises was to say that a broader standard would "open to prosecution . . . conduct that in a very real sense is unavoidable so long as election campaigns are financed by private contributions or expenditures, as they have been from the beginning of the nation" (*McCormick v. U.S.* 1991, 1816).

24. The small academic literature on the subject has tended to be critical of the standard (Morgan 1992; Roberts 1985, 177–89; but see also Kappel 1989, 154–71). A helpful (and rare) discussion of the appearance standard by a contemporary philosopher is Driver 1992.

25. The potential effect on the conduct of others is the principal reason that Thomist ethics has traditionally treated appearing to do wrong under certain conditions as a distinct wrong. The wrong is called "giving scandal" and is defined as providing the "occasion for another's fall." It is considered a sin if one's otherwise permissible action is of the kind that is in itself conducive to sin, and it remains sinful whether or not one intends it to have any effect on others (Aquinas 1972, vol. 35, 109–37).

26. Some further specification of what should count as a general political orientation or a salient issue may be necessary in some circumstances, but it should be clear that agreement on the value of constituent service itself (the principle on which Keating and the Keating Five evidently most strongly agreed) is not sufficient. Constituent service, as has been suggested, may itself undermine the democratic process. Furthermore, in this case it seems plausible to conclude on the basis of his actions that Keating was less interested in constituent service justified as a general practice for all citizens than in the specific services provided for one constituent.

27. Lowenstein proposes a similar distinction between contributions "intended to influence official conduct and accepted with the knowledge that they are so intended" and those "intended solely to help the candidate get elected"

(1985, 847). The distinction drawn in the text differs in at least two respects: (1) it takes the function, rather than actual intentions, as the criterion; and (2) it treats elections as only one of the relevant parts of the political process. Noonan also distinguishes contributions from bribes (1984, 696–7); but the two characteristics he regards as critical – size and secrecy – are better interpreted as indicators of the more basic distinction made in the text. If a contribution is small relative not to the total contributions but to other contributions a candidate receives and if it is public (or if the pattern of which it is a part is made public), then the contribution could be more plausibly seen as support for the candidate, rather than an attempt to influence official conduct.

28. This may be part of the rationale underlying the Supreme Court decision upholding a law that places limits on the ability of corporations to make independent expenditures on behalf of political candidates (*Austin v. Michigan Chamber of Commerce* 1990). Wealth accumulated by a corporation has "little or no correlation to the public's support for the corporation's political ideas" and therefore has "corrosive and distorting" effects on the political process (p. 1397). The idea is presumably that though the corporation is using the money to express substantive political views, the corporation's ability to do so does not derive from any substantive political support; its economic success ought not be translated so directly into political influence. See also Taylor 1991 and, more generally, Stark 1992.

29. An example of such a standard – already followed by some members – would be a rule requiring separation of the fundraising from other functions in the offices of members (see U.S. Senate, Select Committee on Ethics 1991b, *Additional Views*, 102).

30. A public official may act more directly than did the senators in this case. For example, when inserting a tax break for a particular company or individual in legislation, a member is more plausibly regarded as the direct agent than is the Internal Revenue Service. However, the corruption may still count as largely mediated because the other elements of corruption (the gain and the gain-benefit connection) continue to be mediated through the political process.

31. See Cohen 1989, 17–34; Larmore 1987, esp. 59–66; Manin 1987. For a valuable analysis of the relation of deliberation specifically to problems of political finance, see Beitz 1989, 192–213.

32. Montesquieu, who among traditional political theorists most explicitly discusses corruption in branches of government, writes that a state will "perish when its legislative power becomes more corrupt than its executive" (1949–51, vol. 2, 407). More generally, see his "Corruption of Principle in the Three Governments" (vol. 2, 349–66).

33. For criticisms and further citations to the "functionalist" literature, see Rose-Ackerman 1978, 88–92; see also Friedrich 1972, pt. 3.

References

Abramson, Jill, and David Rogers. 1991. "The Keating 535: Five Are on the Grill, but Other Lawmakers Help Big Donors, Too." *Wall Street Journal* (January 10).

Adams, James Ring. 1990. *The Big Fix: Inside the S&L Scandal.* New York: Wiley.

Aquinas, Thomas. 1972. *Summa Theologiae.* New York: McGraw-Hill.

Austin v. Michigan Chamber of Commerce. 1990. 110 S. Ct. 1391.

Banfield, Edward C. 1975. "Corruption as a Feature of Governmental Organization." *Journal of Law and Economics* 18: 587–605.

Beitz, Charles R. 1989. *Political Equality: An Essay in Democratic Theory.* Princeton, NJ: Princeton University Press.

Berke, Richard L. 1991. "Cranston Rebuked by Ethics Panel." *New York Times* (November 21).

Cain, Bruce, John Ferejohn, and Morris Fiorina. 1987. *The Personal Vote: Constituency Service and Electoral Independence.* Cambridge, Mass.: Harvard University Press.

CBS News/*New York Times.* 1991. Telephone interview, National sample of 1280 adults, October 5–7. (Roper Center for Public Opinion Research, University of Connecticut).

Cohen, Joshua. 1989. "Deliberation and Democratic Legitimacy." In *The Good Polity,* ed. Alan Hamlin and Philip Pettit. Oxford: Basil Blackwell.

Cohen, Joshua, and Joel Rogers. 1983. *On Democracy.* New York: Penguin.

Dahl, Robert A. 1989. *Democracy and Its Critics.* New Haven, Conn.: Yale University Press.

DeNardo, James. 1980. "Turnout and the Vote: The Joke's on the Democrats." *American Political Science Review* 74: 406–20.

Dobel, J. Patrick. 1978. "The Corruption of a State." *American Political Science Review* 72: 958–73.

Douglas, Paul. 1952. *Ethics in Government.* Cambridge, Mass.: Harvard University Press.

Downs, Anthony. 1957. *An Economic Theory of Democracy.* New York: Harper & Row.

Driver, Julia. 1992. "Caesar's Wife: On the Moral Significance of Appearing Good." *Journal of Philosophy* 89: 331–43.

Etzioni, Amitai. 1984. *Capital Corruption.* New York: Harcourt Brace Jovanovich.

––––––. 1990/91. "The Keating Six?" *Responsive Community* 1: 6–9.

Fenno, Richard. 1978. *Home Style: House Members in Their Districts.* Boston: Little, Brown.

Friedrich, Carl J. 1972. *The Pathology of Politics.* New York: Harper & Row.

Gottlieb, Stephen. 1989. "The Dilemma of Election Campaign Finance Reform." *Hofstra Law Review* 18: 213–300.

Hamilton, Alexander, James Madison, and John Jay. 1961. *The Federalist Papers,* edited by Jacob E. Cooke. Middletown, CT: Wesleyan University Press.

Heidenheimer, Arnold, Michael Johnston, and Victor T. LeVine, eds. 1989. *Political Corruption: A Handbook.* 2d ed. New Brunswick: Transaction.

Hugick, Larry. 1991. "Majority Disapproves of Congress." *Gallup Poll Monthly* (August), 45–6.

Hugick, Larry, and Graham Hueber. 1991. "Pharmacists and Clergy Rate Highest for Honesty and Ethics." *Gallup Poll Monthly* (May): 29–31.

Kappel, Brett G. 1989. "Judicial Restrictions on Improper Congressional Influence in Administrative Decision-Making: A Defense of the Pillsbury Doctrine." *Journal of Law and Politics* 6: 135–71.

Larmore, Charles. 1987. *Patterns of Moral Complexity.* Cambridge: Cambridge University Press.

Lindblom, Charles. 1977. *Politics and Markets.* New York: Basic Books.

Lowenstein, Daniel H. 1985. "Political Bribery and the Intermediate Theory of Politics." *University of California Los Angeles Law Review* 32: 784–851.

————. 1989. "On Campaign Finance Reform: The Root of All Evil Is Deeply Rooted." *Hofstra Law Review* 18: 301–67.

McCormick v. U.S. 1991. Ill S.Ct. 1807.

McCubbins, Mathew D., Roger Noll, and Barry R. Weingast. 1987. "Administrative Procedures as Instruments of Political Control." *Journal of Law, Economics, and Organization* 3: 243–77.

McCubbins, Mathew D., and Thomas Schwartz. 1984. "Congressional Oversight Overlooked: Police Patrols Versus Fire Alarms." *American Journal of Political Science* 28: 165–79.

Manin, Bernard. 1987. "On Legitimacy and Political Deliberation." *Political Theory* 15: 338–68.

Montesquieu, Baron de. 1949–51. "De l'esprit des lois". In *Montesquieu: Oeuvres Completes*, edited by Roger Caillois. Paris: Gallimard.

Morgan, Peter W. 1992. "The Appearance of Propriety: Ethics Reform and the Blifil Paradoxes." *Stanford Law Review* 44: 593–621.

NBC News/ *Wall Street Journal.* 1990. Telephone interview, National sample of 1002 registered voters, December 8–11. (Roper Center for Public Opinion Research, University of Connecticut).

NBC News/ *Wall Street Journal.* 1992. Telephone interview, National sample of 1001 registered voters, April 11–14. (Roper Center for Public Opinion Research, University of Connecticut).

Noonan, John T., Jr. 1984. *Bribes.* Berkeley: University of California Press.

Peters, John G., and Susan Welch. 1978. "Political Corruption in America: A Search for Definitions and a Theory." *American Political Science Review* 72: 974–84.

Pizzo, Stephen, Mary Fricker, and Paul Moulo. 1989. *Inside Job: The Looting of America's Savings and Loans.* New York: McGraw-Hill.

Rawls, John. 1971. *A Theory of Justice.* Cambridge, Mass.: Harvard University Press.

Richardson, Henry S. 1990. "Specifying Norms as a Way To Resolve Concrete Ethical Problems." *Philosophy and Public Affairs* 19: 279–310.

Roberts, Robert N. 1985. "Lord, Protect Me from the Appearance of Wrongdoing." In *Public Personnel Policy*, edited by David H. Rosenbloom. Port Washington, NY: Associated Faculty.

Rose-Ackerman, Susan. 1978. *Corruption: A Study in Political Economy.* New York: Academic.

Rosenberg, Morton, and Jack Maskell. 1990. "Congressional Intervention in the Administrative Process: Legal and Ethical Considerations." Washington, DC: Congressional Research Service Report, 1–78.

Schumpeter, Joseph. 1962. *Capitalism, Socialism, and Democracy.* 3rd ed. New York: Harper.

Sorauf, Frank J. 1992. *Inside Campaign Finance: Myths and Realities.* New Haven: Yale University Press.

Stark, Andrew. 1992. "Corporate Electoral Activity, Constitutional Discourse, and Conceptions of the Individual. *American Political Science Review* 86: 626–37.

Taylor, Samuel M. 1991. "*Austin v. Michigan Chamber of Commerce.* Addressing a 'New Corruption' in Campaign Financing." *North Carolina Law Review* 69: 1060–79.

Thompson, Dennis F. 1987. *Political Ethics and Public Office.* Cambridge, Mass.: Harvard University Press.

Tucker, Harvey J., Arnold Vedlitz, and James DeNardo. 1986. "Controversy: Does Heavy Turnout Help Democrats in Presidential Elections?" *American Political Science Review* 80: 1292–1304.

U.S. Senate, Select Committee on Ethics. 1991a. *Preliminary Inquiry into Allegations Regarding Senators Cranston, DeConcini, Glenn, McCain, and Riegle, and Lincoln Savings and Loan.* 101st Congress, 2d sess., 15 Nov. 1990 to 16 Jan. 1991.

U.S. Senate, Select Committee on Ethics. 1991b. *Investigation of Senator Alan Cranston Together with Additional Views.* 102d Congress, 1st sess., 20 Nov. 1991.

U.S. v. Brewster. 1977. 408 U.S. 521.

Wilkinson, Francis. 1991. "Rules of the Game: The Senate's Money Politics." *Rolling Stone* (August 8).

Wilson, James Q. 1974. "Corruption Is Not Always Scandalous." In *Theft of the City,* edited by John A. Gardiner and David J. Olson. Bloomington: Indiana University Press.

Yoder, Edwin M., Jr. 1991. "The Keating Five: Was It All in a Day's Work?" *Washington Post* (January 18).

8

Election Time

An election marks a moment of politics – a discontinuous phase in a continuous process. The electoral moment can be specified by three temporal properties: periodicity (the intervals at which citizens vote); simultaneity (the range of time in which citizens vote); and finality (the extent to which the result of their votes is conclusive until the next election). The temporal properties are so familiar that they are usually taken for granted, but the way they structure the electoral process has significant theoretical and practical implications that have not been sufficiently appreciated.

The temporal properties are grounded in basic values shared by most conceptions of democracy. All three support popular sovereignty – the capacity of majorities to control government – in different but related ways. Because elections take place periodically, current majorities can overcome the dead hand of past majorities. To the extent that voting takes place simultaneously, elections express the will of a determinate majority rather than the preferences of a series of different majorities. Because elections produce final results, they legitimate the authority of a current majority until the next election. Other democratic values, such as fairness and civic engagement, are also strengthened to the extent that the electoral process realizes these temporal properties.

The temporal properties come in different combinations and take on different values in different systems. In the United States, citizens vote at regular intervals (more regular than in parliamentary systems), mostly all on the same day for any given election, and with conclusive results that are not normally reversible until the next election. This particular combination of temporal properties creates the distinctive rhythm of election time in the United States. But because electoral practice in the United States does not consistently follow this rhythm, it produces anomalies that undermine the democratic values that the temporal properties support. By examining three of those anomalies (each corresponding to one of the temporal properties), we can see more clearly the significance of election time, and the implications of taking its properties seriously.

The first anomaly concerns the process for drawing electoral districts. Elections are supposed to choose representatives; yet representatives or their colleagues control the drawing of the electoral districts and thereby decide who the representatives will represent. The second anomaly refers to the way that voting is scheduled. Elections are held on one day so that citizens can vote more or less at the same time with access to the same information; yet television networks call elections before the polls have closed, citizens in some states vote many days earlier, and state legislatures have the power to choose presidential electors after they see how other states have voted. A third anomaly involves the division between electoral and other periods of political activity. Electoral politics are more strictly regulated than other kinds; yet the demand for freedom from regulation in campaigns is no less great than in ordinary politics.

These anomalies have not escaped critical notice, but the conventional criticisms do not recognize that the anomalies arise from the same source, and therefore do not identify the fundamental error that produces them. What the anomalies have in common is that they all result from failing to appreciate the special character of election time. If we take the temporal properties seriously, we can see more clearly how the anomalies should be resolved. For each anomaly, we should accept its first claim (which respects the temporal property), and reject its second claim (which undermines the property). An analysis based on temporal properties provides a more cogent basis for eliminating the anomalies than do conventional approaches.

PERIODICITY: WHY REPRESENTATIVES SHOULD NOT CONTROL THE UNITS OF REPRESENTATION

In most states in the United States, the legislature still has the dominant role in the contentious process of redrawing electoral districts to reflect shifts in population since the previous census. Even in most of those states that have a redistricting commission, political parties choose at least some of its members.[1] Typically, districts are drawn to protect the party in power and the seats of incumbents. The party fortunate enough to control the state legislature thus controls the redistricting. Less directly but usually no less effectively, parties in each state govern the process that draws the Congressional districts.

On its face, this practice seems objectionably undemocratic. It undermines popular control by giving the representatives who are to be controlled significant influence over the means by which they are controlled. The representatives or their party colleagues create the districts, and therefore define the electorate. They determine the set of citizens who are to be represented and who are to judge the performance of the representatives. The process appears not to be one "in which the people select their representatives," but one in which "the representatives have selected the people."[2]

The problem could be avoided, or at least mitigated, by adopting a different electoral system. For example, district boundaries would be much less important in a system of multimember districts, which could be much larger than current districts. A multimember district would also permit the use of cumulative voting. Because in this system each citizen may cast as many votes as there are seats to be filled, the district would not be as likely to be dominated by one party. More radical reforms would abolish districts altogether and elect representatives by statewide or national forms of proportional representation. In many of these systems, voters in effect form their own districts, and each representative has a unanimous constituency. The various systems have comparative advantages and disadvantages.[3] Yet none has been adopted on the national level in the United States, and in most of its jurisdictions the winner-take-all district systems are likely to continue to prevail. As long as districts exist in their current form, they will need to be redrawn periodically.

The current practice of granting redistricting authority to legislators has frequently been criticized, but none of the usual arguments against it is entirely satisfactory. First, it is claimed that redistricting should not be subject to a political process at all because the standards of a fair electoral process are objective. They express a form of perfect procedural justice, rather than pure procedural justice. The districts should match the population within certain limits, allowing for some variation to existing political jurisdictions. As far as possible, districts should respect the constitutional standard of "one person, one vote."

But this standard is not very helpful in making the hard choices involved in redistricting. Strictly interpreted as requiring every vote to count equally, it would prohibit patterns that give any category of voter more weight than any other; only a random distribution would be acceptable. Even in random redistricting, votes would not be weighted equally for most categories because people do not distribute themselves randomly among districts. Interpreted more permissively, as it has been in practice, the standard allows officials to take into account some of the factors that have traditionally determined the boundaries of districts – such as geographical features, historical communities, partisan advantage, and even incumbency protection. Armed with powerful computer technology scarcely imagined at the time the standard was proposed, politicians can now create equal districts that give more weight to any of a wide range of different categories.

Redistricting therefore involves making choices among a complex set of values. There is no objective or neutral standard that can determine these choices. Choosing is an unavoidably political process. The criteria adopted by Arizona (Constitution, art. IV, pt. 2, § 1[14]) are typical of those found in many other states: equal population, compactness, contiguity, community of interest, geographical saliency. Plainly, the criteria can yield conflicting results, and choosing among them requires deciding which should weigh more or less heavily. Interpreting and applying the criteria, as well as making the other choices between the various goals we have canvassed, calls for political judgment (Butler and Cain 1992). As long as minority rights are not violated, the political process – specifically the legislature – would seem to be the appropriate place to decide these inherently political questions. The argument from objectivity or neutrality thus does not support the case against legislative control of redistricting.

A second argument appeals to the importance of competition. Letting legislatures control redistricting, it is said, is likely to reduce the competition necessary for a healthy democratic system.[4] Competition requires that voters have real alternatives. Partisan balance may shift from election to election, and in some states and the nation as a whole the division between the parties may be close. The 2002 midterm congressional election was in that respect highly competitive. Even in safe districts competition in primaries can be keen. But the choice that most voters face is in the race in the general election in their own districts. That is the competition that matters most for their voting decision.

In most states, citizens can vote only for the candidates in their own party primary. In most districts, incumbents almost always win, and by large margins. One of the most striking patterns in contemporary legislative politics in the United States is the high rates of reelection of incumbents not only in Congress but also in state legislatures (Ferejohn 1977; Gelman and King 1990; Cox and Katz 1996; Ansolabehere and Snyder 2002a; and Center for Voting and Democracy 2002). The high rates of reelection may indicate that most voters are satisfied with their incumbents, or that incumbents have an unfair advantage from the resources of office, or simply that incumbents and strong challengers do not run when they expect to lose.[5] Even if legislative control of redistricting is not the principal cause of the lack of competition, continuing to give the most power over the redistricting process to incumbents or to the currently dominant party would not seem to be the most effective way to encourage more of it.

Although more competition may be desirable in most district elections in the United States, the case against legislative control over redistricting cannot rest mainly on this goal. In the first place, electoral competition is not an end in itself, but a means of allowing change that voters may want. It may also be a necessary means of discovering whether voters want change, or helping them recognize that they want it. But even as an instrumental goal, electoral competition can be misleading if it is conceived, as it usually is, on the model of economic competition.[6] It neglects forms of contestation that do not readily fit within the categories assumed by market analogies. It gives more attention to the interplay of interests and preferences than to the interaction of principles and ideas. Furthermore, the preoccupation with making electoral contests more competitive distracts attention from other equally worthy goals, such as recruiting and retaining better-qualified candidates and controlling the growth of the cost of campaigning. More generally, concentrating too much on promoting competition may distract citizens and legislators from attending to the business of government. The goal should be to find the optimal level of competition, not to maximize it.

In the second place, although there is still some dispute about the explanation of the high rates of incumbent reelection, there is little evidence that partisan control of redistricting is the main cause (Persily 2002). States that have redistricted do not consistently have higher rates of reelection than states that have not. Incumbents also tend to be reelected in elections that have no districts (such as gubernatorial and senatorial races). Furthermore, politicians usually produce plans with districts that are more competitive than those that existed prior to redistricting. More precisely, redistricting tends to increase responsiveness (the degree to which the partisan composition of the legislature responds to changes in voter partisan preferences), and to reduce partisan bias (the degree to which an electoral system favors one political party in the conversion of the total vote into the partisan division in the legislature).[7] Two factors seem to account for this unexpected result: parties have multiple and conflicting goals (protecting the party may require sacrificing incumbents), and the electoral effects of any redistricting plan are more uncertain than is often assumed.

A third argument against legislative control of redistricting comes closer to capturing its fundamental problem. Giving politicians or their partisan colleagues control of their own means of reelection, it is claimed, undermines accountability, one of the main purposes of elections.[8] Politicians are accountable if they must face an electorate that can decide on the basis of their past performance whether or not to remove them from office. When politicians can adjust the boundaries of their district and manipulate other electoral rules to preserve or increase their relative advantage, they weaken the ability of voters to decide their fate. Some of these effects continue throughout their term until the next redistricting. When representatives believe that they are less vulnerable to defeat, they may, while in office, pay less attention to all constituents, and even less attention to constituents who are not in the majority who elected them. Also, as a result of redistricting, voters who wish to decide on the basis of the past record more than future performance may find that the representative whose record they would judge is running in another district. Further, they may find themselves placed in a district where they are no longer in the majority and are now unable to discipline the party whose record they wish to judge.

Although control over redistricting does give politicians a tool to avoid being called to account, the argument against control cannot rest entirely on the value of accountability. First, even representatives in safe seats generally act as if their reelection is in doubt and therefore tend to be responsive to their constituents (Mann 1977). Second, some voters vote prospectively, rather than retrospectively (Fearon 1999; and Powell 2000). The fact that your district has been altered,

that you find yourself in a different district, does not matter so much
if you are choosing on the basis of a prediction about how candidates
may act in the future. Third, the argument from accountability is incomplete because it does not recognize the significance of changes
in the identity of the legislators to be held accountable, and the voters who are to hold them accountable. With respect to the identity
of legislators, it does not cover the many cases where politicians do
not run for reelection. They cannot be held accountable even if the
districts remain the same. With respect to the identity of the voters,
the argument does not take into consideration the shifts in the composition of the district. The majority who elected the representatives
in the last election will not be the same majority that calls them to
account in this election. New voters arrive, some move, and others
die. The greater the interval, the more the change in the identity of
the electorate, but some significant change is likely to occur between
most elections. Consequently, an argument based on accountability
that assumes a link over time between specific representatives and
a determinate set of constituents cannot constitute a complete case
against letting politicians control the process.

The more fundamental objection is that legislative control of redistricting does not adequately respect periodicity.[9] Elections are not
one-time events. An election is not like the ratification of a constitution or its amendments, a popular initiative or referendum or even
a typical plebiscite. Each election, though a discrete event, stands
in an indefinite series. Because one purpose of periodicity is to enable voters to hold representatives accountable for their actions, the
accountability objection is to that extent correct. But that objection
depends on assuming that there is more continuity in the electorate
and the elected from one election to the next than there usually is.

Even if there were no continuity, periodicity would be important. It
provides the means by which present majorities can escape the dead
hand of past majorities. Elections must be held periodically so that,
when new majorities replace old majorities in the electorate, they can
then decide to what extent to replace an old with a new legislature.
Periodicity keeps open the possibility of change – specifically, change
in the membership of the legislature and thereby in the nature of the
people's representation. In this respect, periodicity is an expression
of the democratic value of popular sovereignty.[10]

To complete the objection to legislative control of redistricting,
periodicity must be combined with a principle of authority, which

specifies who should decide the rules that determine whether and to what extent change occurs in the legislature. The principle holds that decisions about such rules should not be made by people who have a preponderant interest against (or for) change in the membership of the institution in question (Thompson 2002, 133–4, 166–8, 179–80). The point is not that change is always desirable. The aim is to try to ensure that choices between change and continuity – in this case, decisions about redistricting – should be made on their merits, giving due weight to the many relevant factors that affect the democratic process. The assumption is that these decisions are more likely to be made on the merits if legislators and their parties do not make them. When an old legislature elected by the old majority sets the rules that define the new majorities that will elect the new legislature, this possibility of renewal and change in membership is less likely. Legislators, like members of most institutions, generally approve of the mechanisms by which they were selected.

The principle extends an idea originally expressed by James Madison during the debates on the Constitution. He sharply distinguished ordinary legislation from electoral regulation. We can trust the normal process of representation, he said, provided that the issue under consideration is one in which representatives share a common interest with their constituents, not one in which they "have a personal interest distinct from that of their constituents" (Madison 1966). But when representatives decide questions that affect their own status or that of their party, they will tend to give more weight to preserving the privileges and more generally perpetuating the practices of the institution. They will give less weight to promoting other values of the democratic process. On such issues, we should be "jealous" of assigning the representative body final authority.

We do not have to assume that the only problem is the "personal interest" of individual legislators in reelection, or even that this interest is always opposed to the interest of their constituents or the public interest on questions concerning the electoral process. Legislators may conscientiously (sometimes even correctly) believe that the best interest of the institution and the democratic process lies in preserving the current membership or at least the current rules for choosing members. But with regard to the rules that determine who is to be elected, citizens have good reason to doubt that legislators and their parties are impartial judges. If legislators do not pursue their individual or partisan self-preservation, they are likely to engage in institutional self-perpetuation. Whatever differences the parties in the legislature may have, they share a common interest in minimizing challenges from outside. They are likely to join in opposing term limits and campaign finance regulation, which reduce the influence of incumbency; and they are likely to work together to discourage fusion candidacies, which help third-party challengers.[11] Redistricting and other electoral measures – and the choice between change and continuity – are more likely to receive consideration on their merits if those who are deciding whether to adopt them are not the same as those whose electoral future they would determine.

The Madisonian principle refers to the circumstances of judgment rather than any particular conclusion that politicians might reach. It is concerned with the reasons that redistricting officials are likely to consider (and the institutional incentives that favor some reasons over others), rather than the results officials reach (and the institutional legitimacy of any particular result). The principle therefore does not necessarily require more (or less) competition in elections or more (or less) turnover in legislatures. Nor is it satisfied by showing that the competition in the system as a whole is greater than it is in most districts, or that representatives in safe districts are responsive and accountable to their constituents.

Moreover, even if the high rate of reelection of incumbents is the result of strategic entry or exit decisions rather than any advantages incumbents may enjoy, the principle would still cast doubt on giving the dominant party control over redistricting. That party would still be deciding how to redistrict in circumstances in which it would be less likely to give due weight to all the relevant values at stake. For example, a party attempting to maintain control of the legislature could decide it had to pit two experienced and popular incumbents against each other, even if the decision caused one to withdraw from the race. Or a party seeking to create safe districts may need to produce more ideologically homogenous districts, which could have the effect of increasing partisan polarization. A party could prefer a Democrat who is more liberal or a Republican who is more conservative than might be optimal for the political health of the process. A redistricting decision that has the effect of favoring less moderate and less centrist candidates may be justifiable under some circumstances. But as with other decisions that have systematic effects on the democratic process, the Madisonian principle implies that the parties are not the best judges of whether the results of such a choice serve constituents, let alone the public interest.

The value of periodicity combined with the Madisonian principle implies that the authority for governing elections in general and redistricting in particular should be located outside the ordinary legislative process. The need for independent judgment may suggest that courts should have this authority. Certainly, courts have an important role to play in regulating the electoral process. They are well suited to protecting individual rights, notably the constitutional requirements of equal protection and free speech, and are appropriately involved in redistricting cases that involve racial justice.[12] But questions about change in the composition of majorities – to what extent districts should permit or encourage new majorities to form – raise issues that are less about individual voters than about institutional structures and the nature of representation itself. The conflicting demands of democratic majorities neither state legal claims that individuals usually have standing to bring, nor permit remedies that courts usually have competence to apply. They involve the form of government – in constitutional terms, the "guaranty clause" – which courts are not well placed and are usually reluctant to adjudicate.[13] Furthermore, courts are expected to respect precedents, and therefore are bound, more than other institutions, to the will of past majorities and to the decisions of supermajorities in constitutional ratification.

A more promising way to exercise control over redistricting (and potentially other aspects of the electoral process as well) is through an independent commission. Australia (since 1902) and Canada (since 1964) have relied with evident success almost completely on nonpartisan commissions for this purpose.[14] In the United States, six states now authorize commissions to redraw their own legislative districts, and eight more states use commissions to revise congressional as well as legislative districts.[15] The most recent state to join this movement is Arizona, whose voters in the 2000 election approved an initiative "creating an independent commission of balanced appointments to oversee the mapping of fair and competitive congressional and legislative districts."[16]

A well-composed commission is better placed to give due weight to all the relevant considerations that should be considered in drawing districts – equal population, compactness, contiguity, community of interest, geographical saliency, and even partisan politics. Members of

commissions can view their role not as registering preferences of constituents, or even acting on their own conscience and convictions, but
as working together to identify and express the will of the appropriate
majority.

Most states acknowledge the unavoidably political nature of redistricting decisions by permitting former politicians to serve on their
commissions (though most bar current and recent office holders).
Commissions are properly political creatures, but they can cultivate a
politics different from, or at least more wide ranging than, the ordinary kind. They can be designed so that they do not serve entrenched
majorities of any time or place.

But politics probably intrudes too much into the appointment process of most commissions now. Legislative leaders typically appoint
the majority of the commission members, sometimes from a restricted
pool of candidates (for example, nominated by a judicial committee).
If the selection process were more independent of the legislature,
commissions could better take into account all the political factors
that legislatures consider, but give greater priority to providing opportunities for changes in membership than to preserving the privileges
of current members.

Commissions are less democratic than legislatures in the sense that
they are less directly accountable. But the democratic authority of a
commission could be maintained in various ways: by ensuring that voters have an opportunity to approve its constitutional role (its scope
of authority and general procedures) and the nature of its membership (the qualifications of members and their method of selection).
The loss of some direct democratic control in the present is surely
worth the gain of greater democratic control in the future. Commissions have that negative virtue so critical to the democratic process:
they are not self-perpetuating. In this way, they help fulfill a central
democratic purpose of electoral periodicity.

SIMULTANEITY: WHY CITIZENS SHOULD VOTE AT ABOUT THE SAME TIME

On election night 2000, before all the polls had closed in Florida,
the networks called the state for Al Gore. (By then, Florida's electoral
votes were seen as critical to victory.) Some four hours later, the networks changed their minds, and declared George Bush the winner.
Still later, they retracted that call, but only after Gore had phoned

Bush to concede. The reports may have caused some people not to vote.[17] In addition to the effects on turnout, the projections continued to shape the opinion and events in the month-long controversy that followed. In the House hearings devoted to election night coverage, Democratic representative Henry Waxman argued that Gore's "concession" prompted by the networks' projection of a Bush victory "set in motion a chain of events that were devastating to Al Gore's chances. And it immeasurably helped George Bush maintain the idea in people's minds that he was the man who won the election" (U.S. House Committee on Energy and Commerce 2001; Political Staff of the Washington Post 2001). Republicans also complained that the earlier call for Gore caused some of their supporters in the western states to stay home (Political Staff of the Washington Post 2001; Correspondents of the New York Times 2001).

In the aftermath of this election, much of the criticism centered on the errors the networks made rather than the effects their projections had on turnout and legitimacy. In the House hearings, several network witnesses conceded that they had made errors and needed to change their methods, but said they doubted that projections had any harmful effects (U.S. House Committee on Energy and Commerce 2001). The president of the Associated Press heatedly declared that the mere act of holding these hearings was itself a threat to freedom of the press. Some of the networks seemed inclined to make modest reforms, but none wanted Congress to legislate in this area. An outside group recommended that the networks cease using exit polls to call elections, stop relying on one source to collect and collate data, and undertake organizational changes to ensure that accuracy in reporting takes priority over speed (Konner, Risser, and Wattenberg 2001). Clearly, these and similar reforms, whether legislated or not, would be desirable. If the media are to make projections and report polls, it is important that they do so accurately.

But the preoccupation with accuracy neglects the more general problem – the potential damage to the democratic process that results from reporting projections even when they are accurate. It is not simply inaccurate projections that we may wish to limit, but any projection that gives some people but not others information relevant to deciding how or whether to vote while the election is in progress. (In this respect, the greater the perceived accuracy, the greater the potential harm.) We can begin to develop the justification for limiting such projections by examining two common arguments against doing so.

The first appeals to freedom of the press. Although merely hold-ing hearings on proposals to regulate projections does not of course violate freedom of the press, prohibiting the press from publicizing projections could do so. An outright ban on reporting exit polls would rightly be considered a violation of the First Amendment. Yet freedom of the press is not absolute in the electoral sphere. The courts have permitted greater regulation of the media in election-related speech than in many other areas.[18] Electoral politics, as will be shown more directly in the next section, should be regarded as a special sphere, potentially subject to greater regulation than ordinary politics.

But even without directly regulating the media, the government could discourage electoral projections. There is no First Amendment objection to mandating uniform poll closings or embargoing the re-lease of official returns (Ortiz 2002). Uniform closings would make the projections less significant. Embargoes on returns would make exit polls less reliable or more expensive.[19] Furthermore, the net-works could voluntarily agree to forgo making projections until all the polls are closed in all states. Finally and most importantly, the main purpose of freedom of the press is to protect not the press but citizens and the democratic process.

The second argument against limiting projections invokes the free-dom of voters. Restricting election night projections, it is said, would deprive voters of the chance to vote on the basis of information some think they need to make a decision, and therefore would impair their free choice. A "true freedom to vote as one chooses" includes "the right to not vote at all or even to vote as everyone else does" (Barlow 1990, 1020). The assumption evidently is that free choice requires pro-viding the option of deciding not to vote because you believe other voters have already determined the outcome, and the option of bas-ing your vote on how others are voting. "Neither the networks, nor the lawmakers should be permitted to decide which information is useful to voters and which is not.... The choice must belong to the individual" (Barlow 1990, 1020).

This argument misconceives the nature of free choice. In a pro-cess in which projections are publicized, citizens may choose what information they wish to use, but they are denied some other kinds of choices. They cannot choose how information about their own choices and those of others is used. They vote in secret but they do not have the option of keeping the results of their votes secret until all of their fellow citizens have voted. They would have that option in a different system, but the choice of the system does not "belong to the individual." Free choice is not simply a matter of individual decision, but also of institutional structure, which only citizens acting together can choose.

Although restrictions on publicizing projections would limit free choice in some respects, they could enhance it in others. Citizens may reasonably decide that the choices they make in an election are more valuable if no one has information about how they voted until the polls have closed. When citizens decide to limit the range of choice for the sake of improving the value of choice, they are choosing between different aspects of liberty, not between liberty and other values. Their decision may of course also take into account other values, such as the quality of the democratic process, but it is not correctly characterized as favoring collective over individual choice. Other countries that respect individual choice regulate not only publication of election results but also public opinion surveys in the period immediately before the election (Feasby 1997, 242).

But why should citizens choose a system that reports the results all at once? The argument so far shows only that there is no presumption in favor of publicizing projections – that freedom of press and voters would not be violated by restricting projections – but it does not provide any positive reason for such restrictions. We can formulate a positive justification for restricting projections if we take notice of the second temporal property of elections – simultaneity.

In Congress and many other legislative bodies, members vote one at a time (as in a roll call vote), and then at the conclusion have the chance to change their votes after they see the provisional totals. How they vote is affected by how others vote. In an ordinary election, each voter acts as if he or she is voting at the same time as every other voter. No voter knows how others have voted until everyone has voted. No one can change a vote in response to how others have voted. And everyone votes with at least potential access to the same information. The constitutional requirement that all states hold elections on the same day (art. II, § 1) may be read as an expression of the idea that the electoral experience should be, as far as possible, the same for everyone. No more than twenty-four hours elapse from the casting of the first vote (usually just after midnight Eastern Standard Time in Hart's Location and Dixville Notch, New Hampshire) to the closing of the polls at 6 p.m. Hawaiian-Aleutian Time. Election day customs similarly reinforce the idea: while voting continues, politics ceases.

Candidates stop campaigning when the voting starts, and supporters are not permitted to demonstrate near the polling places.

The simultaneous character of an election is not an arbitrary or merely conventional procedural requirement. It has a normative rationale. We should distinguish two aspects of simultaneity, because each rests on somewhat different values. The first is voting at the same time; the second, voting without regard to how others vote.

The practice of requiring citizens to cast their ballots at more or less the same time, usually on the same day, rests partly on the value of popular sovereignty. The more that voting is concentrated in time, the more the election expresses the will of a determinate majority (or plurality). The outcome can then be seen as more the result of a single collective decision than the product of a series of decisions made by different majorities (or pluralities). Simultaneous voting in this way creates a more coherent popular sovereign.

Simultaneity rests even more importantly on the democratic value of fairness. If citizens vote at the same time (or have only information they would have had if they were voting at the same time), the value of each citizen's choice is no greater than that of any other citizen. All make their choices with equal access to relevant information. Election projections deny some voters information that other voters have. Also, to the extent that election projections discourage efforts by parties and candidates to mobilize voters in the western states, some citizens who might have voted do not make a choice at all. When information is unevenly distributed, the election is less fair.

The unfairness can be seen most clearly by considering a purer case of the potential breakdown of simultaneity. In the aftermath of the 2000 presidential election some people proposed to resolve the controversy by rerunning the election in several counties in Florida.[20] Even if a rerun had been practicable, it would have clearly violated the simultaneity norm. The Palm Beach county voters would have been voting with the specific knowledge that the election was very close. Many probably would have voted differently (shifting their votes from Nader to Gore, for example).

Such a violation of simultaneity should be distinguished from a different kind of strategic voting: the decision in a single election to vote for your second-choice candidate (for example Gore) instead of your first-choice candidate (for example Nader) in order to decrease the chances of your third-choice candidate (in this example Bush). This kind of strategic voting is neither a violation nor a consequence of simultaneity. It is consistent with simultaneity because it takes place in a single election. It is a consequence of the winner-take-all rule of most current systems in the United States. It would not be necessary, for example, in a system that uses forms of proportional representation or even one that employs the instant runoff method. The latter method provides a way of combining what would otherwise be sequential elections into a single simultaneous election.[21]

Fairness is not the only value at stake in simultaneous voting. When citizens go to the polls on the same day, publicly participating in a common experience of civic engagement, they demonstrate their willingness to contribute to the democratic process on equal terms. Going to the polling station and standing in line with one's neighbors may not rank among the most exciting moments in life, but voting on election day serves an important expressive purpose in a democracy. It enables citizens to express their commitment to a common project in which they participate on equal terms – the process of choosing the leaders who will represent them. When the media publicize projections, they undermine this sense of participating in an important civic activity. Voters in the western states, for example, lose the chance to take part with their fellow citizens in an event that is still in progress rather than one that is already on its way to the history books. The same media practice that causes the electoral process to treat some citizens unfairly also causes it to convey to all citizens the message that civic engagement is not all that important.

The expressive value of simultaneity has further practical implications. It strengthens the case for making election day a national holiday.[22] Because most people who are registered already go to the polls on election day, making election day a national holiday is not likely to increase turnout. It could even reduce turnout if people decide to travel instead of vote. However, the reform could enhance civic engagement in other ways. Holding the election on a national holiday would not only strengthen the sense of participation in a shared civic activity, but would also increase the number of election workers and polling locations. The improved facilities would promote civic engagement on equal terms by making voting more accessible.

The norm of simultaneity also casts doubt on the increasingly widespread use of early voting – absentee ballots and voting by mail. The incidence of voting before election day has nearly doubled since 1980.[23] In Oregon all statewide elections since 1995 have used a mail-in ballot. In the 2000 presidential election, a quarter of the California vote and two-fifths of the Texas vote was by absentee ballot. Early voting weakens the value of the experience of participating in a civic activity. The public affirmation of voting together openly on the same day is quite different in meaning from the private transaction of filling out and mailing in an absentee ballot. In addition to this expressive value, such activities can contribute in modest ways to the development of the capacities of equal citizenship. Participating openly with others is more likely to reinforce civic attitudes than is voting alone at home. Voting alone may be worse than bowling alone.

To be sure, the value of this kind of civic engagement is not so important that it should take precedence over fairness. Absentee voting is certainly justified for citizens who would otherwise have difficulty in going to the polls on election day – especially some older voters, disabled persons, and members of the armed forces. Absentee or other forms of early voting could also be justified if they substantially increased turnout, especially among groups that are now underrepresented at the polls. But so far absentee voting has increased turnout only modestly, if at all.[24] Unrestricted absentee voting and the further extension of other kinds of early voting may even reduce voter participation by discouraging efforts to mobilize voter turnout. Furthermore, the effects of any increase in turnout have not been equally distributed. Whites are twice as likely as blacks to vote by absentee ballot. Thus, while measures that erode simultaneity may be warranted if they make voting fairer, they are harder to justify when implemented only for the purpose of making it more convenient.[25]

The second aspect of simultaneity is independence of voting – a norm that holds that citizens should not adjust their votes according to how others have voted. This partly rests on fairness. An election that enables citizens to adjust their votes in this way privileges strategic voting. Strategy of course has a place in the campaign, but the value of a vote should not depend on the strategic savvy of the voter.

The norm against strategic voting does not rest entirely on the value of fairness, however. We can imagine an Internet voting system that enabled each voter to vote at more or less the same time (with access to the same information and with the opportunity for the same civic engagement), but with the option of changing his or her vote after seeing the provisional totals. There would of course be significant practical difficulties with any such system. A limit on the number of times voters could change would need to be established, and a deadline by which all voting would cease would have to be set. Protections against the use of "sniper" software would be required so that users could not exploit the advantage of switching at the last possible moment, as occurs in some online auctions. But assume that we could adequately protect against the many forms of potential fraud and manipulation, and also ensure that the technology is highly reliable and the devices readily accessible to all citizens. Is there any objection in principle against this kind of interdependent voting? What is wrong with adjusting your vote in light of how others are voting? It might seem that deliberative democrats especially ought to welcome this kind of interaction.

Although voters may certainly take into account the views of their fellow citizens, the kind of vote switching that would occur in a typical online system would be more likely to reflect conformist attitudes than anything resembling deliberative interaction. This vote switching would not only undermine the norm that voters should make up their minds on the basis of what they hear in the campaign, but also the norm that voters should exercise independent judgment. Of course, many voters do not exercise much independent judgment in the current system, but online nonsimultaneous voting would create additional and specific incentives for voters to decide – suddenly and often irreversibly – to follow the crowd. It would invite politicians and their campaign managers to encourage just that kind of decision making. Whether or not voters or politicians generally acted in these ways, such a system would express in an especially pure form the denigration of independent judgment.

Simultaneity applies not only to individual voters but also to institutions. In the midst of the disputes after the 2000 presidential election, the Republican-led Florida House of Representatives resolved on December 12 to appoint its own slate of presidential electors, all reliably committed to George W. Bush (State of Florida 2000). The House majority feared that the courts or Congress would challenge the state's presidential electors. To ensure that Florida's electoral votes would go to Bush, the legislators invoked this rarely used constitutional authority. Had the state Senate followed suit, the House would have decided the outcome of the presidential election for the nation. (As it turned out, the resolution proved unnecessary because the U.S. Supreme Court stopped the recounts, and the Florida Senate adjourned without taking action.)

The problem is not that legislators were acting as partisans. Indeed, it could be argued that this is exactly how they should have acted because they were elected on the basis of their party affiliation. The problem is rather that legislators were deciding the election in light of how other voters had cast their ballots (as well as information about the vote totals in other states, and the totals and margins of the candidates). Deciding the outcome under such conditions undermines simultaneity (Thompson 2002, 151–61).

The norm of simultaneity applies directly only to single elections, and therefore does not necessarily rule out sequential elections such as the presidential primaries that the national parties hold in many states. Some of the same considerations (such as strengthening the sense of civic engagement) that support same-day voting would also favor a national primary or at least regional primaries. But sequential primaries do not raise fairness concerns to the same extent as does the strategic legislative selection of presidential electors. Although the outcome of the New Hampshire primary often has substantial influence on the subsequent primaries, the decision is not final in the way that the Florida legislature's would have been. In the absence of a compelling argument that the lack of simultaneity in successive elections is unfair, other considerations carry more weight. Preserving some version of the current mixed system of state primaries and caucuses may then be justified by pointing to the greater opportunities it provides for challenging candidates in many different settings, and the lesser scope for influence it gives money and the media in the nominating process (Polsby and Wildavsky 2000, 232–9).

Simultaneity in its various forms is thus important for reasons of fairness and civic engagement. Not merely voting, but voting at more or less the same time, plays an essential role in the democratic process. Democracies should therefore try to avoid the anomaly created by practices that permit citizens increasingly to choose the time they vote, and should preserve as far as possible the practices that encourage voting together on a single election day. They should disfavor publishing the results of exit polls, expanding the use of absentee balloting, and granting legislatures the authority to select presidential electors on their own schedule.

FINALITY: WHY CAMPAIGNS SHOULD BE REGULATED MORE STRICTLY THAN ORDINARY POLITICS

In declaring the expenditure limitations of the 1974 campaign finance law unconstitutional, the Supreme Court in *Buckley v. Valeo* held that "only expenditures for communications that in express terms advocate the election or defeat of a clearly identified candidate" may be regulated (424 U.S. 1 [1976] at 44). The distinction is between financial support for advocating the election of candidates (which may be regulated), and support for advocating a particular policy or general program (which must be left unregulated). Candidate advocacy is part of a campaign, and is only partially protected under the First Amendment. Issue advocacy is part of ordinary political debate, and is fully protected under the Amendment.

But the line between the two kinds of advocacy was anything but clear in the Court's opinion, and subsequent attempts to clarify it have proved difficult. The problem goes beyond the disputes about the differences between contributions and expenditures, the distinctions between money and other kinds of influences, and the controversies about private and public financing (Issacharoff, Karlan, and Pildes 2001a, 533–45). The problem is not completely resolved by any reform proposed so far. It would remain even if *Buckley* were overturned. Although the problem of issue advocacy has received less attention than that of "soft" money, its practical effects have been no less pernicious, and its theoretical implications may be even more significant.[26]

For many years after *Buckley*, the criterion for express advocacy was whether a communication used what became known as the magic words: "vote for," "elect," "support," "cast your ballot for," "Smith for Congress," "vote against," "defeat," and similar terms. Subsequent court decisions broadened the test somewhat to include statements such as those that "provide in effect an explicit directive" to vote for named candidates.[27] Communications that merely discuss public issues, even if their purpose is to influence elections, could not be regulated at all.

The ambiguities of the distinction between express and issue advocacy began to be exploited in the 1996 election in a major way. By the time of the 2000 election the proliferation of sham issue advocacy ads (together with soft money) had for all practical purposes completely subverted the purpose of the regulations. Here is a now notorious example of a sham issue ad (broadcast in the final weeks of the 1996 state election in Montana):

Who is Bill Yellowtail? He preaches family values, but he took a swing at his wife. Yellowtail's explanation? He "only slapped her," but her nose was broken. He talks law and order, but is himself a convicted criminal. And though he talks about protecting children, Yellowtail failed to make his own child support payments, then voted against child support enforcement. Call Bill Yellowtail and tell him we don't approve of his wrongful behavior. Call 406 443 3620 (quoted in Briffault 1999).

The Campaign Reform Act signed into law in March 2002 seeks to deal with these sham issue ads by adopting a broader concept than express advocacy. It defines an "electioneering communication" (which is subject to regulation) as a broadcast ad that clearly identifies a federal candidate within thirty days of a primary or sixty days of a general election and is targeted to his or her constituency (U.S. Congress 2002). Evidently uneasy about the constitutionality of this definition (or eager to invite a challenge), the legislators added this provision: if the primary definition is held "constitutionally insufficient," then an "electioneering communication" should be taken to mean any ad that supports or opposes a candidate and can be plausibly interpreted only as an "exhortation" to vote for or against a specific candidate. This fallback definition is not quite the express advocacy test again (that test is expressly repudiated in the legislation), but it is so close to current practice that it would probably not deal with the problem of sham issue ads.[28] The primary definition (identifying a candidate in the specified period) is much better than the current practice, but it still calls for interpretation and is likely to continue to generate disputes.[29]

The practical problem has been to formulate a criterion that is strict enough to rule out sham issue ads but loose enough to permit robust debate about issues. The theoretical challenge, which has received less attention, is even greater. It can be brought out by asking: why should we regulate any kind of advocacy during a campaign? After all, no one would propose trying to control candidate advocacy all the time (even though it certainly takes place months before the official campaign period). The problem is not how to distinguish different kinds of advocacy, but how to distinguish electoral from non-electoral politics. Why are elections special? This challenge goes beyond the advocacy problem. We have to justify a distinction between electoral and ordinary politics to defend even minimal campaign reforms, such as financial disclosure. (Presumably we would not want to require everyone who takes part in ordinary political activity to reveal all of his or her sources of financial support.)

The usual answers to the challenge are not adequate. First, some try to deny that the regulations assume any fundamental distinction between campaigns and other political periods. The aim of most campaign finance regulation is to control political fundraising, which takes place continually. Ads are regulated during a campaign simply because that is when the money is spent. But this reply does not sufficiently recognize that the purpose of the fundraising, whenever it occurs, is for the campaign, and therefore that the regulation still assumes that there is something special about the campaign period. Funds raised for other purposes (even funds raised during the campaign) are not subject to regulation.

Second, some argue that the regulations in question do not create a significant difference between campaigns and other political periods because they do not prohibit any citizen from engaging in candidate advocacy. "No speech is 'banned' under the new Act... The only restrictions apply to the sources of funding, not to the speech itself" (Potter 2002). It is true that under the law individuals can still advertise for or against a candidate as much as they wish – or can afford (U.S. Congress 2002). They have to disclose only the funding above certain thresholds. Corporations and labor unions may not use their treasury to sponsor electioneering ads, but even they can continue to run ads in the middle of the campaign, provided they use only funds from their political action committees (which must be funded voluntarily by individual employees, shareholders, or union members). National political parties can sponsor electioneering ads if they use "hard" money (which consists of funds raised within strict limits and is subject to disclosure).

Although these considerations may adequately defend the new law against the charge that it bans important forms of free speech, they still do not explain why the regulation of the sources of funds targets only campaign-related activities. Even if no one's liberty is seriously impaired and the integrity of the democratic process is significantly enhanced, the fact remains that the campaign finance law still constrains election-related activity more than other kinds of political activity. It imposes limits on campaigns that are not tolerated in other parts of political life. We are still left with the question: Why single out election-related activity?

A third set of arguments emphasizes the critical importance of the discussion that takes place in the campaign. Elections are periods of "heightened value debate and political opinion formation," and likewise periods of heightened opportunity for citizens to transmit those values and opinions to their representatives (Baker 1998). Citizens pay more attention to political communications during this period, and the amount and variety of political debate is greater than at most other times. Although many citizens may make up their minds before the campaign, undecided voters are more susceptible to political advertising during the campaign. Finally, the stakes are higher because voters are choosing their leaders, not simply trying to influence particular policies or decisions.

The trouble with these arguments is that they are double-edged. The very importance of campaign discussion provides a reason for restraining it less. The more attentive and the more receptive citizens are, the more vigorous and freewheeling the debate should be. The stakes are no less high between elections in the discussion of some issues (such as decisions to take military action or to cut taxes). Furthermore, privileging noncampaign over campaign debate could give political advocates "a perverse incentive to conceal their electoral preferences in order to avoid burdensome regulations" – amounting to "the closeting of electoral speech" (Sullivan 1998). Encouraging citizens and politicians to disguise their electoral positions as general policy positions is "inconsistent with the notion of robust, uninhibited, and wide-open debate about the policy bases for choosing among our representatives."

Despite the difficulty of distinguishing electoral from non-electoral politics, the need for some distinction remains. Without it, we are faced with the dilemma of either abandoning any attempt to control the excessive influence of money in elections, or imposing overly broad prohibitions that risk stifling debate in the wider political process.

Beyond campaign finance reform, many other sensible rules depend on the assumption of the distinctiveness of the electoral process; we reasonably accept many regulations in the electoral realm that would be intolerable in the general domain of public discourse. We accept limits on what voters are permitted to express at the ballot box, as well as requirements to disclose the identity of political speakers; and content-based regulations of electoral speech, ranging from constraints on electioneering near polling places to selective bans on contributions from some speakers, such as corporations (Schauer and Pildes 1999).

The suggestion that the stakes are higher at election time, while not correct in the form that it is usually presented, points in the right direction. What raises the stakes is not the relative importance of the questions that elections decide, but the relative finality of the result that elections produce. Finality, the third temporal property of elections, provides a more fundamental basis for treating electoral politics differently from other kinds of politics.[30] Finality is the flip side of periodicity. Elections occur at intervals but once an election takes place its results are final for the intervening period.

Electoral finality has two aspects. First, unlike ordinary political activity, elections (and the campaigns that precede them) come to a definite conclusion at a foreseeable time. An election takes place at a particular moment, which, until the next election, marks an end to the process of deciding who will hold office. The results of elections are not reversible until the next election. Electoral accountability is not continuous so that those elected can govern effectively for a period without the risk of immediate removal from office.[31]

Second, unlike ordinary political activity outside government, elections result in decisions that are binding on all citizens. Although noncampaign activity also often affects the outcome of elections, its purposes are broader. It is not directed exclusively at influencing a decision that, without any further political discussion or representational mediation, immediately obligates all citizens. The winner of an election gains the authority to act for all citizens.

These two aspects of finality together justify subjecting electoral politics to more stringent standards than those that govern the rest of politics outside government. Because of their finality, elections and the campaigns leading up to them should be considered more a part of government than a part of politics that influences government. Consequently, all citizens not only have an interest in the integrity of the process, but also a claim to participate in setting the standards that govern it. The standards that control the conduct of elections are therefore more appropriately determined by collective decision than by individual choice. Citizens acting together should set the standards for the process that determines who will make and execute the laws by which they all are to be bound.

Finality thus provides in principle a normative basis for adopting stricter regulations for campaigns than for other political activity, but it does not supply a criterion for distinguishing between the two kinds in practice.[32] Like many other normative distinctions, such as that between private and public, the difference between electoral and other kinds of politics can be more readily established in theory than in practice. That is why any practical criteria – both those that specify the length of the campaign and those that identify campaign-related content – are arbitrary in the sense that there is no compelling reason to draw the line at the point they designate rather than at any of an indefinite number of other points. Why sixty days before an election rather than ninety? Why not shorten the campaign period itself as many European countries have done? Why is "referring" to a candidate a necessary or sufficient test? Why not consider whether the intention of the ad is to influence the election? To answer these and similar questions that arise in devising practical criteria, we must take into account a variety of considerations such as administrative convenience, enforceability and transparency. Yet the criteria need not be objectionably arbitrary if they represent a good faith effort to capture, within the limits of these practical considerations, the principled difference between electoral and ordinary politics.

CONCLUSION

Electoral politics runs on a different rhythm than other kinds of politics. Its character is expressed by three temporal properties – periodicity, simultaneity, and finality. Elections take place at intervals, citizens vote on the same day, and the electoral outcome is irrevocable until the next election. These properties are grounded in important values that any adequate democratic process should promote. Different systems realize these properties in different ways and to varying degrees. The specific ways and particular degrees found in the current U.S. system create a rather peculiar electoral rhythm and give rise to the three anomalies criticized here.

Understanding how the electoral rhythm generates these anomalies and why they should be eliminated illuminates the important theoretical values at stake in the electoral process, and the relationships among them. Periodicity serves popular sovereignty by enabling new majorities to escape the control of old majorities, and to effect change when they believe it is needed. It highlights the importance of a key form of that control – the power to draw electoral districts. Simultaneity promotes fairness by increasing the chances that each citizen will have access to the same information and the opportunity to participate on equal terms in an important democratic rite. It can also separately enhance civic engagement and protect independent judgment. A more temporally concentrated election more adequately expresses on equal terms the will of all voters. It also more clearly manifests the will of a determinate majority and therefore more fully realizes popular sovereignty.

Finality also supports popular sovereignty by giving continuing legitimacy to the will of an electoral majority until the next election. Finality works together with periodicity but emphasizes a different and sometimes conflicting aim. While periodicity stresses the need to permit change in representation from time to time, finality recognizes the need to support stability in government over time. It gives leaders the opportunity to govern by temporarily freeing them from the threat of removal.

Respecting the temporal properties also has significant practical implications. If we appreciate the distinctive character of election time, we can see more clearly why and how we should try to resolve some of the anomalies that characterize the current U.S. electoral process. We will have stronger justifications than those that are conventionally given for establishing institutions that give citizens more control over how their representatives are chosen, enhancing opportunities to participate in elections on equal terms, and granting greater authority to regulate campaigns.

Together the temporal properties mark off electoral politics as a sphere that requires special attention, and demands different and often more stringent standards than does political life that lies outside government. Periodicity requires that critical decisions that affect the membership of representative institutions – such as redistricting – are not biased in favor of either continuity or change, and therefore are not based mainly on considerations of incumbent protection or partisan advantage. Coupled with the Madisonian principle that cautions against letting representatives control their own future, periodicity strengthens the case for giving independent commissions the responsibility for redistricting. Simultaneity suggests that we should resist publishing the results of exit polls, expanding the use of absentee balloting, and granting legislatures the authority to select presidential electors on their own schedule. Finality points to the fundamental reasons that electoral procedures and campaign practices require more regulation than do the activities of ordinary politics. Finality justifies, for example, requiring disclosure of funding sources for electioneering ads and imposing stricter limits on organizations that raise funds for such ads. That the results of an election are temporarily irrevocable and binding on each citizen means that all citizens have a legitimate interest in overseeing the standards that govern the whole electoral process.

The three properties considered together yield yet another implication. They create the characteristic rhythm of a healthy democracy – periods of ordinary politics interrupted by campaigns, punctuated by simultaneous voting, concluded by a final decision. This rhythm is disrupted by the increasing length of campaigns in recent years in the United States. When campaigns go on indefinitely, the difference between electoral and ordinary politics begins to blur. When representatives are continually running or preparing to run, campaigning and governing begin to merge. The hybrid political creature that this trend creates – the permanent campaign – does not serve well the goals of either campaigning or governing. To respect the distinctive temporal character of the electoral process, we should resist this trend, and sharpen the difference between running for office and acting in office.

The sphere of electoral politics that these three properties identify is not a clearly defined area with unambiguous boundaries. A line dividing the electoral process from the rest of political life is not to be discovered by undertaking only empirical explorations in the political world, as if we were setting out to look for some natural boundary like a river. It has to be constructed, often one case at a time, as we seek to create and sustain an electoral process that promotes democratic values. The general principles of democratic theory, including the values brought together by the temporal properties described here, can guide those political constructions. Delineating and regulating the content of the electoral process will proceed more democratically and with a better chance of achieving democratic results if we attend to its temporal character. To preserve that character and the values of the democratic process it promotes, we need to make sure that our political life runs on election saving time.

Notes

For comments on an earlier version of this chapter, the author is grateful to Heather Gerken, Amy Gutmann, Richard Pildes, and several anonymous reviewers and the editor of the *American Political Science Review*. Portions of the chapter in a slightly different form were presented in lectures at Harvard, Indiana, Oxford, and Princeton universities, where many colleagues and students offered helpful criticisms in the discussions that followed. Some sections of this chapter draw on parts of Thompson (2002), which benefited from advice also from Charles Beitz, Elizabeth Garrett, Mark Hansen, Sanford Levinson, Stephen Macedo, Thomas Mann, Nancy Rosenblum, T. M. Scanlon, Frederick Schauer, Sidney Verba, and Raymond Wolfinger.

1. For current information on the practices in the states, see the National Conference of State Legislatures: http://www.ncsl.org/programs/legman/ elect/statevote2000.htm. Also see the state government websites of the individual states. An earlier survey can be found in National Conference of State Legislatures (1999), Appendices E, F.

2. The quotation comes from the opinion of Judge Edith H. Jones in a district court decision *Vera v. Richards*, 861 F. Supp. 1304, 1334 (S.D. Tex. 1994), which struck down racial districting in three congressional districts in Texas. She wrote that "the Legislature obligingly carved out districts of apparent supporters of incumbents, as suggested by the incumbents, and then added appendages to connect their residences to those districts.... The final result seems not one in which the people select their representatives, but in which the representatives have selected the people." Guinier and Torres (2002, 168–83) object not only to politicians' control over redistricting, but also to geographical districting itself as well as the winner-take-all rule. It is important to distinguish the objections to this control and the objections to other aspects of the electoral process because each requires different arguments.

3. For a helpful survey and further citations, see Issacharoff, Karlan, and Pildes (2001a, 1089–151). The argument from periodicity focuses on redistricting control.

4. The most recent advocate of this view among constitutional scholars is Issacharoff (2002a and 2002b). Although many of his criticisms of partisan control of redistricting are consistent with the argument presented here, his theoretical rationale gives "competition as an independent value" an excessively privileged position in democratic theory. See the critique by Persily (2002).

5. Cox and Katz (2002) show that strategic decisions to enter or exit a race account for much of what is usually attributed to incumbency advantage. Incumbents and strong challengers are "getting better at avoiding one another," in part as a result of the predictable regularity of redistricting, rather than party control (198). But Ansolabehere and Snyder (2002b) argue that "strategic retirement and entry...cannot explain either the magnitude of the incumbency advantage in state elections today or the growth of the incumbency advantage over the past years."

6. One of the most sophisticated applications of the market analogy to electoral politics is Issacharoff and Pildes 1998. In other writings, one of the authors recognizes the significance of other forms of competition. See, for example, Pildes 2001. For a further criticism, see Thompson 2002, 7–8, 96, 158–9, 175–7, 185.

7. The leading analysis is Gelman and King 1994; but see Cox and Katz 1999, who argue that partisan control may affect responsiveness and bias.

8. Competition is an important means of maintaining accountability, since it gives voters a positive alternative to the reelection of an incumbent, but it is a distinct concept. A race between two candidates who have never served in

office and therefore are not yet accountable can be competitive. A race can be non-competitive but still an instance of accountability as when an incumbent decides not to run because he anticipates defeat. Competition can also work against accountability: if competition results in very high rates of turnover in legislatures, voters may be less able to find legislators to hold accountable for legislation. For other interpretations of accountability, see Przeworski, Stokes, and Manin 1999. A useful critique of the conventional view of accountability is Philp 2002.

9. Manin 1997 provides a helpful discussion of a concept ("repeated character") that is similar to the idea of periodicity.

10. More specifically, the value may be interpreted as an expression of the principle of majority rule (suitably constrained by the values of liberty and equality). Majority rule implies, inter alia, that a current majority should have the power to override past majorities. For a defense of the moral basis of majority rule, see Waldron 1999. For other analyses of the justification of majority rule, see Beitz 1989; Dahl 1989; and Gutmann and Thompson 1996.

11. The leading court case on fusion is *Timmons v. Twin Cities Area New Party*, 520 U.S. 351 1997, which upheld the Minnesota legislature's ban on fusion candidacies.

12. While active in assessing racial redistricting, courts have generally avoided ruling on partisan gerrymandering. Yet partisan gerrymandering can make it more difficult to accomplish constitutionally acceptable racial gerrymandering. When legislators are trying to protect incumbents, they do not have as many possibilities for creating majority-minority districts, and are more likely to draw unusual and irregular boundaries. The "bizarre" shape of the notorious majority-black District 12 in North Carolina, cited by the Supreme Court in finding the redistricting unconstitutional, could have been avoided if the state had not given such a high priority to protecting incumbents. See Justice White's dissent in *Shaw v. Reno*, 509 U.S. 630, 674 n. 10 (1993). For an argument that racial and partisan gerrymandering should be treated similarly in some respects, see Frient 1998. For an argument that partisan gerrymandering does not violate any equality principle (at least none that should be adjudicated by the courts), see Schuck 1987. Also see Guinier and Torres 2002, 176–83, 194–202.

13. The Court has rarely invoked this clause (art. IV, § 4), generally treating claims that might arise under it as "political questions," not appropriate for judicial resolution. The classic case is *Luther v. Borden*, 48 U.S. (7 Howard) 1 (1849). For an argument that more cases involving political rights should be decided under the guaranty clause, see McConnell 2000.

14. See Courtney 2001; and Australian Electoral Commission Information Center 2003. The Boundary Commission for England is chaired by the Speaker of the House of Commons, but it has functioned in a relatively nonpartisan way. See Rallings and Thrasher 1994; and McLean and Butler 1996 (which also includes some discussion of the Australian and New Zealand systems).

15. The states in the first group are Alaska, Arkansas, Colorado, Missouri, Ohio, and Pennsylvania; in the second group are Arizona, Hawaii, Idaho, Maine, Montana, New Jersey, Rhode Island, and Washington. Vermont's

reapportionment board drafts the initial legislative redistricting plan, but the legislature has final authority. Texas has a backup commission, which acts if the legislature fails to adopt a plan. This information is based on the state government websites of the individual states (as of August 2002); and National Conference of State Legislatures 1999, Appendices E, F. On commissions in the United States more generally, see Kubin 1997; and Thompson 2002, 168–79.

16. State of Arizona, Proposition 106, available online: http://www.sosaz.com/election/2000/info/pubpamphlet/english/prop106.htm (June 19, 2003).

17. Jackson 1983 presents one of the few analyses based on information about individuals (using the American National Election Study, University of Michigan). The studies that do not find this effect on turnout mostly use aggregate data, which ignore the large regional differences in the campaigns, relative salience of issues, and variations in the weather. Jackson acknowledges that early reporting of projections may affect turnout only in elections in which the projections differ from prior expectations, as when people expect a close race but the projections indicate a clear victory (632). See also the analysis by Hansen (2002a).

18. See, for example, *Red Lion Broadcasting Co. v. FCC*, 395 U.S. 367 (1969), and *Turner Broad. Sys. v. FCC*, 520 U.S. 180, 227 (1997) (Breyer, J., concurring in part) (citing Red Lion as supporting policy that "seeks to facilitate the public discussion and informed deliberation, which . . . democratic government presupposes and the First Amendment seeks to achieve"); and *Denver Area Educ. Telecomm. Consortium, Inc. v. FCC*, 518 U.S. 727, 741 (1996). Generally, see Schauer and Pildes 1999.

19. In a close election the typical poll's margin of error is likely to be greater than the vote difference between the candidates, and the pollster needs the precinct and county returns in order to call the election with any confidence. Without these returns, the pollster needs to increase the sample size, and thereby the expense of the survey (Hansen 2002a).

20. Occasionally, new elections have been ordered, but only in specific districts or localities, never in whole states or in a presidential election. See Issacharoff, Karlan, and Pildes (2001b, 108–16).

21. For an application of the instant runoff method, see Vermont Commission to Study Instant Runoff Voting 1999. For a description of the system in other countries, as well as a survey of alternative methods, see Farrell 2001.

22. The National Commission recommended that in even-numbered years the Veterans Day holiday be held on the Tuesday next after the first Monday in November and serve also as election day (National Commission on Federal Election Reform 2002).

23. For this data and further analysis, see Hansen 2002b.

24. See Hansen 2002b; Oliver 1996; and Stein 1998.

25. Significantly, all three of the major studies prompted by the 2000 election recommended against increasing absentee voting (National Commission on Federal Election Reform 2002; Caltech/MIT Voting Technology Project 2001; and the Constitution Project 2001).

26. For an application of democratic principles to campaign finance more generally, see Thompson 2002, 105–18.

27. See, for example, *Federal Election Commission v. Massachusetts Citizens for Life, Inc.*, 479 U.S. 238 (1986), at 248–50.

28. The Federal Election Commission seems to have adopted the language of the fallback position without waiting for any constitutional challenge in its definition of a "public communication" (which it defines as a communication that "promotes or supports, or attacks or opposes any candidate"). Code of Federal Regulations, 100.14, (b) 3 as amended by the Commission on June 22, 2002. "Public communication" includes print as well as broadcast ads, but is not regulated as stringently as electioneering communications.

29. For some suggestions about how to draw the line, see Brennan Center for Justice 2000.

30. The basis for the distinction developed here is closest to that presented by Briffault (1999). Other important contributions by legal scholars who are developing the idea of an electoral domain distinct from ordinary politics are: Schauer and Pildes 1999; and Baker 1998. The electoral verdict is also final in a sense similar to that of the concept of finality as a formal condition in a theory of justice: "when the course of practical reasoning . . . has reached its conclusions, the question is settled . . . We cannot at the end count [existing social arrangements and . . . self-interest] a second time because we do not like the result" (Rawls 1999).

31. Recall is unusual, and its desirability is rightly questioned by many democratic theorists (see, for example, Cronin 1999). In most parliamentary systems, the government is subject at any time to a vote of no confidence and a consequent general election, but it still usually enjoys at least as much security as do representatives in other systems. Bringing down a government is more difficult – because party discipline is greater and also more perilous – and therefore less likely, because the representatives of all parties have to face the voters.

32. See the objection raised by Sullivan (1998).

References

Ansolabehere, Stephen, and James M. Snyder Jr. 2002a. "The Incumbency Advantage in U.S. Elections: An Analysis of State and Federal Office, 1942–2000." *Election Law Journal* 1 (3): 315–38.

———. 2002b. "Using Term Limits to Measure Incumbency Advantages When Officeholders Retire Strategically." Available online: http://web.mit.edu/polisci/research/ansolabehere/using_term_limits.pdf (June 19, 2003).

Argersinger, Peter H. 1980. "'A Place on the Ballot': Fusion Politics and Antifusion Laws." *American Historical Review* 85 (April): 287–306.

Australian Electoral Commission Information Center. 2003. "Redistributions." Available online: http://www.elections.act.gov.au/redis.html (June 19, 2003).

Baker, C. Edwin. 1998. "Campaign Expenditures and Free Speech." *Harvard Civil Rights-Civil Liberties Law Review* 33 (winter): 1–55.

Barlow, Anthony M. 1990. "Restricting Election Day Exit Polling: Freedom of Expression vs. the Right to Vote." *University of Cincinnati Law Review* 58: 1003–21.

Beitz, Charles R. 1989. *Political Equality: An Essay in Democratic Theory*. Princeton, NJ: Princeton University Press.

Brennan Center for Justice, Policy Committee on Political Advertising. 2000 (May). "Five New Ideas to Deal with the Problems Posed by Campaign Appeals Masquerading as Issue Advocacy." Available online: http://www. brennancenter.org/programs/cmag_temp/cmag_recs.html (June 19, 2003).

Briffault, Richard. 1999. "Issue Advocacy: Redrawing the Elections/Politics Line." *Texas Law Review* 77 (June): 1764–6.

Butler, David, and Bruce Cain. 1992. *Congressional Redistricting: Comparative and Theoretical Perspectives.* New York: Macmillan.

Caltech/MIT Voting Technology Project. 2001. *Voting: What Is, What Could Be.* Available online: http://web.mit.edu/newsoffice/nr/2001/VTP_report_all. pdf (June 19, 2003).

Center for Voting and Democracy. 2002. *Monopoly Politics 2002: How "No Choice" Elections Rule in a Competitive House.* Available online: www.fairvote.org/2002/mp2002.doc (June 19, 2003).

Constitution Project. 2001. Forum on Election Reform, *Building Consensus on Election Reform.* Washington, DC: Election Reform Initiative.

Correspondents of the New York Times. 2001. *36 Days: The Complete Chronicle of the 2000 Presidential Election Crisis.* New York: Times Books and Henry Holt.

Courtney, John C. 2001. *Commissioned Ridings: Designing Canada's Electoral Districts.* Montreal: McGill-Queens University Press.

Cox, Gary W., and Jonathan N. Katz. 1996. "Why Did the Incumbency Advantage in U.S. House Elections Grow?" *American Journal of Political Science* 40 (May): 478–97.

———. 1999. "The Reapportionment Revolution and Bias in U.S. Congressional Elections." *American Journal of Political Science* 43 (July): 828–33.

———. 2002. *Elbridge Gerry's Salamander: The Electoral Consequences of the Reapportionment Revolution.* Cambridge: Cambridge University Press.

Cronin, Thomas E. 1999. *Direct Democracy: The Politics of Initiative, Referendum, and Recall.* Cambridge, Mass.: Harvard University Press.

Dahl, Robert A. 1989. *Democracy and Its Critics.* New Haven, Conn.: Yale University Press.

Farrell, David M. 2001. *Electoral Systems: A Comparative Introduction.* New York: Palgrave.

Feasby, Colin C. J. 1997. "Public Opinion Poll Restrictions, Elections, and the Charter," *University of Toronto Faculty of Law Review* 55 (spring): 241–67.

Fearon, James. 1999. "Electoral Accountability and the Control of Politicians." In *Democracy, Accountability and Representation,* edited by Adam Przeworski, Susan C. Stokes, and Bernard Manin. New York: Cambridge University Press.

Ferejohn, John A. 1977. "On the Decline of Competition in Congressional Elections." *American Political Science Review* 71 (March): 166–76.

Frient, Megan Creek. 1998. "Similar Harm Means Similar Claims: Doing Away with *Davis v. Bandemer's* Discriminatory Effect Requirement in Political Gerrymandering Cases." *Case Western Reserve Law Review* 48 (spring): 617–58.

Gelman, Andrew, and Gary King. 1990. "Estimating Incumbency Advantage without Bias." *American Journal of Political Science* 34 (November): 1142–64.

———. 1994. "Enhancing Democracy through Legislative Redistricting." *American Political Science Review* 88 (September): 541–59.

Guinier, Lani, and Gerald Torres. 2002. *The Miner's Canary: Enlisting Race, Resisting Power, Transforming Democracy.* Cambridge, Mass.: Harvard University Press.

Gutmann, Amy, and Dennis Thompson. 1996. *Democracy and Disagreement.* Cambridge, Mass.: Harvard University Press.

Hansen, John Mark. 2002a. Task Force on the Federal Election System. "Uniform Poll Closing and Reporting." In *To Assure Pride and Confidence in the Electoral Process: A Report of the National Commission on Federal Election Reform.* Washington, DC: Brookings Institution Press.

———. 2002b. Task Force on the Federal Election System. "Early Voting, Unrestricted Absentee Voting, and Voting by Mail." In *To Assure Pride and Confidence in the Electoral Process: A Report of the National Commission on Federal Election Reform.* Washington, DC: Brookings Institution Press.

Issacharoff, Samuel. 2002a. "Gerrymandering and Political Cartels." *Harvard Law Review* 116 (December): 593–649.

———. 2002b. "Why Elections?" *Harvard Law Review* 116 (December): 684–95.

Issacharoff, Samuel, Pamela S. Karlan, and Richard H. Pildes. 2001a. *The Law of Democracy: Legal Structure of the Political Process.* New York: Foundation Press.

———. 2001b. *When Elections Go Bad: The Law of Democracy and the Presidential Election of 2000.* New York: Foundation Press.

Issacharoff, Samuel, and Richard H. Pildes. 1998. "Politics as Markets: Partisan Lockups of the Democratic Process." *Stanford Law Review* 50 (February): 643–717.

Jackson, John E. 1983. "Election Night Reporting and Voter Turnout." *American Journal of Political Science* 27 (November): 615–35.

Kirschner, William R. 1995. "Fusion and the Associational Rights of Minor Political Parties." *Columbia Law Review* 95 (April): 683–724.

Konner, Joan, James Risser, and Ben Wattenberg. 2001. *Television's Performance on Election Night 2000: A Report for CNN.* Atlanta: CNN, 29 January.

Kubin, Jeffrey C. 1997. "The Case for Redistricting Commissions." *Texas Law Review* 75 (March): 841–51.

McConnell, Michael. 2000. "The Redistricting Cases: Original Mistakes and Current Consequences." *Harvard Journal of Law and Public Policy* 24 (fall): 103–17.

McLean, Iain, and David Butler. 1996. *Fixing Boundaries: Defining and Redefining Single-Member Electoral Districts.* Aldershot: Dartmouth Publishing.

Madison, James. 1966. *The Records of the Federal Convention of 1787* (10 August 1787, 2: 249–50), edited by Max Farrand. New Haven, Conn.: Yale University Press.

Manin, Bernard. 1997. *The Principles of Representative Government.* New York: Cambridge University Press.

Mann, Thomas. 1977. *Unsafe at Any Margin: Interpreting Congressional Elections.* Washington, DC: American Enterprise Institute.

Moglen, Eben, and Pamela S. Karlan. 2001. "The Soul of a New Political Machine: The Online, the Color Line, and Electronic Democracy." *Loyola of Los Angeles Law Review* 34 (April): 1089–114.

National Commission on Federal Election Reform. 2002. *To Assure Pride and Confidence in the Electoral Process: A Report of the National Commission on Federal Election Reform.* Washington, DC: Brookings Institution Press.

National Conference of State Legislatures. 1999. *Redistricting Law 2000.* Denver, CO.

Note. 1996. "Fusion Candidacies, Disaggregation, and Freedom of Association." *Harvard Law Review* 109 (April): 1302–37.

Oliver, J. Eric. 1996. "The Effects of Eligibility Restrictions and Party Activity on Absentee Voting and Overall Turnout." *American Journal of Political Science* 40 (May): 498–513.

Ortiz, Daniel. 2002. Task Force on Legal and Constitutional Issues. "Congressional Authority to Regulate When Presidential Votes Can Be Counted." In *To Assure Pride and Confidence in the Electoral Process: A Report of the National Commission on Federal Election Reform.* Washington, DC: Brookings Institution Press.

Persily, Nathaniel. 2002. "In Defense of Foxes Guarding Henhouses: The Case for Judicial Acquiescence to Incumbent-Protecting Gerrymanders," *Harvard Law Review* 116 (December): 649–82.

Philp, Mark. 2002. "Mill, Tocqueville and the Corruption of Democratic Accountability." Presented at the 2002 Annual Meeting of the American Political Science Association, Boston.

Pildes, Richard H. 2001. "Democracy and Disorder." In *The Vote: Bush, Gore and the Supreme Court*, ed. Cass R. Sunstein and Richard A. Epstein. Chicago: University of Chicago Press.

Political Staff of the Washington Post. 2001. *Deadlock: The Inside Story of America's Closest Election.* New York: Public Affairs Press.

Polsby, Nelson W., and Aaron Wildavsky. 2000. *Presidential Elections: Strategies and Structures of American Politics.* New York: Chatham House.

Potter, Trevor. 2002. "New Law Follows Supreme Court Rulings." BNA's Daily Report for Executives, 22 April 2002. Available online: http://www.capdale.com/db30/cgi-bin/pubs/New%20Law%20Follows%20Supreme%20Court%20Rulings.pdf (June 19, 2003).

Powell, G. Bingham, Jr. 2000. *Elections as Instruments of Democracy.* New Haven, Conn.: Yale University Press.

Przeworski, Adam, Susan C. Stokes, and Bernard Manin, eds. 1999. *Democracy, Accountability and Representation.* New York: Cambridge University Press.

Rallings, Colin, and Michael Thrasher. 1994. "The Parliamentary Boundary Commissions: Rules, Interpretations and Politics." *Parliamentary Affairs* 47 (July): 387–404.

Rawls, John. 1999. *A Theory of Justice.* Rev. edition. Cambridge, Mass.: Harvard University Press.

Schauer, Frederick, and Richard Pildes. 1999. "Electoral Exceptionalism and the First Amendment." *Texas Law Review* 77 (June): 1803–36.

Schuck, Peter H. 1987. "The Thickest Thicket: Partisan Gerrymandering and Judicial Regulation of Politics." *Columbia Law Review* 87 (November): 1325–84.

State of Florida. 2000. *Journal of the House of Representatives.* First Special Session, "A," of 2000–2002. December 12, 2000.

Stein, Robert M. 1998. "Early Voting." *Public Opinion Quarterly* 62 (spring): 57–69.

Sullivan, Kathleen. 1998. "Against Campaign Finance Reform." *Utah Law Review* 1998: 311–29.

Thompson, Dennis F. 2002. *Just Elections: Creating a Fair Electoral Process in the United States.* Chicago: University of Chicago Press.

U.S. Congress. 2002. Bipartisan Campaign Reform Act of 2002, PL 107-55, March 27, 2002, 116 Stat 81, Title II, Sec. 201.

U.S. House Committee on Energy and Commerce. 2001. *Hearings on Election Night Coverage*, 107th Cong., 1st sess., February 14, 2001.

Vermont Commission to Study Instant Runoff Voting. 1999. *Final Report.* Presented to the Vermont House of Representatives pursuant to H.R. 37, January 1999. Available online: http://www.fairvote.org/irv/vermont/index.html (June 19, 2003).

Waldron, Jeremy. 1999. *The Dignity of Legislation.* New York: Cambridge University Press.

9

Hypocrisy and Democracy

No criticism of politicians in liberal democracies is more common than the charge of hypocrisy. If true, the charge would seem to constitute a serious wrong. Hypocrisy, after all, is a species of deception, and no vice is more dangerous to democracy than deceit. As both politicians and philosophers have long emphasized, veracity is a precondition of democracy. To hold their leaders accountable for any decision or policy, citizens must have truthful information about what leaders and their opponents have done and intend to do.

No theorist insisted more consistently or eloquently on the need for accountability in moral and political life than did Judith Shklar. From her criticism of theorists of historical inevitability for their political evasions to her castigation of public officials for their indifference to passive injustice, she expressed nothing but contempt for people who exercise power without responsibility.[1] Nor did Shklar, in her own writing or speaking, personally or professionally, hesitate to speak openly and candidly. "Facing up to" whatever problem was at issue (as in "Facing up to Intellectual Pluralism")[2] was her consistent counsel.

It is therefore surprising to find her, in *Ordinary Vices*, singing the praises of hypocrisy. In the most penetrating theoretical discussion of the subject since Hegel's critique of the "age of hypocrisy," Shklar vigorously defends hypocrites against their critics. She argues that "hypocrisy is one of the few vices that bolsters liberal democracy" (248).[3] Her "liberalism of fear" not only accommodates hypocrisy but welcomes it.

This benign view of hypocrisy is partly the consequence of the ordering of the vices that her liberalism prescribes: it puts cruelty (a form of violence) ahead of hypocrisy (a form of deceit). It is also partly the result of this liberalism's fear that "those who put hypocrisy first" will, like the Puritans or like Orgon in Molière's *Tartuffe*, promote oppression and tyranny (50–1). Shklar seems prepared to sacrifice democratic honesty to save liberal security. Her "liberalism without illusions," it appears, needs one grand illusion to sustain it: that its public officials are as moral as they say they are.

If we examine her arguments closely, however, we find that she generally does not make such broad claims, and, when she occasionally does, she cannot sustain them. Her strongest arguments call for tolerance of only a certain kind of hypocrisy – that which is ascribed primarily to individuals. She does not try to justify, and indeed (along with most writers) mostly ignores another kind of hypocrisy – that which is imputed to institutions. By examining her arguments, and trying to sort out tolerable from intolerable kinds of hypocrisy, we come to better understand the relationship between veracity and democracy. The connection between these values, she in effect suggests, is not as tight as it might first appear. There are reasons to believe that pushing veracity too far, calling for perfect candor, will actually harm democracy.

Shklar is surely right to urge us to pay less attention to individual hypocrisy, currently a dominant strain in the discourse of our democratic politics. But in her charity toward the individual forms of hypocrisy, she disregards the dangers of its institutional forms. If this neglect is an objection to her analysis, it is an objection that can nevertheless proceed in the spirit of the method she recommends. Within the realm of hypocrisy, we should still try to put the worst forms first. We should still try to identify and protect the core of veracity that democracy presupposes. That core may be – like her barebones liberalism – only a barebones veracity, but it is no less essential for democracy.

TWO CONCEPTS OF HYPOCRISY

Among the varieties of individual hypocrisy that Shklar considers in political life, "moral hypocrisy" is the most clearly deceptive.[4] This vice involves pretending that one's "motives and intentions and character are irreproachable when [one] knows that they are blameworthy"

(47). This fits precisely the standard conception of deception – causing or intending to cause someone to have a belief that one knows or should know is false. But it is a specific form of deception. The belief that one seeks to cause is about oneself, not about an impersonal state of affairs (and not even about one's own belief about an impersonal state of affairs). Nor is it a belief about the virtuousness of one's friends, political allies, or the parties and organizations to which one may belong. Moral hypocrites seek to make us believe that they themselves are better than they know they are.

This kind of hypocrisy is individual because it refers primarily to the motives and actions of individuals. But the individuals in question are thoroughly social creatures. Their hypocrisy is deeply embedded in the moral culture in which they live. With Hegel she sees hypocrisy not as an isolated failing, but "a total environment."[5] It is "systematic, not occasional" (63). Hegel blamed the hypocritical character of our moral age on Kant, whose morality demanded "such inner purity and self-perfection" that only a hypocrite would claim to act morally.[6] That is hardly fair to Kant, who (as Shklar notes) abhorred hypocrisy no less than Hegel did.[7] But Kant's followers, those who make personal conscience the sole basis of morality, may deserve much of the blame.

Shklar agrees with Hegel that this exaltation of conscience has contributed to a culture in which hypocrisy has become "a logical and psychological necessity of moral life."[8] But she declines to accept Hegel's prognosis – that conscience will so completely dominate moral discourse that charges of hypocrisy will cease to have any force. Other moralities persist, and they offer other perspectives – based in convention or tradition – from which the claims of conscience can be challenged. There is still plenty of room for antihypocrisy. Instead, "what we have to live with is a morally pluralistic world in which hypocrisy and antihypocrisy are joined to form a discrete system" (62).

In this system, it is still the individual characters who attract Shklar's keenest interest. The most memorable and attractive of her hypocrites is Benjamin Franklin, who knew that in a democracy "a public man should try to make himself acceptable to his fellow citizens" (72). To this end, he deliberately concealed his superior intelligence, affected an air of uncertainty when his beliefs were really dogmatic, and cultivated an appearance of a humility quite beyond his natural character (75). Franklin saw "with perfect clarity what the demands of democratic assemblies were, even in their infancy" (74). His character could also take on whatever shape his many public roles required in the various worlds in which he moved – whether in the elegant society of Versailles, the provincial politics of Philadelphia, or the intellectual milieu of the Royal Society.

Shklar's psychological portraits of historical and literary figures who, like Franklin, keep the system of hypocrisy humming are compelling. They are much more subtly drawn and richly analyzed than the brief sketch of her only example of hypocrisy that could be deemed institutional. The institution in question is "American representative democracy," and its hypocrisy lies in its failure to live up to its own ideals (68–9). With a subject so general as a whole system of government, it is not surprising that Shklar does not pause to examine the specific ways in which this institution is hypocritical. She quickly moves on to the psychological traits of the individuals who must use hypocrisy to defend this democracy, and of those who criticize them. If we are prepared to consider institutions of lesser scope than whole systems, however, we may find that some of her arguments about individual hypocrisy may apply to the institutional kind, though sometimes with opposite results.

Institutional hypocrisy involves a disparity between the publicly avowed purposes of an institution and its actual performance or function. This disparity often develops over time as an institution comes to serve purposes other than those for which it was established. In some cases, no one is deceived, and no harm is done to the democratic process. The electoral college may once have been supposed to provide an additional forum for democratic deliberation, but most citizens today would be more than surprised if the delegates decided to conduct a serious debate about the merits of the candidates and cast their votes according to their own best judgment.

But in other cases the divergence between the official purpose and the actual function is not so open and the consequences not so benign. In some – especially those involving almost any agency that can claim to be protecting national security – the institutional hypocrisy is often deeply deceptive. The National Security Council (NSC) is supposed to provide the president with an independent source of advice and control over the conduct of foreign policy. When it becomes a tool for evading congressional oversight, as it did in the Iran-Contra affair, an appeal to its official purpose constitutes institutional hypocrisy that has serious consequences for the democratic process.

Oliver North and John Poindexter tried to justify their congressionally unauthorized use of the NSC by arguing that the Boland Amendment banned only operational agencies from intervening in the conflict in Nicaragua. The NSC, they said, was merely a planning and advisory agency.[9] They thus exploited the official purpose of the institution while using it for other illegitimate purposes. The disparity was part of the cause as well as the consequence of the damage to the democratic process.

In all these cases it is individuals, most often public officials, who make the statements and carry out the actions that may be regarded as instances of institutional hypocrisy. To appreciate this kind of hypocrisy, it is not necessary to treat institutions as moral agents. Nor is it necessary to try to reduce all the actions of institutions to actions of individuals. But it is important to recognize that institutional hypocrisy and individual hypocrisy are not only distinct but often opposed. Institutional hypocrisy is sometimes made possible by the absence of individual hypocrisy.

Oliver North was not a hypocrite in any conventional sense.[10] He did not believe that his motives or intentions were reproachable. He could not be accused of acting out of self-interest in any of its usual disreputable forms. He believed in his cause, and believed that he was serving both his president and his nation in carrying out his scheme to trade hostages for arms to Iran and divert some of the proceeds to the Contras in Nicaragua. He was not even trying to make himself appear better than he thought he was, since he believed that if most citizens fully understood what he was doing they would consider him a hero. Had North been a conventional hypocrite, he would not have been so successful in enlisting others in support of his cause, and thereby in effecting the institutional hypocrisy that should count as his gravest wrong. His main moral fault was not that he failed to be true to himself, but that he failed to be true to those to whom he was accountable. In his individual sincerity, he created and sustained an institutional hypocrisy.

Four arguments in defense of hypocrisy emerge in the course of Shklar's reflections on the vice. All four assume that democracy requires that public officials be held accountable for their decisions and policies, and then seek to show either that hypocrisy directly encourages accountability or that it supports other values that are equally necessary to responsible democratic government. In all four it is individual hypocrisy that is shown to serve democracy. Applied to institutional hypocrisy, as we shall see, the arguments are more equivocal.

DELIBERATION

The best to be said for hypocrites, Shklar believes, is that they are better than their critics. Antihypocrisy does more damage to democratic deliberation than hypocrisy does. Since it is especially difficult in politics to prove that one's motives are pure, the best response to a charge of hypocrisy is often to hurl a countercharge of the same nature. "As each side tries to destroy the credibility of its rivals, politics becomes a treadmill of dissimulation and unmasking" (67). As citizens watch this spectacle, they confirm their impression that the motives of all politicians are suspect, but they will not learn much about the "actual misdeeds" of politicians, let alone their past and future policies (66).

With their obsession with motives, antihypocrites distract political attention from the decisions and policies that politicians make. What Shklar has in mind recalls Jeremy Bentham's objection on motive-based criticism. In Bentham's inventory of political fallacies, "imputation of bad motive" is branded one of the weakest forms of argument.[11] The fallacy consists in inferring from the alleged bad motives of the person who proposes a policy that the policy is also bad. This is a mistake, Bentham notes, because "(1) motives are hidden in the human breast, and (2) if the measure is beneficial, it would be absurd to reject on account of the motives of its author."[12]

This fallacy, like its companion, "imputation of bad character," are expressions of a general "distrust": citizens are encouraged to oppose otherwise desirable policies on the grounds that "there lurk more behind them of a very different complexion."[13] Debate about motive and character in this way produces a political discourse that is accessible only to those who can see what is "hidden," what is "behind" policies, rather than in them. This is not a discourse that would support a common perspective from which democratic citizens could deliberate about policies and hold public officials accountable.

But, we may ask, does not Shklar herself encourage this general distrust by promoting a "liberalism of fear" that itself "institutionalizes suspicion"? "Only a distrustful population can be relied on to watch out for its rights" (238). The answer surely must be that everything depends on what the object of distrust is. A suspicious attitude directed toward the present and future policies of politicians is perfectly appropriate. Even some suspicions based on motives do not corrupt democratic discourse. Although Shklar does not make the distinction, we should acknowledge a difference with respect to the political effects of what may be called specific and general anti-hypocrisy.

Specific antihypocrisy is a criticism based on definite statements and actions attributable to an individual politician. The politician who opposes legalized abortion but helps his or her daughter obtain an abortion, the candidate who preaches family values but is guilty of marital infidelity, the mayor who gives antidrug lectures in the public schools while addicted to cocaine – all invite criticism pointing to the inconsistency between what they say and what they do. This may not be the most edifying form of political criticism, but it is relatively benign. These politicians bring the criticism on themselves. It is thus avoidable. More important, it is also answerable at least in principle. The charge and the evidence for it are sufficiently definite that citizens can determine whether the politician's explanation is satisfactory, and then move on to the policy issues.

Quite different are the effects of general antihypocrisy – the familiar charge that a politician is taking a position for "political" reasons. Although this charge could be made specific, it is usually based only on a general assumption that politicians act in their political self-interest. The legislator may say she is voting for this bill because it is in the public interest, but we know better: the real motive is that it will benefit her district and improve her chances of reelection. The candidate may say he is in favor of capital punishment on moral grounds, but we suspect that his view has more to do with the anticrime sentiments of voters. The trouble with such criticisms is that there is often nothing a politician can do to avoid or answer them. At best the criticism leads to a discursive draw; at worst, it becomes one more move in the "unending game of mutual unmasking" that Shklar dissects (67).

The general form of antihypocrisy is insidious because the assumption on which it rests is in an important sense valid. The charge of political motivation exploits a feature of democratic institutions that is both inevitable and desirable: representatives act on mixed motives. In any electorally based representative system, legislators are not only permitted but also required to take into account many different kinds of considerations in making decisions. They act for the benefit of particular constituents, for the good of the whole district or state, for the good of the nation, for their own interest in reelection or future political goals. Some of these motives may be more admirable than others, but none is illegitimate in itself, and all are in some measure necessary for accountability in our democratic system. So the assertion that a politician is politically motivated might be taken as a compliment instead of a criticism. It might even be better not made at all.

Under the circumstances of mixed motives, it is hard enough for any official, however conscientious, to separate proper from improper motives, and more generally to find the right balance of motives in making any particular decision. It is harder still for citizens, even well-informed and nonpartisan ones, to judge at a distance whether the official has actually found that balance. The charge that a politician is politically motivated therefore does not advance the political debate. Because it is inherently ambiguous, it leads to a deliberative dead end.

Recognizing the institutional dimensions of antihypocrisy in this way should help us see that some forms may be worse than others. But the critique is still directed against individual hypocrisy. What might institutional antihypocrisy look like? A case in point is the social security system – more specifically, the criticism that exposes the inconsistency between the rationale by which the system has often been defended and the way the system actually operates. The political popularity of social security is partly due to the widespread belief that the pensions that citizens receive when they retire come from the tax contributions they have made in the past. Public officials who want to expand or protect the program find it convenient to encourage this mistaken view of the rationale for the system. But this same view makes it difficult to reduce benefits for wealthy citizens or otherwise to bring under control a system that in fact depends largely on current tax revenues. Pointing out the discrepancy between what has often been taken as the official purpose of the system and how it actually operates may enhance democratic debate. In this respect, the charge of institutional hypocrisy can constitute a necessary step toward making officials more accountable for social security policy as it actually operates.

No doubt the greatest institutional hypocrisy in our history was the disjunction between the principles of liberty and equality so grandly proclaimed in our Constitution and the practice of slavery also legitimized in the same document. Although Shklar does not regard it as a form of hypocrisy, it is precisely the historical contradiction that animates her study of American citizenship: "From the first, the most radical claims for freedom and political equality were played out in counterpoint to chattel slavery . . . the consequences of which still haunt us. . . . The equality of political rights . . . was proclaimed in the accepted presence of its absolute denial."[14] It would be hard to deny that pointing out this discrepancy, even today, is a contribution to democratic accountability. It should also be clear that this kind of criticism is more constructive than the parallel charge of individual hypocrisy such as that traditionally leveled against Thomas Jefferson and Patrick Henry, the most celebrated of our predecessors who defended liberty while owning slaves.

LEGITIMACY

To sustain the consent of the governed on which any democracy depends, the "rhetoric of legitimation" in democratic discourse sets high standards and raises great expectations (78). Political leaders in a democracy not only have to devise good public policies, but also have to convince citizens that these policies fulfill the legitimating ideals of the society (69). The "disparity between what is said and what is done" is bound to be great, and is likely to be greater the higher the political leader aims. This is why presidents like Abraham Lincoln and Franklin Delano Roosevelt who raise the moral expectations of citizens are especially vulnerable to charges of hypocrisy. It is also why politicians inevitably disappoint us if we insist, with Nathaniel Hawthorne, that we should take the "private and domestic view of public men" (74). Shklar prefers Franklin's view, which measures true character by the "manner of acting one's roles," instead of by the conformity of one's actions to some singular "private self" (74). In these and other ways, the needs of democratic legitimation are bound to produce much disappointment, and therefore to breed much hypocrisy. To prevent the disappointments from undermining the system, and thereby tempting citizens to seek remedies that would be worse, we should tolerate the pretense that leaders are better than they are.

Shklar is surely right that we should learn to tolerate some inconsistency between the promises and performances of politicians, and perhaps even more between their private and public lives. No representative democracy, not even one that institutionalizes distrust, can endure unless citizens maintain some degree of confidence in the government and its leaders. One of the most striking trends in democratic politics of the past several decades is the massive decline in trust in government.[15] Whether part of the cause or only an effect, "professional antihypocrites" (46) further erode public trust and encourage a public cynicism that impedes efforts to restore that trust.

No doubt politicians have done too little to earn our trust. But in a healthy democracy our criticism would focus more on the public deeds of leaders and less on their political promises or private lives. The value of this more specific, more accessible criticism lies not only in the improvement in accountability already noted, but also in the cultivation of legitimacy invariably needed. It is difficult for politicians to regain public confidence, even if they promise less and perform better, as long as they are judged mainly by how far they fall short of their expressed ideals, whether in public or private life. In the climate of pervasive cynicism promoted by the "unending game of mutual unmasking," legitimacy is bound to lose. Politicians (and governments more generally) stand a better chance of winning the kind of trust that democracy needs if they are judged by how well they do their job relative to how well their rivals are likely to do it.

Dwelling on the discrepancies between institutional promise and performance may also damage democratic legitimacy in some of these same ways. But in at least one important respect institutional hypocrisy is less tolerable than individual hypocrisy, and its critics therefore are more useful. When an institution systematically fails to fulfill its purposes, it cannot be so readily replaced as can an individual who habitually falls short. To preserve the legitimacy of such an institution, usually the only alternatives are to ignore its failures or to correct them. The first is usually not sustainable, since the effects of the failures become obvious to those whom the institution is supposed to serve, even if critics do not point them out.

The second and more constructive alternative calls for institutional reform, a task to which the critics of institutional hypocrisy can make worthwhile contributions. It was Montesquieu who saw most clearly the need to criticize an institution for betraying its "principle" and its distinctive "end."[16]

The legislator, whether founding or reforming institutions, needs the insight that such criticism can provide. In our time on a less grand scale, criticisms of governmental agencies help set the agenda for institutional reform. The critics who charge a federal regulatory agency with serving the interests of the industries it is supposed to regulate more than the interests of the citizens it is supposed to serve not only can identify the need for reform but can indicate the form it should take. The long-term legitimacy of these and other such institutions depends on establishing more coherence between their official purposes and their actual practices.

The "politics of persuasion," Shklar emphasizes, is inherent in "any openly competitive political system" (75). The "back-and-forth of charges and counter-charges" that make up the rituals we call elections provides an ample "fund of hypocrisy" (70). To win political support in a pluralist society, candidates have to appeal to many different audiences, whose interests and ideals conflict with those of the candidates and with each other. This means first that politicians have to appear better than they are, or (like Franklin) worse than they are. They "pretend to a common touch, youthful poverty and inordinate virtue" (72). But the demands of persuasion go further. They also require politicians to adapt their public statements to the prejudices and opinions of their audience; they may have to compromise with what they regard as their true beliefs. Some earlier liberals like John Morley may have hoped that free discussion would gradually eliminate the need for compromise and the hypocrisy that inevitably accompanies it; they assumed that the pursuit of truth would gradually shrink the realm of politics (67–8). But contemporary liberals, Shklar suggests, should know better. Compromise is a desirable part of the art of democratic politics, and therefore so is whatever hypocrisy is necessary to sustain its artists.

Shklar would not accept on this point the claim of the modern theorists such as Hannah Arendt who argue that the "political realm" is "at war with truth in all its forms."[17] It is not that Shklar denies the possibility of objective truth; it is rather that she thinks the kind of truth appropriate for political theory and democratic politics is quite different from that which most of those who condemn compromise and hypocrisy have in mind. Political theory as a form of persuasion is "closer to what Aristotle called rhetoric, than the sort of discourse which is clearly scientific or purely formal."[18] If "all political theorists must be ... competent rhetoricians," then a fortiori so must all politicians.

Perhaps, then, we should not be so hard on the politician who alters his campaign speech to cater to the opinions or prejudices of the audience to whom he is speaking. On the campaign trail in Florida in 1976 where his chief rival in the Democratic primary was

George Wallace (the darling of reactionary southern whites), Jimmy Carter conveniently dropped Martin Luther King from the standard list of "great Americans" he had used in his speeches in northern states.[19] John F. Kennedy and Eleanor Roosevelt were quite enough. Although we may wish that Carter had shown more courage, we surely must acknowledge Shklar's point that in our electoral system such hypocrisies are inevitable, perhaps even desirable. If we accept that point, though, it is partly because we know that the inconsistency can be readily discovered, and that citizens can then make up their own minds about its significance. It is quite another matter when a candidate (such as Lyndon Johnson) is elected on a promise to end a war, even while he is planning to escalate it.

Institutions not only have to make compromises to accomplish their goals, but the goals themselves may constitute a compromise. When they promote the competing purposes of different groups, they may have to present themselves to one audience as serving one purpose, and another as serving a quite different purpose. Bentham made this point more explicitly than most theorists or legislators would think sensible. Recognizing that in a representative democracy legislators must represent both the general interest and particular interests of their constituents, Bentham asks how these contradictory demands can be resolved. His answer, characteristically mechanical in form, is an institutional procedure that assigns each demand a specific role. He designs a legislature in which representatives speak for their own views of the public interest but then vote according to the views of their constituents.[20] To their constituents, the representatives can say "I voted for you." To those who care about the public interest, the representative can say that at least he spoke for it, even if he could not act on it.

Bentham's procedure is not entirely pointless. The speeches might change the minds of constituents, as Bentham in fact hoped, and thus enable representatives in the future to bring their votes into line with their words. But in the absence of further social and political reforms to encourage public-spirited citizenship, this institutional hypocrisy could scarcely be thought to serve any useful democratic purpose.

There is, of course, no danger that Bentham's proposal will be adopted, but there is some point in identifying the sources of its mischief. They represent, in only a slightly more extreme form, features of some existing institutions in contemporary democracies. One source is the tendency of one of the avowed purposes of an institution simply to be ignored. The problem is not merely that the institution presents a different face to different audiences, but rather that it pays only symbolic attention to one of them. The public interest gets the glory while the particular interests get the gains.

This institutional lip service is common in all branches of democratic government, but because of the conflicting roles of its members, legislatures may be even more prone to its temptations than other institutions. In the United States Congress, members running for reelection must solicit contributions from wealthy groups and individuals, many of whom expect favors in return. The norms of the institution frown on favoritism: members publicly proclaim that contributions do not influence their legislative judgment, and most members also insist that they consider the claims of all constituents equally on the merits. Although money may not buy votes, it often still buys access.[21] Further, some members privately remind contributors, in subtle and not so subtle ways, that it does.

Some of these practices were dramatically exposed in the early 1990s during the hearings of the "Keating Five." The case involved a group of United States senators charged with assisting savings and loan financier Charles Keating in his dealing with the government while accepting large contributions that he had raised for their campaigns. One of the five made the connection between the contributions and the favors explicit in a now famous episode when he "came up and patted Mr. Keating on the back and said, 'Ah, the mutual aid society.' "[22] In this way, members tell some constituents that money does not matter and tell other constituents that it does. The institution does not force members to practice this hypocrisy, but it creates the conditions that encourage it.[23] To the extent that the contradictory demands are built into the institution, the resulting hypocrisy is more institutional than individual.[24]

CIVILITY

Liberal democracy "cannot afford public sincerity," Shklar argues. "Honesties that humiliate . . . would ruin democratic civility in a political society in which people have many serious differences of belief and interest" (78). In modern democracies, citizens "heartily dislike one another's religious, sexual, intellectual and political commitments." They also privately disdain the ethnic, racial and class character of many of their fellows. If their public conduct really mirrored their "private, inner selves," racist and anti-Semitic remarks would be expressed freely and frequently. We may not be convinced that all our fellow citizens are entitled to a certain minimum of social respect, but most of us always act as if we believe that they are, and "that is what counts."

Shklar's sharp separation of "public manners" and "private laxities" should not be taken as implying (or requiring) any deep view about the comparative moral status of human nature and society. She does not intend to reverse the Rousseauian story of the social corruption of the goodness of natural man.[25] Nor is she committed to any part of the Kantian anthropology that finds "man is evil by nature."[26] Insofar as she is presupposing any moral psychology, it is more in the spirit of Aristotle. She hopes that as citizens practice good civic habits in public, they will eventually bring their private attitudes into line with their public postures. But she does not count on this process of internalization to eliminate the need for a separation of private views and public positions. Her main concern is political – the health of democratic politics in a pluralist society – and she does not expect, or wish, that the differences that divide citizens disappear. She hopes that by behaving "better as citizens and public officials than as actors in the private sphere," we can make democracy safe for disagreement.

That is why theorists are seriously mistaken who believe, as Michael Walzer does, that the antihypocrisy reveals moral agreement. Walzer writes that "the exposure of hypocrisy . . . may be the most important form of moral criticism" because it appeals to a shared commitment that goes "deeper than partisan allegiance and the emergencies of the battle."[27] It is the tribute that vice pays to virtue. Shklar has no patience with this defense. Rather than being a sign of shared moral knowledge, the discourse of antihypocrisy manifests "moral confusion and ideological conflict" (79). In the absence of shared commitments, political rivals can criticize each other only for failing to live up to their own commitments; they cannot attack the commitments directly. The moral argument has no substance, and democratic civility suffers.

Shklar's advice on democratic manners may not present the most edifying portrait of democratic citizens, but it provides a fitting framework for democratic politics in the conditions of conflict that are likely to persist in a pluralist society. Although her advice applies primarily to individuals in their social relations with each other, it also has implications for political institutions. In particular, it suggests a view about what kinds of arguments or justifications are appropriate in public forums. In the contemporary debate about the nature of public reason in liberal theory, a chief point of contention is the extent to which private or personal views (such as moral and religious convictions) should be brought into the public forum.

It might seem that the institutional analogue of Shklar's advice implies that the public forum remain neutral: the terms of public justification should not presuppose any conception of the good, whether moral or religious. We should seek "political neutrality" based on "a universal norm of rational dialogue."[28] Shklar's counsel to keep some of our deepest commitments to ourselves may seem to fit well with this idea of a neutral public forum.

Such strict liberal neutrality is not sustainable in theory or practice. It cannot be coherently justified because any attempt to defend the restrictions it would place on other moral views exposes its own substantive moral assumptions. It cannot be consistently practiced because so many important issues of public policy are inseparable from their moral implications.

Indeed, Shklar herself could accept these objections. Despite the drift of some of her comments on hypocrisy, her own liberalism makes no claims to this kind of neutrality at all. On the contrary, she is committed to the principle that "a diversity of opinions and habits is not only to be endured but to be cherished and encouraged," and that this principle itself is as much an ideology as any other.[29] Years before the debate on public reason assumed its current shape, Shklar argued forcefully against the neutralist idea that political language and institutions could ever make good any claim to stand independent of ideology.[30] Even (perhaps especially) legal institutions cannot escape the ideological conflicts that characterize a healthy democratic politics.

The institutional implications of her defense of hypocrisy fit somewhat better with the later work of John Rawls. When discussing and voting on the most fundamental political questions, citizens, Rawls argues, should not appeal to "the whole truth as they see it."[31] They should limit themselves to public conceptions of justice, principles that could not be reasonably rejected by any citizen, rather than those based on distinct religions or comprehensive moralities held only by some citizens. Rawls explicitly denies that public reason and his own theory more generally are morally neutral in the sense that they "ensure all citizens equal opportunity to advance any conception of the good they freely affirm."[32] His theory depends on a fundamental moral conception of citizens as free and equal persons, and it gives priority to the right over the good.

Shklar's objection to philosophical theories of justice such as Rawls's is not so much against what they assert as what they neglect. She complains that philosophers refuse to think about injustice as deeply or subtly as they do about justice.[33] Instead of constructing only "accounts of what we ought to be and do," we should look more closely at "our many injustices." In this spirit, the debates in Shklar's public forum would range more widely and welcome more diversity than theorists of justice may imagine. Imitating her own writings, they would include literary stories, historical chronicles, and cultural myths, along with weighty philosophical claims and ordinary political rhetoric. It may not be politically realistic to expect citizens to check their moral and religious convictions at the door of the public forum, but it is morally reasonable to require citizens to don a mantle of civility as they join the democratic debate. That is the least that should be demanded by a liberalism that makes tolerance a "primary virtue."[34] Civility may still depend on the lesser vice of hypocrisy, but it should enjoin citizens to aspire to the higher virtues of democratic citizenship.

In Dante's *Inferno*, the circle in hell reserved for the deceitful is closer to the center than is the circle for the violent.[35] Deceit is worse than violence, presumably because its victims have no way to defend themselves. Dante did not have government in mind, but his insight is just as relevant to liberal democracy as to personal morality. Deception is the worst democratic vice because it makes possible all the others. To put it more positively, veracity is the political precondition for democratic virtue. We might suppose this ordering to be no less applicable to hypocrisy, which after all is a species of deception.

Yet Shklar, always alert to the ironies of political life, is not so sure. She suspects that in our age, moral vice serves political virtue more often than we like to admit. Like it or not, some kinds of hypocrisy facilitate democracy. Some hypocrites therefore may not deserve to burn in hell and certainly not as much as those who criticize them. In this ordering of the vices she may also be true to Dante, who assigned the "sowers of dissension" an even hotter circle than the hypocrites.[36] Yet both Dante and Shklar are less sensitive to institutional hypocrisy. Its machinations do democracy no good and often much harm. Its perpetrators may also be entitled to a special place in hell.

Notes

1. See for example, *After Utopia* (Princeton, NJ: Princeton University Press, 1969), 263–4, and *The Faces of Injustice* (New Haven, Conn.: Yale University Press, 1990), 6–7, 63–4, 125–6.
2. See "Facing up to Intellectual Pluralism," in D. Spitz, ed., *Political Theory and Social Change* (New York: Atherton Press, 1967), 275–95.
3. Page references in the text are to *Ordinary Vices* (Cambridge, Mass.: Harvard University Press, 1984), unless otherwise indicated. The relevant sections of Hegel's *Phenomenology* and *Philosophy of Right* are discussed by Shklar in *Freedom and Independence* (Cambridge: Cambridge University Press, 1976).
4. The other varieties are "religious hypocrisy," which is less relevant to politics, and states of mind such as "complacency and self-satisfaction," and "insincerity and inauthenticity," which are not intended to deceive other people and may not count as deception at all in the usual sense.
5. Shklar, *Freedom and Independence*, 192.
6. Ibid., 186.
7. See Immanuel Kant, *Religion Within the Limits of Reason* (1793), trans. Theodore M. Greene and Hoyt H. Hudson, 2d ed. (La Salle, Ill.: Open Court, 1960), 37–8, 168, 176–7. Nevertheless, in fairness to Hegel we should also notice that the hypocrisy that Kant most severely criticized was that which involved acting on the moral law from any motive other than pure duty: "All homage paid to the moral law is an act of hypocrisy, if, in one's maxim, ascendancy is not at the same time granted to the law as an incentive sufficient in itself and higher than all other determining grounds of the will" (37 n.).
8. *Freedom and Independence*, 193; and *Ordinary Vices*, 57, 61.
9. Theodore Draper, *A Very Thin Line: The Iran-Contra Affairs* (New York: Hill and Wang 1991), 25–6, 33–7, 344.
10. It may be thought that North fits the profile of the Hegelian hypocrite whose life is "wicked" but whose heart is "pure" and who can justify "any sort of crime as long as it can be said to promote some noble personal ideal" (*Freedom and Independence*, 192–3). But this self-deception or inauthenticity is quite different from the moral hypocrisy that leads officials to conceal their base motives. It does not in itself require, or lead to, deception of other people. Furthermore, as Shklar points out, no one could escape being a hypocrite if states of mind such as self-deception, inauthenticity, and insincerity, rather than acts intended to deceive others, were grounds for charging hypocrisy (*Ordinary Vices*, 47).
11. Jeremy Bentham, *Handbook of Political Fallacies* (New York: Harper, 1962) 86–7.
12. Ibid.
13. Ibid., 100.
14. Judith N. Shklar, *American Citizenship* (Cambridge, Mass.: Harvard University Press, 1991), 1.
15. See Arthur H. Miller and Stephen A. Borelli, "Confidence in Government During the 1980s," *American Politics Quarterly* 19 (April 1991): 149–50.
16. *Montesquieu* (Oxford/New York: Oxford University Press, 1987), 75, 78–9.
17. Hannah Arendt, "Truth and Politics," in *Philosophy, Politics and Society*, 3d ser., edited by Peter Laslett and W. G. Runciman (Oxford: Blackwell, 1967), 113. This is not of course to imply that Arendt's thought in general is Platonic.

18. Judith N. Shklar, *Men and Citizens* (Cambridge: Cambridge University Press, 1969), chs. 1–2.

19. So as not to single out Jimmy Carter, one may wish to take note of a bipartisan list of similar hypocrisies: Michael Oreskes, "Thrust of TV Campaign Ads Can Vary with the Territory," *New York Times* (1 Nov. 1988), A1, 28.

20. Jeremy Bentham, *Constitutional Code*, edited by Frederick Rosen and J. H. Burns (Oxford: Oxford University Press, 1983), vol. 1, VI.1.A11, 44.

21. In a careful study of three House committees, two political scientists found that although political action committee money did not purchase members' votes, it "did buy marginal time, energy, and legislative resources" during formal markups and committee action behind the scenes. See Richard L. Hall and Frank W. Wayman, "Buying Time: Moneyed Interests and the Mobilization of Bias in Congressional Committees," *American Political Science Review*, 84 (Sept. 1990): 797–820. This study also shows that the distribution of mobilization favors financially better-off groups.

22. U.S. Senate, Select Committee on Ethics, *Preliminary Inquiry into Allegations Regarding Senators Cranston, DeConcini, Glenn, McCain, and Riegle, and Lincoln Savings and Loan*, 101st Cong. 2d sess., 15 Nov. 1990 to 16 Jan. 1991, part 4, 14 Dec. 1990, 178. See Chapter 5 in this volume.

23. The conditions produce other anomalies, which members themselves see as forms of hypocrisy. During a debate on gift reform, Senator John Glenn remarked, "It is a little *hypocritical* for members to say they could be bought for a $21 lunch, yet turn around and pick up a phone to a PAC and ask for a contribution over 200 times that amount" (Congressional Record, daily edition, 5 May 1994, S5229 [emphasis added]).

24. A paragraph on the criminal justice system, which apppeared in the original article, is omitted here. It is reproduced in a somewhat different form in Chapter 7 of this volume.

25. *Men and Citizens*, chs. 1–2.

26. Kant, *Religion Within the Limits of Reason*, 27.

27. Michael Walzer, *Just and Unjust Wars* (New York: Basic Books, 1977), xv, 19–20.

28. Charles Larmore, *Patterns of Moral Complexity* (Cambridge: Cambridge University Press, 1987), 53–9; see also Bruce Ackerman, *Social Justice in the Liberal State* (New Haven, Conn.: Yale University Press, 1980), 11, 61.

29. Judith N. Shklar, *Legalism* (Cambridge: Harvard University Press, 1986), 5.

30. Ibid., 5–28.

31. John Rawls, *Political Liberalism* (New York: Columbia University Press, 1993), 216.

32. Ibid., 192–3.

33. *The Faces of Injustice*, 16.

34. *Legalism*, 5.

35. Dante Alighieri, *The Divine Comedy* (1321), trans. Carlyle-Wicksteed (New York: Modern Library, 1950), 3–5, 123–7.

36. Ibid., 5.

10

Private Life and Public Office

The preoccupation with private vice has become a public vice. Debate about the personal lives of public officials is capturing a disproportionate share of public attention and is distorting the character of political discussion. The various social and political causes of this preoccupation have been frequently discussed, but the underlying moral assumptions that support it have been less often analyzed. The increased attention to private lives gains legitimacy from mistaken moral assumptions concerning the nature of political ethics, the basis of privacy of public officials, and the criteria that justify publicizing their personal lives. To begin to restore discursive balance in our politics, we need to understand more clearly how personal and political ethics differ, and why the claims of privacy of public officials and the criteria that justify publicizing their personal lives should rest on the needs of the democratic process.

THE DIFFERENCES BETWEEN PERSONAL
AND POLITICAL ETHICS

Political ethics prescribes principles for action in public institutions, and in a democracy its foundation lies in the principles governing the democratic process. It differs from personal ethics in origin, function, and content. Personal ethics originates in face-to-face relations among individuals. It fulfills a social need for principles to guide actions toward other individuals across the familiar range of personal relations. Political ethics originates in institutional circumstances. It arises from the need to set standards for impersonal relations among people who may never meet and must judge one another at a distance.

The function of personal ethics is to make people morally better or, more modestly, to make the relations among people morally tolerable. Political ethics also serves to guide the actions of individuals, but only in their institutional roles and only insofar as is necessary for the good of an institution. Political ethics uses personal ethics only as a means – not even the most important means – to the end of institutional integrity, specifically the needs of the democratic process.

In their most general form, the content of the ethical principles of public and private life have a common foundation. Certainly, one wishes both friends and officials to respect the rights of others, to fulfill their obligations to their communities, to act fairly and speak truthfully. But in this form the principles are too general to guide conduct in the complex circumstances of political life. Once the principles are translated into the particular standards suitable for public institutions, they often recommend conduct that is distinct from, and sometimes even contrary to, the conduct appropriate for private life. As a result, the content of political ethics differs from that of personal ethics.

For example, some conduct that may be wrong in private life is properly ignored by political ethics. The public may think less of politicians who enjoy hardcore pornography or commit adultery, but as long as they keep these activities private and do not let them affect their public responsibilities, political ethics does not proscribe them.

Conversely, some conduct that is permissible or even praiseworthy in personal ethics may violate the principles of political ethics. Returning a favor or giving preference to a friend is often admirable in private life but, though occasionally useful in public life, such an act is more often ethically questionable and sometimes criminal. Furthermore, many of the problems of political ethics, such as restrictions on the types of employment that officials can follow after the end of their public career, do not arise in private life. Others, such as conflict of interest, do not arise in the same form or to the same extent. .

The contrast between the ethical demands of private and public life has never been more plainly put than it was by an anonymous supporter of Grover Cleveland in the presidential campaign of 1884. Cleveland's opponent, James G. Blaine, had corruptly profited from public office but lived an impeccable private life. Cleveland had a reputation for public integrity but had been forced to acknowledge fathering an illegitimate child. One of Cleveland's supporters remarked:

> I gather that Mr. Cleveland has shown high character and great capacity in public office, but that in private life his conduct has been open to question, while, on the other hand, Mr. Blaine, in public life has been weak and dishonest, while he seems to have been an admirable husband and father. The conclusion that I draw from these facts is that we should elect Mr. Cleveland to the public office which he is so admirably qualified to fill and remand Mr. Blaine to the private life which he is so eminently fitted to adorn (Howe 1932, 151).

The separation between private and public life is not, of course, quite as sharp as these observations imply. Some kinds of otherwise private immorality may affect an official's capacity to do a job. As citizens, we may not care if the chair of the House Administration Committee has an affair, but we may legitimately object if he gives his mistress a job on the Committee staff, especially if she says: "I can't type. I can't file. I can't even answer the phone" (Congressional Quarterly 1992, 89). Even if the member does not misuse the powers of office, his private life may become so scandalous that it casts doubt on his judgment and undermines his effectiveness on the job. Perhaps the chair of the Ways and Means Committee should be able to date an Argentinean striptease dancer, but when he appears on a Boston burlesque stage to praise her performance, citizens properly take notice.

Sexual conduct that would otherwise be private becomes a legitimate subject for investigation and reporting by the press when it violates the law (provided of course that the law itself is morally justified). Sexual harassment is not a private matter. Even some conduct that does not strictly violate the law may still be relevant if it reveals a pattern of unwanted sexual advances to persons in subordinate positions. The press therefore could not be faulted for publicizing Senator Bob Packwood's sexual encounters, which the Senate Ethics Committee found constituted a "pattern of abuse of his position of power and authority" (Senate Ethics Counsel 1995, 125).

THE BASIS OF PERSONAL PRIVACY OF PUBLIC OFFICIALS

Just because personal ethics differs from political ethics does not mean the claims of privacy made by public officials can be dismissed. In political ethics itself there are strong reasons to grant public officials some substantial privacy. We can best see what they are by first considering three common but inadequate justifications for the privacy of officials.

Individual Rights

In general, privacy may be understood as a claim to protect information about an individual that he or she is entitled to control: personal activities that should not be known, observed, or intruded upon without his or her consent. The most common justification for this claim invokes the right of privacy that all citizens should enjoy. Like all citizens, officials surely have some right to the kind of control implied by this right. No democracy should make the price of public service the sacrifice of all one's rights, especially when the consequences may be permanent and follow the individual long after leaving office.

But citizens become public officials by choice, and they may be assumed to consent to whatever limitations on their privacy are reasonably believed to be necessary for the effective functioning of the democratic process. What their rights are, then, depends on what these limitations are. We have to know what the democratic process requires before we can determine what rights officials have.

Political Recruitment

Another (related) justification points to effects on the recruitment of public officials. If the press constantly probes the private lives of public officials, who would want to serve in public office? The prospect of exposing to public scrutiny family finances and personal indiscretions (however minor) hardly is a positive incentive to seek public office.

Although many complain about the glare of publicity, many more continue to seek public office in spite of it. The question is not *whether* some decide not to seek office because of the possibility of public exposure, but *which kinds* of people decide not to seek office because of it. No doubt some admirable citizens who would be fine public servants decline to serve. But certainly some less admirable citizens, who have much to hide, decline to serve because they fear that their past (and present) transgressions may come to light. If the latter group is larger (and the number of quality people who are willing to serve does not decline), we should consider the prospect of public exposure a *favorable* effect on recruitment.

There are at least three reasons to doubt that there is a strong net negative effect on recruitment. First, some of the most talented citizens may be more attracted to service in a government that maintains higher standards and greater respectability. Second, the decision to seek and hold public office is affected by so many weighty personal and political factors that the burden of public exposure is likely to be a minor consideration. Third, studies of the federal executive branch, where restrictions have been more stringent for a long time, generally find no effect on recruitment. In its study of the problem, the General Accounting Office concluded that it is "extremely difficult, if not impossible, to attribute any specific degree of federal recruiting difficulty to the Ethics Act or to any of its provisions" (1983, Appendix I, 1).

Moral Skepticism

Another justification sometimes given for protecting the privacy of public officials is based on moral skepticism (see, for example, Himmelfarb 1998). Who is to say what is right or wrong, moral or immoral, in private life? If these moral judgments are a matter of personal preference or even individual conscience, then the public has no business judging the private behavior of officials and therefore has no need to know about it (unless of course it is illegal and therefore subject to a more objective standard).

This justification proves too much. If moral judgments are so subjective, then who is to say that the press (or anyone else) is wrong when it publicizes private conduct? Moral skepticism is a double-edged instrument here. If it exempts officials from moral criticism of their private conduct, it also exempts the press from criticism for exposing private conduct.

Nor does moral skepticism provide any support for those who favor a laissez-faire policy in this matter. Permitting the press to report whatever it thinks the public wants, letting each individual make his or her own moral judgments, does not represent a neutral default position. Any such permissive policy also rests on a set of moral judgments about what kind of practices best serve society and protect individuals. Moral skepticism thus does not help either side in this dispute because it treats all moral judgments as equal, when the dispute is about which moral judgment is right.

DEMOCRATIC ACCOUNTABILITY

The common failing of all these justifications is that they do not connect the rationale for privacy to the needs of the democratic process. As a result, the justifications are incomplete or inadequate. Once we recognize that public officials do not have the same rights as ordinary citizens, the argument from the right to privacy does not provide much help in determining what the limits on publicity should be. The recruitment argument is inadequate because it offers no criteria for balancing the desire for privacy and the legitimate demands of office. It often seems to presume that the less publicity there is, the better. And the skeptical argument is indeterminate: it supports opposite views of the democratic process equally well.

These failings suggest that any adequate justification for privacy will have to rely on a view about what the democratic process requires. Although there are of course many different conceptions of democracy, we can posit a minimal requirement that should be acceptable on almost any conception. The requirement is *accountability*: citizens should be able to hold public officials accountable for their decisions and policies, and therefore citizens must have information that would enable them to judge how well officials are doing or are likely to do their job.[1]

It is plain enough that the requirement of accountability provides a reason to override or diminish the right of privacy that officials would otherwise have. The requirement would clearly justify making some conduct public that is ordinarily private, such as information about mental or physical health, family finances, and personal friendships. It also provides grounds for making conduct more public that is partially private (such as old court or employment records).

The accountability requirement has another implication that is less noticed but no less important. The requirement provides a reason to limit publicity about private lives. When such publicity undermines the practice of accountability, it is not justified. How can publicity undermine accountability? The most important way is through the operation of a political version of Gresham's law: Cheap talk drives out quality talk. (Not because people hoard the quality talk in the hope that they might be able to enjoy it later, as Gresham thought people would hoard higher-value currency. Rather, the cheap talk attracts readers and viewers, even those who, in their more reflective hours, would prefer quality talk.)

Talk about private lives is "cheap" in two ways. First, the information is usually more immediately engaging and more readily comprehensible than information about job performance. Most people (understandably) think they know more about sex than tariffs. Second, the information about private life is less reliable because it is usually less accessible and less comprehensive. Furthermore, to establish reliable generalizations about the effects of private conduct on public performance in any present case, we need information about past cases. This information is likely to be even less reliable.

Given these characteristics, information about private life tends to dominate other forms of information and to lower the overall quality of public discourse and democratic accountability. Informing citizens about some matters makes it harder for them to be informed about other matters. Even in its early phases, the coverage of the Clinton-Lewinsky affair dominated media discussion of not only important new policy proposals on social security, health insurance, and campaign finance reform but also attempts to explain the U.S. position on Iraq in preparation for military action.

Journalists argue that they are only responding to what the public wants, and if the only test is what the public reads or views they may be right. But the considered judgments of most citizens in this and similar cases is that they do not need to know so much about the sexual affairs of their leaders[2] and that the press pays too much attention to the private lives of politicians.[3] It is perfectly consistent to believe that the political process would be better with less publicity about such matters, and even to prefer to know less about them, while at the same time eagerly reading whatever the press reports about them.

We do not have to assume that in the absence of the scandals citizens will necessarily pay more attention to the more important issues of the day and the more important qualities of candidates. Some citizens would no doubt simply ignore political reporting completely. Reporting scandals might sometimes even increase interest in politics. Some viewers might turn on the news to find out the latest about Clinton and Lewinsky, and then stay to see a report on Iraq that they would have otherwise missed.

What exactly are the effects of the coverage of scandalous private conduct? This is an empirical question that unfortunately has not received much serious investigation by social scientists.[4] But there are plenty of examples to support the plausible assumption that serious issues of public policy and substantive statements of candidates for public office are likely to receive less coverage and less discussion when they have to compete with stories featuring the vices of private life. Even if the tilt of political attention from the public to the private affects only opinion leaders and the political classes, it can still have the effect of weakening the system of accountability.

This tendency to dwell on personal ethics also means that some conduct of legitimate public concern is viewed almost entirely from the perspective of personal ethics. This doubly distorts the problem. First, it gives the transgression of personal ethical standards more prominence than it deserves compared to other problems. The overdrafts by members in the House Bank that caused such a public outcry in 1991 is a case in point. Because the scandal seemed to fit easily into the category of personal ethics, it generated more outrage than more serious problems, such as the failures in the regulation of the savings and loan industry, where individual villains in government were less easy to find.

Second, the perspective of personal ethics can also distort the nature of the transgression itself. In the case of the House Bank scandal, it emphasized individual greed and arrogance more than institutional negligence and incompetence. Yet it was the institutional faults – the management practices and appointment procedures – that needed attention and represented the more enduring and potentially far-reaching problem. Individuals were to blame for these faults, and individuals could be held accountable for correcting them. But they were faults in the institution, not flaws in the character of its members – at least not the kind usually found in a catalog of personal vices.

THE RELEVANCE OF PERSONAL LIFE TO PUBLIC OFFICE

Democratic accountability permits exposure of the private lives of officials when such information is necessary for assessing past or likely future performance in office. This is the basis of a familiar "relevance" standard: private conduct should be publicized to the extent that it is relevant to the performance in public office. But an essential point, often neglected in applying this standard, is that relevance is a matter of degree. The standard does not draw a bright line between private and public life, and then permit conduct that is deemed relevant to be publicized without limit. The standard, properly interpreted, seeks a proportionate balance between degree of relevance and extent of publicity. We can see more clearly what this means by considering some of the criteria that should guide judgments about what to publicize about the private lives of public officials.

Publicness of Conduct

Consider the case of John Fedders, who in the mid-1980s was forced to resign as chief of the enforcement division of the Securities and Exchange Commission after the *Wall Street Journal* reported that he had repeatedly beaten his wife (Jackson 1985). Although his wife's charges had appeared in the public record at the start of the divorce proceedings nearly a year and a half earlier, virtually no one had taken notice until the *Journal*'s story appeared. The first justification that almost all editors gave for publicizing this case is that the conduct was already on the public record.[5] Abe Rosenthal, the executive editor of the *New York Times*, took this as a sufficient justification: "When stories of repeated wife-beating by a public official . . . become part of the public record, they must be printed" (Taylor 1985).

This kind of justification is not sufficient. We should require some independent test of the plausibility of the charges, beyond the fact that the charges are made in public. This case illustrates that the press itself can determine how public a fact that is on the public record will become. For John Fedders, the difference between a court record and the front page of the *Journal* was the difference between holding public office and resigning in disgrace. More generally, the simple fact that conduct has come to light – whether as a result of court proceedings or (more commonly) through less reputable means – does not automatically justify giving it still more exposure. Just because an activity is public (even legitimately so) does not mean that it should be more widely publicized. Failure to make this distinction leads journalists to evade responsibility for the consequences of a decision that determines whether an activity remains only nominally public or becomes detrimentally public.

Similarly, the fact that a story is likely to be published elsewhere ("If we don't run it, somebody else will") is not in itself sufficient. With this justification, almost any story can be considered legitimate, whether actually public already or imminently so – if not in the *Wall Street Journal* then in the *Daily News*, or if not in the *Daily News* then in the *Drudge Report*. On the relevance standard, properly interpreted, it makes a difference where the story is published. Contrary to what is often assumed, this difference is becoming more important in the era of cyberpublicity. Publication in the *Journal* (or its local counterpart) gives a story more credibility, and has more effect on political discussion and accountability, than does publication in the tabloids or on the Internet.

Editors sometimes face the dilemma of choosing between reporting unsavory private conduct or ignoring a story that may have public significance. The respectable press often tries to avoid the dilemma by a technique that may be called *metareporting*: writing about the fact that the less respectable press is writing about the private scandal. Thus the *New York Times* publishes a story about unsubstantiated rumors that the *Daily News* has published about Clinton and Lewinsky – complete with miniature reproductions of the front pages of the *News* (Scott 1998). This technique might be more justifiable if the respectable press were not inclined to engage in metareporting about stories that feature sex so much more than about stories that reveal other failings of their fellow journalists.

Unity of Character

A second criterion is that the private conduct should reveal important character flaws that are relevant to the job. Citizens may reasonably want to know about someone's tendency toward domestic violence when he is responsible for enforcing the law and regulating the finances of other people. But the appeal to character must be more specific than the way it is commonly used to justify publicizing private conduct. The general claim that private conduct reveals character flaws that are bound eventually to show up on the job is a psychological version of the classical idea of the unity of the virtues. A person who mistreats his wife is likely to mistreat his colleagues; a person who does not control his violent temper is not likely to resist the temptation to lie.

We should be wary of any justification based on this idea because many people, especially politicians, are quite capable of compartmentalizing their lives in the way that the idea denies. Indeed, for some people, private misbehavior may be cathartic, enabling them to behave better in public. And private virtue is no guarantee of public virtue. We should remember that most of the leading Watergate conspirators led impeccable private lives. So did most of the nearly one hundred political appointees who were indicted or charged with ethics offenses during the early years of the Reagan administration (Lardner 1988).

As far as character is concerned, we should be primarily interested in the political virtues – respect for the law and Constitution, a sense of fairness, honesty in official dealings. These virtues may not be correlated at all with personal ones. And the vices in which the press seems most interested – the sins of sex – are those that are probably least closely connected with the political vices.

Character is sometimes thought to be relevant in a different, more symbolic way. Officials represent us by who they are as much as by what they do. We need to know if they have the character fit for moral leadership – for serving as role models for our youth and virtuous spokespersons for our nation. But this conception of public office is too demanding, as most citizens seem to recognize. They seek leaders whose character displays the political virtues to a high degree, but most do not believe that even the president should be held to higher moral standards in his private life than are ordinary citizens.[6] The question is not whether it would be desirable to have a leader who is as moral in his private as in his public life, but whether it is worth the sacrifice of privacy and the distortions of public debate that would be required to make private probity a job qualification.

If the character trait is specifically related to the job, the case for considering it relevant is stronger, even if the connection is only symbolic. This is part of the reason that Fedders's domestic violence was relevant to his role as a law enforcement official. The point is not that Fedders might actually condone violence or other lawbreaking on the job, but that his private conduct symbolically repudiated the specific values that an official in his position is sworn to uphold. Even smoking cigarettes in the privacy of one's home may be a legitimate target in the case of some public officials. Responding to stories in the press, William Bennett had to give up smoking when he was head of the Drug Enforcement Agency.

Reactions of the Public

Private conduct may affect job performance not only because of what the officials themselves do but also because of the reactions of other people when they find out about the conduct. In the early days of the Lewinsky scandal, many people said that although they themselves did not think the conduct was relevant to Clinton's performance, the expectation that other people, including foreign leaders, would have less confidence in him made it relevant. But we need to be careful about appealing to reactive effects. The anticipated reaction of other people should almost never count as a sufficient reason to publicize further what would otherwise be private. The missing step in the argument – the factor that is often ignored – is the assumption that the private conduct itself is morally wrong, and that therefore the anticipated reactions of other people are morally justified.

Why this step is essential can be seen more clearly if we consider cases of homosexuals in public office being outed. The fact that constituents will vote against their conservative congressman if they find out he is gay is surely not a reason for publicizing his sexual orientation. The mainstream press was right not to disclose the fact that the chief spokesman for the Pentagon during the Gulf War was gay, even though some opponents of the policy of excluding gays from the military sought to publicize that fact. If the congressman had actively opposed gay rights or if the Pentagon spokesman had prominently defended the military's policy, the press would have had a reason to expose their sexual orientation. But justification for the exposure should not be that these officials deserved to be punished for their hypocrisy or even that hypocrisy is in itself always inexcusable, but that their hypocrisy is serving a morally wrong cause.

There is an important qualification to the general rule that public reactions should not count as a reason for exposure unless those reactions are morally justified. If the official flagrantly and for no public purpose disregards moral sensitivities – in effect inviting scrutiny of private conduct that offends many people – the press may be justified in exposing it, whether or not it is in itself wrong. Perhaps the press should not spy on a prominent senator who goes off on a yacht for a rendezvous with his mistress, but when he declares himself a family man and dares the press to prove otherwise, the press has a reason (though not necessarily a sufficient reason) to expose his activities (Dowd 1998).

The senator is guilty of failing to take into account the reasonable reactions of citizens. Officials who behave in these ways display a form of the traditional vice of "giving scandal." In Thomist ethics, "giving scandal" is defined as providing the "occasion for another's fall" (Thomas Aquinas 1972). In secular terms, we could say that a public official who fails to take into account the reasonable reactions of citizens fails to fulfill an important public duty, and citizens deserve to know about that failure. In his escapades with Monica Lewinsky,

President Clinton was inter alia guilty of "giving scandal." Except for the issues of perjury and obstruction of justice (which arose later), this ultimately may be the strongest justification for the press's treating his affair differently (in the early phase) from the more discreet relationships that Robert Dole and George Bush were alleged to have had.

If we invoke reactive effects when applying the relevance standard, we cannot escape making substantive moral judgments. Even when editors decide to disclose private conduct on the grounds that citizens themselves should decide whether that conduct is justifiable, they are in effect judging that the anticipated reactions are not bad enough to outweigh the value of informing citizens about the conduct. Once the story is out, the decision has been made. Without judging to what extent the reactions they are anticipating are justifiable, editors (and citizens more generally) will not be able to distinguish between outing a homosexual and exposing a wife beater.

Priority of Process

The last criterion relates private conduct to other public issues. To what extent does knowing about the conduct help or hinder citizens' learning about *other* matters they need to know to hold officials accountable? Even when private vices bear some relation to the duties of public office, public discussions of politicians' ethics have an unfortunate tendency to dwell on private conduct to the neglect of conduct more relevant to the office. Senator John Tower's drinking problem may have deserved some discussion during the hearings on his nomination to be secretary of defense, but it surely deserved less than his activities as a consultant for defense contractors (Babcock and Woodward 1989). Yet because of the public preoccupation with private immorality, citizens heard little about these financial dealings, which probably would have revealed much more about his record as a senator and his capacity to head the Department of Defense.

In the confirmation hearings of Clarence Thomas, the press, the public, and the Senate Judiciary Committee paid more attention to Thomas's relationship with Anita Hill than to his judicial qualifications. The Gresham effects are especially damaging when, as in this case, irreversible decisions are made under tight constraints of time, so that any distortions in the process of accountability cannot be corrected as they might be in the normal course of politics.

The Gresham effects go well beyond particular cases such as Clarence Thomas and Bill Clinton. The cumulative consequences of many cases, as they increase in number and prominence, create a pattern of press coverage that distorts our essential practices of democratic deliberation. Habits of discourse – the considerations we easily identify, the distinctions we readily make, the reasons we immediately accept – become better adapted to controversies about private life than to public life. The more citizens hone their skills of deliberation on the finer points of sexual encounters (would he have really put her hand there?), the less they are prepared to develop their capacities to deliberate about the nuances of public policy (should he support this revision of social security?). Democratic deliberation is degraded, and democratic accountability thereby eroded.

Publicity about the private lives of public officials can damage the democratic process by distracting citizens from more important questions of policy and performance of government. When deciding whether to publicize what would otherwise be private conduct or when judging such decisions made by others, including the press and officials themselves, the key questions concern the effects on accountability. Is the conduct of a type about which citizens generally need to know in order to hold officials in this position accountable? If the conduct is relevant in this sense, is the degree of the publicity proportionate to the relevance? Are the character flaws revealed by the conduct closely and specifically connected to the office (are they political rather than only personal vices)? If negative public reaction to the conduct is part of the reason for publicizing it, is the reaction morally justified? Is the publicity about the conduct unlikely to distract citizens from paying attention to other political matters they need to know to hold officials accountable (will there be no Gresham effects)? If more journalists, officials, and ordinary citizens would more often take these questions seriously, we might notice some improvement in the quality of democratic discourse. In the meantime, we will remain hostage to the vagaries of a political version of Gresham's law.

Notes

1. For analysis of the principle as part of deliberative democracy, see Gutmann and Thompson 1996, 128–64. Also see the discussion of "publicity" at pp. 95–127. Accountability applies not only retrospectively but also prospectively. Citizens can hold an official accountable for what they reasonably

predicted on the basis of what they learned about the official as a candidate for office.

2. Sixty-four percent of respondents in a February 1998 survey (Bennet 1998) said it is not important for the public to know "what the relationship was" between Clinton and Lewinsky. Distinguishing the relationship from legal testimony about it, 61 percent said it is important for the public to know whether Clinton encouraged Lewinsky to lie.

3. In a February 1998 Roper Center national survey, 80 percent of the respondents said they thought the media coverage of the Clinton-Lewinksy story was "excessive" (February 6, 1998). Sixty percent agreed with the more general proposition that the media had "gone too far in disclosing the details of Clinton's private life," while only 9 percent thought the media had not gone "far enough." Even before this scandal, 60 percent of respondents in May 1994 (Roper Center 1994) said that the news media paid too much attention to Clinton's private life. Since the 1980s there has been a steady and substantial increase in the number of people who say that the "increased attention being given to the private lives of public officials and candidates" is a "bad thing" (from 39 percent in 1989 to 47 percent in 1993) (Gallup Organization, 1989; 1993).

4. A comparative content analysis (Payne and Mercuri 1993) of the press coverage of Gary Hart in the 1988 campaign and Bill Clinton in 1992 found that the stories of the affairs dominated the coverage of Hart's campaign, but "did not fully eclipse" discussion of Clinton's stand on issues because the press "cast more doubt on the accuser, Gennifer Flowers, and the medium, *The Star*" (298).

5. Norman Pearlstine, the *Wall Street Journal* editor, was more careful. For him, Fedders's public admission of guilt, not just the publicness of the proceedings, was essential.

6. About 53 percent of the respondents in a national survey in 1998 (Roper Center, February 23, 1998) in the aftermath of the Lewinsky publicity said that "when it comes to conduct in one's personal life," the president should be held to the same standard you hold yourself, while 44 percent said he should be held to a higher standard. An overwhelming majority, 84 percent, agreed that "someone can still be a good President even if they do things in their personal life that you disapprove of."

References

This article draws on some of my previously published work: "Privacy, Politics, and the Press," *Harvard International Journal of Press/Politics* 3 (Fall 1998): 103–13; "Paradoxes of Government Ethics," *Public Administration Review* 52 (May–June 1992): 254–9; and *Ethics in Congress: From Individual to Institutional Corruption* (Washington, DC: Brookings Institution, 1995). For an earlier and more general discussion (written not only before Monica Lewinsky but even before Gary Hart), see "The Private Lives of Public Officials," in Joel L. Fleishman, Lance Liebman, and Mark Moore, eds., *Public Duties: The Moral Obligations of Government Officials* (Cambridge, Mass.: Harvard University Press, 1981), 221–47; and a revised version in *Political Ethics and Public Office* (Cambridge, Mass.: Harvard University Press, 1987), 123–47.

Babcock, C. R., and B.Woodward. 1989. "Tower: The Consultant as Advocate." *Washington Post*, February 13, A1, A10.

Bennet, J., with J.Elder. 1998. "Despite Intern, President Stays in Good Graces." *New York Times*, February 24, Al, A16.

Congressional Quarterly. 1992.*Congressional Ethics: History, Facts, and Controversy.* Washington, DC: Congressional Quarterly.

Dowd, M. 1998. "Change of Hart." *New York Times*, March 22, Week in Review, 15.

Gallup Organization. 1989. *Gallup, Newsweek* (Conducted June 1–2) [Public Opinion Online]. Storrs, Conn.: University of Connecticut, June.

———.1993. *Gallup, Newsweek* (Conducted March 9–10) [Public Opinion Online]. Storrs, Conn.: Roper Center, University of Connecticut, March 20.

General Accounting Office. 1983. *Information on Selected Aspects of the Ethics in Government Act of 1978.* Washington, DC: U.S. Government Printing Office.

Gutmann, A., and D. Thompson. 1996. *Democracy and Disagreement.* Cambridge, Mass.: Harvard University Press.

Himmelfarb, G. 1998. "Private Lives, Public Morality." *New York Times*, February 9, A19.

Howe, M. A. D. 1932. *Portrait of an Independent: Moorfield Storey, 1845–1929.* Boston: Houghton Mifflin.

Jackson, B. 1985. "John Fedders of SEC Is Pummeled by Legal and Personal Problems." *Wall Street Journal*, February 25, 1, 22.

Lardner, G., Jr. 1988. "Conduct Unbecoming an Administration." *Washington Post National Weekly Edition*, January 3, 31–2.

Payne, J. G., and K. Mercuri. 1993. "Private Lives, Public Officials: The Challenge to Mainstream Media." *American Behavioral Scientist* 37 (November): 291–301.

Roper Center for Survey Research and Analysis. May 1994. Princeton Survey Research Associates, *Newsweek* (Conducted May 6) [Public Opinion Online]. Storrs, Conn.: University of Connecticut.

———. February 6, 1998. *Clinton-Lewinsky News Coverage* (Conducted January 30 to February 4) [Public Opinion Online]. Storrs, Conn.: University of Connecticut.

———. February 23, 1998. *CBS News, New York Times* (Conducted February 19–21) [Public Opinion Online]. Storrs, Conn.: University of Connecticut.

Scott, J. 1998. "Focus Turns Elsewhere in Newspapers and on TV." *New York Times*, February 4, A19.

Senate Ethics Counsel. 1995. *The Packwood Report.* New York: Times Books.

Taylor, Stuart. 1985. "Life in the Spotlight: Agony of Getting Burned." *New York Times*, February 27, A16.

Thomas Aquinas. 1972. Question 43, "Scandal." In T. C. O'Brien, ed. and trans., *Virtues of Justice in the Human Community*, 35: 109–37, London: Blackfriars.

PART III

EXTENSIONS OF INSTITUTIONAL RESPONSIBILITY

11

Restoring Distrust

The questions asked in practical ethics most often take this form: What is the right thing to do? But equally important is a question that is less often asked: What is the right thing to do when others do not do what they ought to do? The ethics of oversight addresses this question. It focuses on the moral responsibility for seeing that other people act rightly and, when they do not, the responsibility for acting to correct the problem.

Overseers now play a more important role than ever, and so, therefore, should the ethics of oversight. In modern society, particularly in organizations, we have to trust the decision makers to act rightly because we cannot monitor everything they do. We trust them in part because we trust the people charged with overseeing them. When both the decision makers and their overseers betray our trust, the violation is more than just a double failure of individual responsibility. It points to a systematic problem of institutional responsibility.

THE SCANDALS: THE FAILURE OF OVERSIGHT

We have seen some striking failures of this kind of responsibility in recent years. I concentrate on three cases from the United States – involving a corporation, a church and a government agency – but their general features, especially the responses to the failures, are relevant to organizations in many other countries. What is striking is how similar the responses are, even though the organizations and the wrongs are quite different. Although only one of the organizations is part of government, all three are political in the sense that they and their members are involved in the exercise of power in a public institution.

Enron

A widely praised energy trading company and the seventh largest corporation in the world, Enron filed for bankruptcy in the fall of 2001 after it became clear that most of its profits over the previous four years had been the result of accounting manipulations.[1] Several top executives had conspired to arrange offshore partnerships to conceal the company's debt (and to make personal profits for themselves). The company's Board and various oversight committees, its long-time auditor Arthur Andersen, and its law firm Vinson and Elkins had either helped with the arrangements, or seen nothing wrong with them. Wall Street analysts, major banks, and government regulators also failed to catch the problems, though there were warnings, including from a high-level executive who later was celebrated as a courageous whistleblower. Before the company collapsed many of the top executives managed to sell their stock, but the rank-and-file employees whose stock was locked into their retirement funds could not. There were a half dozen other major corporate scandals of a similar kind in this period, including the even larger collapse of WorldCom. Enron was not alone.

The Catholic Church

When the *Boston Globe* forced the release of court documents in a suit against Father John Geoghan in January 2002, the public learned that Cardinal Bernard Law and his administrative bishops had not taken any serious disciplinary action against Geoghan or many other priests accused of molesting minors.[2] Most had simply been reassigned to other parishes. As the scandal unfolded, it was revealed that some eighty priests had committed offenses over the past forty years. Nationwide the responses were similar to the more than 1,200 cases that are now known. Again there were plenty of warnings, but little action. Even after the scandal came to light, the National Conference of Bishops declined to censure or call for the resignation of their colleagues who had failed in their oversight duties. Cardinal Law eventually resigned, but two years later none of the other negligent bishops had.

The FBI

Before the attack on the World Trade Center and the Pentagon in September 2001, FBI agents in various field offices had accumulated a significant amount of information that might have exposed at least some of the terrorists' plans.[3] The Minnesota office had been denied permission to seize the computer of Zacarias Moussaoui, the so-called twentieth hijacker. In retrospect, many critics concluded that the supervisors in the Washington office were at fault for the failures. But more relevant for our purposes is the conduct of Director Robert Mueller. In this cast of characters of negligent overseers his motives seem purest. He did not join the Bureau until after 9-11. But for more than nine months he ignored calls for a far-reaching investigation, and disregarded letters from a credible whistle-blower.

These failures took place in very different organizations with different purposes. The failures represented very different degrees and kinds of wrongs, driven by different motives – lust, greed, and other self-interested motives – but also excessive loyalty to an organization and misplaced zeal. (Some of the motivations were bizarre. Consider Father Robert Meffan, a priest who enticed teenage girls preparing to become nuns into sex acts by claiming to be "the second coming of Christ" [Pfeiffer 2002]. Exposed many years later, he explained his motive: "What I was trying to show them is that Christ is human . . . I felt that by having this little bit of intimacy with them that this is what it would be like with Christ.")

Despite the differences in the organizations and the motivations, most of the excuses (and the conception of moral responsibility they express) are very similar. They are all failures of ethical oversight – a failure to take responsibility for dealing with the wrongs that others commit. We can say that these leaders violated our trust. That kind of violation is all the more important in an organizational society because we count on trusting leaders like these to ensure that others fulfill *their* trust.

THE INDIVIDUALIST RESPONSE: DEMANDS FOR
MORE TRUST

The public and press certainly viewed all these failures as violations of trust. In each case, the dominant responses were framed in terms of the need to restore trust. The U.S. Conference of Catholic Bishops titled their official response to clergy abuse: "Restoring Trust" (2003). *Business Week*'s cover story about Enron was headlined: "Restoring Trust in Corporate America" (Byrne 2002). Alan Greenspan in his congressional testimony in July 2002 stated: "our market system depends critically on trust – trust in the word of our colleagues and trust in the word of those with whom we do business." (U.S. Senate 2002a). Coleen Rowley, the FBI agent who blew the whistle on the bureau's failures before 9-11 wrote: It "almost always boil[s] down, in the final analysis to one thing: trust. It's hard to [do our job if the public] . . . refuses to trust what you're saying about how the law or policy is applied in practice" (U.S. Senate 2002d).

These lamentations about trust resonate with the more general trend in social criticism and social theory in the past decade (Braithwaite and Levi 1998; Nye, Zelikow, and King 1997; O'Neill 2002b; Putnam 2001; Warren 1999a). Many writers have worried about the decline of trust in government, in the professions, and among ordinary citizens. Voters are increasingly cynical about government; people are increasingly suspicious of professionals. Social capital is eroding, and more people are bowling alone.

It is therefore not surprising that we are hearing more calls for restoring trust. I am not opposed to the efforts to try to reestablish trust in government, in the professions, and in civil society more generally. (I would not even oppose giving a boost to bowling leagues.) But in devoting all this attention to trust, we are neglecting the importance of *distrust*. The efforts to try to restore trust are missing an essential point: we should not trust our institutions unless we can be confident that someone is distrusting the officials who run them.

The priests who abused children, the CEOs and CFOs who cooked the books, and the FBI desk officers in Washington – they were all trusted too much by their overseers. The most conspicuous example is Arthur Andersen – Enron's auditors (Nanda 2002; U.S. Senate 2002c). These auditors did not ask hard questions partly because they had an especially close relationship with Enron executives. More than a hundred Arthur Andersen auditors had their permanent offices in the Enron headquarters. Also, like many accounting firms, Arthur Andersen had a large consulting contract with the firm it was auditing, which was more lucrative than the auditing. The management consultants from Arthur Andersen had their offices on the same floor with the auditors. And many of the financial executives at Enron had earlier worked at Arthur Andersen. This cozy arrangement was praised as "integrated accounting" (Dugan, Berman, and Barrionuevo 2002). In these and the many similar cases, what we need is not more trust, but more distrust.

The preoccupation with trust reflects a broader fixation on the individualist approach to practical ethics. Trust is an interpersonal interaction, commonly understood as a relationship between two individuals (or small groups of individuals).[4] I can trust you because I know you well enough to know that you are trustworthy: I know that you have good character. I can rely on you to act on my behalf even if I cannot always monitor your behavior. The reactions if you violate the trust are also individualist: I criticize your character, give you unfavorable recommendations, impose penalties, break off relations with you, and so on. Or if I think you can be rehabilitated, as the Cardinal and his bishops believed that the priests might be, I may take less punitive measures, though they would still be tailored to the individuals in question.

In contrast, the concept of distrust points toward a more institutional approach to practical ethics – an approach that is more appropriate for the organization-dominated public life in which we now live and work. If we recognize the importance of distrust, we will make sure that the institutions on which we depend are designed in a way to encourage good behavior in the absence of good character, and in the absence of trusting personal relations (see Warren 1999b; Offe 1999).

Creating institutions founded in part on distrust is following the counsel of Hume: "It is a just political maxim that every man must be supposed a knave, though at the same time ... [it] is false in fact" (Hume 1994). The rationale for much of the American Constitution, as presented especially by Madison in the *Federalist* papers, assumes that "enlightened statesmen will not always be at the helm" (Madison 1961). But this approach has new relevance and takes new forms in an organizational age, because it is needed not only for the constitutions of states but also for the constitutions of many other kinds of institutions. It provides a foundation for shifting our political ethics – from an individualist to an institutional mode – as we make judgments of blame and responsibility, and offer prescriptions for reform and prevention.

THE INSTITUTIONAL RESPONSE: DEVICES OF DISTRUST

To show why we need to make this shift toward a more institutional approach, consider the responses to three different types of agents in the three dramas featuring Enron, the Church, and the FBI: those who committed the offenses; those who accused them; and those who should have been monitoring them. In each case, I shall argue that our responses have been too individualist, and show why an institutional approach is more appropriate.

The Offenders

In all of these scandals, the first and most intense condemnation was directed at the primary wrongdoers – the offenders who committed the crimes or misdeeds. The abusive priests, the devious executives, the evil hijackers – these people of course did not all commit the same kinds or degrees of wrongs, but they were identifiable individuals. They were individuals who acted deliberately and with full knowledge of what they were doing. The language in which they were condemned was characteristically individualist: it referred most often to the vices, to the bad character of the offenders. Alan Greenspan captured the mood of condemning individual vice when he diagnosed the problem of corporate corruption as a result of "infectious greed" (U.S. Senate 2002a).

The leaders and other officials who were responsible for preventing these wrongs – the overseers – do not have the same kind of bad character. And for the most part they did not do wrong deliberately or with full knowledge of the consequences. That is why they felt comfortable using the excuses of ignorance, such as "we cannot be criticized for failing to address . . . problems that have been concealed from us" (U.S. Senate 2002b, 14). When they took responsibility or apologized, as many of them did, they engaged in a ritual of responsibility. Taking responsibility becomes merely a political tactic that has no negative effect on a leader. It often effectively blocks further inquiry into the actual moral responsibility of all the officials who might have prevented the offense in question, and who ought to be doing something more about it.

The excuses – and these ritualistic takings of responsibility – sometimes work. They can protect the overseers because of what I call the problem of many hands (discussed in Chapter 1). In any complex organization, an offense is often the result of a pattern of conduct or series of harms to which many different individuals contribute, often in relatively small ways and often under some pressure or without full knowledge. The individual offense seems much less serious than the collective offense. The moral whole is greater than the sum of its parts. This is especially so in the cases of the failure of oversight. However negligent the Enron Board, the Cardinal and his bishops, or the Washington officials in the FBI may have been, their individual guilt pales in comparison with that of the Skillings, Geoghans, or the Moussaouis of the world.

Yet this focus on individual guilt or responsibility – more precisely, the focus on the responsibility for specific actions by individuals considered one at a time – misses the difference that the institutional roles make. If we recognize the great harm that individuals in an institution acting or failing to act together can cause, we can begin to shift our attention to the institutional structures that cause the harm. We will focus more on the institutional failures and less on the individual faults.

There are two main types of institutional failures of oversight. The first is what I call prospective oversight, a failure to support institutions that can prevent the wrongs. Each of the cases supplies examples. Enron's Board rescinded the ethics rules that had prevented their executives from owning stock in corporations with whom Enron did business (U.S. Senate 2002b). CEO Skilling and CFO Fastow exploited this leniency to establish Raptor and the other notorious offshore partnerships. The Church, as Cardinal Law himself noted, suffered from a lapse of "institutional memory": it did not keep adequate personnel records or adopt any procedures that would inform parishes where the problem priests were transferred (Law 2002b). After the *Globe*'s legal actions forced the Church to open up all its records, it became clear that there was more information than the Cardinal had implied. The FBI (and its overseers in Congress) supported a "bureaucratic culture" that discouraged "risk taking" and downgraded the role of analysts (Johnston and Van Natta 2002). The culture also reinforced suspicion of other agencies, especially the CIA, making it difficult to share information about terrorists. In this respect, there was excessive personal trust within units inside the organization (within each field office, and within headquarters), and too little trust between the field office and headquarters, and between the Bureau as a whole and outside agencies (Lazarus 2002).

The second type of institutional failure involves retrospective oversight. It has been even less appreciated, and it is even more important for the ethics of oversight. FBI Director Mueller is an especially apt example because he joined the agency after 9-11. He cannot himself be blamed for any of the institutional failures of the first type – the failures to prevent the hijackings or at least to discover the connections between the various pieces of information that the government had gathered about the hijackers. These failures did not happen on his watch. That is why he welcomed the question, which was repeatedly posed by the public and the press: could the hijackings have been prevented? No, he answered, plausibly enough (U.S. Senate 2002d). But he ignored Coleen Rowley's early whistle-blowing. He did not initiate major investigations or institute any serious reforms until many months later when public pressure forced him to take further action, and responded only when she released her letter to the public. Under his regime, other officials continued to harass an agent who had blown the whistle on mistakes in the Ruby Ridge incident (Leahy 2002). None of Mueller's reforms included improving the oversight institutions (including rights of whistle-blowers, who are not covered by the protections that other federal workers enjoy). He cut even the staff of the Law Enforcement Ethics Unit in the Bureau (Eggen 2002).

The Church also failed in retrospective oversight. The charter published by the Conference of Catholic Bishops in November 2002 concentrated almost entirely on the offenses of the priests (U.S. Conference of Catholic Bishops 2002). It did not even mention the bishops who transferred the priests without reporting their offenses. The conference rejected proposals to institute a lay council that could audit the finances and other practices (Goodstein 2002). The Vatican then further diluted the conference's own recommendations. Neither the bishops nor Vatican officials were prepared to do anything about the excessive secrecy and abuse of confidentiality that had been part of the reason the oversight had failed so badly in the past.

In the case of Enron, the most telling example is the corporation's own attempt at an investigation: the internal committee the board appointed concluded that the board and most of the outside advisers had been misled by key managers such as the CEO and the CFO (Enron Board of Directors 2002). The focus on the individual culprit not only protected the board and other gatekeepers, but distracted attention from the need for major reform of corporate governance, the auditing profession, and government agencies such as the SEC.

In urging that we pay more attention to institutional failures such as the neglect of retrospective oversight, I am not rejecting the idea of individual moral responsibility in favor of some notion of collective responsibility. Perhaps corporations and the Church should be sued, perhaps the FBI should be sanctioned. But organizational liability should not replace personal responsibility. We would still hold individuals responsible, but for the oversight of their institutions. What I am suggesting is a shift in focus away from individual responsibility for committing the primary offenses to individual responsibility for failing to monitor the institutional practices that permit those offenses. It is individuals whom we should hold responsible for creating and maintaining the conditions for proper institutional oversight.

This change of focus to the ethics of oversight calls for some modifications of our ethical concepts and practices of individual responsibility itself. We may need to modify the standard notions of individual responsibility so that we are prepared to condemn and punish overseers for acts of omission as much as for acts of commission; gross negligence as much as for intentional wrongdoing; offenses of oversight as much as for the primary offenses over which the oversight is exercised; and inappropriately trusting friends and colleagues as much as for mistakenly trusting enemies and rivals. Judgments of individual character certainly have a place in the ethics of oversight. But it focuses less on the vices and virtues of primary decision makers in organizations (greed or honesty, for example), and more on the vices and virtues of the monitors (carelessness or vigilance, for example). On this approach, a watchful official is no less admirable than a benevolent one.

The Accusers

Among the many parallels in the three scandals, one of the most striking is that in each case there was a prominent whistle-blower who played an important role in bringing the scandal to light. Rowley, who was the general counsel in the FBI's Minnesota office, wrote to Director Mueller in May 2002 describing earlier refusals by headquarters officials to grant the Minnesota office permission to apply for a search warrant to examine the computer of Zacarias Moussaoui, the so-called twentieth hijacker (Rowley 2002; U.S. Senate 2002d). When Mueller appeared to do nothing to correct the alleged errors of headquarters, she wrote again criticizing him personally – in effect charging him with a failure of retrospective oversight. In the case of Enron, there was Sherron Watkins, a middle level executive in the finance section of the company. She first wrote an anonymous letter, then went in person to see the company chairman, Kenneth Lay. He instructed lawyers to investigate. Unfortunately, the lawyers he chose were the company's own outside counsel, Vinson and Elkins, who had earlier signed off on some of the same partnerships and other arrangements that were in question. In the Church, one of the first and most significant accusations against a priest came from Margaret Gallant, who complained to Cardinal Law as early as 1982 about Father John Geoghan (Investigative Staff of the Boston Globe 2002). She charged that he had molested seven young members of her family. The Cardinal wrote back: "sinners can be forgiven." It was not until 1996 that Geoghan was forced to take a permanent leave.

These whistle-blowers are certainly to be admired – they and others have been widely praised. Three appeared on the cover of *Time* magazine as "persons of the year" (Lacayo and Ripley 2002). Because whistle-blowing is a manifestation of distrust, it might seem that I should be arguing in favor of more of it. I am not of course opposed to it. But I do not believe that it is the most appropriate model for the ethics of oversight.

The celebration of whistle-blowers is a further manifestation of the excessively individualist approach to organizational ethics. In this kind of oversight, the villains are despicable individuals, and the heroes (or heroines) are admirable individuals. The organization is harmed by individuals, and then saved by individuals. We trust that when the organization goes bad, some individual – someone, somewhere – will blow the whistle. Concentrating on whistle-blowing distracts us from seeking a more systematic institutional response to organizational failures.

It is perhaps no accident that the whistle-blowers in these cases were all women. (In one of the other major corporate scandals of the year, Worldcom, the whistle-blower was also a woman, Cynthia Cooper.) These women all held important positions in their organizations, but they did not expect to become CEOs, or advance much higher than their current level. They were not part of the old-boy networks of their companies. They were not part of the inner circle where personal trust smoothes over disagreements, and puts to rest potential doubts about one's colleagues. They were more willing to take risks with their careers, and less willing to trust colleagues who seemed to be engaging in questionable conduct. Does this mean that as more women rise in the power structures of large organizations, there will be more potential whistle-blowers? We should not count on it. As women's opportunities in the corporate world increase, one of the less happy consequences may be that they will act in this respect more like men.

For at least three reasons, we cannot count on whistle-blowing as a reliable method of oversight (Johnson 2002; Glazer and Glazer 1989). First, when someone blows the whistle, even as publicly and about such a prominent issue as terrorism after 9-11, she does not necessarily produce results. Whistle-blowing was not sufficient in any of these cases, and probably was not even necessary in some of them. Second, whistle-blowing is not particularly well suited to exposing patterns of abuse – the systematic failures of the institution and especially the defects in the methods of oversight. Usually, only people at relatively high levels of the organization are in a position to see the patterns, and they are the least likely to blow the whistle. Rowley herself may not have been fully informed. There is now some reason to believe that she in fact may have been partly mistaken in her complaint. Some experts believe that her fellow agents did not have a sufficient case for a search warrant after all (Lazarus 2002; U.S. Senate 2002f). Third, because whistle-blowing is risky, it is not likely to occur as often as abuses occur. It underinsures against institutional failure, and is therefore not a reliable basis for putting our trust in leaders and institutions. Even when whistle-blowers do not suffer retaliation, their careers almost always suffer.

Whistle-blowing is a form of distrust but not the most appropriate form. In effect, whistle-blowing as a practice universalizes distrust. It makes everyone an overseer. No one in the organization is specifically responsible for discovering and reporting problems. Every priest, agent, or employee is a potential guardian of the organization's integrity. This seems to fit better with common individual morality. We all have the duty to help people in trouble, or to report a crime when we see it. When it comes to natural duties, there is no specialization of moral labor.

But organizations are defined in part by specialization: a division of labor is the essence of organizational life. Organizational ethics should in part mirror that structure. Of course we want to preserve some of the general responsibility that everyone should have to act when things go wrong. But at the same time we should assign specific and continuous responsibility to certain roles within the organization.

We should promote some specialization in distrust – roles and institutions specifically dedicated to oversight.

The Overseers

The ethics of oversight does not call for completely new kinds of institutions. It could function quite well with some of the institutions that already exist, such as inspectors general, ombudspersons, and "trustee" members of boards of directors. But the ethics of oversight does require that we conceptualize these and other similar institutions in different ways. They should have a more prominent role and should be designed so that they display more distrust – so that they are more consistently and constructively vigilant than they have been. The aim would be not to populate the institutions with a different kind of people – people who are more prone to distrust. Too much distrust in the individual mind is a form of madness (Hertzberg 1988). The aim instead should be to create structures in which normal, ordinarily conscientious people will understand their main responsibility to be watching for problems and warning the appropriate officials about them.

Three broad ethical principles should guide our assessment of any reforms of the structures of oversight. Each tracks an aspect of the concept of moral responsibility: a responsible person or institution is one that acts not under compulsion, with knowledge, and on public reasons. The first two are familiar criteria in the literature since Aristotle, and the third adds a more modern requirement suggested by Kant and developed later by Rawls.[5] Applied in practice to institutions, the criteria track some of the conditions that deliberative democrats have proposed for holding public officials accountable (Gutmann and Thompson 1996).

Independence. The most important principle is that the overseers be independent enough to make judgments on the basis of the good of the organization as a whole, rather than the interests of particular executives or officials within it, and (equally important) with due regard for the rights and welfare of citizens who are not members of the organization. Financial dependence is the most obvious way this principle can be violated. Because Arthur Andersen depended on Enron for a significant share of its profits from management consulting, its auditors were less likely to take a hard look at Enron's dubious accounting practices. That is why the law should prohibit accounting firms from selling management consulting services to the companies they audit.

Some critics have objected that this kind of proposal carries the idea of conflict of interest too far.[6] After all, we have to trust the auditors to act honestly despite the fact that they are getting paid for the auditing. They already have a conflict of interest because they have an interest in keeping large accounting contracts. So why not trust them with management consulting?

There is an important difference between auditing and consulting in these circumstances. Firing your auditor is a dramatic, high-visibility event, almost certain to raise suspicions among investors and the press. Hiring a different management consultant is common enough, and can easily be presented as a routine business decision, like changing ad agencies. Publicity can serve as a deterrent for firing your auditor, but not for changing your consultant. A good practical precept in organizational ethics is this: where publicity loses its grip, prohibition must come to the rescue. (I return to the idea of publicity later.)

Personal loyalty (another form of trust) can also be an obstacle to independence, especially in nonprofit organizations such as the Church, or in civil service careers such as the FBI. To counter the excessive loyalty that develops, we need lay councils of the kind urged by groups such as Voice of the Faithful, but so far rejected by the Conference of Bishops. An Office of Professional Responsibility might serve this function for organizations such as the FBI if it broadened its mandate beyond the issues on which the Bureau's Office now concentrates, such as the use of cars for personal purposes (Johnston and Van Natta 2002).

Knowledge. Overseers cannot monitor an organization unless they know a lot about it. The most common excuses that offending leaders give appeal to ignorance: "I didn't know." In the case of Enron and the Church, the excuses were exaggerated. There were plenty of warnings about the misconduct. But for truly effective oversight you need to know not only about specific misdeeds, but patterns and tendencies, which may not yet have caused problems but are likely to do so in the future. This kind of knowledge, often specific to the organization, can come only from experience within the organization. It is more likely to come to overseers who over the years have developed friendships with colleagues who give them inside information. In this way, the knowledge principle may conflict with the independence principle. Knowing more may require depending more.

Nevertheless, it is possible to structure oversight institutions so that members with extensive experience in the organization, or at least in an organization of a similar type, have incentives to reach independent judgments. A temporal division of labor may be one solution: officials could be rotated through the oversight agency as part of their career advancement. Some police departments have found that their internal affairs unit works better if they follow this practice (U.S. Senate 2001). It is essential, however, that the officials serving in such units know that their future career advancement depends on performing well in their role as overseer.

For any of these practices to work well, the performance of the oversight agency itself has to be judged independently. That means that its operation has to be subject to public scrutiny. The conduct of overseers themselves must be accessible to public inspection.

Publicity. To reconcile the independence and knowledge criterion, therefore, we call on a third principle – publicity. Kant designated this principle as a criterion of morality: "All actions which relate to the right of other men are contrary to right and law [if their] maxim . . . does not permit publicity."[7] But for organizational ethics we need to turn what for Kant is a hypothetical condition for morality and justice into an actual requirement for responsibility.

Many of the initial oversight problems in the recent scandals were partly the result of too much confidentiality. The organizations have certain rights to privacy and can make legitimate claims for confidentiality. Protecting the privacy of the priests (and the victims), the rights of suspects, and the secrecy of business deals from competitors can be worthy ends. But at the oversight level, these claims lose much of their force. Appealing to them begins to look less like a protection of the innocent and more like a cover up for the guilty. The victims no longer need protection, the suspects have been exposed, and so have the business deals. Who is left to be protected? Mostly the overseers themselves.

Unlimited openness is neither realistic nor desirable. Too much transparency may make it harder for overseers to do their job. People may be reluctant to bring forward information if they think that anything they report will be made public immediately. But oversight bodies can function more openly than they have in the past. They can make clear in advance the types of information they will keep secret, the reasons for the secrecy, and the possibilities for future access to the information. They can maintain comprehensive records, which could be available for inspection at some future time for specified purposes. Even if the publicity is too late to make any difference in the instant case, the prospect of future publicity could act as a deterrent for overseers who are tempted to neglect their duties.

OBJECTIONS

All this emphasis on distrust may make some readers uneasy about the approach proposed here – perhaps even distrustful of it. At least three kinds of objections may be brought against the approach. All of them in one form or another suggest that trying to increase distrust is self-defeating. There are philosophical, sociological, and constitutional versions of the criticism.

Philosophical

The philosophical versions usually seek to show how distrust undermines the trust that is necessary for successful human relations in any context.[8] In one form, the objection takes an ethical turn. To the extent that an institution creates rules and procedures that imply distrust (and assume that people cannot be trusted), members of the institution are justified – ethically justified – in acting as if they are not trustworthy. "If you don't trust me, I don't see why I should go out of my way to act as your trusted agent. I'll follow the rules but no more than that." This kind of attitude could logically generate a spiral of distrust (and, practically, a culture of distrust) in an organization.

The objection can also be stated in a somewhat different form: the practices of a distrustful institution unfairly shift the burden of proof. All members of the organization are presumed to be untrustworthy until proven trustworthy. It is as if the criminal system picked defendants randomly and asked them to defend themselves. Oversight based on distrust in effect declares, before any evidence has been presented, that everyone in the organization is an offender.

The objection in all its forms treats the relationships in organizations in personal rather than the impersonal terms more appropriate to oversight practices. In this respect, it relies too much on an individualist notion of trust. The procedures of oversight imply distrust only in the impersonal sense that they assume that anyone could potentially be an offender, not that everyone is actually an offender who has merely not yet been discovered. The procedures prescribe prophylactic and punitive measures, but do not logically presume that everyone subject to them is untrustworthy. Oversight is intended to prevent violations of trust from occurring, and if successful will keep everyone trustworthy.

From this perspective, the practice of oversight is one that all members of the organization can see as necessary for their mutual protection against potential failures – their own as well as those of others. In principle, the overseers are performing a role that any member should reasonably accept. They are a kind of devil's advocate for distrust, who in order to ensure that members are trustworthy must act, within limits, as if they are not. Understood in this way, oversight practices do not lessen the obligation of any member to be trustworthy, and therefore do not provide any ethical basis for the retaliatory responses that can set off the spiral of distrust.

Although this objection presents itself as philosophical, it depends in significant measure on an empirical premise. The premise is that institutional rules (such as prohibitions of conflict of interest) tend to cause people to act as if they are not trusted, and generate actual spirals of distrust and actual shifts in burdens of proof. This raises questions about the sociology of trust and brings us to the second type of objection.

Sociological

Some studies have shown that, in organizations, professionals who are trusted are more likely to be trustworthy (Braithwaite 1998). That is, the more that people are treated as if they are the kind of people who fulfill their obligations, the more likely they will be to fulfill their obligations even when they are not monitored. The most extensive evidence comes from – of all places – Australian nursing homes. The findings resonate with much management and personnel literature and with common sense. If you treat people as worthy of respect and trust, they are more likely to act that way.

But these findings apply more to people at the lower and middle levels of an organization. There is less evidence that they hold for the executives in charge, and there is no evidence that they apply to overseers. We should also keep in mind that nursing homes have elaborate regulations, which are enforced by authorities that are independent, knowledgeable, and public.

Certainly, we should not favor more rules and regulations – engaging in what has been called "the ritual of accountability" – if they result mainly in filling out forms, multiplying routine reports, and proliferating review committees (Power 1999). But a robust set of institutions of oversight, properly designed, could enable us to have *fewer* rules and regulations and could allow *more* discretion, because it would ensure that the most egregious violations and most damaging patterns of abuse would be identified promptly and dealt with effectively.[9] Effective oversight, while intensifying distrust, concentrates it in specific roles and practices in an organization, permitting other roles and practices to function in a less distrustful environment.

Constitutional

The third objection is a variation of the age-old question of constitutionalism: "Who will guard the guardians?" becomes "Who will oversee the overseers?" A completely hierarchical system of accountability is subject to a regress of authority (Braithwaite 1998; Power 1999: 134–6); overseers overseeing overseers all the way up. But in the absence of a single trustworthy guardian – a cadre of philosopher kings (and queens) – the answer must be to multiply the overseers at various levels, and allow them to check one another.

While this must be part of any answer to this question, it raises a further question itself. That question is a variation of the problem of many hands. It might be called the problem of many overseers. The most salient feature of the Enron scandal is just how complete and widespread was the failure of oversight (Coffee 2002, Nanda 2002). Every single one of the gatekeepers failed: the board of directors, the outside auditors, the law firms, the Wall Street analysts, the banks that arranged the credit, the Security and Exchange Commission, the Federal Energy Regulatory Commission, and even the financial press.

Instead of providing fail-safe and backup protections, the existence of multiple overseers gave everyone a false sense of security. After the fact, it also provided a bountiful fund of excuses. The board relied on the accountants who relied on the auditors who depended on the government who depended on the auditors, and so on.

The allocation of responsibility in this kind of multiple-monitor system thus has to be done carefully. We need multiple overseers, and each should have distinct spheres of responsibility, but each should also have some specific responsibility for overseeing other overseers. The problem in the Enron case was that the lawyers did not question the auditors because accounting was assumed not to be the business of lawyers, though the lawyers knew enough to suspect that something was wrong with the accounting. Similarly in the Church and the FBI, the problem was not too much overlap of oversight but too little.

What we need are stronger bodies that are specifically responsible for monitoring the primary overseers themselves. Examples include the lay councils of the Church, offices of professional responsibility for law enforcement agencies, and professional associations and government agencies for the accountants. The Public Company Accounting Oversight Board created by the recently enacted Sarbanes-Oxley bill would be an appropriate model, if its members can be made truly independent (*Sarbanes-Oxley Act of 2002*, Title 1).

What we do not need are more rules and regulations, especially those that require more forms and reports, indiscriminately imposed, as many have been in the past. Such an approach manifests the pathologies of distrust. It runs contrary to a healthy ethics of oversight. Requirements imposed without regard to their wider effects not only erode desirable forms of trust, and impede and frustrate organizational efficiency, but they also provide false assurance and may even increase the incidence of misconduct in an organization. The focus should be on the overseers themselves: they should be held accountable for monitoring the organization in ways that do not impair its central goals, and for providing information and analysis to all those who are significantly affected by its actions. They should be prepared to give their colleagues and their fellow citizens accounts that are independent, knowledgeable, and public. In this way they can contribute to the continuing deliberation that should take place about the role of their organization in the wider democratic society.

CONCLUSION

These three scandals show why practical ethics should pay more attention to the question of what might be called second-order responsibility: What ought to be done when others do not do what they ought to do? What ought to be done is to make sure that those responsible for oversight systematically distrust the leaders who hold positions of trust in major organizations. We should more diligently and more deliberately institutionalize distrust.

I have suggested that an individualist approach to ethics obscures this aim, and produces a deficient ethics of oversight. We are better served by an institutional approach, which still holds individuals responsible for oversight. If we want to restore trust in our leaders and our institutions, then we should begin by restoring some distrust.

Notes

1. Useful overviews of the Enron scandal are: Coffee 2002; Fox 2002; Gordon 2002; and Nanda 2002. The U.S. Senate reports provide the most detailed accounts so far: U.S. Senate 2002b; and U.S. Senate 2002c. The report of the Enron Board's special investigative committee is more critical than one might expect, except on the role of the board itself (Enron Board of Directors, Special Investigative Committee 2002).

2. A wide-ranging account of the scandal and its background is: Investigative Staff of the Boston Globe 2002. The extensive depositions in the civil case filed against the Church should be consulted for more detail and for the perspective of the Church officials. See, for example, Law 2002a.

3. For the FBI case, government reports and congressional testimony are the most useful sources: U.S. Senate 2001; U.S. Senate 2002d; U.S. Senate 2002e; U.S. Senate 2002f; U.S. Senate 2002g; and U.S. Department of Justice 2002. Also see Coleen Rowley's memo to Director Robert Mueller (Rowley 2002).

4. For analyses of the concept of trust, see O'Neill 2002a; 2002b; Uslaner 2002; Hardin 2002; Becker 1996; Baier 1986; Hertzberg 1988; and chapters in Braithwaite and Levi 1998.

5. Aristotle 1963, 1109b–11b. Cf. Glover 1970, esp. 60–1; and Donagan 1977, 112–42. For Rawls and Kant, see note 7.

6. Coffee (2002) raises the objection but provides an answer consistent with that suggested in the text.

7. Kant 1996. For John Rawls (1971), a similar principle is a necessary condition of justice: "The point of the publicity condition is to have the parties [to the original position] evaluate conceptions of justice as publicly acknowledged and fully effective moral constitutions of social life." From the very different perspective of utilitarianism, Bentham also insisted that publicity is essential: "Let us place at the head of [the political assembly's] regulations the fittest law for securing the public confidence, and causing it constantly to advance towards the end of its institution . . . [the] law . . . of publicity" (Bentham 1962).

8. The philosopher who has provided the most extended criticism of increased accountability is Onora O'Neill. The philosophical objections I presented in the text are suggested by her comments though she does not present them in exactly the same form. See O'Neill 2002a; and 2002b. Petit (1998) also raises and then attempts to answer what might be termed a philosophical objection (the paradox between trusting in leaders and maintaining vigilance, which he sees as characteristic of "republican theory").

9. Accounting standards in the United States are generally more detailed and rule-based than those in Europe. Many experts believe that the former permit auditors and their clients to escape responsibility (for example, by exploiting loopholes), and the latter encourage a broader and more reliable responsibility for the overall integrity of the accounts (for example, by granting auditors greater discretion) (*Financial Times* 2002).

References

Aristotle. 1963. *The Works of Aristotle, Ethica Nicomachea*, edited by W. D. Ross. Oxford: Oxford University Press.

Baier, Annette. 1986. "Trust and Antitrust." *Ethics 96* (January): 231–60.

Becker, Lawrence C. 1996. "Trust as Noncognitive Security about Motives." *Ethics* 107 (October): 43–61.

Bentham, Jeremy. 1962. "Essay on Political Tactics," "Of Publicity." Vol. VIII, *Works*, edited by John Bowring. New York: Russell & Russell.

Braithwaite, John. 1998. "Institutionalizing Distrust, Enculturating Distrust." In *Trust and Governance*, edited by V. Braithwaite and M. Levi. New York: Russell Sage, 343–75.

Braithwaite, Valerie, and Margaret Levi, eds. 1998. *Trust and Governance*. New York: Russell Sage.

Byrne, John A. 2002. "Restoring Trust in Corporate America." *Business Week*, 24 June.

Coffee, John C. 2002. "Understanding Enron: 'It's About the Gatekeepers, Stupid.'" *The Business Lawyer* 57 (August): 1403–20.

Donagan, Alan. 1977. *The Theory of Morality*. Chicago: University of Chicago Press.

Dugan, Ianthe Jeanne, Dennis Berman, and Alexei Barrionuevo. 2002. "On Camera: People at Andersen." *Wall Street Journal*, 15 April.

Eggen, Dan. 2002. "FBI Whistle-Blower's Case Reexamined." *Washington Post*, 11 November, A02.

Enron Board of Directors, Special Investigative Committee. 2002. *Report*, 1 February.

Financial Times. 2002. "Honest Numbers: Accounting and Auditing." 19 February.

Fox, Loren. 2002. *Enron: The Rise and Fall*. New York: John Wiley.

Glazer, Myron Peretz, and Penina Migdal Glazer. 1989. *The Whistleblowers: Exposing Corruption in Government and Industry*. New York: Basic Books.

Glover, Jonathan. 1970. *Responsibility*. London: Routledge & Kegan Paul.

Goodstein, Laurie. 2002. "Bishops Pass Plan to Form Tribunals in Sex Abuse Cases." *New York Times*, 14 November, A1.

Gordon, Jeffrey N. 2002. "What Enron Means for the Management and Control of the Modern Corporation." *University of Chicago Law Review* 69 (summer): 1233–50.

Gutmann, Amy, and Dennis Thompson. 1996. *Democracy and Disagreement*. Cambridge, Mass.: Harvard University Press.

Hardin, Russell. 2002. *Trust and Trustworthiness*. New York: Russell Sage.

Hertzberg, Lars. 1988. "On the Attitude of Trust." *Inquiry* 31: 307–22.

Hume, David. 1994. "Of the Independency of Parliament." In *Political Essays*, edited by Knud Hakkonssen. Cambridge: Cambridge University Press.

Investigative Staff of the Boston Globe. 2002. *Betrayal: The Crisis in the Catholic Church*. Boston: Little, Brown.

Johnson, Roberta Ann. 2002. *Whistleblowing: When it Works – and Why*. Boulder, Colo: Lynne Rienner.

Johnston, David, and Don Van Natta, Jr. 2002. "Wary of Risk, Slow to Adapt, F.B.I. Stumbles in Terror War." *New York Times*, 2 June, sec. 1, 1.

Lacayo, Richard, and Amanda Ripley. 2002. "Persons of the Year: Sherron Watkins of Enron, Coleen Rowley of the FBI, Cynthia Cooper of WorldCom." *Time Magazine*, 22 December.

Law, Cardinal Bernard. 2002a. *Deposition in connection with civil lawsuits... [regarding] Rev. Paul R. Shanley*. August, October. Available online: http://www.boston.com/globe/spotlight/abuse/shanley/law_deposition/081302_entire.htm (1 April 2003).

———. 2002b. *Letter to priests of the Boston Archdiocese*, 12 April. Available online: http://www.boston.com/globe/spotlight/abuse/documents/law_letter_041202_a.htm (1 April 2003).

Lazarus, Edward. 2002. "At the F.B.I., It's Always Been Washington vs. the Field." *New York Times*, 11 August, sec. 4, 4.

Leahy, Sen. Patrick. 2002. "The DOJ Inspector General's Report on Allegations of a Double Standard at the FBI." 15 November. Available online: http://leahy.senate.gov/press/200211/111502a.html (1 April 2003).

Madison, James. 1961. *The Federalist* No. 10, edited by Benjamin Fletcher Wright. Cambridge: Harvard University Press.

Nanda, Ashish. 2002. *Broken Trust: Role of Professionals in the Enron Debacle*. Cambridge, Mass.: Harvard Business School, Division of Research, Working Paper.

Nye, Joseph S., Jr., Philip D. Zelikow, and David C. King, eds. 1997. *Why People Don't Trust Government*. Cambridge, Mass.: Harvard University Press.

Offe, Claus. 1999. "How Can We Trust Our Fellow Citizens?" In *Democracy and Trust*, edited by Mark Warren. Cambridge: Cambridge University Press, 42–87.

O'Neill, Onora. 2002a. *Autonomy and Trust in Bioethics*. Cambridge: Cambridge University Press.

———. 2002b. *A Question of Trust*. Cambridge: Cambridge University Press.

Pettit, Philip. 1998. "Republican Theory and Political Trust." In *Trust and Governance*, edited by V. Braithwaite and M. Levi. New York: Russell Sage.

Pfeiffer, Sacha. 2002. "He Invoked Religion for Sexual Acts." *Boston Globe*, 4 December, A1.

Power, Michael. 1999. *The Audit Society: Rituals of Verification*. Oxford: Oxford University Press.

Putnam, Robert. 2001. *Bowling Alone: The Collapse and Revival of American Community*. New York: Simon and Schuster.

Rawls, John. 1971. *A Theory of Justice*. Cambridge, Mass.: Harvard University Press.

Rowley, Coleen. 2002. "Memo to FBI Director Robert Mueller." Edited version by *Time Magazine*, 21 May. Available online: http://www.time.com/time/nation/article/0,8599,249997,00.html (1 April 2003).

Sarbanes-Oxley Act of 2002. U.S. Public Law 107–204. 107th Cong., 2nd sess., 23 January 2002.

U.S. Conference of Catholic Bishops. 2002. *Charter for the Protection of Children and Young People, Revised Edition.* 19 November 2002. Available online: http://www.usccb.org/bishops/charter.htm (26 August 2003).

———. 2003. *Restoring Trust: Response to Clergy Sexual Abuse.* 11 March. Available online: http://www.usccb.org/comm/restoretrust.htm (26 August 2003).

U.S. Department of Justice. 2002. Office of the Inspector-General. *A Review of the Federal Bureau of Investigation's Counterterrorism Program.* September.

U.S. Senate. 2001. Committee on the Judiciary. *Reforming the FBI Management: The Views from Inside and Out.* 18 July.

———. 2002a. Committee on Banking, Housing, and Urban Affairs. *Oversight on the Monetary Policy Report to Congress Pursuant to the Full Employment and Balanced Growth Act of 1978.* Testimony of Chairman Alan Greenspan, U.S. Federal Reserve Board. 107th Cong., 2nd sess., 16 July.

———. 2002b. Committee on Governmental Affairs, Permanent Subcommittee on Investigations. *The Role of the Board of Directors in Enron's Collapse.* 107th Cong., 2nd sess., 8 July.

———. 2002c. Committee on Governmental Affairs, Report of the Staff. *Financial Oversight of Enron: The SEC and Private-Sector Watchdogs.* 107th Cong., 2nd sess., 8 October.

———. 2002d. Committee on the Judiciary. *Oversight Hearings on Counterterrorism.* Testimony of Coleen Rowley and Robert Mueller. 107th Cong., 2nd sess., June 6.

———. 2002e. Select Committee on Intelligence and House Permanent Select Committee on Intelligence. *The F.B.I.'s Handling of the Phoenix Electronic Communication and Investigation of Zacarious Moussaoui Prior to September 11, 2001.* Testimony of Eleanor Hill, Director, Joint Inquiry Staff. 107th Cong., 2nd sess., 24 September.

———. 2002f. Select Committee on Intelligence and House Permanent Select Committee on Intelligence. *Open Hearing: Joint Investigation.* Testimony of Robert S. Mueller. 107th Cong., 2nd sess., 17 October.

———. 2002g. Select Committee on Intelligence and House Permanent Select Committee on Intelligence. *Proposals for Reform within the Intelligence Community.* Testimony of Eleanor Hill, Director, Joint Inquiry Staff. 107th Cong., 2nd sess., 3 October.

Uslaner, Eric. 2002. *The Moral Foundations of Trust.* Cambridge: Cambridge University Press.

Warren, Mark, ed. 1999a. *Democracy and Trust.* Cambridge: Cambridge University Press.

Warren, Mark. 1999b. "Democratic Theory and Trust." In *Democracy and Trust,* edited by Mark Warren. Cambridge: Cambridge University Press, 310–45.

12

The Institutional Turn in Professional Ethics

One of the most important developments in the study of professional ethics in recent years is what may be called its institutional turn. This refers to a shift toward the study of ethical issues that are more salient in institutions than in relations among individuals or in structures of whole societies or states. This turn has only just begun and needs to be encouraged – but in the right direction. We can go further in that direction by analyzing some of the implications that follow from taking seriously the institutional context of professional ethics.

The institutional turn is a response to an underlying social trend that has been going on for much longer: the institutionalization of the professions. This trend has been described as a shift from "social trustee professionalism" to "expert professionalism" (Brint 1994, 203–5). The traditional ideal in which professionals alone or in small groups serve their patients and clients in accord with a public-spirited goal has moved more toward practices in which professionals serve in organizations that value mainly their expertise and expect them to act in accord with the organization's goals. Often those goals are determined by the market, and economic pressures are an important part of this trend. But the organizational dimensions of the trend have been less discussed. They are also more general because they apply to both market and non-market institutions.

Professional ethics has been slow to take account of these social trends (see, for example, Chapter 13 in this volume). In the academic literature on ethics, whether applied or theoretical, the institutional dimension has rarely been prominent. Ethics has been studied mainly on either the micro level or on the macro level. In moral philosophy, the main questions concern relationships between individuals (whether the issue is the trolley problem or the doctor-patient relationship). In political philosophy, the main focus is the basic structure of society or the constitution of the state (whether the issue is distributive justice or free speech).

What has been neglected is the ethics at the midlevel – the vast range of institutions that operate between the world of families, friends, and neighbors on one side and the realm of governments on the other – institutions such as hospitals, schools, corporations, and the mass media. Yet these are the structures with which most people, including professionals, interact during most of their daily life (more than with governments and often as much as with their families and friends). The ethical problems of these institutions deserve at least as much attention as those on which both philosophers and professionals have tended to concentrate.

This charge of neglect has more force against the more individualist professions like law and medicine than against the more organizational professions like engineering, business, government, and social work. But even these organizational professions could benefit from giving more attention to institutional problems.

If the problems of institutional ethics were essentially the same as the problems of individual and social ethics, then their neglect would not matter so much. But they are not. To show why they are not, I consider two general kinds of ethical problems that are more critical, or take on a different character, in institutional settings. The nature of these problems can be brought out by considering the reaction to a case in medical ethics presented to a class of twenty practitioners – lawyers, doctors, government officials, and business executives. All were leaders in their professions, but none had any substantial background in ethics. The case was based on an actual incident in a Massachusetts hospital affiliated with a health maintenance organization, though the names and facts were modified. (See the Appendix for a fuller description of the case.)

The ethical drama begins when a cancer patient asks his doctor for a prescription for a drug that the doctor believes his patient will use to commit suicide. The patient is not in pain and could continue to function at least for some months, but his prognosis is poor. He is amply informed and perfectly competent, and his doctor knows him well. The conditions seem favorable for allowing physician-assisted suicide, and the instructor presenting the case expected that most members of the group would agree that, if this episode were taking place in private practice, the doctor should be ethically permitted, though not required, to write the prescription. The instructor planned to move immediately to the next step in the discussion – to explore what difference the institutional setting makes.

But it turned out that several members of the class were strongly opposed to suicide, even more so to physician-assisted suicide, and they were very articulate in expressing their opposition. In the face of this spirited disagreement, even those members who had said at first that the decision was easy were now trying to avoid answering the question the instructor kept pressing – what should the doctor do in this case?

Several members at first tried a tactic of evasion familiar in ethical discussion: "We need more information about the case." But the instructor had brought along one of his colleagues who had been the physician in this very case. He was able to give them all the information they could possibly want (which, of course, did not make the decision any easier).

But then one member of the class said: "Obviously people of good will are going to disagree about this case. Maybe there is no right answer for everyone. So I think each person should follow his own conscience and do what he thinks is right." Many heads nodded, and the class thought they had the right answer: individual discretion. But then the instructor asked: "Do you really think that this should be the hospital's policy? That each doctor (and then why not also each healthcare professional) should decide on his or her own whether to grant a patient's request for help in committing suicide?"

Many members of the class were themselves heads of institutions and members of boards of trustees, and they now saw what they had ignored when they had focused only on the individual doctor and his patient. Letting each individual decide is not a satisfactory solution to the problem of what the institution should do. Or, if it is a possible solution, it is no more neutral or privileged than any other, and it requires just as much moral argument and is likely to produce just as much moral disagreement.

The general point is that an institution needs to have a policy, which means that (a) the rules may require individuals in the institution to act in ways that they may not otherwise act on their own; and (b) someone has to decide what the rules are. The first is the problem of representation, and the second, the problem of authority.

Both expose the challenges that we face when we take institutional context seriously. Each needs to be considered separately, though, as will become clear, they are closely related.

THE PROBLEM OF REPRESENTATION

The physician in this case goes to the General Counsel of the HMO and asks for his advice. The General Counsel's dilemma is a good place to begin, because if anyone in this drama should know how to suppress his own personal moral views in favor of institutional priorities, it is surely the lawyer. This General Counsel is sympathetic toward the patient and also toward the doctor, who is his friend. But he has good reason to believe that the Board of Trustees would oppose physician-assisted suicide even if it were legal. And he thinks that what the doctor intends to do is against state law.

What should he tell the doctor? Some members of the class suggested a neutral statement of the facts: As a lawyer he should simply tell the doctor what the law is and what the institution's policies are. But this impersonal approach is hard to sustain because, first, the doctor is his friend. (Imagine how the conversation would go: "Come on, Bob, I know what the law is. I need your help in deciding what to do here.")

But the more general problem is that the status of the law itself was uncertain. A U.S. Appeals Court had recently held that individuals have a constitutional right to assisted suicide, and though the decision did not apply directly to Massachusetts, it cast doubt on the future viability of the state law and confirmed that some respectable legal opinion supported a right to assisted suicide (*Compassion in Dying v. Washington* 1996, later reversed in *Washington v. Glucksberg* 1997; *Quill v. Vacco* 1996; *Vacco v. Quill* 1997). To say anything at all helpful about the law, the General Counsel would have to appeal to moral values, including the risk to the institution, the benefit to the patient, and the importance of a potential constitutional right. Once he begins this moral deliberation, he has to ask himself: Whose values should I appeal to? This leads directly to the more general question: Whom do I represent?

The question of representation points to two different issues. The first, more familiar one is the conflict of roles. An enchanting instance of this problem occurs in Gilbert and Sullivan's Mikado (Cohen 1966–1967). It illustrates a moral mistake in dealing with role conflict that may be called Pooh-Bahism in honor of Pooh-Bah, the Emperor's Adviser in the operetta. Pooh-Bah, assuming several different roles in turn, gives conflicting advice, and then finally offers to resolve the conflict if he receives a bribe simply "as Pooh-Bah." (See the discussion in Chapter 2.)

The example serves the purpose here well because we cannot immediately conclude that the lesson is that Pooh-Bah should have ignored his roles and acted on his personal views of what is right. Because some professionals' consciences are not as well developed as they should be, relying on personal views is not the best solution. But even if Pooh-Bah as Pooh-Bah had shown more rectitude, we still would not want him to have ignored any of his roles. The better approach would be to try to balance the claims of each role. He should try to represent all his constituencies – in this case, the claims from all the various departments of the institution.

Part of the problem of representation, then, concerns the conflict of loyalties that attorneys and other professionals typically experience. Among these are: conflicts between personal moral views and a client's views, conflicts between justice and professional obligations in an adversary system, and conflicts between obligations to friends and colleagues in the organization (which are obligations that institutions themselves should also respect).

The second, less appreciated problem of representation is: Whom does the individual professional represent when acting as an official of the institution? Even if we assume that the primary client is the institution, the General Counsel in this case is in a position to influence what the institution's policy is and how it is interpreted. He is also in a position to influence whether the institution should press for a change in the law (for example, whether it should join others in sponsoring legislation in the state or filing briefs in federal courts). And his own professional identity is bound up with the institution just as much as it is with his profession. In a sense he is representing himself. But it is a self that is defined by the traditions and purposes of the institution, and those traditions and purposes are subject to change by him and by his colleagues.

The colleagues in this case include the doctor, too. The doctor's first loyalty may be to his patient, but he also knows that he has a responsibility to other patients (both present and future) whom the institution may serve. And he knows that what he does in this case, and what positions he supports on rounds and in internal meetings, will influence what the institution does. He too is representing many different "clients," and he too should have something to say about what is in the interest of one of the principal ones – the institution itself.

Some division of moral labor is necessary in any complex institution. The doctor at the bedside should not have cost containment uppermost in his mind, and the CEO of the HMO (even if he is a doctor) cannot give absolute priority to the individual welfare of each patient. How individuals should maintain their personal integrity and how they can balance the claims of these different roles when they serve in more than one are important questions in institutional ethics. But the even more significant point is that the questions themselves must be addressed from an institutional perspective. The General Counsel and the doctor share some responsibility for creating and changing the structures that define that division of labor. They not only act within it, but sometimes must step outside it and seek to change it when it does not function as it should.

The institutional perspective encourages professionals to consider their responsibilities over time. Recognizing this dynamic aspect of the problem of representation does not, of course, tell the General Counsel or the doctor what to do in this or any other case. But it does put their decisions in a different light. It expands both the range of questions they should ask and the factors they should consider in answering them. To decide what to advise the doctor, the General Counsel has to ask not only what his friend and colleague should do but also what the institution should do. And he has to consider both questions from several different, potentially conflicting perspectives, all of which may change over time.

THE PROBLEM OF AUTHORITY

When the General Counsel and the doctor ask what the institution should do, they are only a step away from asking the second question, which constitutes the problem of authority. This problem addresses the question of – not what is the right decision to make but – who has the right to make the decision.

One aspect of this question – the rights members should have who disagree with an institutional decision – has received considerable attention in the literature on professional ethics under the rubric of whistle-blowing (Bok 1981; Bowman 1989). Discussions of the ethics of the organizational professions have extensively addressed this question. The discussions of ethics in the organizational professions – in engineering ethics and business ethics, for example – is increasingly relevant to the practice of law and medicine as these professions become more and more institutionalized.

But even the work on the ethics of the organizational professions does not have much to say about the broader question of who should make institutional policy. In the discussion of this case, most of the class assumed that the board of trustees had the right ultimately to decide the policy for the HMO. Although this assumption was no doubt correct in some formal sense, it raises more questions than it answers. How much weight should the board give to the views of those who work for the institution? Those who are served by it? Should professionals have more say than others? Who should sit on the board? In the absence of an explicit policy, which seemed to be the situation in this case, should the doctors try to formulate their own informal rules, and, if so, whom should they consult? And to what extent should outside institutions, including the state, have anything to say about the institution's policies?

The question of who should decide is increasingly important in professional ethics because more people are making legitimate demands to participate in setting institutional policies and are also finding themselves disagreeing about what the policies should be. When institutional decisions were made by a relatively small group of professionals who came from similar backgrounds and who shared more or less the same conventional moral outlook, moral controversy was less frequent or at least less frequently made public. As the number and range of persons whose views need to be taken into account expands, we should not be surprised that the incidence of moral controversy increases. Even the seemingly like-minded group of professionals in the class discussing this case found themselves disagreeing sharply about physician-assisted suicide. Imagine if the issue had been abortion, or capital punishment, or affirmative action.

It would be hard to deny that at least some of the new and diverse voices demanding to be heard deserve a role in the process of decision making in institutions. There is no reason to assume that physicians, lawyers, or any other professionals have a monopoly on moral wisdom on the questions that institutions now have to decide and that affect all of us. But neither is there any reason to assume that the only solution is to give equal weight to any individual or group who thinks they have something to contribute.

The institutions in which professionals serve therefore should not be treated exactly like single-purpose organizations, such as professional associations, or like political entities, such as the state. In the former, authority goes only to those who can be clearly recognized as having the expertise to promote its purpose; in the latter, authority rests ultimately with all citizens. In the institutions in which professionals work, authority is necessarily and legitimately divided. Professional ethics thus faces the challenge of formulating principles to deal with the problem of authority in institutions that are half professional and half political.

Under these conditions, the solution to the problem of authority cannot be simply a matter of deciding which particular procedure (majority rule, informed consent, shareholder proxies) should settle such disputes fairly but finally. Professional ethics needs to pay attention to the moral quality of the process itself. The most promising approach relies on democratic deliberation. This is a process that involves a continuing interaction in which the way the disputants relate to each other is as important as the decision about who has the right to make the final decision.

Many concepts in the growing literature on deliberative democracy are relevant for a professional ethics that takes institutions seriously, but one can serve as an illustration. The concept is called the economy of moral disagreement (Gutmann and Thompson 1996). In a deliberative process, participants distinguish between opponents who hold positions about which reasonable people may disagree, and opponents who hold positions about which there should be no reasonable disagreement. With opponents who hold morally respectable positions, participants try to practice the economy of moral disagreement. They try to minimize the range of their disagreement by promoting policies on which their principles converge, even if they would otherwise place those policies significantly lower on their own list of political priorities. Pro-choice liberals, for example, would treat pro-lifers differently from white supremacists.

In the HMO hospital in this case, the concept of an economy of moral disagreement implies that those who oppose physician-assisted suicide should work harder than they might otherwise to ensure that end-of-life therapies and facilities are comfortable and humane. They should also support, or at least not oppose, an institutional policy that would provide information to patients who want to find other ways to end their lives (perhaps at another institution). Those who favor physician-assisted suicide should make sure that if the hospital decides to permit the practice, any physician or staff member who opposes it could, without fear of reproach, decline to participate in it.

The professionals in the class that discussed this case seemed to sense the need for something like a deliberative process. Their tendency to say that each person should decide what is right, mistaken though it is as a principle of institutional ethics, expressed a recognition that the question of physician-assisted suicide is one about which there is reasonable moral disagreement. That recognition does not settle what the policy should be, but it does imply that within the institution both sides of the dispute should continue to be heard, and to be heard in a spirit of mutual respect.

Whatever the right answers in this case may be, the more general conclusion should be clear. Professional ethics can no longer be adequately studied or effectively practiced by attending only to individuals or to associations of individuals, even professional associations. The principles of professional ethics must take seriously the special circumstances of institutional life. That does not mean that institutional ethics rests on different moral foundations, or that the problems it poses are of a completely different kind from ordinary ethics. But if we take the institutional context seriously, we will ask some questions that we might not otherwise ask and consider some answers that we might otherwise neglect. The agenda of the study of professional ethics will then turn in a more fruitful direction and address problems that are more relevant for the practice of professionals today.

APPENDIX
PHYSICIAN-ASSISTED SUICIDE IN AN INSTITUTIONAL SETTING

DG is a successful professional who had enjoyed excellent health until he was diagnosed with metastatic colon cancer at age sixty-five. His primary care physician for the past ten years, an oncologist in a hospital-based HMO, prescribed a course of chemotherapy. After undergoing the treatment, DG felt somewhat better and was able to continue with his work and to take a vacation with his wife.

But after several months he began to suffer from frequent vomiting caused by the cancer. His doctor told him he had only two options: palliative care or major surgery. The doctor recommended palliative care, but DG chose to undergo surgery. It did not improve his condition.

Three days after DG's discharge from the hospital, the doctor visited him at home. He was comfortably sedated yet able to converse with his family and visitors.

The next morning DG called his doctor, saying that he could no longer tolerate the extreme discomfort and that he wanted help in ending his life immediately. The doctor told him that his morphine infusion could be increased up to the point of loss of consciousness, but that his life could not be intentionally ended. DG then asked the doctor to prescribe Seconal for sleep. The physician believed but was not certain that DG knew that Seconal is the drug recommended by the Hemlock Society for suicide.

Sympathetic to the patient's request but recognizing that complying with it might violate the law or hospital policy, the doctor called the General Counsel of the hospital for advice. The General Counsel, a long-time friend of the doctor, personally believed that patients should have the right to end their lives in some circumstances and that physicians should have the right to assist them. He knew that state law prohibited prescribing medication if a doctor has reason to believe that the patient intends to use it to commit suicide. But he was also aware that a recent decision by the Ninth Circuit Court in California had held that patients have an almost unlimited constitutional right to physician-assisted suicide.

Many of the healthcare professionals in the hospital believe that physicians should be able to assist patients in such circumstances, and in the past some had probably done so covertly. The board of the hospital has never considered the question, but it is likely that a majority of the members would oppose a policy that permitted physician-assisted suicide, even if it were not against the law.

- What should the General Counsel tell the doctor?
- What should the doctor do?
- What policy should the hospital adopt?

Notes

An earlier version of this chapter was presented at a Workshop on "Ethics in the Professions and Practice," sponsored by the Association of Practical and Professional Ethics and held at the University of Montana, Missoula, in July 1996. I am grateful to Ezekiel Emanuel for the preparation of the case reproduced in the Appendix and to him and David Wilkins for advice on the issues raised by the case.

References

Bok, S. 1981. "Blowing the Whistle." In *Public Duties*, edited by J. Fleishman, L. Liebman, and M. H. Moore. Cambridge, Mass.: Harvard University Press, 204–20.

Bowman, J. 1989. *Professional Dissent: An Annotated Bibliography and Resource Guide*. New York: Garland.

Brint, S. 1994. *In the Age of Experts: The Changing Role of the Professions in Politics and Public Life*. Princeton, NJ: Princeton University Press.

Cohen, G. A. 1966–1967. "Beliefs and Roles." *Proceedings of the Aristotelian Society* 67: 17–34.

Compassion in Dying v. Washington, 79 F.3d 790 (U.S. App. 9th Cir. 1996).

Gutmann, A., and D. Thompson. 1996. *Democracy and Disagreement*. Cambridge, Mass.: Harvard University Press.

Quill v. Vacco, 80 F.3d 716 (U.S. App. 2d Cir. 1996).

Vacco v. Quill, 117 S. Ct. 2293 (U.S. Supreme Court 1997).

Washington v. Glucksberg, 117 S. Ct. 2258 (U.S. Supreme Court 1997).

13

Hospital Ethics

Hospital ethics, familiar enough in practice but surprisingly neglected in the literature, deals with the ethical problems that arise distinctively or typically in hospitals and similar healthcare institutions. More precisely, it consists of the ethical principles that should govern the conduct of healthcare professionals and other staff in their capacities as members of the hospital as an institution, and the conduct of the hospital itself as an institution. It is a species of institutional ethics, which focuses on the ethical problems created or significantly shaped by the institutional setting in which they occur.

It is surprising that hospital ethics – and institutional ethics more generally – has been so neglected. After all, we live most of our lives with institutions – working for them or dealing with them one way or another. But ethics (both as an academic discipline and as concrete practice) has tended to focus on either relations among individuals or on the structures of society as a whole, not on that middle range of intermediary associations of which institutions are the most durable and influential.

In medical ethics, this dichotomy is reflected in the common distinction between microethics, which deals with such issues as doctor-patient relations, and macroethics, which is concerned with questions such as the just distribution of healthcare. Hospital ethics falls between micro- and macroethics; it examines the problems that arise at the point where they intersect.

Because institutional ethics has been neglected, there is a tendency in our institutional life to apply moral principles with which we are familiar from our personal life. However, principles from individual ethics often distort institutional ethics. Ethical problems in the hospital are not exactly the same as ethical problems that arise when individual doctors treat individual patients. And when the problems are similar, the ethical principles by which we should resolve them are likely to be quite different.

To begin to make a case for taking hospital ethics seriously, I briefly examine two familiar principles of individual doctor-patient ethics that look different, or should look different, in the setting of a hospital. I then discuss ethics committees – one of the most important ways in which hospital ethics is put into practice.

CONFIDENTIALITY IN HOSPITALS

The first familiar principle or practice that looks different in the hospital from the way it appears in individual doctor-patient relationships is confidentiality. "Things I may see or hear in the course of the treatment or even outside of treatment . . . things which one should never divulge outside, I will keep to myself. . . ." The noble declaration of the principle of confidentiality in the Hippocratic oath, although qualified in the ensuing centuries, remains an important value in the ethics of physicians and healthcare professionals today.[1] But confidentiality takes a quite different form in the modern hospital from what one would expect from the traditional statements of the principle. The qualifications to patient confidentiality are not merely exceptional; they are routine.

First, consider the number of people who have access to the records of a patient: attending and consulting physicians, residents, radiologists, nurses, physical therapists, administrators, among others. Then recall how much information about patients passes informally through the corridors. Although no doubt much of this access is necessary and beneficial for the patient, most patients are not aware of, let alone have consented to, such widespread disclosure. It is unrealistic, if not disingenuous, then, to ask patients to disclose information purportedly under the protection of the traditional doctor-patient confidentiality, and then dispense the information under an institutional system that offers much less protection.

The problem is especially difficult in those cases in which the patient would probably not consent to the release of certain information, but the hospital believes that the information is necessary, either for the patient's own benefit or (more commonly) for the benefit of other patients and the staff. The testing and identification of AIDS patients is a case in point. The government now recommends a policy of "universal precautions" that should make some of the more blatant violations of patient confidentiality unnecessary.[2] But according to a survey of 560 randomly selected nongovernment hospitals, two-thirds of these institutions still do not comply.[3] (One surgeon proudly reported that his hospital had solved the problem by "testing all patients and marking their charts with stickers – green for those who did not have the virus, red for those who were infected or who refused to be tested.") The right balance between patient confidentiality and institutional disclosure apparently has yet to be established in a form that is widely accepted.

There are other ways in which confidentiality looks different in hospital ethics. We usually assume that confidentiality applies only to the patient: information about the patient is supposed to be kept confidential. But what about information about doctors, other members of the staff, and the institution itself? Some kinds of information (about the personnel process, say, or about the quality of care in the institution) may be useful to patients, potential patients, and the wider community (including the staff itself). But surely some of this information should also be kept confidential.

THE BEST INTERESTS OF THE PATIENT

The second example that illustrates the importance of the institutional dimension of ethics is the principle that the physician (and the whole healthcare team) should put the best interests of the patient first. This is the traditional and still dominant duty in medical ethics.

As we hear more and more about the growing cost of healthcare, we also hear more about the need to limit the use of scarce medical resources. The plea for limiting (or as some say "rationing") is not simply a conservative reaction against escalating governmental expenditures. It is one increasingly accepted in some form by liberals, including those in the healthcare community.[4] The issue is no longer so much whether there are to be limits, but rather how the limits are to be imposed.

The standard way of dealing with this problem is to distinguish sharply between macro- and microdecisions, assigning the former to the political or administrative process and the latter to the physicians and health professionals. The doctor at the bedside is insulated from the macrodecisions: within whatever level of resources is set by the community or the hospital, the doctor pursues the best interests of the patient.[5]

In most individual cases, this is no doubt the right role for the individual doctor.[6] But in many other circumstances (especially in urban hospitals and HMOs), this dual-role solution is too easy. In these institutions, macro- and microethics meet face to face. Neither the institution nor the medical professionals working within it can escape confronting the problem of how to reconcile their duties to individual patients and their responsibilities for the just allocation of resources.

One example of this conflict concerns intensive care units (ICUs). In many urban hospitals, the ICU is under great and increasing pressure. Rationing or limiting care is unavoidable, and in fact is already taking place at least informally. Indeed, rationing may even be taking place in a reasonably fair and efficient manner. A study of the de facto allocation in an ICU in an acute-care hospital in Seattle, Washington, found that patients admitted when the unit was crowded were more seriously ill than those admitted at other times, and that in general the relative risk of discharge was inversely related to empty bed availability, illness severity, and age.[7] A study done at Massachusetts General Hospital found similar results.[8]

Informal rationing may work in small hospitals and perhaps for a while in large institutions. But when the decisions and treatment involve many different members of the staff on rotating shifts, the absence of an explicit policy is likely to result in unethical if not harmful allocations. In some hospitals, ICU allocations have become political; they actually involve bargaining of a kind that political scientists who study congressional logrolling would find familiar. An intensive care physician described the process this way: "We'll say to neurosurgery, 'O.K. we'll take Mr. Jones, but you have to get your patient Mr. Smith out because we think he'll probably do O.K. on the floor.' 'You take Mrs. Jones, and we'll find room for Mr. Smith. You owe us one next time.'"[9]

The Von Stetina case illustrates the possible consequences of the failure to set and maintain explicit standards in the ICU.[10] A previously healthy 27-year-old woman recovering well from severe injuries in an automobile accident was accidentally disconnected from her ventilator in the ICU, suffered brain damage, and lapsed into a permanent coma. During the subsequent trial, it became clear that the

ICU was overcrowded and understaffed and had no effective policies on admission and discharge. At the time, nurses were busy with several patients who probably should have been discharged from the ICU and one who came close to meeting the criteria for brain death. The trial court's opinion, in favor of the plaintiff, implied that hospitals may be legally obliged to discharge borderline patients in order to be able to maintain an adequate standard of care for the new arrivals.

Whether or not such a discharge policy becomes a legal requirement, it surely is an ethical one. In an institutional setting, ICU allocations should not be left to the discretion of individual doctors and nurses or to informal understandings that may be the result of no one's deliberate decision. The institution should decide as a matter of policy, for example, whether the likelihood of benefit from the ICU should be the primary criterion or whether other factors (perhaps first-come-first-served) should have some weight.

A similar point can be made about the growing controversy over cardiopulmonary resuscitation (CPR). There is emerging evidence that CPR is performed on too many people with too little chance of success,[11] and there are increasing calls for greater selectivity in its use.[12] A physician's order is generally required to withhold CPR but not to perform the procedure; consequently many paramedics, nurses, and others feel they must perform it unless they can document reliable postmortem signs. The situation is further complicated by the proliferation of variations on do-not-resuscitate (DNR) orders – "slow," "partial," "chemical," or "pharmacological" codes. Under these circumstances, it is not surprising that "nurses, house officers, or cross-covering physicians are often forced to make life-and-death decisions without clear direction . . ."[13]

In dealing with these and related problems that raise conflicts among patient needs, physician prerogatives, and institutional priorities, the dual-role model will work only if all the members of the hospital team are prepared to take on, from time to time, each role – patient advocate and institutional trustee. Patients themselves and the whole staff must also understand clearly the institutional limits under which the doctors and nurses are making decisions in particular cases.

All members of the hospital must appreciate the full dimensions of ethical problems, and this understanding should affect how the ethical standards of the hospital are set. The principles of hospital ethics should be the product of extensive discussions by representatives of all members of the hospital. As such, they will be more likely to be accepted as reasonable limits under which doctors and nurses can pursue – and be seen by patients as pursuing – the best interests of their patients.

THE GOVERNANCE OF HOSPITAL ETHICS

The old-time hospital – the "doctors' workshop" where physicians ruled without challenge – is fading from the scene, as lay administrators, nurses, employee unions, patients' rights organizations, and lawyers struggle to assert their authority in many different domains of the institution.[14] This is the problem of ethical disagreement – a problem that does not arise in the same way in individual ethics. An individual, of course, may disagree with other individuals about ethical issues, but, unlike an institution, an individual does not normally disagree with himself. An institution experiences real and legitimate internal disagreement and thus faces the problem of how to reach moral judgments in the face of such disagreement. In the hospital, the problem is further complicated by the fact that among the various voices in conflict are some whose claims are based on professional expertise and some whose claims are not.

The increasing controversy over ethical issues in medicine is not merely the result of technological progress or even the expanding demand for healthcare. It is also the result of a broader social phenomenon: the increase in the number and diversity of people who are making, or who claim to have a voice in making, the decisions that affect medical care in particular cases as well as for society as a whole. As the group of persons whose views must be taken into account expands, the likelihood of moral controversy increases. The more people who participate in making healthcare decisions, the more diverse their backgrounds and perspectives are likely to be, and the more frequent their disputes about moral issues. In these circumstances, we should not be surprised to see more moral controversy in public debates about healthcare.

Because much of this controversy has a legitimate place in medical decision making, we face the problem of how to balance the competing claims. Neither physicians nor any other group has a monopoly on moral wisdom in these matters. But that does not mean that the best solution is to give equal weight to each group who has a stake in the decision. We need to design institutions that are representative but also deliberative.

ETHICS COMMITTEES

The institutional mechanism that many have recently seen as a partial solution to dealing with the problem of ethical disagreement or uncertainty in the modern hospital is the ethics committee (or, as it is sometimes called, the optimum care committee). In 1982, less than 1 percent of American hospitals had ethics committees; today at least 60 percent of large hospitals have ethics committees (some estimates put the proportion as high as 80 percent).[15] Although these committees have become common and familiar institutions around some hospitals, their role is still controversial. Three general questions have been raised about ethics committees.

1. Who should serve on the committee? The typical committee includes some doctors, nurses, other health professionals, an ethicist, and sometimes a layperson. The key challenge is to find the right balance of representation among these various groups or interests. The optimal distribution will no doubt vary depending on the nature of the hospital and the community, but all members of the institution should have a voice in determining the form of the representation itself.

There has been some controversy about what at first seems a relatively unimportant question: Should administrators serve on the committee? Many medical ethicists say no.[16] They argue that administrators necessarily represent the interests of the institution, which are primarily financial, and the administrative presence may therefore cast doubt on the "ethical purity" of the committee's decisions. The ethics committee should be "the one decision-making body that remains fully insulated from the need to act as a team player in a competition which rewards narrow institutional gains, rather than success in meeting community needs." However, if ethical judgments should be understood as "all things considered" conclusions reached after taking all the relevant factors into account (including financial and legal ones), then a broader view of the committee's membership is required, and administrators should not be excluded.

2. What kinds of issues should the committee decide? In the past few years, committees throughout the country have reported that they are doing fewer and fewer case consultations; many committees evidently are beginning to play a larger role in setting policy.[17] This policymaking role is coming under criticism. The criticism depends partly on a mistaken belief about the nature of hospital ethics – the view that an institution should take a stand only on particular cases, not on general principles. The critics argue that because ethics committees represent a diverse range of moral views, they cannot reach consensus on the principles on which they base their conclusions, although they may be able to agree on the particular conclusions.[18] Discussions about the principles, it is said, merely cause the members to express their religious or ideological prejudices.

This objection confuses foundational principles (such as religious doctrines or moral theories) with the general principles that constitute policies in a hospital. There is a considerable distance between these foundational principles (such as the greatest good for the greatest number) and the principles that express institutional policies (allocate ICU beds to those most likely to benefit). We do not have to decide the foundational questions to agree on institutional principles.

Ethics committees should consult on particular cases, but they should examine the cases with an eye toward establishing ethical principles for the institution. The apparent trend against case consultations should be reversed, but at the same time the policymaking role of these committees should be strengthened.

3. What authority should the committee's decisions have? It would be easier to promote the idea of a broader membership and expanded jurisdiction of ethics committees if the authority of the committees remained as modest as originally intended. In most hospitals, ethics committees, in the beginning and still in principle, take only cases that are brought voluntarily and issue opinions that are only advisory.

Many critics of ethics committees doubt that the authority of the committees is as optional as official policies imply. One critic reports a case that is supposedly typical of disputes that come to ethics committees. It involved a disagreement between an attending pediatrician and a neonatologist. Although the committee did not vote or issue a formal recommendation, its discussion

appeared to show a slim majority favoring continuing treatment. . . . The committee chairman said to the attending [pediatrician], "Of course, the committee has no power to make decisions: the choice is still up to you." To which the attending replied, "Poppycock!" Understandably, he felt enormous social pressure to continue treatment and knew that he would be going upstream against colleagues if he chose otherwise.[19]

According to this same critic, ethics committees, unlike individual physicians, "lack specific medical knowledge, have not been trained in the ethic of caring, have little responsibility or accountability for decisions and have not been sanctioned by the patient to make such decisions."[20] Thus, he concludes, it may be unethical for physicians or hospitals to delegate decision making to such committees.

There are two different objections here, and they do not go well together. The first – that despite their formal authority ethics committees pressure physicians into accepting decisions against their judgment – presents a portrait of a physician who is too weak willed to resist "social pressure" and stick to a decision he or she regards as medically correct (though the physician described does have the courage to exclaim "Poppycock!"). The second objection – that ethics committees lack all the virtues that physicians possess for making decisions in the best interest of the patient – assumes a quite different picture of the physician. It suggests an omnicompetent professional who combines medical knowledge, a capacity for caring, and a determination to take responsibility for decisions.

A more balanced and realistic picture of the capacities of both physicians and ethics committees would recognize the strengths and weaknesses of each. In the face of legitimate ethical disagreement, we must find a way to give voice to a variety of perspectives. Ethics committees represent one way of doing so – at present the only widely institutionalized way. This need for inclusion, of course, has to be balanced with the need to give physicians and other healthcare professionals the primary responsibility for medical decisions in their respective spheres of competence.

Ethics committees under the kind of expanded authority suggested here would not make clinical decisions. Physicians, nurses, and other staff could ask for advisory opinions, but they would still have the primary responsibility for making those decisions. In difficult or controversial cases, the committee would issue an opinion, which would be intended not specifically as criticism or approval of the physicians or nurses in the instant case but rather as a guide for the future decisions of others and as a basis for the policies of the hospital.

Ethics committees are not the only way – and certainly not a perfect way – to deal with moral uncertainty and disagreement within the hospital. But the immediate alternative may be not the revival of the consensual hospital of our fond memory, but rather the extrapolation of the externally regulated hospital of our familiar present.

If hospitals do not find a way to institutionalize ethical discussion, their internal conflicts will spill out into the community and reinforce the growing pressures that seek to control hospitals and the practice of medicine more generally. A hospital that sustains a robust forum for raising and resolving ethical issues is better prepared to resist the illegitimate intrusions of external forces and is better positioned to channel the legitimate external influences toward constructive results. A hospital that minds its own ethics is in a better position to tell outsiders to mind theirs.

CONCLUSION

Hospital ethics should take a different form from ethics of individual relations between doctors and patients. Some of the familiar ethical principles and practices that govern those relations – such as confidentiality and best interests of the patient – must be revised if they are to serve the purposes of institutional ethics. They cannot be left to individual doctors and patients. All members of the institution – and others who have a stake in its decisions – should have a voice, directly or indirectly, in shaping its policies.

Respecting the institutional dimensions of hospital ethics has three important implications. All point to ways of encouraging hospitals to take more control of their own ethics, and thereby to resist the efforts of outside forces to determine their ethical fate.

First, the traditional principle of confidentiality is no longer adequate. Hospitals should establish and enforce more explicit standards for institutional confidentiality that balance the interests of patients, physicians, staff, and the institution as a whole.

Second, the conventional dual-role conception of medical ethics is too simple. Hospitals should encourage doctors, nurses, and other staff to develop the capacity to see, and at appropriate times to act on, the perspectives of both individual patients and institutional needs.

Third, hospitals should establish strong ethics committees with a broad mandate to help develop standards and policies in these and related areas. The committees should include a wide range of representatives of various interests in the hospitals (including administrators); serve as forums for discussing all institutional policies that raise serious ethical issues; and have the authority to review particular care decisions and recommend general guidelines and policies.

Notes

1. A. R. Jonsen, M. Siegler, and W. J. Winslade, *Clinical Ethics*, 2nd ed. (New York: Macmillan, 1986).
2. P. Baldrige, S. Kauffman, and C. Hopkins, *Institution and Documentation of Universal Precautions*, Internal Memo to Department Heads, Massachusetts General Hospital, January 19, 1988.
3. P. J. Hilts, "Many Hospitals Found to Ignore Rights of Patients in AIDS Testing," *New York Times*, February 17, 1990, 1.
4. One of the most serious versions of the charge that we are spending too much on healthcare is a humane essay by a liberal: D. Callahan, *What Kind of Life: The Limits of Medical Progress* (New York: Simon and Schuster, 1990).
5. For an early statement of rationale for this role division, see C. Fried, "Rights and Health Care – Beyond Equity and Efficiency," *New England Journal of Medicine* (1975) 293: 241–5. See also B. A. Brody, "The Macro-allocation of Health Care Resources," in *Health Care Systems: Moral Conflicts in European and American Public Policy*, edited by H. M. Saas and R. U. Massey (Dordrect: Kluwer Academic Publishers, 1988), 213–36.
6. The American system, unlike the more centralized British system, offers no assurance that resources not spent on one patient will be used on other more needy patients. See N. Daniels, "Why Saying No to Patients in the United States Is So Hard: Cost Containment, Justice and Provider Autonomy," *New England Journal of Medicine* (1986) 314: 1381–3.
7. M. J. Stauss, J. P. LoGerto, J. A. Yeltatzie, et al., "Rationing of Intensive Care Unit Services, *Journal of the American Medical Association* (1986) 255: 1143–6.
8. Faced with a reduction of ICU beds from 18 to 8 (because of a shortage of nurses), physicians informally rationed beds so that patients at greatest risk of myocardial infarction were more likely to be admitted. See D. E. Singer, P. L. Carr, A. G. Mulley, et al, "Rationing Intensive Care – Physician Responses to a Resource Shortage." *New England Journal of Medicine* (1983) 309: 1155–60.
9. E. Rosenthal, "Crowding Causes Agonizing Crisis in Intensive Care." *New York Times*, August 22, 1989, C11.
10. H. T. Engelhardt and M. A. Rie, "Intensive Care Units, Scarce Resources, and Conflicting Principles of Justice," *Journal of the American Medical Association* (1986) 255: 1159–64.
11. G. Taffet, T. A. Teasdaale, and R. J. Luchi, "In-hospital Cardiopulmonary Resuscitation," *Journal of the American Medical Association* (1988) 260: 2069–72.
12. S. J. Younger, "Do-not-resuscitate Orders: No Longer Secret, But Still a Problem," *Hastings Center Report* (1987) 17(1): 24–33.
13. Ibid., 25.
14. A. B. Flood and W. R. Scott, *Hospital Structure and Performance* (Baltimore: Johns Hopkins, 1987); and J. R. Hollingsworth, *Controversy about American Hospitals: Funding Ownership and Performance* (Washington, DC: American Enterprise Institute, 1987).
15. C. B. Cohen, "Ethics Committees: Birth of a Network." *Hastings Center Report* (1988) 18(1): 11.
16. D. Wikler, "Institutional Agendas and Ethics Committees," *Hastings Center Report* (1989) 19(5): 21–3.

17. C. B. Cohen, "Ethics Committees: Is Case Consultation in Retreat?" *Hastings Center Report* (1988) 18(5): 23–4.
18. T. Murray, "Where Are the Ethics in Ethics Committees?" *Hastings Center Report* (1988) 18(1): 12–13.
19. N. Fost and R. E. Cranford, "Hospital Ethics Committees: Administrative Aspects. *Journal of the American Medical Association* (1985) 253: 2687–92.
20. M. Siegler, "Ethics Committees: Decisions by Bureaucracy," *Hastings Center Report* (1986) 16(3): 22.

14

Conflicts of Interest in Medicine

The problem of conflicts of interest began to receive serious attention in the medical literature in the 1980s. Studies have described a wide range of conflicts involving physicians, medical researchers, and medical institutions. Among the areas of concern that have been identified are self-referral by physicians, physicians' risk sharing in health maintenance organizations (HMOs) and hospitals, gifts from drug companies to physicians, hospital purchasing and bonding practices, industry-sponsored research, and research on patients. Yet the concept of conflict of interest itself has been inadequately analyzed, and consequently its elements, the purposes of regulation, and standards for assessment are still often misunderstood.[1]

ELEMENTS OF CONFLICTS OF INTEREST

A conflict of interest is a set of conditions in which professional judgment concerning a primary interest (such as a patient's welfare) tends to be unduly influenced by a secondary interest (such as financial gain). Conflict of interest rules, informal and formal, regulate the disclosure and avoidance of these conditions.

In general terms, the primary interests are the health of patients, the integrity of research, and the education of students. The professional duties of physicians, researchers, and teachers give these interests priority. Although what the duties mean may sometimes be controversial (and the duties themselves may conflict), most people agree that whatever else they may imply, they should be the primary consideration in any professional decision that a physician, researcher, or teacher makes.

The secondary interests are usually not illegitimate in themselves. Indeed, they may even be a necessary and desirable part of professional practice. Only their relative weight in professional decisions is problematic. The aim is not to eliminate or necessarily to reduce financial gain or other secondary interests (such as preference for family and friends or the desire for prestige and power). It is rather to prevent these secondary factors from dominating or appearing to dominate the relevant primary interest in the making of professional decisions.

Conflict of interest rules usually focus on financial gain, not because it is more pernicious than other secondary interests but because it is more objective and more fungible. Money is easier to regulate by impartial rules, and it is also generally useful for more purposes.

It is therefore a mistake to object to the constraints on financial gain by complaining that there are other kinds of influence, such as "an interest in obtaining provocative results" or pressure to favor "previously published findings of colleagues, friends, or researchers in collaborating groups" (Rothman 1991; Rothman 1993) that can have equally bad or worse effects on professional judgment. Just because we cannot do much about the other secondary interests, it does not follow that we should do little about financial gain. This point also applies to the differential regulation of types of financial interests; we might choose to proscribe one type, but not another (McDowell 1989).

It is also a mistake to treat conflicts of interest as just another kind of choice between competing values. They should be distinguished from ethical dilemmas involving termination of care, confidentiality, or the use of human subjects in research. Failure to do so dilutes the concept of a conflict of interest and encourages the attitude that conflicts are so pervasive that they cannot be avoided. In ethical dilemmas, both of the competing interests have a presumptive claim to priority, and the problem is in deciding which to choose. In the case of financial conflicts of interest, only one of the interests has a claim to priority, and the problem is to ensure that the other interest does not dominate. This asymmetry between interests is a distinctive characteristic of conflicts of interest.

REASONS FOR REGULATING CONFLICTS OF INTEREST

A common criticism of rules governing conflicts of interest is that they unfairly punish ethical physicians and researchers for the misdeeds of the few unethical ones. Rules regulating conflicts in research are said to be a "serious insult to the integrity of scientists" who have any financial connections with commercial enterprises (Rothman 1991). "To ascribe a conflict of interest automatically in such situations amounts to an assumption that the sponsor's interests have influenced the investigator . . . and that the research findings are different from what they would otherwise have been" (Rothman 1991).

Similarly, rules regulating self-referral are said to impugn the motives of physicians by implying that they would prescribe drugs or order diagnostic tests in which they have a financial interest without regard to whether the drugs or the tests are in the patient's interest (McCormick 1992). Defenders of self-referral arrangements argue, on the contrary, that patients benefit because a physician's financial interest in the facility to which he or she refers patients creates a strong incentive to ensure that it provides high-quality care (McDowell 1989; Bureaus of Competition 1987).

Criticisms of this kind rest on a mistaken view of the basic purposes of conflict of interest rules. The first purpose is to maintain the integrity of professional judgment. The rules seek to minimize the influence of secondary interests that should be irrelevant to the merits of decisions about primary interests. The rules do not assume that most physicians or researchers let financial gain influence their judgment. They assume only that it is often difficult if not impossible to distinguish cases in which financial gain has improper influence from those in which it does not. It is difficult even in one's own case – and all the more so in the case of people one does not know personally – to determine what motives have influenced a professional decision. Given this general difficulty of discovering real motives, it is both more prudent and ethically more responsible to decide in advance to remove, as far as possible, factors that tend to distract professionals from concentrating on medical and scholarly goals.

Why not simply judge professional decisions by their results? One reason is that many treatment or referral decisions are never reviewed by anyone other than the physicians directly involved. Neither is the market an adequate test of results; it provides only limited protection against the harmful effects of conflicts of interest (McDowell 1989).

In the conduct of research, peer review of results offers greater protection. But the objectivity of a particular piece of research is not the only concern, as many commentators suppose it is (Rothman 1991). The more far-reaching issue, which peer review does not usually address, is the choice of topics and the direction of research – for example, the tendency of industry-sponsored researchers to put more emphasis on commercially useful research than on basic research (Blumenthal et al. 1986). Nor is it correct to say that conflict of interest rules "focus attention on the circumstances of the writer *rather than* on the substance of the writing and thereby stifle objectivity" (Rothman 1993, emphasis added). There is no reason why we cannot seriously consider both the circumstances and the substance. We should keep in mind that the point of the rules is to protect the substance of the research. The rules seek to eliminate or reduce the influence of certain kinds of circumstances so that researchers (and their critics) can concentrate on the substance.

The second purpose of conflict of interest rules is to maintain confidence in professional judgment. This purpose depends even less on the assumption that physicians neglect patients or researchers produce biased results because of the influence of financial gain. The aim is to minimize conditions that would cause reasonable persons (patients, colleagues, and citizens) to believe that professional judgment has been improperly influenced, whether or not it has.

Maintaining confidence in professional judgment is partly a matter of prudence. To the extent that the public and their representatives distrust the profession, they are likely to demand greater regulation of clinical practice and research and are likely to supply fewer resources for both. Patients may be less likely to trust physicians generally. Since the actions of individual physicians and researchers can affect public confidence in the whole profession (Kassirer 1993), individual professionals have an obligation, both to the public and to the profession, to make sure that their own conduct does not impair their colleagues' capacity to practice medicine or conduct research.

A failure to avoid a conflict of interest may therefore be wrong even when one is not influenced by secondary interests at all. When professionals do not take reasonable precautions to avoid situations of conflict or do not observe rules regulating such conflicts, they have acted unethically. Contrary to the view of some commentators (Rothman 1993), a charge of a conflict of interest may indeed constitute an accusation, even in the absence of an otherwise improper motivation.

STANDARDS FOR ASSESSING CONFLICTS OF INTEREST

Standards for assessing conflicts of interest identify factors that make conflicts more or less problematic. The severity of a conflict depends on (1) the likelihood that professional judgment will be influenced, or appear to be influenced, by the secondary interest, and (2) the seriousness of the harm or wrong that is likely to result from such influence or its appearance.

In assessing likelihood, we may reasonably assume that, within a certain range, the greater the value of the secondary interest (for example, the size of the financial gain), the more probable its influence. Below a certain value, the gain is likely to have no effect; this is why de minimis standards (which define that value) are appropriate for some gifts. Also, the value should generally be measured in relation to typical income and to the scale of the practice or research project.

Also affecting likelihood is the scope of conflict, in particular the nature of the relationship that generates the conflict. Longer and closer associations increase the risk. A continuing relationship as a member of the board or a limited partner of an industrial sponsor, for example, creates a more serious problem than the acceptance of a one-time grant or gift.

The extent of discretion – that is, how much latitude a physician or researcher enjoys in exercising professional judgment – partly determines the range of probabilities. The more routine the treatment or the more closely it follows conventional professional practice, the less room there is for judgment and hence for improper influence. Also, the less independent authority the professional has in a particular case, the less latitude there is for improper influence. A conflict involving a laboratory technician, for example, is generally less severe than one involving a principal investigator.

In assessing the seriousness of a conflict, we consider first the value of the primary interest – the effects on a patient's welfare or the effects on the integrity of the research. These effects include not only the possibility of direct harm to the patient or the research, but also the indirect harm that results from a loss of confidence in the judgment of the physician or researcher.

The greater the scope of the consequences, the more serious the conflict. Beyond its effects on the particular patient or research project, a conflict may have effects on the practices of other physicians or on the research projects of colleagues. Questions such as these should be considered: Will this physician's association with a commercial laboratory raise doubts about the objectivity of all the physicians in his or her hospital or HMO? Will the fact that this drug company is sponsoring this research project tend to undermine confidence in the results of the work of other scholars in the institution and their ability to raise funds from other sources? Claims of physicians' independence or academic freedom should not be allowed to obscure the fact that the actions of any particular physician or researcher may substantially affect the independence of colleagues.

Finally, the more limited the accountability of the physician or researcher, the more serious the conflict. If the decision of a physician is reviewable by colleagues or authorities (who do not themselves have conflicts of interest), then there is less cause for concern. But the reviewers must be and be seen to be genuinely independent and effective. Even if professionals are accountable for particular decisions, they may escape scrutiny for the cumulative effects and broader policy implications of their decisions. The informal norms and policies of a hospital or HMO represent judgments that, no less than explicit decisions in particular cases, may be improperly influenced by secondary interests.

REMEDIES

Historically, the trend has been from less to more extensive control of conflicts of interest – from individual discretion to collective regulation. The more severe the conflicts, the more justifiable are more extensive forms of control.

Relying on the good character of individual physicians and researchers to ensure that they avoid conflicts, or deal with them judiciously when they arise, is the least intrusive procedure. It also has the advantage of maintaining conditions of mutual trust between physicians and patients and between researchers and their public. It is, however, more effective in face-to-face relations that continue over time – in small communities, for example, in which patients know their physicians personally. It is less likely to be adequate in large organizations and in the impersonal encounters or distant relationships that characterize much of the practice of modern medicine and medical research.

Regulation by the profession provides more assurance that conflicts will be avoided than does individual discretion. As compared with government regulation, it also has the advantage of involving those who know and care personally about professional practice. Rules are more likely to fit the special circumstances of the clinic and the laboratory when they are written by those who know these circumstances well and who have a personal stake in maintaining the integrity of the profession. The disadvantage of relying exclusively on the profession is that physicians – not only individually but also collectively – confront a conflict between their primary interest in maintaining the integrity of the profession and their secondary interest in promoting the economic welfare of its members. Unlike many other professions, the medical profession did not formally address conflicts of interest in its codes until the 1980s, and even then it in effect left the problem to the discretion of individual physicians (Rodwin 1993). Only in 1991 did the American Medical Association declare that self-referral, for example, was "presumptively inconsistent" with a physician's obligation to patients (Council on Ethical and Judicial Affairs 1992).

The growing role of governments in regulating conflicts of interest is in part a response to the failure of physicians and scholars to deal adequately with the problem and in part a result of the greater stake that society has in medical practice and research. Despite the claim of some physicians that ethics cannot be legislated (Todd 1992), law and morality overlap and interact in many ways, most of which are mutually reinforcing. The chief advantage of government regulation is that it includes more people in the process of making and enforcing the rules, thereby reducing the conflicts of interest that the profession faces when it regulates itself. An important disadvantage is the uniformity and procedural complexity that normally characterize the legal process. These create difficulties in matching the rules to the variety of conflicts that may arise and could even decrease the probability that violations will be prevented or punished.

Whether the responsibility for dealing with conflicts of interest falls to individual physicians and researchers, the profession, or governments, disclosure is the remedy most commonly prescribed. A physician is required, for example, to tell patients about his or her financial interest in the laboratory to which they are being referred and to let them decide whether to go to a different laboratory. A principal investigator is expected to indicate the sources of financial support for his or her research. Disclosure may be more or less public: the information may be provided to colleagues, hospital or HMO administrators, professional boards, state boards, or the general public. An advantage of disclosure is that it gives those who would be affected, or who are otherwise in a good position to assess the risks, information they need to make their own decisions.

A deficiency of disclosure is that those who receive the information may not know how to interpret it and may not in any case have reasonable alternative courses of action in the circumstances (McDowell 1989; Rodwin 1989). Disclosure could even exacerbate some of the indirect consequences of conflicts of interest, such as the effects on confidence in the profession or in the research enterprise. By itself, disclosure may merely increase levels of anxiety, causing patients and readers generally to suspect physicians and researchers but providing no constructive ways to restore trust. Disclosing a conflict only reveals a problem, without providing any guidance for resolving it.

Because of the limitations of disclosure, more stringent methods of enforcement deserve consideration, especially in cases of more severe kinds of conflict of interest. Other methods (roughly in order of increasing stringency) include mediation (devices such as blind trusts that insulate the physician from the secondary interest), abstention (an analogue to judicial recusal that would have physicians or researchers withdraw from cases in which they have substantial secondary interests), divestiture (which would eliminate the secondary interest), and prohibition (which would have physicians or researchers withdraw permanently from fields in which they have substantial secondary interests).[2]

The problem of conflicts of interest in medicine is more complex than is often recognized. A more systematic framework is desirable for specifying and applying rules to regulate conflicts. A better understanding of the nature of conflicts of interest and a clearer formulation of standards could increase confidence in the medical profession. Physicians and scholars could then concentrate more fully on their main missions – treating patients, teaching students, and conducting research.

Notes

I am indebted to those who participated in the Clinical Ethics Lecture Series, sponsored by the Harvard University Division of Medical Ethics and Massachusetts General Hospital, Boston, at which an earlier version of this chapter was presented – especially Dr. David Blumenthal, Dr. Linda Emanuel, and Daniel Steiner.

1. Important earlier discussions of conflict of interest in medicine include: Relman 1980; and Relman 1985. The most comprehensive study is by Rodwin 1993. On self-referral, see Rodwin 1993; Mitchell and Scott 1992; and Council on Ethical and Judicial Affairs 1992. On risk sharing, see Hillman, Pauly and Kerstein 1989. On gifts from drug companies, see U.S. Senate 1990; and Kusserow 1991. On purchasing and bonding practices, see Rodwin 1993. On research, see Council on Scientific Affairs 1990; Blumenthal et al 1986; and Shimm and Spece 1991.
2. On mediation, see Council on Scientific Affairs 1990; and McDowell 1989. On forms of abstention and prohibition, see *Ethics in Patient Referrals Act of 1989*; McDowell 1989; and Green 1990.

References

Blumenthal, D., M. E. Gluck, K. S. Louis, M. A. Stoto, and D. Wise. 1986. "University-Industry Research Relationships in Biotechnology: Implications for the University." *Science* 232: 1361–6.

Blumenthal, D., M. E. Gluck, K. S. Louis, and D. Wise. 1986. "Industrial Support of University Research in Biotechnology." *Science* 231: 242–6.

Bureaus of Competition, Consumer Protection and Economics. 1987. *Comments Concerning the Development of Regulations Pursuant to the Medicare and Medicaid Anti-kickback Statute*. Washington, DC: Federal Trade Commission.

Council on Ethical and Judicial Affairs. American Medical Association. 1992. "Conflicts of Interest: Physician Ownership of Medical Facilities." *Journal of the American Medical Association* 267: 2366–9.

Council on Scientific Affairs, Council on Ethical and Judicial Affairs. 1990. "Conflicts of Interest in Medical Center/Industry Research Relationships." *Journal of the American Medical Association* 263: 2790–3.

Ethics in Patient Referrals Act of 1989. (The "Stark Bill.") 101st Cong., 1st sess., H. R. 939.

Green, R. M. 1990. "Physicians, Entrepreneurism and the Problem of Conflict of Interest." *Theoretical Medicine* 11: 287–300.

Hillman, B. J., C. A. Joseph, M. R. Mabry, J. H. Sunshine, S. D. Kennedy, and M. Noether. 1990. "Frequency and Costs of Diagnostic Imaging in Office Practice – a Comparison of Self-referring and Radiologist-referring Physicians." *New England Journal of Medicine* 323: 1604–8.

Hillman, A. L., M. V. Pauly, and J. J. Kerstein. 1989. "How Do Financial Incentives Affect Physicians' Clinical Decisions and the Financial Performance of Health Maintenance Organizations?" *New England Journal of Medicine* 321: 86–92.

Kassirer, J. P. 1993. "Medicine at Center Stage." *New England Journal of Medicine* 328: 1268–9.

Kusserow, R. P. 1991. *Promotion of Prescription Drugs through Payments and Gifts*. Washington, DC: Department of Health and Human Services.

McCormick, B. 1992. "Referral Ban Softened." *American Medical News*. July 6/13: 1, 52.

McDowell, T. N., Jr. 1989. "Physician Self-referral Arrangements: Legitimate Business or Unethical 'Entrepreneurialism.'" *American Journal of Law and Medicine* 15: 61–109.

Mitchell, J. M., and E. Scott 1992. "New Evidence of the Prevalence and Scope of Physician Joint Ventures." *Journal of the American Medical Association* 268: 80–4.

Relman, A. S. 1980. "The New Medical-industrial Complex." *New England Journal of Medicine* 303: 963–70.

———. 1985. "Dealing with Conflicts of Interest." *New England Journal of Medicine* 313: 749–51.

Rodwin, M. A. 1989. "Physicians' Conflicts of Interest: the Limitations of Disclosure." *New England Journal of Medicine* 321: 1405–8.

———. 1993. *Medicine, Money and Morals.* New York: Oxford University Press.

Rothman, K. J. 1991. "The Ethics of Research Sponsorship." *Journal of Clinical Epidemiology* 44: Suppl 1: 25S–8S.

———. 1993. "Conflict of Interest: the New McCarthyism in Science. *Journal of the American Medical Association* 269: 2782–4.

Shimm, D. S., and R. G. Spece, Jr. 1991. "Industry Reimbursement for Entering Patients into Clinical Trials: Legal and Ethical Issues." *Annals of Internal Medicine* 115: 148–51.

Todd, J. S. 1992. "Must the Law Assure Ethical Behavior?" *Journal of the American Medical Association* 268: 98.

U. S. Senate. Hearings Before the Committee on Labor and Human Resources. 1990. *Advertising, Marketing and Promotional Practices of the Pharmaceutical Industry.* 101st Congress, 2nd Session, December 11–12.

15

The Privatization of Business Ethics

During a conference on business ethics for corporation executives, the director of a large supermarket chain enthusiastically declared that he was in favor of more ethics in business. He then described a problem faced by many of his store managers in poorer urban areas: some customers were taking shopping carts home and using them as baby carriages. He commented:

> We must teach customers that it is unethical to take shopping carts. I realize we should not blame them now, because they may not understand that it is wrong – that it is really stealing – to take the carts. But better training in ethics will help them to understand this and become better people.

No doubt this executive was sincere, and no doubt it would be better if customers did not steal shopping carts (for whatever reason). But to think of ethics first in these terms is misguided, and misses the larger, more systematic ethical problems in our society.

This executive's approach to ethics is a common way of thinking about ethics that in various forms pervades not only the world of business but also much of public life in the United States. It reflects a tendency to make individual ethics the only kind of ethics in public life. Individual ethics refers to the moral principles that guide the face-to-face relations of individuals – the ethics of the family, friendship, small groups, and the behavior of individuals in society generally. It is to be distinguished from institutional ethics, which governs the relations among individuals as members of organizations and as citizens. The tendency to let individual ethics dominate institutional ethics – what may be called the privatization of ethics – is a mistake. The various forms of that mistake, and the obstacles they create to a more institutional kind of business ethics, deserve greater attention.

There are two principal types of the privatization of ethics. First, there is the tendency to transfer ethical principles that are appropriate for relations among individuals in private life to the context of organizations, where they are less appropriate. This is the tendency to *personalize* business ethics. Second, there is the tendency to try to keep ethics out of organizations by stipulating that they and their officers should be ethically neutral. This is the tendency to *depersonalize* business ethics.

These types of mistake may at first glance seem to be opposites, but they both have a common source. They both assume that the only kind of ethics appropriate in organizations is individual ethics. The first mistake – personalizing business ethics – tries directly to reproduce individual ethics in organizations, while the second – depersonalizing ethics – does the same indirectly. It imports individual ethics into the organization by insisting the only kind of ethics on which an executive can legitimately act is the ethics of other private individuals, specifically those to whom he or she is responsible (for example, owners or shareholders).

By considering several examples of each of these types of mistake, we can see why they are mistakes, and why they stand in the way of developing a business ethics more suitable for a social environment of large organizations and interdependent relationships. We should be seeking a business ethics that is neither personalized nor depersonalized – but rather is based on widely shared principles, formulated through open discussion among all citizens in a society.

PERSONALIZING BUSINESS ETHICS

The three most important ways of personalizing business ethics privilege the moral status of the individual. One emphasizes the character of individual leaders, and another their limited responsibility for the consequences of their organizations. A third would shift responsibility to the organization but by treating the corporation as the moral equivalent of an individual.

Personal Character

What is the most important factor in making business ethical? According to many commentators on business ethics, it is the good character of the corporate executives.[1] The CEO should be someone of high moral reputation in the community, preferably someone with deep religious commitments. When executives are interviewed about business ethics, many refer primarily to personal qualities in managers, such as integrity, conscientiousness, and honesty. The assumption is that if managers are good persons, they will act ethically on the job, and their organizations will be moral.

No advocate of business ethics should wish to speak against the value of good moral character. It is no doubt valuable, certainly in itself and probably in its effects. But as a factor in business ethics, it is vastly overrated. It is neither a sufficient, nor even a necessary, condition of moral action by executives or corporations.

It is not sufficient because many corporate misdeeds can be attributed to the actions of executives whose personal character is otherwise exemplary. Executives convicted of price fixing are typically described as upstanding members of the community. The vice-presidents convicted in the celebrated price fixing conspiracy in the heavy electrical equipment industry in the United States in the early 1960s were not only good family men, but also respected corporate leaders. The corporate culture and other features of organizational life apparently created conditions in which men of good character could not resist breaking the law.[2] Even in more egregious cases, where direct harm to other people results from corporate action – as in product liability cases – the corporate culprits hardly seem like criminals. No one had any basis in advance to criticize the character of the Ford executives who in the Pinto case in the late 1970s deliberately failed to correct the design of a fuel tank that they knew to be dangerous and which resulted in numerous fatal accidents.[3]

Neither is good personal character a necessary condition. One reason that it is mistakenly thought to be necessary is that it is often confused with the appearance of good character. It is certainly useful to *seem* to be a person of unquestioned integrity, someone who in public and private life treats everyone honestly and fairly. But some people are able to conceal even their most objectionable flaws, and perform well even in positions of high visibility and responsibility. One of the most successful and respected executives in the Securities and Exchange Commission resigned in 1985 after admitting that he had for many years repeatedly and violently beaten his wife. His performance as chief of the enforcement division had been outstanding, and his personal viciousness came to light only inadvertently.[4] Many people are capable of leading dual lives, keeping their personal vices from affecting their public actions. Indeed, individuals who are the most successful at maintaining this separation must be those about whose private vices we never hear, and whose character defects we never suspect.

Another reason personal character should not play a more important role in business ethics is that many of the moral virtues that we praise in individual relations can produce bad consequences in organizational life. Loyalty to family and friends is a quality we admire in private life, but it is a common source of favoritism and corruption in public life. Loyalty to employees or to shareholders may be a desirable trait, but it is not the same quality as loyalty to family and friends. Loyalty calls for different inclinations and judgments in organizational life from those it requires in personal relations. So does compassion. Not only do corporate executives sometimes have to overcome their compassion for individuals (when, for example, they fire employees, or close a plant) – a Machiavellian point many may already appreciate too well – but they also have to develop a capacity for compassion for distant and unidentifiable victims (including those who appear only as "statistical lives"). The harm to potential victims may have to take precedence over the harm that actual victims suffer more immediately, and to which a personally compassionate person normally reacts more strongly. The gap between private virtue and public virtue is great. It casts doubt on a business ethics that would identify the good person with the good executive.

Personal Responsibility

A second way of personalizing business ethics involves a mistake, not about moral virtue or moral principle, but about moral responsibility – about the extent to which we hold each other accountable for moral wrongs (whatever they might be). This mistake consists in limiting moral responsibility to one's own direct actions, and avoiding taking any responsibility for the actions of other people.

This limited view of moral responsibility makes some sense in everyday life. After all, it is not your fault if other people lie, break promises, or fail to do their fair share. You may not like what they do, and you may want to criticize them. But in the absence of any special connections to them, you would not expect to be blamed or criticized for what they do. Nor would you necessarily think it your responsibility to report them to some moral or legal authority. It is enough that you stay virtuous yourself.

When this limited view of personal responsibility is transferred to organizational life, it produces an anemic set of responsibilities. It suggests an ethics of merely keeping your own hands clean. Indeed, what it produces might be more accurately called an evasion of responsibility. It becomes a way for individuals to avoid responsibility for the organizations with which they are associated.

One consequence of this anemic conception of responsibility is to discourage whistle-blowing in organizations. There are already many obstacles facing an employee who would protest when he or she sees others doing wrong. But if employees also think that it is none of their moral business to protest, they are even less likely to do so.[5]

Some writers on business ethics argue that whistle-blowing is unethical, or at least morally ambiguous. Peter Drucker writes:

"Whistle-blowing," after all, is simply another word for "informing." And perhaps it is not quite irrelevant that the only societies in Western history that encouraged informers were bloody and infamous tyrannies – Tiberius and Nero in Rome, the Inquisition in the Spain of Philip II, the French Terror and Stalin....For under "whistle-blowing," under the regime of the "informer," no mutual trust, no interdependencies and no ethics are possible.[6]

Whistle-blowing is surely not the same as informing. Whistle-blowers sooner or later make their protests public (and are often penalized rather than rewarded). But even if they do not, and to this extent come to resemble informers more closely, they are "informing" for the good of the organization or the good of society (whatever their motives). If the organization or the society is worth preserving (as "bloody and infamous tyrannies" are not), we should encourage, not condemn, the whistle-blower. We may decide we do not like the kind of person who is capable of blowing the whistle: we may still think that he or she is too much like a "squealer" or "tattletale." But to let that attitude determine how we act in corporate life and how we design institutions would be again to confuse individual ethics with institutional ethics.

This limited notion of responsibility is no less a mistake when applied to organizations as when applied to the individuals who work within them. To be sure, we should praise corporations that accept that they have a moral responsibility, like that of individuals, for the harmful consequences of their own actions. (This has been one of the aims of the "corporate responsibility" movement.) Under normal circumstances this may be responsibility enough for a corporation. We may assume, for example, that a corporation should not generally be held accountable for harms that its customers cause by using its products, or its suppliers cause in producing their products. But when customers themselves are corporations, and when the product or its manufacture can cause great harm to many people, we should rethink this assumption. Under these conditions, it seems excessively individualist.

In the 1970s, Allied Chemical Corporation, which produced a highly profitable DDT-like pesticide called Kepone, contracted with outside producers to supplement their supply of the chemical.[7] One of the contractors produced Kepone under appalling working conditions that caused severe damage to the health of workers and others in the area. Executives at Allied apparently assumed that the contractor was producing the chemical under conditions as safe as Allied had maintained in its own plant, and at first denied responsibility for the negligence of its contractors. But then Richard Wagner, president of Specialty Chemicals at Allied, insisted that the company should recognize its moral obligation to the people the contractor had harmed. Wagner also implemented a new program called Total Product Responsibility, which made Allied responsible for foreseeing and preventing the harmful effects of their products before and after the company had control over them. One of the guidelines stated: "A product should not be sold to a customer where it is known that the end use application is not proper."

In this way, Allied moved beyond a limited concept of responsibility that might have been appropriate for an era when the harm that corporations could cause was on the scale of harm that individuals could cause. Allied adopted a broader concept of responsibility – one that is more suitable for an age of large institutions with great potential to cause widespread and systematic harm to many more people.

Corporate Persons

Although we may speak of corporations such as Allied as having moral responsibility, we should remember that it is the corporations's officers and other executives who are charged with acting on that responsibility. The idea of moral responsibility of the corporation is a metaphor, a way of identifying what actions its officials, present and future, should take on behalf of the organization. The danger with taking this metaphor literally is that we may begin to think that the corporation has the moral status and enjoys the moral rights of persons. This tendency to ascribe moral rights to corporations is a third way of personalizing business ethics.

An illustration of this tendency can be seen in the rules of confidentiality adopted by the American Bar Association (ABA) in 1983. The rules permit lawyers – including those working in or representing corporations – to reveal the confidences of their clients under only the most extreme conditions.[8] The ABA rejected a rule that would have required lawyers to reveal information necessary to prevent "death or serious bodily harm." The rules finally adopted merely *permit* a lawyer to reveal information necessary "to prevent the client from committing a criminal act that the lawyer believes is likely to result in imminent death or substantial bodily harm." This stricter standard of confidentiality – giving greater priority to the clients' confidences than to possible harm to third parties – was originally developed to protect important individual rights, especially the right to a fair trial in the adversary system. But whatever its value in protecting the rights of individuals, the zealous protection of confidentiality does not look so appealing when the clients are corporations.

First, the basic rationale for confidentiality is that it is necessary to encourage the client to tell the lawyer all the facts he or she needs to know in order to conduct the best possible defense. This rationale makes some sense when the client is an individual who is accused of a crime. But it makes less sense when the client is a corporation. In this context, lawyers have an ongoing relationship with their "client" (indeed they are often employees of their client), and can usually acquire all the information they need.

Second, if the rules referred only to individuals, it may be justifiable to limit disclosure to cases of "imminent death or serious bodily harm" because those are among the most serious harms that individuals are likely to cause. But imminent death and serious bodily harm are not always the most, or at least not the only, serious harms that corporations can cause. Corporate harms are more likely to be statistical and remote than imminent (for example, pollution of the environment or the harmful effects of cigarettes[9]), and are just as likely to be intangible as bodily (for example, racial discrimination or political bribery).

In the case of confidentiality rules, as with other corporate activities, we should not assume that what seems right for individuals will also be right for organizations. Indeed, the opposite may be the case.[10] Ethics for individuals is not ethics for corporations, at least not without some substantial changes. If we wish to develop a business ethics appropriate for the complex world of corporate life, we have to revise some of the assumptions that serve us well in our personal life.

DEPERSONALIZING BUSINESS ETHICS

The cure for the tendency to personalize business ethics is not, as one might at first suppose, to try to depersonalize it. Depersonalizing ethics is no less a mistake than personalizing it. Indeed, as already suggested, it is at root the same mistake. It also assumes that individual ethics is the only kind of ethics we need.

Depersonalized business ethics in its pure form assumes that corporations and corporate executives in their official capacity are responsible only to their shareholders, and only for maximizing the profit of the corporation (within the limits of the law). Except insofar as ethical principles have been enacted into law, executives should not take them into account. Not only should executives not let their own personal moral values affect their business decisions (as a personalized ethics suggests), but they should also try as far as possible to exclude moral values from their decisions. They should strive to keep business and ethics completely separate.

There are three main arguments in favor of this depersonalization. Each has some merit, but none is ultimately satisfactory. All fail for a similar reason: they do not recognize the institutional nature of ethics in public life. They treat ethics as a purely private matter.

Corporate Power

The first argument is that in a society where citizens disagree about moral values, it is wrong for corporations to use their power to impose their own values on the rest of society. They and their executives should stay morally neutral. During the civil rights struggles in the American South in the 1960s, corporations were sometimes asked to take a stand against racial discrimination. Arthur Wiebel, the president of a division of U.S. Steel in Birmingham, Alabama, at this time, was an active leader in community efforts to protect the civil rights of blacks. But when asked to use his corporation's influence in the community for the same purposes, he refused. He explained the company's policy:

As individuals we can exercise what influence we may have as citizens, but for a corporation to attempt to exert any kind of economic compulsion to achieve a particular end in the social area seems to me to be quite beyond what a corporation should do . . . [It would be] an abuse of corporate power . . . [11]

The appeal of this position even (or perhaps especially) to liberals should be obvious. If executives can enlist the power of their company to further good objectives (such as civil rights), then they may also use them to further less benign objectives (such as the unregulated pollution of the environment).

But the retreat to neutrality – the separation of the role of citizen and the role of executive – is a spurious solution to this problem. It ignores the fact that the corporation inevitably influences community values and practices, one way or another, whatever the corporate executive does. When the executives of U.S. Steel tried to keep the corporation neutral on civil rights issues, they contributed to maintaining the status quo. They reinforced racist values that neither citizens nor business executives should countenance.

To be sure, the business executive should not use the corporation to further his or her own personal ideology. That is personalized ethics again, and in this case might have justified corporations' attempts to preserve racial discrimination in their communities. The values behind which the executive might throw the weight of the corporation must be public values – principles of justice that have legitimate standing in the nation as a whole.

How we decide which values qualify for this status – and how we distinguish them from mere personal values and from local prejudices – are difficult questions. I offer some suggestions later about the kind of process that may help us to answer such questions in practice. But they are questions that a depersonalized ethics not only does not address, but also leads us to believe do not need to be addressed.

Another case illustrates why ethical neutrality is not really possible. In modern society corporations cannot avoid becoming entangled in moral questions. In the late 1980s the French corporation, Roussel-Uclaf, announced that it had developed a new drug, RU 486, which is an effective method of terminating pregnancy within the first nine weeks of gestation.[12] The healthcare community welcomed the drug as a safe and relatively private substitute for surgical abortion, but antiabortion activists immediately condemned it as a potentially dangerous drug and a "baby-killing poison." (If the pill were widely available, they suggested, it might be used at later stages of pregnancy, without proper medical supervision, when it could cause fatal hemorrhaging.) Antiabortionists and Catholic hospitals announced that they would stop buying any product made by Roussel, its parent company (the German conglomerate Hoechst), and all of the subsidiaries. On the other side, doctors at the World Congress of Obstetrics and Gynecology threatened to boycott Hoechst products if Roussel did not release the drug.

The Board Chairman of Roussel at first decided that the company would not distribute the drug: "If I were a lone scientist, I would have acted differently. But we have a responsibility in managing a company... Imagine your workers going back on the evening train and their children saying, 'Father, is it true that you are an assassin?'"[13]

But then the French government intervened. The Health Minister threatened to transfer Roussel's patent to another company (allowable under French law since the government owned part of Roussel). He argued that no one should "deprive women of a product that represents medical progress. From the moment government approval for the drug was granted, RU 486 became the moral property of women, not just the property of the drug company."[14] Roussel began distributing the drug in France, but for some time refused to sell it in any other country.

Whatever we think of the merits of Roussel's decisions (before and after government intervention), we should recognize that the corporation did not, and could not have, maintained a morally neutral position. Whatever its decision, the company would have foreseeably favored one side of the moral controversy about abortion. Even after the government had intervened, Roussel could not disavow moral responsibility for the distribution of the drug. The company still had to decide whether to sell the drug in other countries, including some where the drug was likely to be misused.

Competitive Disadvantage

The second argument for depersonalized ethics points to the competitive disadvantage that a corporation or executives are likely to suffer if they try to act ethically in an environment when others do not. The argument tries to appeal to the idea of justice: it is not fair that our company should play by the rules when our competitors do not. Even if we agree that a certain practice is wrong, we have to put aside our moral scruples and act on our (impersonal) business judgment.

Some American business executives invoked this argument in defending the bribes their corporations paid to promote sales in foreign companies. In the 1970s, some 400 corporations (including 117 of the Fortune 500) admitted to the Securities and Exchange Commission that they had made foreign political payments in the previous decade. In 1977, the U.S. government enacted the Foreign Corrupt Practices Act, which prohibits corporations and their executives from offering or giving payments to officials of foreign governments for the purpose of obtaining or retaining business.

Many business executives (a majority, according to a more recent poll) still oppose this law, and believe there is nothing wrong with such bribes. They argue that in many countries, this kind of bribery is an accepted way of life, and we should not try to impose our moral standards on them. The bribes in effect help government officials make up for low salaries and lack of retirement benefits; bribes are in this way a kind of tax on companies, and are essentially harmless.[15] Because officials take the bribes from almost everyone, the bribes do not cause them to act differently from the way they would otherwise have acted. If any particular company decided not to offer bribes, it would simply lose business to some other company.

The same kind of argument is also used in domestic contexts. Within one country, certain kinds of ethically improper and even illegal practices may be common in some sectors of the business community. Types of misleading accounting practices may be widespread, and corporations may try to justify their own wrongdoing on grounds of fairness: why should they be obligated to reveal unfavorable financial information when other corporations do not?

It may sometimes be unfair to insist that any particular company, or even all companies in a particular country, should refrain from engaging in a morally questionable practice when other companies or countries do not operate under similar constraints. But it does not follow that a particular corporation has no moral obligations in such situations. If bribery is wrong, each corporation has an obligation to work to establish enforceable agreements, and (where necessary) to press for enforceable laws that apply to all corporations – first in their own country, then through international cooperation in other countries. In the meantime, corporations and their executives should also recognize that their own conduct serves as an example, for good or ill, in the struggle to enforce the ethical standards that they purport to favor.

One reason that corporations and their executives have not taken the lead in such efforts may be that they assume (as depersonalized ethics suggests they should) that morality is none of their business. Even corporations and executives who are convinced that such bribery is wrong act as if they believe that it is not part of their role to campaign for more stringent laws in this area. Those who doubt that such bribery is wrong also evidently assume that ethics has no place in business (at least this kind of business). They criticize their fellow citizens for trying (through the legislative process) to impose moral standards that are not accepted by everyone in their own country, let alone in foreign countries.

Although the argument from competitive disadvantage is sometimes right (indeed, even ethically justified), it is neither supported by, nor supports, a depersonalized ethics. On the contrary, it is justifiable only if those corporations and executives who invoke it are prepared to act with others in their society and elsewhere to arrive at common ethical standards for the conduct of their common affairs. Neither their own individual ethics (on which a personalized ethics allows them to act) nor the individual ethics of others (to which a depersonalized ethics encourages them to defer) is adequate.

Good Business

The third argument for depersonalized ethics is in a sense the reverse of the one just discussed. Instead of claiming that the ethical corporation is at a disadvantage, this argument asserts that ethics is good business.

On this view, the corporation and its executives are still depersonalized, ethically speaking. They are not supposed to act directly on ethical principles; they are supposed to consider only what will maximize profit. But if they make business decisions reflectively with a regard to long-term consequences, they will find themselves making decisions that are ethical. A corporation with a reputation for ethical behavior will win and keep the good will of its employees, customers, competitors, and the general public – and thereby strengthen its capacity as a long-term competitor in the marketplace. The profitable corporation becomes, through the medium of a kind of invisible conscience, an ethical corporation.

This view is not the monopoly of business executives. At least one moral philosopher evidently holds it. In workshops for executives at his center in Arizona, and in his book on business ethics, this philosopher has produced numerous arguments intended to show that ethics is good business, and various prescriptions for "Gaining the Ethics Edge" (the subtitle of the book).[16] A newsletter from his center includes a section of advice entitled "Ethics – a Better Way to the Bottom Line," and testimonials from satisfied customers ("Now that I have taken your course, I can put ethics to work for my company. I will attempt to insinuate ethics into almost every corner of my organization").

In the book, in a section entitled "Shopping Mall Ethics," we learn about Mel, a real estate developer in Indiana, who had nearly won approval from the city council for building a huge shopping mall, after investing three and a half million dollars in planning.[17] But then a citizen group conducted its own study, which showed that any benefits of the shopping mall would go mostly to new residents and that the effects on the environment, traffic, and crime would be costly. It looked as if Mel would now lose the vote in the city council.

But, just in time, ethics came to the rescue. With the help of this philosopher (brandishing something that looked vaguely like John Rawls's difference principle), Mel was able to show that the least advantaged residents of the town would benefit after all (the townies more than the yuppies), and that these benefits should take priority over the costs, resulting in a net gain of social utility. The philosopher concedes that some council members were suspicious of Mel's newfound concern for the least advantaged, but ethics nonetheless carried the day. In a close vote, Mel won.

The objection to this kind of argument – and the impulse to reconcile ethics and profits that it displays – is not that it is never valid. Certainly, some of the most successful corporations are among the most ethical, and no doubt ethical behavior can often contribute to long-term profits. The objection is that if the only justification for ethical behavior in business is that it promotes profits, then there will be no basis for a call for ethical action that constrains profits. Many practices that we would agree are unethical may sometimes appear to be, and may actually be, in the long-term interest of a company, and perhaps a whole industry. Polluting the environment at home, marketing hazardous products abroad, perpetuating unsafe working conditions – all may enhance profits and may not even hurt the reputation of the corporation (especially if done incrementally or – better yet – secretly).

The complaint in the shopping mall case should be not so much about Mel, who may have been using the right principle for the wrong reason. Rather, our criticism should be directed against the shopping mall philosopher, who promotes the idea that the best reason for the principle is that it is a better way to the bottom line. Reducing all motivations to material gain – recognizing only self-interested motives even for moral action – leaves business executives with little basis for moral action in cases where profit and ethics conflict.

The reduction of morality to profitability also corrupts the wider debate in the public forum, where some of the most important arguments about business ethics should take place. If ethics is merely seen as good business, then the only respectable motives, the only acceptable reasons, in public discourse will be those that appeal to self-interest – indeed, only to material interest. Public debate will become (even more than it is now) a perpetual exchange of accusations of ulterior motive. The process of creating an institutional ethics for our common life becomes corrupted when the participants come to expect that the only justification that counts is an appeal to the self-interest of individuals or organizations. When citizens suspect selfish motives behind every declaration of principle, the corporation and the business executive will not be spared. Indeed, they will be the first to be suspected. They will deserve the suspicion if they have no other ethics than the depersonalized kind.

TOWARD AN INSTITUTIONAL ETHICS OF BUSINESS

In recent years, a new view of business ethics has begun to emerge in business schools and in the business world more generally.[18] According to this view, corporate executives are responsible not only to shareholders but to all stakeholders of the corporation. Stakeholders include employees, customers, suppliers, lenders, citizens of the local community, and sometimes even foreign nationals.

This new view of business ethics is not immune to privatization. It can lead quite easily to a personalized ethics. Given such a large and conflicting group of people to whom they are responsible, executives may think they have to fall back on their own personal values.

Alternatively, an executive may suppose that the most responsible way of resolving all these conflicting values is to assume that what they all have in common is the desire for material gain, and that the best way to fulfill his or her wider responsibility is still to try to maximize long-term profits. The executive thus defers to the values (or, more precisely, one of the values) held by indeterminate groups of individuals, and is thus depersonalized.

But if the new business ethics is in this way vulnerable to the twin dangers of personalization and depersonalization, it also can point us toward a broader conception of ethics for business. It can remind us that the moral responsibilities of the business community are more extensive than the concerns of both personal morality and impersonal commerce. The principles and practices that govern the world of business are increasingly everyone's business.

The criticisms presented here against two common approaches to business ethics suggest the direction in which business ethics should move. Both of the approaches fail ultimately for the same reason. By assuming that the only ethics that counts is individual ethics, they both stand as obstacles to a more appropriate ethics that emphasizes institutional principles. Because such principles govern the life of all members of an organization and affect many members of society together, they need to be developed by all members acting together. Our aim then should be to create and sustain a public dialogue in which all citizens (including members of the business community) seek ethical principles and practices for their institutional life based on values that they share, or, through continuing discussion, can come to share.

This institutional ethics calls for virtues that differ from those most prized in private life. It favors compassion that takes into account the distant and remote consequences of actions, and confidentiality that defers to the public interest. It expresses an extended sense of moral responsibility – a willingness to take responsibility for the wrongs that others commit, and for the protection of those who protest against the wrongs that others commit. Among its practical implications are greater institutional protections for whistle-blowers, and broader scope for liability for dangerous products.

An institutional ethics will not let corporate executives decline the invitation to enter the public forum by claiming that their jobs have nothing to do with ethics. Institutional ethics insists that executives account to the public in public for their actions, and give moral reasons that appeal to principles shared with their fellow citizens. At the same time, institutional ethics allows for the possibility that business and businesspeople are capable of doing more than pursuing profit for its own sake.

If this kind of public deliberation is to be both effective and ethical, it will require some new institutions, or at least some reform of existing institutions. Corporations will have to be more open about what they do within their own walls, and more open about what they do in the corridors of government. Political parties will have to transcend their traditional ideological dogmas – for or against government regulation, for or against big business. Professional associations will have to relinquish some of their protective privileges and regain their commitment to public service. Governments will have to take on as much responsibility for encouraging public deliberation about public policy as for trying to influence policymakers. Educational institutions will have to prepare citizens, including men and women who aspire to be leaders in business, to take moral responsibility seriously in both speech and action. Business schools will have to teach more than merely technical skills, and liberal arts colleges more than theories and great books to students bound for careers in business.

No one today would unequivocally declare that "What is good for General Motors is good for the country."[19] But in the complex and interdependent world in which we now live, it is no longer possible to believe in the happy conjunction of any set of particular interests and the public interest. Nor is it sensible to believe that all particular interests conflict with the public interest. Forging a union of the particular and the general – a balance between profit and morality – is the aim of a business ethics that can claim to be an ethics for all citizens.

Notes

1. Joseph Badaracco and Richard Ellsworth, *Leadership and the Quest for Integrity* (Boston: Harvard Business School Press, 1989); Clarence Walton, *The Moral Manager* (Cambridge, Mass.: Ballinger, 1988); Barbara Toffler, *Tough Choices: Managers Talk Ethics* (New York: John Wiley and Sons, 1986); and John W. Newstrom and William A. Ruch, "The Ethics of Management and the Management of Ethics," in *Contemporary Moral Controversies in Business*, edited by A. Pablo Iannone (New York: Oxford University Press, 1989), 143–50.
2. Jeffrey Sonnenfeld and Paul R. Lawrence, "Why Do Companies Succumb to Price Fixing?" *Harvard Business Review* (July-August 1978), 145–57.

3. The case is discussed in Frances T. Cullen, William J. Maakestad, and Gray Cavender, *Corporate Crime Under Attack: The Ford Pinto Case and Beyond* (Cincinnati, Ohio: Anderson, 1987).

4. Brooks Jackson, "John Fedders of SEC is Pummeled by Legal and Personal Problems," *Wall Street Journal* (February 25, 1985), 1. See also chap. 10 in this volume.

5. For a sympathetic review of whistle-blowing in government and industry in the United States, see Myron Peretz Glazer and Penina Migdal Glazer, *The Whistleblowers: Exposing Corruption in Government* (New York: Basic Books, 1989).

6. Peter Drucker, "Ethical Chic," *The Public Interest* (spring 1981), 18–36. Also see his "Is Whistle-Blowing the Same as Informing?" *Business and Society Review* (fall 1981), 4–17.

7. Harvard Business School Case Services, *Allied Chemical Corporation* 379–137 (Harvard University, 1979).

8. Model Rules, Rule 1.6 (b) (1). The old Code, still in effect in many states, also gives strong protection to confidentiality (though in a different way: a lawyer may report a client who intends to commit a crime, but not a client's knowledge of a past crime).

9. It is possible that the confidentiality rules could prevent an attorney formerly employed by a tobacco company from revealing the results of studies conducted by the company itself that confirm even more strongly the Surgeon General's warnings about the harmful effects of smoking. When a corporation invokes confidentiality in such a case, the public and the victims of smoking-related diseases are deprived of important information about the company's knowledge of the effects of its product. (For a case that suggests such a possibility, though the facts of the actual case are somewhat different, see *New York Times* [December 2, 1987], A20.)

10. Protecting corporate rights does not necessarily protect individual rights: individuals cannot claim the protection of a corporation's privilege for themselves if the corporation decides to waive it. See Charles Wolfram, *Modern Legal Ethics* (St Paul, Minn.: West Publishing, 1986), 284.

11. Kenneth Goodpaster, "The Challenge of Sustaining Corporate Conscience," *Journal of Law, Ethics and Public Policy*, 2 (1987), 837–8. (The "company policy" is a quotation from Roger Blough, the corporate President of U.S. Steel.)

12. Joseph Palca, "The Pill of Choice?" *Science* 245 (September 22, 1989), 1319–23.

13. Ellen Benoit, "Why Nobody Wants $1 Billion," *Financial World* (June 27, 1989), 34.

14. Ibid., 245.

15. See David Braybrooke, *Ethics in the World of Business* (Totowa, NJ: Rowman & Littlefield, 1982), 424–6. For an "ethical" argument against the Foreign Corrupt Practices Act, see Mark Pastin and Michael Hooker, "Ethics and the Foreign Corrupt Practices Act," in Iannone, *Contemporary Moral Controversies in Business*, 466–9.

16. Mark Pastin, *The Hard Problems of Management: Gaining the Ethics Edge* (San Francisco: Jossey-Bass, 1986).

17. Ibid., 7–11.

18. For a comparison of the two views, see Norman Bowie, "How Do Corporate Managers Shape Public Policy Issues?" in *The Ethical Contexts for Business Conflicts*, edited by Samuel M. Natale and John B. Wilson (Lanham, MD: University Press of America, 1990) 143–58.

19. This maxim is commonly attributed to Charles E. Wilson ("Engine Charlie"), a Detroit auto executive who became the Secretary of Defense. But Wilson was misquoted; what he actually said was: ". . . what was good for our country was good for General Motors, and vice versa. The difference did not exist. Our country is too big. It goes with the welfare of the country . . ." See William Safire, *Safire's Political Dictionary* (New York: Ballantine, 19–78), 787.

16

Democratic Theory and Global Society

In the early days of the European Union, the Casagrande family left their home in northern Italy to find work in Germany.[1] Although their new jobs as migrant laborers would certainly not make them rich, the prospects for the future looked better, especially for their young son, Donato, who could take advantage of the social services and educational opportunities. They enrolled Donato in the Realschule in Munich, and after his father died his mother applied for the monthly grants that the Bavarian law awards to pupils from low-income families. But the city of Munich denied her application, pointing out that the same law that promises grants to poor schoolchildren declares non-Germans ineligible (unless they are stateless individuals or aliens residing under a right of asylum). The fact that Donato had lived most of his life in Germany did not make any difference.

The Casagrandes appealed this decision – not, as one might expect, to German authorities, but to the European Court of Justice. They relied on Article 12 of a European Council regulation, which provides that children of citizens of other states of the European Union must be admitted to the educational programs on the same conditions as nationals. The Bavarian public prosecutor intervened, challenging the authority of the European Council to issue such a regulation, but the European Court sided with the Council, and Donato Casagrande got his grant.

The case has become a landmark decision in the developing constitutional law of the EU, and raises many interesting issues in the politics and jurisprudence of regional integration and international law. But for my purposes its significance lies in what it illustrates about some larger challenges to the theory of liberal democracy in a global society. Embedded in this case are the key elements of the problems that globalization poses for both liberalism and democracy.

THE EXTENSION OF LIBERAL DEMOCRACY

At first glance, the Casagrande case looks like an instance of the traditional conflict between majority rule and individual rights, or, more broadly, between democracy and liberalism. And indeed it does involve some such conflict: the democratic majority in Bavaria enacted a law that was alleged to violate an individual right. But there is something problematic about both elements in this conflict; neither fits readily into the familiar framework of liberal democracy.

On the democratic side, the Bavarian majority is not the only majority that is relevant. The European Council and Parliament, at least in theory, represent a majority of member states, and also a majority of citizens in the Union. This is not simply a problem about how to allocate authority to various levels of government – as in the jurisdictional issues that arise in a federal system. The authority that EU officials have over the Bavarian governments, though more than an international organization such as the United Nations can claim, is less than that which the central government in a fully developed federal system enjoys.[2] The problem exemplifies a more general difficulty of democracy in a global society: what may be called "the problem of many majorities," the fact that decision-making authority is dispersed, and that no majority has an exclusive and overriding claim to democratic legitimacy. The problem is further complicated by the fact that not only governments but also corporations, nongovernmental organizations, international agencies, and professional associations are making decisions that systematically affect and often bind citizens in many different countries.

On the liberal side, the individual rights being protected in this case are not those of citizens, and the authority protecting them is not that of the national government. Donato Casagrande, however long he lived in Germany, remained an Italian national, and so did his parents. To be sure, any adequate democracy should grant foreigners some basic rights, such as a right to free speech and fair trial. And any decent democracy would provide essential education for the children of foreigners who are working in their country. But to require as a matter of right that a government provide to anyone who happens to come to their country the same educational opportunities that its own citizens enjoy substantially expands the demands of liberalism beyond its traditional understanding and correspondingly reduces the scope of democratic discretion.

Furthermore, the expansion affects not only the content of the right but also its enforcement. To permit an authority that is independent of the national government to impose this requirement is to give the right a status significantly beyond that which liberal constitutions usually have guaranteed. It insulates the right from democratic decision making even more than does judicial review in most national constitutions. Nor is the problem solved simply by noting that the national government has formally consented to the right in question or to the process that establishes and enforces it. The German government has the formal power to demand that the Council rescind the regulation or alter the court's jurisdiction, but in practice any such action would be difficult if not impossible.

In any case, the problem is more general than that of a jurisdictional dispute within a regional authority like the EU. It arises because liberal rights are increasingly being claimed and enforced by authorities outside national jurisdictions (sometimes officially as in the EU, but often unofficially through social and economic pressures exerted by nongovernmental organizations). Furthermore, the liberal rights are not always for the protection of the welfare of individuals like Donato Casagrande. They are also at least as often put forward to protect economic interests of corporations and the growth of the free market.

In these ways, the traditional tension between liberal rights and democratic authority takes on a more challenging form in the global society. The scope of liberal rights is expanding, bringing more disagreement about what their content should be and about who should enforce them. At the same time the locus of the democratic authority that might deal with these disagreements is increasingly dispersed. The tension exists not only within a single state, but between a state and other formal and informal centers of power.

How should democratic theory deal with these problems that globalization poses? Here I focus on the theoretical challenge – how to think about liberal democracy, not immediately how to change it. We should try to clarify our thinking before starting to reform institutions or design new ones. Also, we should not expect a democratic theory to yield a definite answer to any particular policy problem – to declare, for example, that the city of Munich must provide educational grants to noncitizens. Indeed, the most promising democratic theory leaves such questions open.

Two main approaches to the problems of globalization are prominent in democratic theory today. One accepts the tension between liberty and democracy but extends it to the level of interstate or international politics. This is what is sometimes called "cosmopolitan governance" (which I shall refer to simply as cosmopolitanism). The other tries to dissolve the tension by reducing the role of government at all levels. This is the approach of some of those who focus on "civil society" (which I call "civil societarianism"). Neither approach is adequate, and though in some respects they seem to be the opposite of each other, their inadequacy stems from the same source. Both concentrate the search for a solution on sites outside the framework of states, and therefore downplay the need to change the way that states understand their own democratic process.[3]

THE LIMITS OF COSMOPOLITANISM

First, consider cosmopolitanism.[4] Inspired by the universalist aspirations of Enlightenment philosophers such as Kant, the cosmopolitans pin their hopes on strengthening regional and international forums in order both to protect liberal rights and to enhance democratic decision making.[5] Without rejecting democratic politics at the national or local level, they favor encouraging more regional integration ("EU and beyond"), granting international courts compulsory jurisdiction, making economic agencies and corporations accountable to regional and international assemblies, maintaining an international military force, and creating a global parliament.[6]

The vision is attractive, and to some extent its realization is not only desirable but inevitable. The health of liberal democracy depends on making liberalism and democracy more universal at all levels of government. But as a guiding conception for democratic theory, cosmopolitanism has serious defects both in its liberalism and in its democracy, and therefore in the way that it combines them.

First, the liberalism. As long as we think about human rights (such as those prohibiting rape and torture) or even welfare rights (such as those promoting education and health), making liberalism universal is attractive in theory, however difficult in practice. But the form of liberalism that is in ascendance today emphasizes economic rights – the liberty promoted by the free market. As in domestic liberalism, these rights are defended on the grounds that they will benefit individuals, not only the capitalist corporations that exercise them. But in the absence of any political authority to limit these rights when they threaten to undermine other liberal rights, economic liberalism is likely to dominate, even more than it does in domestic contexts. Yet most cosmopolitans recognize that establishing such a political authority is not feasible in the foreseeable future.

The other problem with universalizing liberalism is that as soon as we move beyond the basic liberties recognized in international law and advocated by the human rights movement, internal conflicts break out within liberalism itself. The more communities or nations come under the dominion of liberal rights, the greater the likelihood of disagreement about what the rights should mean. Some of the disagreement is reasonable: neither side can be shown to be morally mistaken, even within its own moral or cultural framework. We do not even have to look to radically different cultures to find such conflicts. The conflict over abortion after the unification of East and West Germany is a case in point. It is not clear that the right to life protected in West Germany is any more liberal than the right to an abortion that had been guaranteed in East Germany.

Even when there is no disagreement about the right itself, there may be reasonable disagreement about the scope of its application or about what needs to be provided to satisfy it. Given limited resources, should a state spend more on preventative healthcare or on lifesaving therapies? May a state prevent (as Canada does) citizens from buying healthcare in the private market beyond what is provided to other citizens? Disagreements over these issues occur now in politics within a state, particularly in multicultural societies, but they multiply as politics spreads beyond the state.

Cosmopolitanism is problematic on the democratic side, too. First, when we look at the experience of extending governmental authority beyond national boundaries, we cannot be encouraged so far by what we see. As the EU has gained more power and become more effective, it has also drawn more criticism for its lack of democratic accountability. A prominent theme in the scholarly literature and popular commentary on the EU is the criticism that it suffers from a "democratic deficit."[7] This deficit shows up both between the EU and the member states (the EU has enacted regulations on a wide range of social policies without any effective electoral accountability), and within the structure of EU government itself (the democratic Parliament has much less effective power than the technocratic Commission).[8]

A second and more general problem with cosmopolitan democracy is its multiplication of decision-making authorities, which is likely to result in a decline of accountability. Cosmopolitans usually do not recommend a single sovereign authority (a world government) or the abolition of the state. One of the most fully developed cosmopolitan theories proposes a "network of regional and international agencies and assemblies that cut across spatially delimited locales."[9] By its very nature, such a network does not give those citizens outside particular agencies or assemblies any significant control, and does not provide any way for citizens within them to deal with the effects of the unco-ordinated decisions of other agencies and assemblies. The dispersal of authority may generate more points of influence and more opportunities for participation, but it is also likely to offer less effective control and coordination.[10] Although accountability in the present system may not be robust, we can see and try to correct its deficiencies more clearly than we could in a system with still more sources of authority.

THE INADEQUACY OF CIVIL SOCIETARIANISM

The other leading approach intended to enable liberal democracy to deal with globalization – strengthening civil society – suffers from this same dispersal of authority. This is again the problem of many majorities. Civil societarianism suffers from the problem to an even greater degree than cosmopolitanism does because, without denying the need for governmental institutions, it neglects the importance of improving and strengthening them.

To be sure, democracy needs robust social institutions – from professional associations and trade unions to choral societies and bowling leagues. At least since Tocqueville democratic theorists of many different persuasions have recognized the importance of civil society, even if they have taken it for granted more than they have theorized about it. And the growth of civil society beyond the state – through transnational associations and similar institutions – represents an important and promising development in democratic politics. But the new civil societarians pay so much attention to social institutions that they disregard governmental ones. Citizens need to make collective decisions about matters that affect the whole society, among them the positive and negative consequences of the many separate decisions made by the institutions of civil society. The civil societarians are in danger of purchasing more democracy in segments of society at the price of less democracy in the whole of society.

"Palermo may represent the future of Moscow," a leading civil societarian has written.[11] This prognosis gives Moscow too much credit, and Palermo too little. The chaos in Moscow was due more to the breakdown of political institutions than to the collapse of civil society. To the extent there has been progress in restoring law and order in Palermo, it is surely the result of the rebuilding not of choral societies but of political institutions, an effort in which the national *government* has played an important role. So politics in the traditional places – local and national government – is still of critical importance for democracy itself, not least for making possible the democratic governance of the institutions of civil society.

Civil societarians, whether liberals or not, usually value liberty, but they differ about which liberties they regard as most important. One group favors social institutions because it believes they provide more opportunities for individuals to develop their various talents and interests, and therefore promote the free pursuit of a diverse range of activities. A robust civil society makes it more likely that all citizens, including those who may be disadvantaged, will find greater support in pursuing their life plans whatever they may be. For the other group, the liberty that matters most in civil society is economic freedom, and the social institution that matters most is the market. This group is more strongly opposed than the first to any collective political action, reflecting the skepticism that classical liberalism has always held toward government.

This conflict between these ways of valuing civil society reveals a problem that they both share. The problem is that while the liberties to which each gives priority are important, they are not always compatible, and neither group offers a way to resolve the conflict even in theory. Each simply reasserts the priority of its own favorite liberty. Should a corporation have complete freedom to decide to close a plant that has been the lifeblood of the residents of a region? Should a trade union or professional association have the right to set qualifications for membership based on political, religious, or other non-economic grounds? Should economic development of the rainforests take precedence over recreational needs? The answers are obvious only if one has already decided in advance to give priority to one kind of liberty, and most citizens in most democracies have not. Choosing between, or balancing among, these conflicting liberties – if the choice is to be justifiable to the people who will be bound by it – is a task that requires a robust process of democratic decision making.

There is another reason to worry about the neglect of government, a reason that has special force against those civil societarians who emphasize the importance of the market. An effective democratic government is a necessary part of the answer to one of the most common objections to free trade in the global society. The objection begins by observing that nations that treat their workers well and protect the environment properly will be disadvantaged in economic competition with nations that do not. As a matter of fairness, nations with higher wages and stronger environmental regulations may seem to be justified in adopting protectionist trade policies. Without such policies, so the fairness objection goes, there is no "level playing field" in international trade.

But, as many economists point out, there does not have to be a level playing field for free trade to benefit all trading partners.[12] Nations do not have to have the same wage levels or the same standards of environmental protection. In fact, differences between countries in these and other respects are to a significant extent what makes free trade advantageous to all the countries that take part. This is simply an implication of the fundamental idea of comparative advantage. But notice – what the economists do not usually emphasize – that whether comparative advantage disposes of the fairness objection depends on a further assumption: that the differences between nations (in wage levels, environmental standards, welfare provisions, and the like) reflect genuine differences in the views of the citizens in these nations. The differences should represent policies that citizens in the trading nations in some sense have endorsed or accepted. This assumption in turn depends on the existence of some form of democratic decision making in which citizens can have some influence on the labor, environmental, and social policy of their governments. Thus, from a liberal perspective, whether the free trade that market-oriented civil societarians favor is justifiable depends on the existence of robust governments of which democrats could approve.[13]

To reaffirm the importance of the state is not to deny the need for transnational democracy, or to privilege the state as the only site of liberal democracy. Even less does this reaffirmation depend on assuming that democracy can exist only as the expression of a common will of a people, rooted in a national culture or identity.[14] The state is simply better placed at present to provide the most justifiable means of exercising collective power for liberal democratic ends, including the ends of strengthening institutions of civil society and transnational politics. Without denying the potential of these other institutions, we should recognize that for the foreseeable future the power exercised by states (and their subgovernmental units) is likely to be more legitimate – more justifiable to the persons bound by them – than that exercised by other institutions.

THE PROMISE OF LIBERAL DEMOCRACY IN THE STATE

But even if it is desirable to try to maintain strong democratic governments in states, is it possible? The "loss of sovereignty" is a much-debated empirical question, and the evidence is not sufficient yet to reach any final conclusions.[15] There is no doubt that the forces of globalization constrain what states can do. In general, these forces probably make it harder for governments to tax capital and to spend more resources on social programs.[16] Capital and labor move more freely and rapidly across borders than ever before, and governments may have less control over their movements. The effects of changes in the financial markets in one nation are felt potently and almost immediately in many other nations. One of President Clinton's advisers emphasized the power of the financial markets in this way: "[In the next life], I want to come back as the bond market."[17]

But it is easy to exaggerate the effects on the autonomy of domestic governments. Governments have always been vulnerable to the forces of international economy; globalization simply intensifies problems that have long been familiar to many governments.[18] The most reliable recent studies show that the effects of international capital mobility are "contingent on the choices of national policymakers" and their domestic institutions.[19] Also, politicians use globalization as an excuse to avoid hard choices in domestic policy. In face of widespread opposition to their proposal for pension and fiscal reforms in 1995, the French government blamed the changes on the EU. Although they were required by the Maastricht criteria, they were also in the long-term interest of France, according to most experts.[20]

In other instances, what may seem to be loss of domestic control is actually the result of "self-limited sovereignty."[21] Why have many nations accepted immigrants or permitted workers who came as "guests" to stay permanently and to enjoy many of the benefits of citizenship? The most convincing analyses show that internal politics largely explain the acceptance of "unwanted" immigrants and guest workers (though of course there are often important differences in how each group is treated). It turns out that they are actually wanted – not by everyone, but by powerful groups within the state who benefit from the presence of workers from other nations.

If liberal democracy can and should be kept alive in the state, what kind of liberalism and what kind of democracy are most suitable in the age of globalization? Any satisfactory theory of liberal democracy must be able to deal with the two general problems that cosmopolitanism and civil societarianism fail adequately to address. On the democratic side, it must deal with the problem of many majorities, and on the liberal side, the problem of disagreement about rights. Deliberative democracy – a theory that is receiving increasing attention in recent years – offers the most promising way of dealing with these problems.[22]

The fundamental premise of deliberative democracy is that laws and policies imposed on individuals must be justified to them in terms that they can reasonably accept. The theory is "deliberative" in the sense that the terms it recommends are conceived as reasons that citizens or their accountable representatives give to one another in an ongoing process of mutual justification. The reciprocal reasons are not merely procedural ("because the majority favors it") or purely substantive ("because it is a human right"). They appeal to moral principles (such as basic liberty or equal opportunity) that individuals who are motivated to find fair terms of cooperation can actually accept. Some reasons that can be accepted in this sense are often not actually accepted because the social and political conditions are not favorable to the practice of deliberation. But deliberative democracy still holds this standard of reciprocity as an ideal against which actual practice can be measured.

How does deliberative democracy deal with the problem of many majorities? It does so by broadening the scope of political accountability: public officials must consider not only their electoral constituents but also what may be called their moral constituents, all those individuals who are bound by the decisions they make, whether de jure or de facto.[23] This moral constituency goes beyond the borders of the nation, but stops short of a cosmopolitan inclusion of everyone in the world who might be affected by a state's decision. It goes beyond the borders because noncitizens are sometimes bound by the state's decisions, such as those involving immigration, import restrictions, and transnational environmental agreements. It stops short of including everyone who may be affected because most noncitizens are not reasonably regarded as participants in the scheme of cooperation that establishes the rights and obligations that the state enforces.

Consider, for example, the policy of exporting hazardous products, notably toxic wastes.[24] For many years, the United States exported to countries such as Bangladesh large quantities of waste designated as hazardous by its own Environmental Protection Agency, contrary to the Basle convention of 1989.[25] The U.S. policy in effect denied that its officials must justify their policies to foreign citizens: U.S. officials should concern themselves only with what is good for their own citizens and their own economy, and let foreign governments and the free market take care of the wellbeing of their citizens and their economies. Two kinds of reasons are offered in support of this position.

One set of reasons refers to the fact that foreign nations voluntarily accept American exports. This is the argument from consent, but it mistakenly identifies the consent of the government, or in some cases the consent of certain business groups, with consent of citizens. The kind of individual or even collective consent that might justify the practice is not usually present. Even in those countries that are democratic, we cannot assume that a majority of citizens consent to the policy in any meaningful way unless they are well informed about the life-threatening risks that the wastes pose. U.S. officials do not usually make strenuous efforts to so inform them.

A second set of reasons try to show that exports actually benefit citizens in other countries by offering products that are less hazardous than others that are available, and by generally improving their standard of living. The evidence for these claims is at best uncertain. In the case of some products (such as carcinogenic pesticides), the risks are high, and tend to fall on the most disadvantaged citizens rather than on those who benefit most from improvements in the economy through international trade. But more than the argument from consent, this argument brings citizens of foreign nations into the moral universe of U.S. officials. An official who appeals to the welfare of these citizens, even for the purpose of justifying the export of hazardous waste, is already acknowledging these citizens as moral constituents. This kind of appeal therefore recognizes the broader scope of deliberative accountability.

This broadened scope of accountability does not of course completely solve the problem of many majorities. It does not dictate a particular answer to the question of whether toxic wastes should be exported or – for that matter – whether children of foreign workers should receive full education benefits. Different majorities could still come to different conclusions. But keeping open that possibility in a wider range of cases than allowed by some other theories is one of the virtues of deliberative democracy. By extending the constituencies of all majorities, deliberative democracy makes it more likely that each will at least consider the interests of some of the same individuals, and seek policies that will at least not harm and may even benefit those individuals. The more deliberative the U.S. legislature or the Munich Landeshauptstadt, the more consideration the claims of the citizens of Bangladesh or the guest workers from Italy are likely to receive.

The broadened accountability in deliberative democracy suggests some institutional changes. For example, a state could establish forums in which representatives could speak for the ordinary citizens of foreign states, presenting their claims and responding to counterclaims of representatives of the host state. The responsibility could even be formalized by establishing a special office – a form of tribunal for noncitizens. Such processes could help correct the bias of commercial and government-to-government negotiations that dominate policymaking on these issues now. The processes could be designed to encourage representatives to take into account the views of transnational agencies and organizations, and to this extent bring closer together the institutions of deliberative democracy and those of some forms of cosmopolitanism.

In the case of guest workers, forums could be provided for representatives to give voice to their concerns, even when they are (legitimately) denied the full rights of citizenship, such as voting in national elections. In such a forum, properly deliberative, Donato Casagrande may or may not have won the right to the same educational support German citizens enjoy, but he would not have been denied the right simply because noncitizens should have no say in such decisions.

Recall that the European Court overruled the Munich officials, and thereby protected Donato's right. Why not adopt a democratic theory that would simply declare certain liberties inviolable and let an authority insulated from political majorities enforce them?

Deliberative democracy does not exclude judicial review as a possible institutional arrangement, but it insists that there will often be reasonable disagreement about what liberties should be inviolable, and that even when there is agreement there will be reasonable dispute about their interpretation and how they should be weighed against other liberties. Most liberties are subject to revision as a result of new philosophical insights or empirical evidence, and, most importantly, challenges raised in actual democratic deliberations.

From the perspective of deliberative democracy, we can say that Donato has a right to basic education, but how much he should get, and how this right should be funded compared to other rights such as healthcare, and to what extent his right should depend on what rights other states grant foreigners are all questions that should not be settled in advance of democratic deliberation. Because rights and liberties are not privileged, because they are not completely set aside from politics, deliberative democracy is quite compatible with changing conceptions of liberty and continuing conflicts among liberties.

This conclusion may seem to exalt democracy at the expense of liberalism. But deliberative democracy does provide protection for liberty. At least as much protection as any *theory* can offer. It holds that some liberties and rights are fundamental, and should not be easily overridden by majority vote or even judicial decision. It assigns special status to those liberties and rights that are necessary for free and equal citizenship, even while declining to see a constitutional court, whether national or supranational, as the sole authority for deciding what they are, and how they should be interpreted. At any particular time, some liberties are properly regarded as rights, which democratic majorities should not override. But majorities themselves must come to view the rights in this way. The rights are more likely to be sustained if not only courts but also citizens and their representatives have opportunities to deliberate about them. This is especially so when people find themselves, as in a global society, needing to cooperate with others who have quite different and competing ideas about liberal rights.

Deliberative democracy does not give democracy any more priority than it gives liberty. It treats the democratic process itself in the same way as it treats the system of rights and liberties. Questions about what is required to make the democratic process more deliberative are themselves to be debated and answered by means of continuing deliberation. The liberties and opportunities – such as free political speech and primary education – that are among the preconditions of democratic deliberation are themselves subject to interpretation and balancing in the democratic process.

Thus deliberative democracy does not privilege either liberty or democracy, and sees the tension between them as a continuing condition that no adequate theory of democracy should expect to resolve. It recommends a reiterative process in which liberties are proposed, established, challenged, and revised in an ongoing process.

What might this process look like in practice? Imagine how it would work in the Casagrande case. After the Munich Landeshauptstadt decides against granting Donato a right to the educational grant, the European Court would issue a preliminary opinion. It would observe that the Landeshauptstadt's action is prima facie inconsistent with the EU Council's regulation, and ask the Munich officials to reconsider their decision. The Munich officials might conclude that they were mistaken, and change their policy. Or they could ask the EU Council to consider whether it intended the regulation to have this implication, and if so whether it wishes to revise the regulation in light of objections raised in this case. Other authorities, such as the EU Parliament and the German national institutions, could also be invited to submit opinions. Deliberation takes place not only within a state but among citizens in different states. This cross-national deliberation is not only compatible with but necessary for viable democratic politics within a state.

By the time a process like this had run its course, Donato would probably have finished school and started worrying about his pension benefits instead of his educational rights. Any reiterative process of this kind would have to include junctures of authoritative decision – times at which a particular case would be decided or a particular policy implemented. Furthermore, the participatory demands of deliberative democracy could be reduced if the deliberation concentrates on the second-order question of what the first-order decision-making processes should be. But whether the question is a policy or a procedural one, the deliberative process would still permit challenges to continue, keeping open more possibilities of revision than other forms of democracy normally encourage. The point is not that continuing deliberation is valuable in itself, but that it is necessary to reach decisions that are mutually justifiable, that can be reasonably accepted by those who are bound by them.

While deliberation may finally produce at least a rough consensus on some issues (as seems likely on educational policy in the EU), it cannot be expected to produce agreement on all. Deliberative democracy explicitly allows for this possibility, and provides some standards for living with moral disagreement. One of the most important (in one version of the theory) is the principle of an economy of moral disagreement, which calls on citizens and their representatives to search for significant points of convergence between their own moral understandings and those of the citizens whose positions, taken in their more comprehensive forms, they reject.[26]

This principle is applicable to disputes in which both sides hold moral positions neither of which can be shown to be wrong. An example is the abortion controversy mentioned earlier – the dispute between pro-life West Germans and pro-choice East Germans. Although this dispute had to be settled in the law by choosing one side, the principle of the economy of moral disagreement reminds citizens and officials on both sides that their deliberative obligations do not cease after an abortion law is enacted. Citizens and officials should try to promote policies on which their principles converge, even if they would otherwise place those policies significantly lower on their own list of political priorities. For example, even if some pro-choice advocates happen to think that publicly funded programs to help unwed mothers care for their own children are less important than some pro-life proponents believe, the pro-choicers should still join in actively promoting these programs and other policies that are similarly consistent with the principles they share with opponents.

CONCLUSION

At its summit in 1996, the Group of Seven issued a communiqué, "Making a Success of Globalization for the Benefit of All," which declared: "In an increasingly interdependent world we must all recognize that we have an interest in spreading the benefits of economic growth as widely as possible..."[27] The sentiment is welcome but the aim is incomplete. In an increasingly interdependent world, we all also have an interest in spreading the benefits of liberty and democracy as widely as possible. This political aim is no less important than the economic one, and though the two may conflict they ultimately stand or fall together. In our eagerness to manage efficiently the global economy, we should not forget that we need to govern democratically the global society that sustains it.

The challenges that globalization poses for liberal democracy are not entirely new, but they call for some new thinking about both the theory and practice of democracy. I have concentrated on the theory here, because I believe that theories, or fragments of theories, influence the way that leaders and citizens act. They often create conceptual obstacles that stand in the way of making practical progress in liberal democracies. Both cosmopolitan and civil societarian theories, while directing our attention toward some promising opportunities in the international arena and in communal associations, neglect the need to adjust our conception of politics in its more familiar site, the state. If we adopt the perspective of deliberative democracy – a theory that favors broader accountability, greater opportunities for revising political decisions, and more economy of moral disagreement – states that aspire to be liberal democracies will be better prepared to cope with the challenges they face in global society.

Notes

An earlier version of this article was presented as a public lecture at the University of Siena. I am grateful for the comments of the participants in the discussion on that occasion, as well as for advice from Michael Doyle, Amy Gutmann, Andrew Moravscik, Sebastiano Maffettone, Robert Goodin, and two readers for the *Journal of Political Philosophy*.

1. European Court of Justice, *Donato Casagrande v. Landeshauptstadt München*, Case 9/74, ECR 773, [1974] 2 CMLR 423.

2. The European Union is already formally a federal system in many respects: see Koen Lenaerts, "Constitutionalism and the Many Faces of Federalism," *American Journal of Comparative Law* 38 (1990), 205–63.

3. It is of course possible to combine the two approaches, as some theorists do – for example, by seeking to strengthen international civil society at the same time as strengthening international governance. But it is more likely that this combination, rather than permitting each approach to compensate for the deficiencies of the other, will simply compound the deficiencies of both.

4. David Held, *Democracy and the Global Order: From the Modern State to Cosmopolitan Governance* (Stanford, CA: Stanford University Press, 1995); and Daniele Archibugi, David Held, and Martin Köhler, eds., *Re-imagining Political Community: Studies in Cosmopolitan Democracy* (Stanford, CA: Stanford University Press, 1998). In a similar spirit but with more philosophical analysis, Thomas W. Pogge proposes a system in which "persons should be citizens of, and govern themselves through, a number of political units of various sizes, without any one political unit being dominant and thus occupying

the traditional role of state"; "Cosmopolitanism and Sovereignty," *Ethics* 103 (1992), 48–75, at 58.

5. Held, *Democracy and the Global Order,* 279–80. Kant, however, would not have approved of extending international government beyond providing collective security, free trade, and free movement.

6. Ibid., and Held, "Democracy and Globalization," in *Re-imagining Political Community,* edited by Archibugi, Held, and Köhler, 21–6.

7. J. H. H. Weiler, "The Transformation of Europe," *Yale Law Journal* 100 (1991), 2403–83, at 2466–7; and J. H. H. Weiler, U. R. Haltern, and F. C. Mayer, "European Democracy and its Critique," *West European Politics* 18 (1995), 4–39, at 6–9.

8. Pogge emphasizes the importance of higher-order democratic control in designing the institutions that make supranational decisions, and even in determining the process for designing those institutions; see his "Creating Supranational Institutions Democratically: Reflections on the European Union's 'Democratic Deficit,'" *Journal of Political Philosophy* 5 (1997), 163–82.

9. Held, *Democracy and the Global Order,* 237. Held sees this network as "a way of strengthening democracy 'within' communities and civil associations by elaborating and reinforcing democracy from 'outside'..." (237) He does not argue that national sovereignty has been "wholly subverted," but his response to globalization centers almost entirely on developing "new institutions and mechanisms" that go beyond those in the state ("Democracy and Globalization," 21, 23).

10. To the extent that cosmopolitans can effectively exercise power for collective international projects, as is sometimes the case now in some peacekeeping operations, they may be in danger of enforcing, without democratic legitimacy, the values and ideologies of the dominant world powers. See Danilo Zolo, *Cosmopolis: Prospects for World Government* (Oxford: Polity, 1997).

11. Robert Putnam, *Making Democracy Work* (Princeton, NJ: Princeton University Press, 1995).

12. Gary Burtless et al., *Globaphobia: Confronting Fears About Open Trade* (Washington, DC: Brookings Institution, 1998), 92–5; and Jagdish Bhagwati and T. N. Srinivasan, "Trade and the Environment: Does Environmental Diversity Detract from the Case for Free Trade?" in *Fair Trade and Harmonization,* edited by J. Bhagwati and R. E. Hudec (Cambridge, Mass.: MIT Press, 1996), 159–224.

13. Democratic determination of trade policy has the further important advantage of increasing the likelihood that those citizens who suffer the major losses will be compensated, a necessary condition if free trade is to maximize welfare rather than only the gross national product.

14. See, for example, David Miller, "The Left, the Nation-state and European Citizenship," *Dissent* (summer 1998), 47–51; and the criticism by Seyla Benhabib, "On European Citizenship," *Dissent* (fall 1998), 107–9.

15. Saskia Sassen, *Losing Control? Sovereignty in an Age of Globalization* (New York: Columbia University Press, 1996); and John Ruggie, "Territoriality and Beyond," *International Organization* 47 (1993), 139–74.

16. Dani Rodrik, *Has Globalization Gone Too Far?* (Washington, DC: Institute for International Economics, 1997), 49–67.

17. James Carville, quoted in Burtless et al., *Globaphobia,* 110.

18. Janice Thomson and Stephen Krasner, "Global Transactions and the Consolidation of Sovereignty," in *Global Changes and Theoretical Challenges*, edited by Ernst-Otto Czempiel and James Rosenau (Lexington, Mass.: Lexington Books, 1989).

19. William Roberts Clark and Usha Nair Reichert, "International and Domestic Constraints on Political Business Cycles in OECD Economies," *International Organization* 52 (1998), 87–120. Also see Louis W. Pauly, "Capital Mobility, State Autonomy and Political Legitimacy," *Journal of International Affairs* 49 (1995), 369–88.

20. Rodrik, *Has Globalization Gone Too Far?* 79–80.

21. Christian Joppke, "Why Liberal States Accept Unwanted Immigration," *World Politics* (January 1998), 266–93.

22. Deliberative democracy now comes in several varieties. For the version that I find most fruitful for addressing these problems, see Amy Gutmann and Dennis Thompson, *Democracy and Disagreement* (Cambridge, Mass.: Harvard University Press, 1996).

23. John S. Dryzek clearly recognizes that one of the virtues of deliberative conceptions of democracy is that they can better "cope with fluid boundaries," though (in my view) he insists too strongly on severing the "link between democracy and the state"; "Transnational Democracy," *Journal of Political Philosophy* 7 (1999), 30–51, at 44.

24. See Gutmann and Thompson, *Democracy and Disagreement*, 148–50, and the references therein.

25. John H. Cushman, "Clinton Seeks Ban on Export of Most Hazardous Waste," *New York Times* (March 1, 1994), A18.

26. Gutmann and Thompson, *Democracy and Disagreement*, 84–94.

27. Quoted in Rodrik, *Has Globalization Gone Too Far?* 3.

Credits

Index